MW00338319

Implementing Microsoft Dynamics 365 for Finance and Operations

Implement methodology, integration, data migration, and more

This book is based on Enterprise Edition

Rahul Mohta
Yogesh Kasat
JJ Yadav

BIRMINGHAM - MUMBAI

Implementing Microsoft Dynamics 365 for Finance and Operations

First published: September 2017

Production reference: 1120917

Published by Packt Publishing Ltd.
Livery Place
35 Livery Street
Birmingham
B3 2PB, UK.

ISBN 978-1-78728-333-6

www.packtpub.com

Credits

Authors

Rahul Mohta
Yogesh Kasat
JJ Yadav

Reviewers

Nicolae Tarla
Madhu Babu Rapolu
Pankaj Sonawane
Sukrut Parab

Commissioning Editor

Aaron Lazar

Acquisition Editor

Denim Pinto

Content Development Editor

Vikas Tiwari

Technical Editor

Subhalaxmi Nadar

Copy Editor

Muktikant Garimella

Project Coordinator

Ulhas Kambali

Proofreader

Safis Editing

Indexer

Francy Puthiry

Graphics

Abhinash Sahu

Production Coordinator

Melwyn D'sa

Disclaimer

This book was prepared by each of author's personal capacity. The opinions and recommendations expressed are the author's own and do not reflect the view of any of the organizations they are associated with.

About the Authors

Rahul Mohta is a cofounder of Real Dynamics and also works as an independent trainer for Microsoft. He has 16 years of experience in ERP, focusing on Microsoft Dynamics 365 for Finance and Operations, Enterprise edition (AX) and has worked for customers and partners worldwide. His experience spans multiple geographies (America, Europe, and Asia) across various domains, such as financials, supply chain and distribution, projects, manufacturing, warehousing, retail, and professional services, where he works as a trusted advisor while undertaking diverse roles across various implementations and initiatives.

He is an enthusiast of ensuring value creation while embracing Microsoft Dynamics 365 for Finance and Operations, Enterprise edition (AX), and he regularly shares his knowledge through blogs and training sessions delivered for Microsoft and other companies.

I would like to thank several people who supported me directly as well as indirectly in my knowledge on Microsoft Dynamics 365 for Finance and Operations, Enterprise edition (AX) and for motivating me to write this book. I sincerely thank my parents, coauthors (Yogesh and JJ), partners in Real Dynamics, mentors, colleagues, and my near and dear ones in my family and circle of friends.

Yogesh Kasat is a founding partner of Real Dynamics, which is one of the first IV&Vs (Independent Verification and Validation services provider) for Microsoft Dynamics 365 for Finance and Operations, Enterprise edition. He has led several large Dynamics AX implementations and turned them into success stories with his unique blend of knowledge of financial and supply chain modules, technical architecture, and business process optimization.

Yogesh brings over 15 years of experience in ERP Consulting and Audits to the team. He has worked as a solution architect and project lead on many enterprise engagements, and as an advisor with the Microsoft Product team. His global customer experience covers the USA, Canada, UK, Ireland, Japan, India, and Singapore.

Yogesh is a returning author, and having previously written the book *Microsoft Dynamics AX Implementation Guide*.

I would like to thank several people who provided me encouragement and valuable feedback on the previous. My sincere thanks to customers, colleagues at Real Dynamics, mentors, and peers in the industry who helped me gain knowledge on Microsoft Dynamics 365 for Finance and Operations, Enterprise edition (AX). I thank my mom, sisters and brothers, wife and kids, and friends and family for their continued support while I was writing.

JJ Yadav has been working on Microsoft Dynamics 365 for Finance and Operations, Enterprise edition for more than 13 years as a solutions architect, project manager, technical lead, and developer. He started working on Axapta 3.0 as a developer with Euro Info Systems in India (now Tectura India). He has experience in leading and managing several Dynamics AX Global implementations and upgrade projects. His core technical expertise includes infrastructure planning, integration services, data migration, and workflow. He has extensive functional experience in financials, procurement, accounts payable, accounts receivable, inventory and warehouse management, and the service modules of Dynamics AX.

Currently, he works as a senior project manager with Hitachi Solutions, America in the central region of the U.S.

JJ Yadav has also coauthored the book *Microsoft Dynamics AX Implementation Guide*, published by *Packt*.

I would like to thank my family, friends, and coworkers for their support and inspiration, and my beautiful wife, Khushboo, for supporting and encouraging me at every walk of life and for all her patience and support during the hours and weekends that I spent writing this book.
My sincere gratitude to my coauthors, Yogesh Kasat and Rahul Mohta, for putting in great teamwork while writing this book. I would like to thank all the reviewers and Packt for providing valuable feedback and comments during the creation of this book.

About the Reviewers

Nicolae Tarla is a Microsoft Dynamics 365 specialist with a focus on solution architecture and technical presales. He has worked on various mid-sized to enterprise-level Dynamics 365, Office 365, and SharePoint implementations for both private and public sectors. He has been awarded the Business Solutions MVP designation for community contributions across several times.

Nicolae has participated as a technical reviewer and author on several books, presented at several events and conferences. He blogs at `https://thecrmwiz.com/`.

Nicolae has also worked as a technical reviewer on the books: *Microsoft Dynamics 365 Extensions Cookbook* and *Microsoft Dynamics CRM 2011: Dashboards Cookbook*. Moreover, he has authored *Microsoft Dynamics CRM 2016 Customizations*, *Microsoft Dynamics CRM Customization Essentials*, and *Microsoft Dynamics CRM 2011 Scripting Cookbook* by Packt.

> *I would like to thank the author and publisher for offering me the opportunity to partake in this review. It was a great experience assisting on this project. In addition, a big thanks goes to the Dynamics 365 community, for supporting the authors.*

Sukrut Parab is senior solutions architect in Dynamics 365 for Operations (AX). He brings 11+ years of technology experience in industry and consulting, exclusively focused on Microsoft Dynamics AX development and related technologies (.NET ,SQL). He has been part of the successful upgrade from Ax 2012 RU 7 to Dynamics 365 for Operations. He has been working on Dynamics AX since Axapta 3.0 and has extensive experience in solution architecture, design, development, integration, data migration, and version upgrade for Microsoft Dynamics AX ERP. He has successfully worked with global teams to implement ERP systems in a variety of industries (finance, trade and logistics, entertainment, retail, and so on). He has also worked extensively on various Microsoft Dynamics AX modules, such as accounts payable, accounts receivable, inventory, product information management, general ledger, expense management, and HR. Sukrut has a bachelor's degree in electronics and telecommunication engineering and is a Microsoft Certified Technology Specialist (MCTS), Dynamics AX.

Madhu Babu Rapolu has 17 years of industry experience, with over 11 years of experience working on the various versions of Microsoft Dynamics 365 for Finance and Operations, Enterprise edition. He has extensive functional experience in the trade and logistics, financials, project management and accounting, and production modules of Microsoft Dynamics AX. He has played versatile roles during his tenure as a business analyst, functional lead, and project manager. He is currently working as a solution architect in the central region of the USA.

Pankaj Sonawane is an accomplished, dedicated, and result-oriented Microsoft Certified Dynamics 365 Consultant. He is a highly motivated Dynamics AX professional with solid track records in AX consulting, solution designs, and the development and delivery of AX projects. He has been working for more than 13 years in the AX space, with strong analytical and problem-solving skills, from Axapta 3.0 to the latest Dynamics 365 for Finance and Operations, Enterprise edition. During his career, he has played various roles in some of the world's largest Dynamics AX implementations and upgrade projects, ranging from senior developer and technical consultant to technical architect, team lead, and AX manager. He has been continuously working in the Microsoft technology stack using MorphX, X++, SQL, C#, ASP.Net, BizTalk, AIF, SSRS, SSAS, data warehousing, Power BI, Visual Studio, and so on. He is also proficient in different AX-functional areas such as trade and logistics, AR, AP, inventory, general ledger, and human resource. He is also skilled in developing user documentation, requirements specifications, technical documentation, and architectural designs. He is the most sought-after ERP expert with an in-depth knowledge of AX as a product.

Recently, Pankaj has successfully completed an upgrade from Dynamics AX 2012 to Dynamics 365 for Finance and Operations, Enterprise edition and has continued working on the same to integrate Dynamics 365 with various SaaS systems.

www.PacktPub.com

For support files and downloads related to your book, please visit www.PacktPub.com. Did you know that Packt offers eBook versions of every book published, with PDF and ePub files available? You can upgrade to the eBook version at www.PacktPub.com and as a print book customer, you are entitled to a discount on the eBook copy. Get in touch with us at service@packtpub.com for more details.

At www.PacktPub.com, you can also read a collection of free technical articles, sign up for a range of free newsletters and receive exclusive discounts and offers on Packt books and eBooks.

https://www.packtpub.com/mapt

Get the most in-demand software skills with Mapt. Mapt gives you full access to all Packt books and video courses, as well as industry-leading tools to help you plan your personal development and advance your career.

Why subscribe?

- Fully searchable across every book published by Packt
- Copy and paste, print, and bookmark content
- On demand and accessible via a web browser

Customer Feedback

Thanks for purchasing this Packt book. At Packt, quality is at the heart of our editorial process. To help us improve, please leave us an honest review on this book's Amazon page at `https://www.amazon.com/dp/178728333X`.

If you'd like to join our team of regular reviewers, you can e-mail us at `customerreviews@packtpub.com`. We award our regular reviewers with free eBooks and videos in exchange for their valuable feedback. Help us be relentless in improving our products!

Table of Contents

Preface

Enterprise Resource Planning (ERP) is a growth pillar in any organization, and this makes it a critical aspect to be used effectively. However, every business is unique, with a distinct business model, organizational culture, and value proposition, which also brings in tons of challenges in embracing and implementing an ERP system. Thus, it is crucial for a businesses to adopt an ERP and for an ERP to adapt to the business model. Such a hybrid approach requires tailor fitting the ERP to various business needs, and to achieve that, you need a solid foundation for all your digital and business transformation initiatives.

Microsoft Dynamics 365 is a business platform providing unified ERP and **Customer Relationship Management (CRM)** to deliver intelligent business applications. The Dynamics 365 ERP solution, Finance and Operations, Enterprise edition, is a modern, cloud-first and mobile-first platform, suitable for medium and large enterprise customers.

With the release of Microsoft Dynamics 365, Microsoft has not only changed the technology stack but also how customers can select, evaluate, and implement these apps in their enterprise. Recent releases, rapid innovation from Microsoft, and the evolution of the cloud have created a need to understand and master several tools and techniques in order to be effective and successful.

The book starts with an introduction to Microsoft Dynamics 365 as a whole platform, describing different apps and tools available under Microsoft Dynamics 365. It then goes through the various phases of implementation of Microsoft Dynamics 365 for Finance and Operations, Enterprise edition. In a phased manner,the book introduces you to the basic concepts, new technology and architecture, tools and techniques, best practices, and recommendations.

Using the book, you will find guidance and practical approaches to manage your entire implementation lifecycle and extended knowledge to avoid common pitfalls with straightforward techniques and step-by-step instructions, thereby increasing your efficiency and effectiveness.

What this book covers

Chapter 1, *Introduction to Microsoft Dynamics 365*, introduces you to Microsoft Dynamics 365 and shares the details of various apps, solution elements, buying choices, and complimentary tools. You will get an insight into the various tools, offerings, and options provided by Microsoft in Dynamics 365.

Chapter 2, *Implementation Methodology and Tools*, explores various implementation methodologies, such as CRP, agile, and waterfall, with a comparative summary of the key attributes to evaluate the best fitting methodology for your project. This chapter also introduces Lifecycle services, various tools for implementation, and the sustenance of Microsoft Dynamics 365 for Finance and Operations, Enterprise edition.

Chapter 3, *Architecture and Deployment*, starts with introducing the conceptual architecture and deployment architecture. It then goes on to explain various application components and architectures, such as identity, data layer, platform, application, client, and so on. This chapter also explains different deployment choices: cloud, local business data (on-premise), and Cloud and Edge (Hybrid), with a detailed comparison to help you decide the best-suited deployment choice for your implementation.

Chapter 4, *Project Initiation and Kickoff*, covers the details and importance of solid project initiation through various topics, such as project team composition, project plan, project charter, the kickoff meeting, project initiation and LCS tools, project deliverables, and best practices in project initiation.

Chapter 5, *Requirements, Business Process Analysis, and Traceability*, explains requirements, processes, and solution blueprints, emphasizing their needs and various other moving parts in managing the scope for your project. It also covers how to use the LCS business process modeler and VSTS to manage your requirement lifecycle throughout the project.

Chapter 6, *Configuration and Data Management*, explores configuration management and data migration through topics, such as strategies for managing configuration, data migration, configuration management, data migration management, data management framework, data management scenarios, and best practices for managing configurations and data migration.

Chapter 7, *Functional and Technical Design*, covers the solution design phase of the implementation project, including finding the right app for your business needs. It discusses common features that can be leveraged as part of your custom solution and also discusses the planning and execution of a functional and technical design.

Chapter 8, *Integration Planning and Design*, covers integration planning, integration technologies, and integration design/development. It explores topics such as integration architecture, basic integration concepts, integration tools and scenarios, Dynamics 365 data integrator, integration design and development, best practices and recommendations, and so on.

Chapter 9, *Building Customization*, explains the development process and tools in Dynamics 365 for Finance and Operations, Enterprise edition. It starts with introducing the development architecture, concepts, and development environment. Then it goes on to cover development planning and process. The chapter also covers the automated build and testing process of Dynamics 365 for Finance and Operations, Enterprise edition.

Chapter 10, *Analytics, Business Intelligence, and Reporting*, discusses the powerful reporting and analytics features in Microsoft Dynamics 365 for Finance and Operations, Enterprise edition. The chapter covers various reporting and analytics topics, for example, Power BI, Cortana intelligence, Office integration, modern reports and SSRS, electronic reporting, and financial reporting.

Chapter 11, *Testing and Training*, discusses what goes on during the testing and training phase of an implementation project. On testing, it covers various topics such as the importance of testing, types of testing, automated testing strategies, and test planning guidelines and recommendations. On training, it covers topics such as the importance of training, training and the help system, planning and executing training, and change management.

Chapter 12, *Go Live*, explains the Go Live phase of a project through topics such as production environment and responsibilities, Go Live activities, organization readiness to Go Live, and Go Live planning and execution.

Chapter 13, *Post Go Live Support*, covers post Go Live activities, spanning support, issue identification, tracking, resolutions, and managing the support Lifecycle.

Chapter 14, *Update, Upgrade, and Migration*, covers activities involving evaluation and processes to get on the latest version from prior versions of Dynamics 365 for Finance and Operations, Enterprise edition. This includes updating to the latest platform releases, applying hotfixes, and upgrading or migrating from previous major versions, such as Dynamics AX 2012 and AX 2009.

What you need for this book

To get the most out of this book, you need to have a basic understanding of the ERP implementation process, IT project management, and software development lifecycle. In addition, you should have access to the Lifecycle Services (LCS) portal and the development environment of Microsoft Dynamics 365 for Finance and Operations, Enterprise edition.

Who this book is for

This book is written from multiple perspectives, encompassing all the areas that any customer, partner, learner, or industry can use to be more successful in the implementation and adoption of Dynamics 365 for Finance and Operations, Enterprise edition. Solution architects, functional consultants, technical consultants, subject matter experts (SMEs), super users, IT managers, project stakeholders, and technology leaders who are in the process of buying, planning, or undergoing a Microsoft Dynamics 365 for Finance and Operations, Enterprise edition implementation are expected to directly benefit with the insights in the book.

For readers completely new to Dynamics 365 for Finance and Operations, or who have worked on prior versions, such as Dynamics AX 2012, this book is a perfect start to learning Dynamics 365 for Finance and Operations, Enterprise edition. The book helps you understand the basic concepts, tools, technologies, best practices, and recommendations. The book will help you during every phase of implementation with what to expect, deliverables across phases, roles/skill set involvement, common pitfalls to avoid, and some tips and tricks learned from our experiences.

Every business has its unique business model and organizational culture, and this brings unique challenges for ERP implementation. While going through this book, you will encounter many recommendations, guidelines, and experiences; however, you may need to fine-tune the recommendations as per your specific needs, based on the particular project size, timeline, business organization structure, and industry.

Conventions

In this book, you will find a number of text styles that distinguish between different kinds of information. Here are some examples of these styles and an explanation of their meaning. Code words in text, database table names, folder names, filenames, file extensions, pathnames, dummy URLs, user input, and Twitter handles are shown as follows: "The OData protocol supports many advance filtering and querying options on entities such as `$filter`, `$count`, `$orderby`, `$skip`, `$top`, `$expand`, and `$select`."

A block of code is set as follows:

```
"phoneNumbers": [
  {
    "type": "home",
    "number": "212 555-1234"
  },
]
```

New terms and **important words** are shown in bold. Words that you see on the screen, for example, in menus or dialog boxes, appear in the text like this: "Setup is available under **System administration | Setup | Azure Active Directory applications**."

Warnings or important notes appear like this.

Tips and tricks appear like this.

Reader feedback

Feedback from our readers is always welcome. Let us know what you think about this book-what you liked or disliked. Reader feedback is important for us as it helps us develop titles that you will really get the most out of. To send us general feedback, simply e-mail feedback@packtpub.com, and mention the book's title in the subject of your message. If there is a topic that you have expertise in and you are interested in either writing or contributing to a book, see our author guide at www.packtpub.com/authors.

Customer support

Now that you are the proud owner of a Packt book, we have a number of things to help you to get the most from your purchase.

Downloading the example code

You can download the example code files for this book from your account at
`http://www.packtpub.com`. If you purchased this book elsewhere, you can visit
`http://www.packtpub.com/support` and register to have the files e-mailed directly to you.
You can download the code files by following these steps:

1. Log in or register to our website using your e-mail address and password.
2. Hover the mouse pointer on the **SUPPORT** tab at the top.
3. Click on **Code Downloads & Errata**.
4. Enter the name of the book in the **Search** box.
5. Select the book for which you're looking to download the code files.
6. Choose from the drop-down menu where you purchased this book from.
7. Click on **Code Download**.

Once the file is downloaded, please make sure that you unzip or extract the folder using the
latest version of:

- WinRAR / 7-Zip for Windows
- Zipeg / iZip / UnRarX for Mac
- 7-Zip / PeaZip for Linux

The code bundle for the book is also hosted on GitHub at
`https://github.com/PacktPublishing/Implementing-Microsoft-Dynamics-365-for-Fina nce-and-Operations`. We also have other code bundles from our rich catalog of books and
videos available at `https://github.com/PacktPublishing/`. Check them out!

Downloading the color images of this book

We also provide you with a PDF file that has color images of the screenshots/diagrams used
in this book. The color images will help you better understand the changes in the output.
You can download this file
from `https://www.packtpub.com/sites/default/files/downloads/ImplementingMicroso ftDynamics365forFinanceandOperations_ColorImages.pdf`.

Errata

Although we have taken every care to ensure the accuracy of our content, mistakes do happen. If you find a mistake in one of our books-maybe a mistake in the text or the code-we would be grateful if you could report this to us. By doing so, you can save other readers from frustration and help us improve subsequent versions of this book. If you find any errata, please report them by visiting `http://www.packtpub.com/submit-errata`, selecting your book, clicking on the **Errata Submission Form** link, and entering the details of your errata. Once your errata are verified, your submission will be accepted and the errata will be uploaded to our website or added to any list of existing errata under the Errata section of that title. To view the previously submitted errata, go to `https://www.packtpub.com/books/content/support` and enter the name of the book in the search field. The required information will appear under the **Errata** section.

Piracy

Piracy of copyrighted material on the Internet is an ongoing problem across all media. At Packt, we take the protection of our copyright and licenses very seriously. If you come across any illegal copies of our works in any form on the Internet, please provide us with the location address or website name immediately so that we can pursue a remedy. Please contact us at `copyright@packtpub.com` with a link to the suspected pirated material. We appreciate your help in protecting our authors and our ability to bring you valuable content.

Questions

If you have a problem with any aspect of this book, you can contact us at `questions@packtpub.com`, and we will do our best to address the problem.

1

Introduction to Microsoft Dynamics 365

Organizations need a system of records to manage data, control it, and use it for their growth. This often leads to embracing business applications for managing their resources well and keep improving. Traditionally, this used to happen via software installed at the customer's location; it later evolved to hosting either internally or at the partner's premises. Now, in this modern world, it has transformed into leveraging the power and elasticity of the cloud.

Dynamics 365 is a cloud service from Microsoft, combining several business needs into a single, scalable, and agile platform, allowing organizations to bring in the much-needed digital disruption.

This chapter will introduce you to Microsoft Dynamics 365 and share the details of various apps, solution elements, buying choices, and complimentary tools. We hope you will get an insight into the various tools, offerings, and options provided by Microsoft in Dynamics 365. This may help you in your business transformation initiatives, and solution and platform evaluation, spanning **Customer Relationship Management (CRM)**, **Enterprise Resource Planning (ERP)**, and **Business Intelligence (BI)**.

Let's explore the topics we are going to cover in this chapter:

- What is Microsoft Dynamics 365?
- Microsoft Dynamics 365 apps
- Complimenting/supporting tools with Microsoft Dynamics 365

- Dynamics 365 for Finance and Operations, Enterprise edition (AX)
- Trail and Buying Microsoft Dynamics 365

What is Microsoft Dynamics 365?

To understand Dynamics 365, let's first understand Microsoft Cloud competencies and the overall cloud vision. Microsoft Cloud has numerous offerings and services; Microsoft categorizes these offerings into four broad categories, namely **Modern Workplace**, **Business Applications**, **Application and Infrastructure**, and **Data & AI**. Each of these categories comprises of multiple applications and services.

The following are the visual highlights of these four categories:

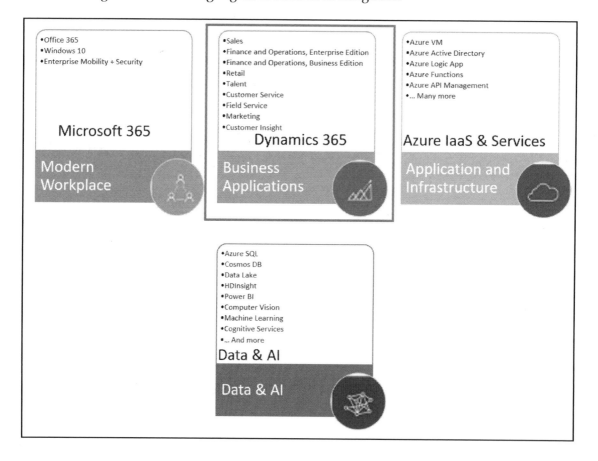

As shown in the preceding visual, **Modern Workplace** combines Office 365, Windows 10, and Enterprise Mobility and Security, and it is offered as Microsoft 365. The **Business Applications** category is a combination of ERP and CRM business applications and is offered as Dynamics 365. The third category is Cloud **Application and Infrastructure**, which is powered by Azure. The last category, **Data & AI**, deals with data, AI, and analytics.

Turning our focus back to the Business Applications category, in the business application word, business leaders are looking for greater business process automation to achieve digital transformation. What gets in the way today is monolithic application suites, which try to solve business process automation as a single application; you need modular applications built for a specific purpose, but at the same time, you need these applications to talk to each other and produce a connected graph of data that can be further used for AI and analytics. Microsoft, from the past several years, has been focused on building modern world purpose-built modular, integrated applications infused with AI and analytics capabilities.

Microsoft Dynamics 365 is the next generation of intelligent business applications in the Cloud. Microsoft Dynamics 365 is a unification of the current CRM and ERP Cloud solutions into one Cloud service, delivered by purpose-built applications. It enables end-to-end business processes driven by unified navigation, has a core user experience in how they look and feel, and also allows seamless integration with each other. Microsoft Dynamics 365 further extends Microsoft's commitment of being a cloud-committed company bringing in world-class business apps together in their overall cloud offering. The Dynamics 365 applications can be independently deployed. A customer can start with what they need, and as the business demands, the customer can adopt additional applications.

Many of you may be new to Microsoft Dynamics 365, and it would be a good idea to register the logo/brand image of this solution from Microsoft. The following is a common symbol that you should expect to gain a lot of traction among organizations embracing business applications in Microsoft Cloud:

Let's now explore the key deciding factors for adopting Microsoft Dynamics 365 in your organization's day-to-day life, with the help of its usage benefits and salient features.

The benefits of Microsoft Dynamics 365

Any business application and its platform decision is often based on benefits, return on investment, and the commitment of product principal with an assured road map. We would like to share the top three among several benefits of leveraging Dynamics 365 as your business solution platform:

- Productivity like never before with purpose-built applications
- A powerful and highly adaptable platform to enable business transformation effectively
- Integrated applications to eliminate data silos
- Insightful intelligence to drive informed decision making

Microsoft Dynamics 365 salient features

What makes Microsoft Dynamics 365 stand apart from its competition and an enabler for organizations lies in its features, capabilities, and offerings.

Here's a quick glance at the salient features of Dynamics 365:

- Cloud-driven, browser-based application
- Generally made available on November 01, 2016 to a number of markets
- Seamlessly integrated with Office 365, all out of the box, to increase productivity and stand apart from others
- Intelligence built in for predictive analysis and decision making support
- Releveled and revolutionized the traditional approach towards business solutions

Dynamics 365 is the next generation of intelligent business applications in the Cloud (public and private) as well as on premises, expected to transform how businesses use technological solutions to achieve their goals.

Microsoft Dynamics 365 apps

The Microsoft Dynamics 365 approach to business applications unifies Microsoft's current CRM and ERP cloud solutions into one cloud service with new purpose-built business applications that work together seamlessly to help you manage specific business functions.

Let's now get an insight at a high level into the various apps available in Dynamics 365. The following visual shows the apps and their association to ERP/CRM:

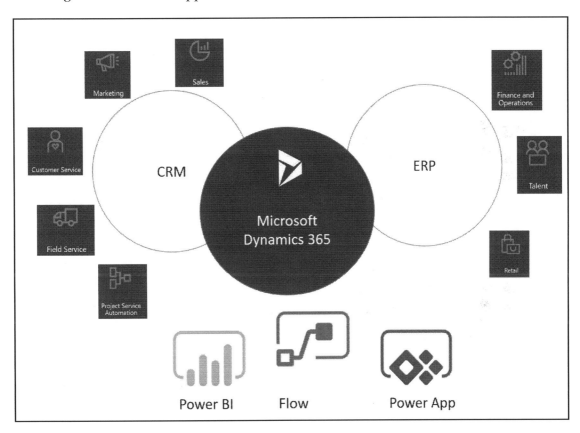

Now let's get personal with these apps starting with their names, their former solution base, and their brand logos. The following are the matrix of business solution enablers in Microsoft Dynamics 365 with their quick URL:

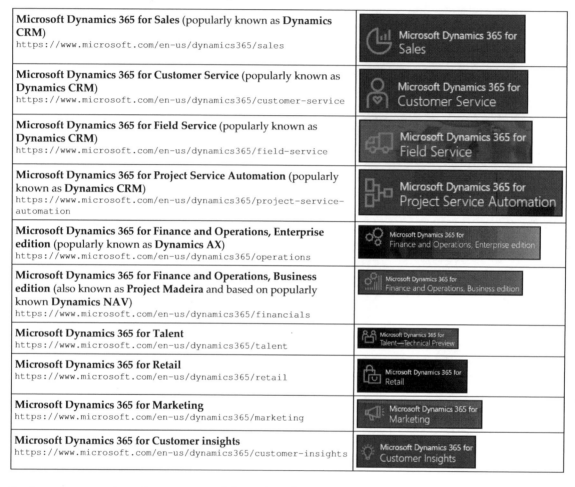

Microsoft Dynamics 365 for Sales (popularly known as **Dynamics CRM**) `https://www.microsoft.com/en-us/dynamics365/sales`	Microsoft Dynamics 365 for Sales
Microsoft Dynamics 365 for Customer Service (popularly known as **Dynamics CRM**) `https://www.microsoft.com/en-us/dynamics365/customer-service`	Microsoft Dynamics 365 for Customer Service
Microsoft Dynamics 365 for Field Service (popularly known as **Dynamics CRM**) `https://www.microsoft.com/en-us/dynamics365/field-service`	Microsoft Dynamics 365 for Field Service
Microsoft Dynamics 365 for Project Service Automation (popularly known as **Dynamics CRM**) `https://www.microsoft.com/en-us/dynamics365/project-service-automation`	Microsoft Dynamics 365 for Project Service Automation
Microsoft Dynamics 365 for Finance and Operations, Enterprise edition (popularly known as **Dynamics AX**) `https://www.microsoft.com/en-us/dynamics365/operations`	Microsoft Dynamics 365 for Finance and Operations, Enterprise edition
Microsoft Dynamics 365 for Finance and Operations, Business edition (also known as **Project Madeira** and based on popularly known **Dynamics NAV**) `https://www.microsoft.com/en-us/dynamics365/financials`	Microsoft Dynamics 365 for Finance and Operations, Business edition
Microsoft Dynamics 365 for Talent `https://www.microsoft.com/en-us/dynamics365/talent`	Microsoft Dynamics 365 for Talent—Technical Preview
Microsoft Dynamics 365 for Retail `https://www.microsoft.com/en-us/dynamics365/retail`	Microsoft Dynamics 365 for Retail
Microsoft Dynamics 365 for Marketing `https://www.microsoft.com/en-us/dynamics365/marketing`	Microsoft Dynamics 365 for Marketing
Microsoft Dynamics 365 for Customer insights `https://www.microsoft.com/en-us/dynamics365/customer-insights`	Microsoft Dynamics 365 for Customer Insights

In the subsequent sections, we are elaborating these apps, giving a brief introduction to them and a summary of their key features.

Microsoft Dynamics 365 for Sales

Dynamics 365 for Sales empowers the sales teams in new and exciting ways by helping them sell more and faster.

The following is a visual from one of the screens showing a configurable dashboard from
Dynamics 365 for Sales:

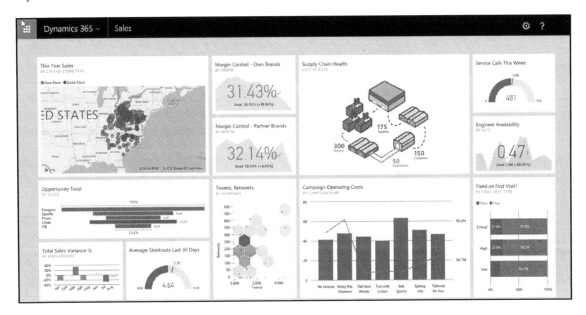

Dynamics 365 for Sales has a built-in digital intelligence and automated business processes
to increase revenue while controlling acquisition costs. It allows you to win new and repeat
business using a personalized sales process, allowing your sales team to quickly and easily
use it day in and day out. By measuring the past and identifying leading indicators for
future sales, it helps in maximizing your sales team's performance by reducing distractions
and helping them focus on the priorities.

We would like to give a full suite coverage of modules/capabilities in Dynamics 365 for
Sales with the help of the following visual:

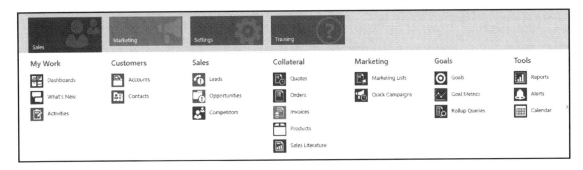

As shown above, there are several modules/capability areas spanning **Customers**, **Sales**, **Collateral**, **Marketing** and other tools.

Also, identification of customers with the most potential and basing strategic decisions on digital intelligence is a great asset here. Personalizing every engagement is needed to gain insights into buyer's decision and using that insight for efficient sales management is possible with Dynamics 365 for Sales. Your sales team will be empowered to close deals faster by collaboration, application of contextual insights, and the ability to work anytime, anywhere with the tools they need.

We would like to share the top features in Dynamics 365 for Sales, which are as follows:

- Full suite opportunity management
  - Generation of new leads
  - Content collaboration
- Social selling capabilities
  - People enabler to share knowledge and participate in social conversations
- High visibility to information contest results
- Onsite services
- Motivates users to perform their best for themselves and their teams
- Increases performance, productivity, and adoption
- Efficiently manage customers
- Actionable insights into your organization sales performance

Microsoft Dynamics 365 for Customer Service

Dynamics 365 for Customer Service is an omni-channel solution to unify the way customers and prospects experience your business.
Similar to Dynamics 365 for Sales, there are a number of dashboards in Dynamics 365 for Customer Service as well. The following image depicts one of the dashboards:

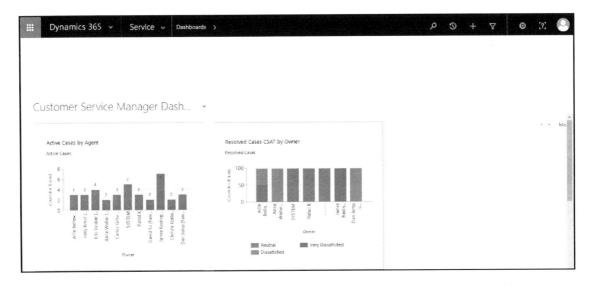

One can create consistency and loyalty at all touch points across various experience channels such as self-service, peer-to-peer service, and assisted service. It also proactively addresses the issues by detecting the customers' intent and social sentiment. Expect an increase in CSAT (customer satisfaction) and retention by providing personalized and consistent engagements and proactive addressing of service issues.

We would like to give a full suite coverage of the modules/capabilities in Dynamics 365 for Customer Service with the help of the following visual:

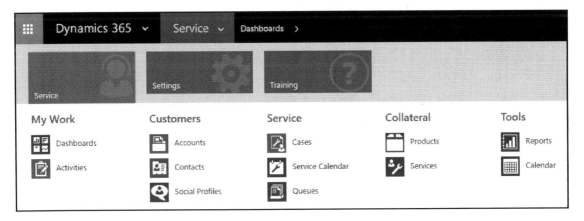

As shown in the preceding image, there are several modules/capability areas spanning **Customers**, **Service**, **Collateral**, and other tools.

Empower your customer service agents to gain actionable insights into customers' case histories, preferences, and feedback and provide guidance on entitlements and service-level agreements. When agents respond quickly to customer and market changes, you get the power of an agile, Cloud-based environment that has digital intelligence built in.

We would like to share the top features of Dynamics 365 for Customer Service as follows:

- Full suite omni-channel experience
- Agent enablement platform
- Leverage relevance search to quickly find information for better service experience
- Enable teams to perform customer oriented activities efficiently and timely
- Enabling customer for self service capabilities
- Knowledge and community management

Microsoft Dynamics 365 for Field Service

Dynamics 365 for Field Service is the new Microsoft Field Service application which drastically reduces your service costs and improves customer satisfaction.
Similar to Dynamics 365 for Sales and Dynamics 365 for Customer Service, there are a number of useful dashboards in Dynamics 365 for Field Service. Here is one such dashboard, utilized for scheduling the field staff:

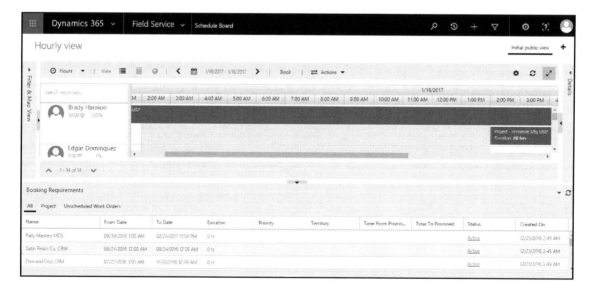

The new solution is an intelligent, world-class Field Service, which includes scheduling, mobile, and resource optimization. This helps in maximizing efficiency, minimizing costs, and improving customer satisfaction.

We would like to give a full suite coverage of the modules/capabilities in Dynamics 365 for Field Service with the help of the following visual:

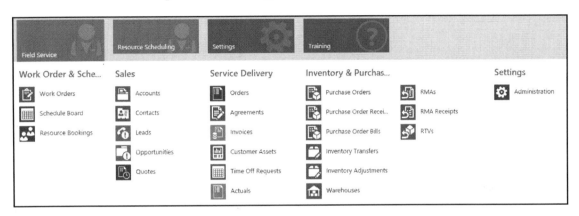

As shown above, there are several modules/capability areas spanning **Sales**, **Service Delivery**, **Inventory & Purchase**, and other tools.

The following are the top features of Dynamics 365 for field service:

- Optimize scheduling and dispatch
- Improve resource productivity
- Management and execution of services
- Asset and warranty management
- Mobility suite
- Service and Inventory management
- 360-degree customer centric experience enabler
- Leverage **Internet of Things (IoT)** to enable preemptive action from field service agents by connecting asset monitoring and anomaly detection so that action can be taken before failures occur, avoiding customer service issues

Microsoft Dynamics 365 for Project Service Automation

Dynamics 365 for **Project Service Automation (PSA)** lets you run your project-based business more productively and profitably. You can create and execute more profitable projects and customer relationships and satisfy your clients.

Similar to other Dynamics 365 apps, there are a number of useful dashboards in Dynamics 365 for Project Service Automation as well. The following screenshot depicts one such dashboard:

It helps in deepening customer engagement and building a trusted customer relationship by developing credibility and increasing customer confidence through a responsive engagement model. It also empowers your professionals with a collaboration-rich experience, enabling transparency across the business and empowering them to use their expertise to increase project productivity with every customer. It also helps you in prioritizing, innovation, and investment in service offers based on actionable insight.

We would like to give a full suite coverage of the modules/capabilities in Dynamics 365 for Project Service Automation with the help of the following visual:

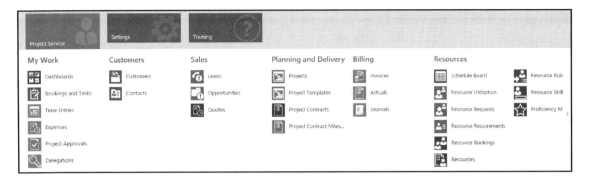

As shown above, there are several modules/capability areas spanning **Customers**, **Sales**, **Billing**, **Planning and Delivery** and other tools.

Here are the the top features in Dynamics 365 for project service automation:

- Contract management
- Resource management
- Time and expense management
- A number of capabilities in opportunity management
- Planning and collaboration platform for resources
- Team collaboration
- Customer billing
- Powerful unified resource scheduling
- Enhanced service billing experience
- Optimum talent utilization
- Analytics in project performance

Microsoft Dynamics 365 for Finance and Operations, Enterprise edition (AX)

Dynamics 365 for Finance and Operations, Enterprise edition is a complete re-architecture of Dynamics AX to be a Cloud-first Azure service. Microsoft offered users an interface that is so natural to use that they just use it with an accelerated adoption, thereby raising productivity.

Working seamlessly anywhere on any device and on any platform is among the key features that make Dynamics 365 for Finance and Operations, Enterprise edition a game changer.

Dynamics 365 for Finance and Operations, Enterprise edition (AX) offers a wide variety of role-specific dashboards and work spaces to make work life easier for folks using day in and day out. The following screenshot shows a dashboard comprising of several work spaces in Dynamics 365 for Finance and Operations, Enterprise edition (AX):

One can imagine a usage choice and Dynamics 365 for Finance and Operations, Enterprise edition addresses it:

- **Enterprise**: End-to-end solution that manages the financials and core operations for a company
- **2-Tier Subsidiary**: Solution that manages the financials and operations for subsidiaries or business units and integrates with the headquarters ERP
- **Operational Workloads**: Manages specific business functions/workloads of a business and integrates with corporate systems

It would be so nice to get a glimpse of all workloads available in Dynamics 365 for Finance and Operations, Enterprise edition (AX) suggesting their core functionality. The following diagram shows a full-suite visual for various workloads:

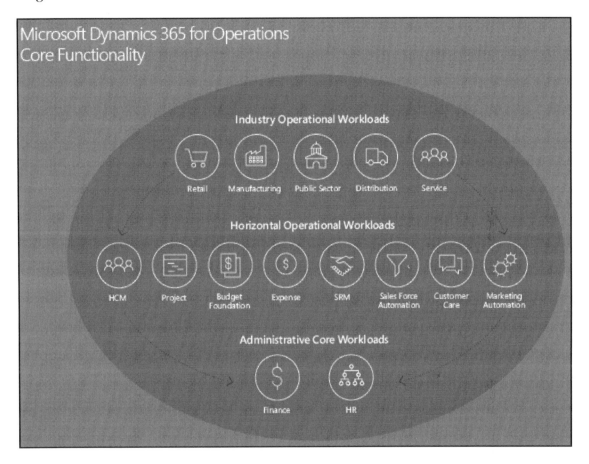

As shown in the preceding diagram, there are several modules/capability areas spanning different workloads viz. vertical, horizontal/operational and administrative. Microsoft Dynamics 365 for Finance and Operations, Enterprise edition (AX) offers several deployment choices to its customers, suggesting the following options:

- Public Cloud/Azure:
    - Fully Cloud
    - Edge mode (Cloud and local)
- Private Cloud
- On-premise

We will be getting into the details of Dynamics 365 for Finance and Operations, Enterprise edition (AX) throughout this book; however there are a few key features that are inline with other business apps as follows:

- Full-suite business management solution including enterprise class ERP functionalities with powerful financials
- Evolution of Dynamics AX on Azure
- Multiple industry capabilities viz. retail, distribution, manufacturing, public sector, and service industries; all built in a single solution
- Availability in 18 countries/markets with local compliance met and local language support
- Choice of running solution on the cloud (public/private) or on the premises

Microsoft Dynamics 365 for Finance and Operations, Business edition (NAV)

Dynamics 365 for Finance and Operation, Business edition is more than accounting software. It is a comprehensive business management solution for small and mid-sized organizations that automates and streamlines business processes. Its pay-as-you-go enterprise-grade software can scale from one to unlimited users making it amongst the most scalable cloud accounting solutions.

Microsoft Dynamics 365 for financials also has dashboards similar to the role drive dashboards in other Dynamics 365 apps:

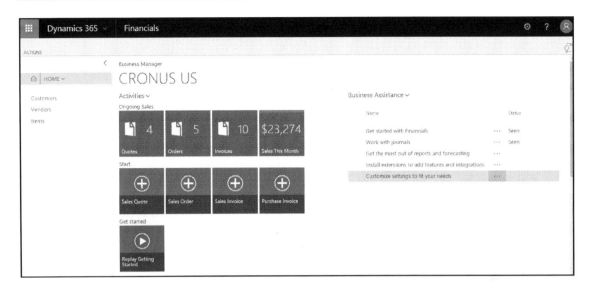

It helps in the easy migration of the existing business data from a legacy system. Dynamics NAV is the pedigree that the Dynamics 365 for Financials platform was built on.

As of July 2017, Dynamics 365 for Finance and Operation, Business edition is available in the United States and Canada and soon other countries are expected as well from Microsoft. It is licensed by named users and has the option to choose between full user and limited user access.

Among several features in Dynamics 365 for Finance and Operation, Business edition, the following are some of the key features for your platform evaluation:

- Comprehensive business management solution for **small and medium-sized businesses (SMBs)**
- As of July 2016, available only in the USA and Canada
- A business management solution for small and mid-sized organizations that automates and streamlines business processes

Microsoft Dynamics 365 for Retail

Earlier, a part of Dynamics 365 for Finance and Operations, Enterprise edition, Microsoft Dynamics 365 for Retail is now separated as its own application as part of the Dynamics 365 product portfolio. Microsoft Dynamics 365 for Retail provides an intelligent platform to enable retailers to combine the best of digital and in-store to deliver personal, seamless, and differentiated customer experiences by empowering people and capturing insights to drive growth.

The following screenshot depicts a **point of sale (POS)** solution:

The following are the key features of Microsoft Dynamics 365 for Retail:

- Personalize customer experiences throughout stores, web, mobile, and call centers
- Provide convenient, flexible ways to shop, such as in-store pickup or home delivery
- Offer cross-channel incentives, such as loyalty programs, gift cards, and promotions

- Deliver better services by giving employees access to real-time product, customer, inventory, and order details
- Offer more product selection and recommendations by blending the best of online and in-store shopping
- Get more control over store operations through automation and advanced operational capabilities
- Give customers the flexibility to buy in store, pick up in other locations, or have it delivered to their doorstep
- Improve employee productivity thorough schedules, time clock, and manager dashboards
- Simplify sales and promotional efforts by centrally managing your products and promotions
- Attract more customers by managing your assortments by channel and personalized offers
- Drive revenue by creating and targeting catalogs across channels, customers, and seasons
- Optimize fulfillment and enable the right level of inventory at right locations
- Get a centralized and cohesive view of your entire operations
- Finish end-of-day activities faster using automated and streamlined workflows
- Meet your changing business needs with a solution built for multi-company, multi-brand, and multi-channel global operations
- Take advantage of the latest innovations and opportunities with continuous application updates

Microsoft Dynamics 365 for Talent

Microsoft Dynamics 365 for Talent was an earlier part of the Finance and Operations, Enterpise edition and is now a separate SaaS-based independent offering out of Dynamics 365 Enterprise edition. If you have Dynamics 365 for Finance and Operations, Enterprise edition, you already have the Talent application. Dynamics 365 for Talent brings your human capital management to the cloud for a mobile, employee-focused, strategic HR approach that helps you find and hire the right people, nurture success, and deliver high-impact, sustainable results.

The following is a talent solution dashboard showing various modules and capabilities:

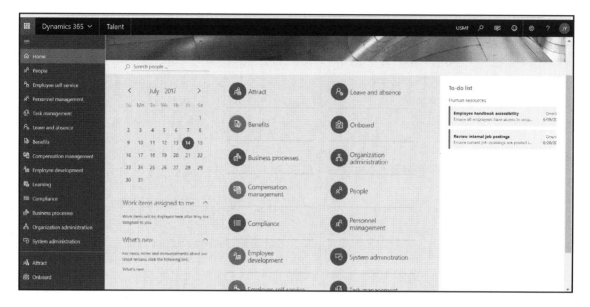

At the high level, Microsoft Dynamics 365 for Talent has the following modules and high-level functions.

Human resources

The human resources module's focus is to streamline the human resource management process. Here are the functionalities at a high level:

- Centralized HR programs such as benefits, leave and absent management, and compliance
- Create a personalized career path. Build competencies to meet future career demand. Increase employee engagement and satisfaction.
- Benefits and compensation management. Integration with payroll system
- Powerful analytics

Attract

The **Attract** experience allows you to build accurate candidate profiles, manage the interview process and shorten the time to hire.

- Integrates with LinkedIn to find and source top candidates
- Create accurate profiles by integrating disparate data
- Interview scheduling (coordinate calendars, automate the scheduling process, communicate with candidates on expectations)
- Allow interviewers to easily provide feedback from a mobile device or desktop
- Keep hiring managers in the loop at every stage

Onboard

The **Onboard** experience aims to enable a seamless on-boarding experience that accelerates the productivity and business impact of new hires.

- Create personalized pre-boarding and on-boarding plans
- Share critical resources and information to get your new hire productive
- Create on-boarding milestones and task lists
- Identify critical contacts and help make connections
- Monitor the success of on-boarding progress

Microsoft Dynamics 365 for Marketing

Dynamics 365 for Marketing is a comprehensive marketing service that can be leveraged to delight customers and personalize their experiences of your company/brand.

This is a unique service/app in Dynamics 365 targeting a crucial aspect in any organization: growth viz. marketing. The following is the landing page in Dynamics 365 for marketing:

As shown in the preceding screenshot, there are several modules/capability areas spanning **Customers**, **Collateral**, **Marketing**, and other tools.

It integrates with Adobe Marketing Cloud to deliver powerful customer experiences and give a holistic customer view. This unified customer profile is the foundation for building and running integrated, cross-channel marketing.

Your marketing teams can provide one-to-one personalized communications and send offers that automatically adapt to a customer's behavior. You can also orchestrate coordinated campaigns across different channels and measure **return on investment** (**ROI**) across the board.

This offering is expected to evolve in the same way as the other Dynamics 365 services/apps and we would like you to make a note of the following key features for Dynamics 365 for Marketing:

- Comprehensive service to address modern marketing needs
- Collaboration with Adobe for Marketing Cloud
- Easily and effectively model and manage customer journeys across marketing and sales, lead management across marketing and sales

Microsoft Dynamics 365 for Customer insights

Dynamics 365 Customer insights is built on top of Azure and Cortana Intelligent. It leverages data services and connects your Dynamics 365 data with any other data source. This enables you to have a 360 view of your customer and to better understand and engage with them.

Managing customers is amongst the dearest goals in any enterprise, and leveraging the Dynamics 365 for Customer insights gives you the power to gain a 360-degree perspective of your customers with actionable information:

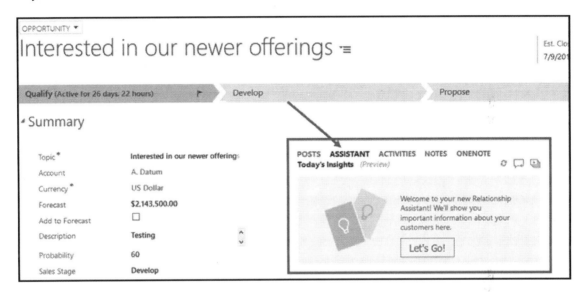

Once the relationship assistant is enabled, you can review action cards that will automatically become available in the social pane in several primary records such as opportunities, accounts, cases, and so on. It uses the information derived from interactions to help guide your customer facing team's daily work, find critical opportunities, manage email communications, identify actionable email messages, and propose follow up activities.

The following are the salient features of Dynamics 365 for customer insights:

- Intelligent customer analytics
- Transform customer data into intelligence
- Completely new solution connecting and analyzing data from Dynamics 365 with business applications, web, social, and IoT sources
- Predictive intelligence applied to create a 360-degree customer view with automatic suggestions to improve customer engagement.

Complimenting/supporting tools with Microsoft Dynamics 365

Dynamics 365 is complimented with tools to make it more personalized and easy for information consumption and informed decision making. Power BI, PowerApps, and Microsoft Flow are all backed by the best-in-class cloud services for enterprise developers and IT professionals to quickly extend capabilities for power users and scale to enterprise-wide manageability easily at any time.

Let's have a visual overview of additional apps/services/tools which could be utilized to measure information, act upon task, and automate stuff as much as possible. The following screenshot shows the apps, Power BI, PowerApps, and Microsoft Flow, addressing each of the aforementioned capabilities:

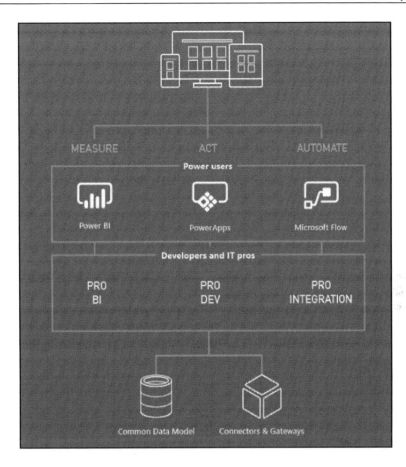

Let's now explore all of these tools one by one.

Power BI

Power BI is a powerful analytical visualization for power users to quickly gain insights into information over cloud or on their premises. It works with Microsoft Dynamics 365 to provide a self-service analytics solution. With Power BI built directly into Dynamics 365, you gain access to powerful business intelligence – real-time on any device no matter where you are in the world – with rich visuals, charts and graphics.

Power BI also has data warehouse capabilities including data preparation, data discovery, and interactive dashboards and can be embedded on most Azure Cloud platforms. The following screenshot shows a sample dashboard from Power BI with several informational parts such as charts, trends, values, tables, and many more:

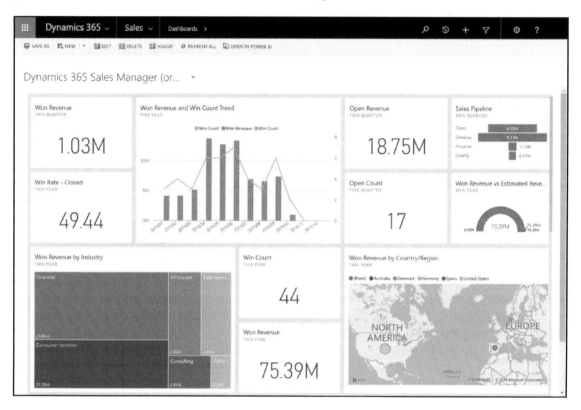

PowerApps

PowerApps is a mobile app with capabilities for power users with faster time to market delivery. It is the foundation to build any web/mobile application on top of Dynamics 365 solutions without writing any significant code.

Let's have a glimpse of a sample mobile app built in no time and ready for usage by business. The following screenshot shows an app built on top of Dynamics 365 for Finance and Operations, Enterprise edition (AX) and its data entities:

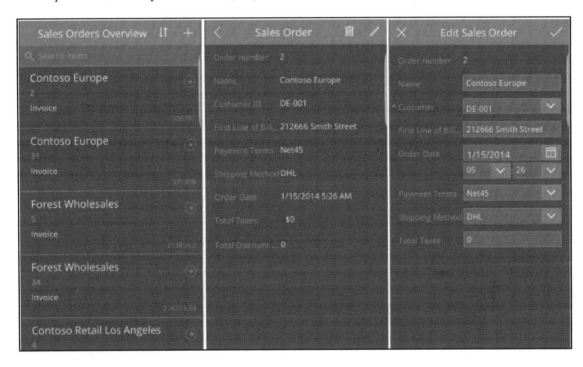

This app is expected to create the much needed disruption in how ERP and CRM data are used.

Microsoft Flow

Flow is the new workflow engine of Microsoft Cloud helping in quickly designing any time consuming task or process as either a complex multi-step process sequence, or a simple one-step task. It is going to be seen more in areas of notifications, sync, and automating approvals. Let's have a look at the chain of events which is so easy to establish in Microsoft Flow as follows:

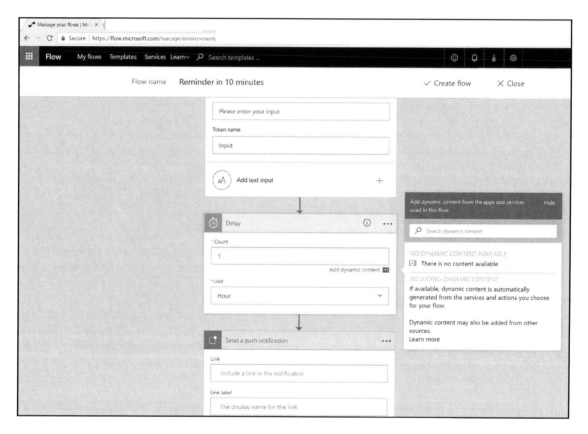

Flow supports a wide variety of data sources to connect to external world applications seamlessly and the list is increasing as you are reading this book.

Common Data Service (CDS)

Common Data Service (CDS) is a shared database for storing business entities that connects to Dynamics 365, Flow, and PowerApps. It is the fabric behind Dynamics 365 and Office 365 to provide consistently structured entities across services spanning solutions within Dynamics 365 as well as external applications.

CDS gives a secure and encrypted business database, comprising of well-formed standard business entities that can be deployed for use in your organization. It provides structured metadata, rich data types, auto numbering, lookups, business data types, such as Address, Currency, capabilities, such as referential integrity, through metadata configuration, and cascade deletes, making a compelling functionality. CDS is licensed together with PowerApps as a standalone solution and is included in two different versions with Dynamics 365.

The following is a glimpse of managing entities within CDS with other tools such as connections, gateways, notifications, and others:

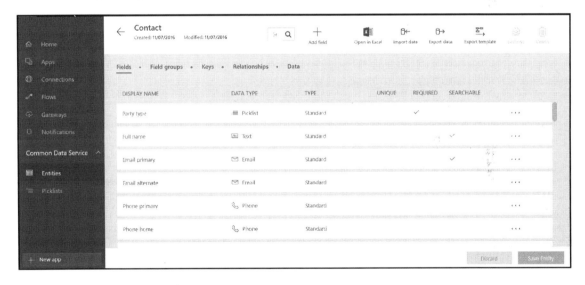

Microsoft AppSource

Think of an ecosystem in cloud which can act as a single destination for business users to discover, try, and acquire line-of-business SaaS applications. That is what Microsoft AppSource is and we see it as a great platform for partners having niche expertise in a specific subject to build, show and sell their expertise and solution on Cloud.

Let's see how the AppSource landing screen looks. The following is a visual showing the AppSource search page along with solution offerings by partners related to one or many Dynamics 365 apps:

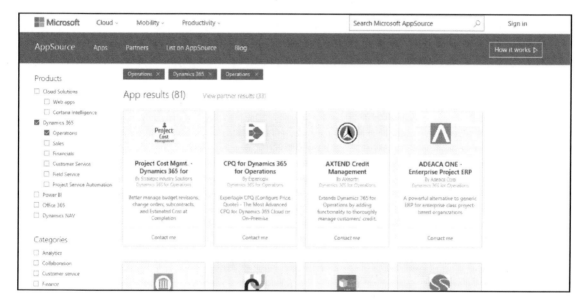

Consider AppSource as an application store, where businesses will be able to find and try out line-of-business SaaS apps from Microsoft and its partners.

AppSource also provides a list of implementation partners who can assist customers in implementing these business apps. Currently, it hosts more than 80 apps for Dynamics 365 for Finance and Operations, Enterprise edition (AX).

For customers, Microsoft AppSource is your destination to easily find and evaluate the apps from Microsoft and our partners that drive your business. Use AppSource to review the details of business application, request trial through implementation partner.

For ISVs, Microsoft AppSource is your destination to market **line-of-business (LoB)** SaaS apps to business users. Drive discoverability and usage of your apps within an existing global network of business customers through co-marketing opportunities, lead generation, and the support of Microsoft's worldwide ecosystem and sales force. Harness Azure's leading, secure, and intelligent Cloud services platform and tools to deliver differentiated apps to customers:

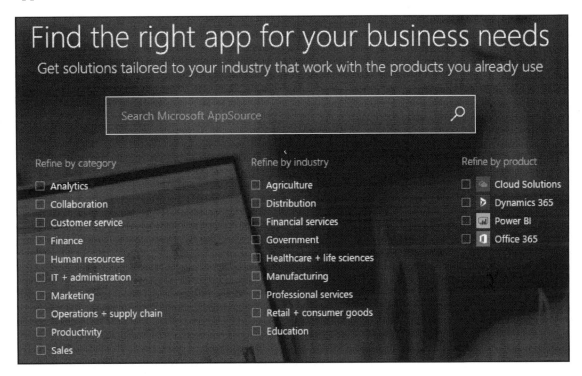

The preceding image shows the AppSource landing page and solution across industry segments for ease in locating the perfect solution.
To learn more about it, you can visit `https://appsource.microsoft.com`.

Dynamics 365 for Finance and Operations, Enterprise edition (AX)

Earlier in this chapter we learned about, Microsoft Dynamics 365 offering and all different components and options available with the offering. Our focus of this book is primarily on Dynamics 365 for Finance and Operations, Enterprise edition. Throughout the book we will be focusing on Finance and Operations, Enterprise edition as product and will go through different phases of ERP implementation cycle in various chapters. We will discover specific tools and techniques applicable to implement it successfully in organizations. In this section, you will learn a little more more about Finance and Operations, its history and highlights.

What is Dynamics 365 for Finance and Operations, Enterprise edition?

As we learned earlier in the chapter, Microsoft Dynamics 365 for Finance and Operations is an ERP offering out of Dynamics 365 enterprise edition. To clarify further, the following image shows how Dynamics 365 for Finance and Operations fits into the overall **Dynamics 365 Enterprise edition** offering. Finance and operations enterprise edition is is available under enterprise edition **Dynamics 365 Plan** or **Unified Operations Plan**:

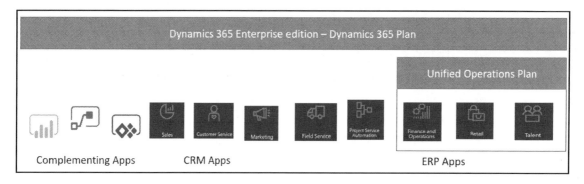

Microsoft Dynamics 365 for Finance and Operations is a modern ERP system built for cloud-first with two decades of proven business functionalities. Dynamics 365 for Finance and Operation is designed for mid-size and large enterprise customers, and is a multi-language, multi-currency Enterprise resource planning solution. Finance and Operations is available in 138 countries and supports more than 40 languages and country specific localization out of the box. On one side, Microsoft Dynamics 365 for Finance and Operations, Enterprise edition seamless integration with Office 365 takes productivity to a new level, on the other hand, out-of-the-box integration with Power BI, Cortana analytics, and machine learning takes decision making to another level.

History of Dynamics 365 for Finance and Operations

Dynamics 365 for Finance and Operations may be a new name but it has been around for the last two decades. Finance and Operations, in the past, was known as Microsoft Dynamics AX and Axapta. It was originally developed by IBM and Danish company Damgard in 1998 and released with the name, IBM Axapta. Later Damgard bought out IBM and got exclusive rights for Axapta. In the year, 2000, Damgard merged with Navision and the product became Navision Axapta. Microsoft acquired Navision in 2002 and Navision became part of the Microsoft Business solution group. Navision Axapta was now called Microsoft Navision Axapta. In 2004, Microsoft released the first major version and renamed the product to Microsoft Dynamics AX 4.0. Other releases under Microsoft are Microsoft Dynamics AX 2009 and AX 2012. In February 2016 Microsoft released the new cloud based modern version with the new name, Microsoft Dynamics AX, later renamed to Dynamics 365 Operations to get into the brand of Dynamics 365 and now called Dynamics 365 for Finance and Operations, Enterprise edition.

The following diagram highlights the history of Dynamics 365 for Finance and Operations, Enterprise edition over the last two decades:

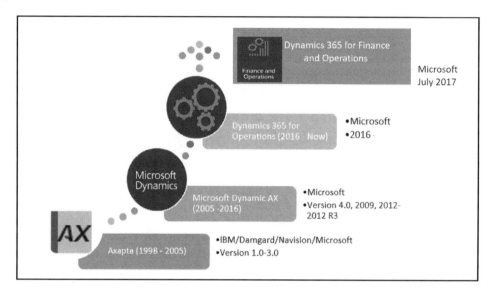

The history of ERP products is important to understand the product growth in the past both in terms of functionality and implemented best practices. The history of Dynamics 365 for Finance and Operations from the last two decades shows the story of growth from an ERP system for small businesses to a tier 1 ERP system for global enterprises.

Highlights of Dynamics 365 for Finance and Operations

The following topics describe the highlights of Dynamics 365 for Finance and Operations:

- **Modern**: Dynamics 365 for Finance and Operations, Enterprise edition is a modern, cloud-first, and mobile-first ERP solution. Microsoft has completely rewritten the technology platform and user interface from its previous version, Dynamics AX 2012. Just to name few advancement, new version comes with; cloud-first Azure deployment, modern HTML 5 client, mobile app, Power BI integration and modern integration capabilities and so on.

- **Work anywhere, anytime, and on any device**: The new user experience is optimized for multiple platforms and mobile apps. The clean, modern and intuitive browser-based UI is a pleasure to use and easy to learn. All business logic is available any time, any place, on any device.

- **Business Intelligence**: Dynamics 365 for Finance and Operations, Enterprise edition brings the power of Cloud to light up state of the art business intelligence options such as Power BI, Cognitive services, and artificial intelligence. Dynamics 365 for Finance and Operations comes with a near real-time operational data store called entity store for analytics and BI reporting. Entity store uses in memory, **clustered columnstore index (CCI)** functionality that is built into Microsoft SQL Server to optimize reporting and queries. Dynamics 365 for Finance and Operations, Enterprise edition comes with many out of the box Power BI content packs from Microsoft and also provides the ability for partners and customers to author their own power bi content pack and distribute it through the market place.

- **Productivity**: Microsoft Dynamics 365 for Finance and Operations, Enterprise edition keeps the productivity as core on its product and user interface design. Integration with productivity tools such as Office 365 has taken things to a new level, and the ability for business users to use their favorite apps such as Excel to export, edit, and publish data back to an application has never been so easy. New concept *workspaces* takes productivity to a new level by providing information around a process. All the dependencies and answers to questions around a given process are available through a single page. Task guides make it easier to on board new staff and train them on process with step by step instructions while minimizing the learning curve.

- **Predictable and repeatable implementations**: Dynamics 365 for Finance and Operations, Enterprise edition brings **Lifecycle Services (LCS)** to the next level. With LCS customer and implementation partners can manage their application Lifecycle and move towards predictable, repeatable, and high quality implementations. LCS is mandatory for any implementation project and allows customers and implementation partners to manage their implementation project from the project planning, deployment, and configuration, to monitoring and post go live support. LCS provides best practices and standards for implementation projects.

Trial of Microsoft Dynamics 365

New customers or consultant who wants to get familiar with Dynamics 365 applications can leverage the trial provided by Microsoft to explore Dynamics 365. To start the free trial, simply follow the link `https://trials.dynamics.com/`, choose an app to explore, provide your work email and get started. Following visual shows the trial sign-up experience as available currently:

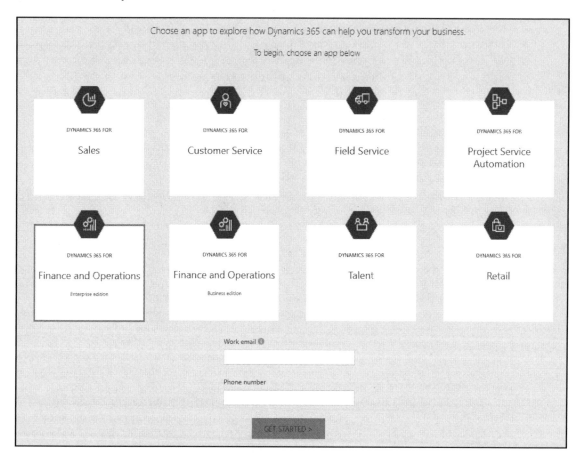

Depending on the application selected, you may have to provide additional details before application can be provisioned for you. Trial application comes with guided experience and demo data to make new users easy to navigate, learn and get familiarize with the application.

Buying Microsoft Dynamics 365

Dynamics 365 is available in two editions which can be leveraged for purchasing. You can always get a trial version by signing up at Microsoft Dynamics 365 website and see all the platform and apps working together for yourself.

There are two Microsoft Dynamics 365 plan subscriptions available namely Enterprise edition and Business edition. The enterprise plan further provides various options to choose from as well as the option to select individual applications to start what you need and then upgrade as your business grows.

The following image shows the enterprise and business edition plans and various product offerings, as of July 2017:

Additional license options for Team members, activity users, and devices are available in both Enterprise and Business edition.

We would like to summarize our understanding of the buying options. Please do validate the current validity of the following options with your solution advisor/partner:

Business edition	• Comprises of Business edition ERP and CRM • Cloud only • Suitable for 10~250 employees • Upper cap of 300 seats at maximum
Enterprise edition	• Comprises of Enterprise version of CRM and ERP Applications • Cloud or on-premise choices; dual user rights • No upper limit on maximum seats • Minimum 20 users related to Finance and Operations/AX SKU's

 Listing of buying option in this section as described as available at the time of writing this book (July 2017). These plans and offer may change in future. To know the current offer, pricing details please refer to Dynamics 365 pricing page at `https://www.microsoft.com/en-us/dynamics365/pricing`.

Summary

In the very first chapter of this book, you started with learning about Microsoft Dynamics 365 and all the different products that are part of it. You also briefly learned about all the product offerings, different plans, buying, and trial options. Then, we shifted the focus to Dynamics 365 for Finance and Operations, Enterprise edition, which is the primary focus of this book ,and we explored its history and key highlights.

In a nutshell, Dynamics 365 is a solution approach with a unified platform and data model. It's an end-to-end full suite business application on cloud. It's a win-win for customers, advisors, partners, and Microsoft, as they have enabled different channels of development, for example, drag-and-drop/wizard-like building capabilities for business users and analysts as well as pure development on Visual Studio, .NET, and Biz Talk.

The following diagram summarizes the the overall theme of Microsoft Dynamics 365, showing the next-generation intelligent applications that work together on the cloud:

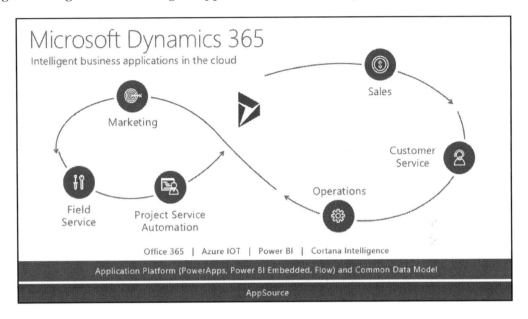

We look forward to Microsoft Dynamics 365 creating infinite possibilities and allowing organizations to leverage their finite resources and a fixed timelines to be able to achieve more.

In the next chapter, we will start our journey of implementing Dynamics 365 for Finance and Operations, Enterprise edition and learn about the implementation methodology and tools.

2
Implementation Methodology and Tools

In the first chapter, you learned about Microsoft Dynamics 365, its various apps/services/offerings, their capabilities, and the disruption in the way business apps are going to be leveraged. From this chapter onward, we will focus solely on the implementation process, architecture, various tools, features, and best practices of Dynamics 365 for Finance and Operations, Enterprise edition.

After you have chosen to implement Dynamics 365 for Finance and Operations, Enterprise edition in your organization and decided on the partner to assist you in this implementation journey, one major decision for the customer and the vendor is to decide the implementation strategy. Let's now learn how to lay down the foundation for your project success. Whether it is an ERP implementation or any other major business transformation initiative, you must chalk out the path, rules, guidelines, processes, and milestones before embarking on your efforts. It is like the route of your journey, which is where a methodology comes into force. A methodology gives the much needed direction and the propelling force to drive your initiative.

In this chapter, we will share information on the various methodologies for selection, the tools for implementation, and the sustenance of Microsoft Dynamics 365 for Finance and Operations, Enterprise edition with the help of the following topics:

- Why select a methodology?
- Methodologies relevant for embracing Dynamics 365
- The Implementation tools in Lifecycle Services (LCS)
- Resources

Why select a methodology?

Methodology is a systematic theoretical analysis of methods applied to achieve one or many goals. This systematic study of methods with a clear process and coupled with best practices ensures a higher success rate for goal attainment. However, a methodology does not guarantee success and hence needs to be customized and refined over the course of the cycle to ensure that it adapts to any changes in an enterprise environment.

A methodology comprises various tools and techniques, such as phased workflows, individual process workflows, process procedures, templates, samples, aids, instructions, responsibility, accountability, authority, risks and issues, and many more, all carried out to deliver the product or service.

By managing every program undertaken in a repeatable manner, your team gains efficiency, works smarter, and can build an environment of continuous process improvement.

In a nutshell, having a methodology provides enterprise initiatives with clear expectations and increases the probability and likelihood of its success.

Let's take a deep dive into the relevant methodologies for Microsoft Dynamics 365 in the next section.

Methodologies relevant for embracing Dynamics 365

The choice of methodology selection is limited but needs to be done carefully. The primary methodologies of Dynamics 365 are as follows:

- **CRP**: This is the latest methodology recommended by Microsoft and other advisers to embrace and implement Dynamics 365 for Finance and Operations, Enterprise edition (AX). As this is a blend of agile and waterfall, one can smartly use this methodology to achieve goals of all sizes, big or small.
- **Agile**: This methodology is good in some scenarios, such as support and enhancements. However, for a greenfield initiative of implementing Dynamics 365 for Finance and Operations, Enterprise edition (AX), this may not be so useful. When the project duration is short and goals are clearly defined and non-changeable, this methodology will be found useful.

- **Waterfall**: This is the traditional and proven methodology, which banks on clearly defined stages and deliverables, and often is used when the duration of the project is longer.

Let's learn about about these methodologies in detail in the next subsection.

The Conference Room Pilot (CRP) methodology

Prototyping models have long existed for the purpose of testing and evaluation to see how the product performs before releasing. A **Conference Room Pilot (CRP)** is very similar to a prototyping model. CRP is the ability to prototype out-of-box capabilities in a software product, including enhancements/customization, and it released the solution/product to the end user in logical connected parts.

The following are the salient features of a CRP methodology:

- The CRP methodology levers pilots, wherein each pilot is designed to target a specific stage, event, or business process of the enterprise during an implementation and should determine the success or failure
- It's a recurring approach and is well utilized when a larger goal is divided into many manageable goals
- This progressive approach brings in *time to value* to implementations and ensures that the acceptance of a solution happens in the early part of the initiative/program
- It is very often said that *a picture is worth more than a 1000 words*; similarly, a CRP is an effective way to communicate the solution in a language that business **SMEs** (**subject matter experts**) can understand more effectively using visual aids and flows

There is a number of benefits of using the CRP methodology in Dynamics 365 implementations:

- Confirms and validates your understanding of business scenarios and requirements
- Less change management
- Quicker go-lives
- Validated proposed solution with early feedback
- Iterative with synergized efficiencies
- Better and faster, and can leverage multiple delivery models

- Opportunity for innovating, learning, and improving in between delivery cycles
- The building of bigger solutions, bit by bit, and in a highly efficient and successful manner

Let's now explore the various steps involved in using the CRP methodology.

Planning

This is an utmost important aspects in any methodology you would select. The planning process should address the core milestones in this approach, which spans scenarios, configured solutions with validation, and feedback, performed in an iterative way.

The following visual shows the various steps and processes, with the flow of information involved in this approach:

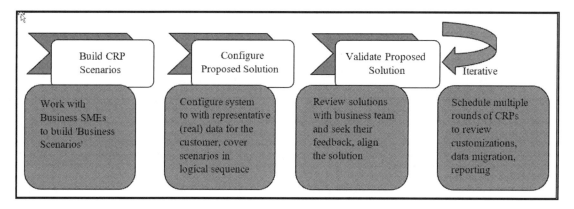

Considering that the CRP's success lies in its pilots, the following factors should be leveraged in arriving at the number of pilots needed:

- Long-term as well as short-term goals of initiative/program:
    - Use of top-down as well as bottom-up attainment of goals
    - Hierarchical map of goals, business processes, scenarios, and requirements
- A standard solution functionality span and fitment
- Enhancements/modifications need
- Localization, country, or legal requirements
- Security and data privacy, or SOX
- Connectivity (network latency) or performance

- Maintainability, deployment, or downtime for maintenance
- Licensing, support, and upgrade costs
- Shared services, inter company transactions, and master data management

Execution

A good plan needs an equally good execution for goal achievement. As part of execution, there are a number of iterative steps needed in CRP. Here are the steps we follow and are recommended to execute in the CRP way:

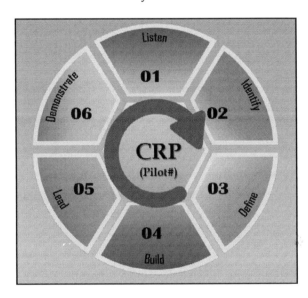

There are six steps and they are all iterative until you figure out the key steps making an impact and adding value to your implementation. The following are a brief guidance to the CRP execution steps:

1. **Listen**: This involves giving a listening ear to all verbal and non-verbal business scenarios to cover in a CRP pilot.
2. **Identify**: This involves figuring out the core scenarios and preparing the solution options.
3. **Define**: This defines the scope for a pilot and gets it validated. Doing so is crucial to the success of the CRP pilot. This must be done for both business scenarios and solution options.

4. **Build**: This step involves building prototypes, visuals, and a working solution once you have the stakeholders on board with the scope and solution.

5. **Lead**: One must have a solution champion who leads the pilot from start to finish.

6. **Demonstrate**: This step demonstrates the solution to all the stakeholders (business, solution, and IT) and seeks feedback for confirmation and optimization.

Let us now explore some best practices while leveraging CRP methodology.

Best practices in using CRP

Every methodology needs best practices as guiding stars in the implementation journey. The following are the best practices that we recommend for using CRP in Dynamics 365 initiatives/programs:

- Always have a big picture agreed upon for the entire future-state solution
- Use multiple conference room pilots for understanding and documenting business scenarios
- Get early feedback on the business scenario understanding
- Jointly work on the number of pilots needed
- Build multiple solution options and validate with stakeholders
- Progressively add scenarios through a series of CRP workshops to gain the stakeholder's acceptance
- Keep iterations short but still maintain the atomicity of each pilot
- While feedback is important in CRP, it is a must to have agreed upon change control and governance procedures
- Maintain the traceability of all the artifacts

Some of you might be new to the CRP methodology; hence, we will elaborate this concept using an example.

An example of a CRP methodology

Our example is based on a typical customer undergoing Dynamics 365 for Finance and Operations, Enterprise edition (AX) implementations and how to leverage the CRP methodology.

Here is the business background:

- Consider a customer who is into hi-tech manufacturing of public safety goods. The customer is keen to know more about how Dynamics 365 for Finance and Operations, Enterprise edition (AX) could support their particular division undergoing business transformation.
- We start the initiative with the CRP goal of going live with a business solution to support their transformation initiative.
- We need to plan for the number of pilots in Dynamics 365 for Finance and Operations, Enterprise edition (AX) by dividing the larger goal into smaller manageable ones.

Let's now see how a CRP approach can be used to accomplish the business goals:

1. Conduct multiple CRP sessions to understand the division operations. You may select a top-down approach or a scenario-driven approach; either way, the goal is to understand the entire business need. This helps in visualizing the big picture.
2. Validate your business scenario understanding and prepare the solution options. The solution preparation needs to give as much emphasis as possible to out-of-the-box capabilities, and where a tailor-fitting situation arises, think of enhancements/customization. Always prepare a solution blueprint, covering end-to-end business scenarios, and validate with the stakeholders that it achieves the business objectives:
    - First prepare all the solution proposals for out-of-box functionalities before even envisioning customization
    - Run CRP sessions to configure, demonstrate, and test the out-of-box functionalities so as to get the stakeholders' early involvement and buy in
    - Once all the out-of-box capabilities are tested, it is a good idea to then envision the solution for gaps
    - As a thumb rule, look for viable workarounds and seek validation with stakeholders
    - When no workaround exists, prepare the solution , present them with visual aids to the stakeholders, and perform a **SWOT (strength, weakness, opportunities, threats)** analysis jointly

3. After conducting solution CRP sessions and getting a confirmation from the stakeholders, it is time to scope the CRP:
   - Prepare a **Requirements Traceability Matrix (RTM)** and ensure that all the business scenarios, requirements, solution, and proposals are well-documented and signed off
   - Emphasis must be given on key decisions, taken collectively by stakeholders
   - Also, set a time to review the contract and make any amendments with more insights into the business and the solution

4. After the stakeholders are on board with the solution, start building a working solution for all out-of-box functionalities:
   - Reuse the visuals and SWOT analysis to build/develop a solution for the gaps
   - Follow the prototyping approach in development and ensure that the core gap is designed first

5. Act as a solution champion/advisor and lead the pilot with all the stakeholders. This one is easier said than done; one must always lead by example and ensure that all the ambiguities are funneled through a detailed brainstorming:
   - Embracing abstractness and converting it into concrete elements is the sign of a true leader
   - Bearer of all the key decisions that are made and going to be made

6. Now is the time to put all the hard work into action. Book several demonstration sessions with the stakeholders, based on the scope of the pilot:
   - Always start with the end-to-end solution blueprint and then demonstrate the business scenarios in the solution
   - It always helps to ensure that the highest impact scenarios are covered first and given priority
   - Seeing feedback is a must and should become part of the RTM as well in-line with change control and governance processes

Now that you have understood the CRP methodology with an example, we will now take a deep dive into some other models.

The agile methodology

Agile is an iterative and collaborative process of applying process and controls to achieve the objective. This methodology is popularly embraced by product development enterprises and can be used for implementing Dynamics 365 solutions.

The following is an end-to-end visual of what needs to happen in the agile methodology:

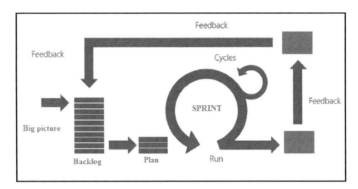

Let's look at all the moving parts:

- While agile is focused on relatively quicker achievement than the other methodologies, the important aspect for its success is knowing the big picture
- Using the big picture, a list of features/requirements/cases are elaborated and carved out into multiple plans
- Each plan is then taken into execution, which is popularly known as a sprint
- A plan tends to have multiple sprint cycles
- While executing these sprints, the feedback is taken and used in the backlog validation/updates

After knowing how an agile methodology functions, let's look at some salient steps in this methodology:

1. **Use case scenarios preparation**: This should comprise of the solution core preparation, solution roll out, support/sustenance, presales, and so on.
2. **Initial requirements analysis**:

   - Typically achieved in a couple of days in each sprint, led by an advisor/consultant, with sponsors and key users
   - This is important, as the list of requirements and use cases are to be prepared per sprint volume

- This is not to be focused on a project basis, as the projects are hardly small when implementing Dynamics 365
- An ideal start would be to first prepare the requirements outline, covering everything at a high level
- In between the days/sessions, we must document the findings and the solution alignment upfront in order to ensure a smooth envisioning of the bigger solution

3. **Solution envisioning workshops**:This is one of the most critical phases, where the solution options using the SWOT technique are discussed.

4. **Prototyping workshops**:

   - These are workshop sessions with sponsors and users, demonstrating the proposed solution (fits, workarounds and gaps)
   - This is used to validate the solution approach and its buy in by stakeholders
   - This phase is conducted in iterations/sprint so that the requirements and key decisions taken are well-documented and are kept up to date with each prototype

5. **Final system build**:

   - After ensuring sufficient confidence in the proposed solution, the final system can be taken for building up
   - This is also iterative in nature and involves leveraging sprint cycles to deliver functionality gradually
   - Following this stage, the classical stages can be undertaken:

     - **System Integration Testing (SIT)**
     - **User Acceptance Testing (UAT)**
     - Training
     - Cut over/transition
     - Go live
     - Support

Agile has some overlap with the CRP methodology, and hence, I am explaining them along with the overlapping components.

After understanding the CRP and agile methodologies, let's now learn about the waterfall methodology.

The waterfall methodology

Waterfall is a classical sequential (non-iterative) approach used in large-scale packaged solution implementations globally. This has been used for initiatives/programs that are big, span multiple businesses, have a large number of requirements, involve complex single-site deployments, developed by global/multi-site organizations, and so on.

This approach is simple to understand and has checkpoints/phases that must be completed before the next phase can start.

The following image shows the Microsoft Sure Step methodology with discrete phases and their deliverables in order to give an end-to-end glimpse of the waterfall methodology:

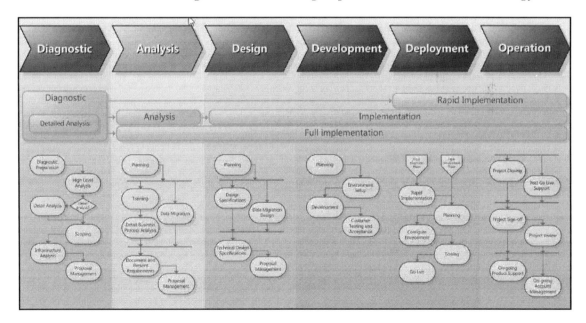

Please check if Sure Step is available or has been stopped by Microsoft, as there are a lot of changes happening in the cloud world.

As shown in the preceding image, there are predefined stages and their associated deliverables. In a typical waterfall implementation, the following phases are expected:

- **Diagnostic**: This is primarily the presales phase, or the requirement gathering phase.
- **Analysis**: This is the phase where an advisor/partner understands the requirements and maps them with the solution. During this phase, the extent of solution fitment will be known and the decision to customize, buy, or build the solution verticals are decided.
- **Design**: This is the phase where a solution blueprint needs to be prepared and which in turn needs to be supported with other designs, such as functional, technical, data migration, security, and so on.
- **Development**: In this phase, all the gaps for which design documents are prepared in the earlier phase are undertaken for development and unit testing. Some implementations perform functional testing as part of this phase or in the subsequent phase.
- **Deployment**: This is the solution validation phase, where the solution is to be tested to fit the business requirements of the initiative. Preparation for go-live also happens in this phase, and so do the activities and deliverables related to data migration, security, training, and so on.
- **Operation**: This is the phase after go-live, often known as support.

Let's now explore some key attributes of this methodology:

- This methodology is highly efficient when the requirements are very clear, fixed, and well-articulated. The scope for ambiguity must be less, as it would reduce the chances of success.
- Sometimes, implementations allow phases to run in parallel.
- There are some shortcomings of this methodology and they must be checked all the time:
    - Ensure that the concept stage is finalized and signed off, as once the system goes into the testing phase, it is very difficult to go back and change anything
    - The entire solution remains a black box and is seen only towards the later phase in the methodology lifecycle.
- Reconsider your methodology when the requirements are to be elaborated out or when the program is an on-going initiative.
    - There can be huge risks, assumptions, and uncertainties involved due to the inherent nature of the methodology.

Comparative summary

Each methodology has both strengths and weaknesses, and no one size fits all in the ERP world. Hence, the project team should carefully evaluate the best fitting methodology to achieve the business goal.

No one size will fit all the situations; however, for easing your effort in a methodology, we are sharing a comparative summary of the key attributes of the preceding methodologies:

Attribute/methodology	CRP	Agile	Waterfall
End-to-end greenfield implementation of Dynamics 365 for Finance and Operations, Enterprise edition or Business edition	This is the latest and most recommended methodology from Microsoft in this modern digital cloud era	Though this could be used, a lot of project management efforts will be needed, as it will not be able to handle all the ambiguities that come with an ERP implementation	Traditional approach, which is still OK to use, but the duration of the project is typically longer before one can start reaping benefits
Enhancements and new feature implementations	Very well-suited to these initiatives	Depending upon the delivery duration and clarity of requirements and technical design, this methodology can be used.	Typically, this one is not used for a shorter duration due to the huge efforts involved
Upgrades/migration	Very well-suited to these initiatives	This methodology may be used in upgrades and could have significant overlaps with the CRP methodology	This methodology could be used; however, for faster ROI and buy in from end users, either CRP or agile should be preferred
Support/maintenance	Very well-suited to these initiatives	This methodology overlaps with the CRP methodology and is suited for support	Typically, this one is not used for a shorter duration due to the huge efforts involved

What has worked for us is the CRP methodology while implementing and embracing Dynamics 365 solutions. As your new ERP is no longer a traditional application, the traditional approach of waterfall may not be the best fit, while agile is not intended for long-running initiatives. Hence, it is also carefully used, based on the situation.

Microsoft Dynamics 365 has created a new trend--customers are implementing multiple Dynamics 365 products, such as Sales and Finance, and Operations, Enterprise editions together. There may be two different teams implementing these two product lines. However, it is critical for these teams to collaborate with each other and align their methodologies for a smooth implementation and roll-out of each product.

After selecting the methodology and project implementation strategy, let's look at the tool sets available to help your implementation project. Microsoft LCS combines all the tools you will need throughout your project lifecycle. The next section provides an overview of LCS, and all the tools available and their use.

Lifecycle Services (LCS) -- implementation tools

Microsoft Dynamics **Lifecycle Services** (**LCS**) provide a cloud-based collaborative workspace that customers and partners can use to manage implementations by simplifying and standardizing the Dynamics 365 Finance and Operations, Enterprise edition implementations.

LCS is a must-have tool for all Dynamics 365 for Finance and Operations, Enterprise edition implementations and helps in improving the predictability and quality of implementations, thereby enabling business value faster. LCS provides regularly updated services. The goal of LCS is to deliver the right information, at the right time and to the right people, and to help ensure repeatable and predictable success with each roll-out of an implementation, update, or upgrade.

LCS is available to customers, partners as well potential prospects. While customers and partners get access for learning, implementation and other purposes, prospects can get access for trial purpose. Following table suggest various ways of getting your LCS access:

For an existing customer of the older version of Dynamics AX	**For partners of Microsoft Dynamics 365 for Finance and Operations - Enterprise Edition**	**For customers of Microsoft Dynamics 365 for Finance and Operations - Enterprise Edition**
Sign into LCS using the CustomerSource credentials	Sign into LCS using PartnerSource credentials	Sign into LCS using Microsoft Azure Active Directory (Azure AD) credentials

Let's now have a quick look at all the tooling available in LCS:

Common tools	Project-specific tools
Common tools in LCS consist of the following: • Manage methodologies • Organization users • Preview feature management • Manage incidents • Shared asset library	Some of the key project-specific tools in LCS consist of the following: • Project settings • Project users • Cloud-hosted environments • Business process modeler • Configuration and data manager • Support • Asset library • Updates • System diagnostic, and so on.

While there are so many tools available, it may easily become confusing if you don't know when and where to use them. We intend to cover this aspect with the help of the following matrix highlighting in brief the timing/segment of the tool, URL of the tool for more details, and its capability and usage:

Segmentation	Tools	Details of the tooling
Foundation	Methodologies	Methodologies provide a tool that you can use to ensure a more repeatable and predictable implementation of projects.
Foundation	Projects	Projects are the key organizers for your experience in LCS. Projects let you invite your partners to collaborate with you, and they also let you track the progress.
Foundation	Upgrade analysis	Upgrade analysis helps you plan your upgrade to the latest version of Microsoft Dynamics 365 for Finance and Operations by analyzing the code artifacts from Microsoft Dynamics AX 4.0, Dynamics AX 2009, or Dynamics AX 2012.
Foundation	Usage profiler	Usage profiler is a data-gathering tool that helps you describe your projected or current usage of application. Usage profile prepared can be used for various purposes, such as hardware sizing, support, and so on.
Foundation	License sizing estimator	License sizing estimator helps you estimate the number of licenses that are required.
OnGoing	Business process modeler	Business process modeler lets you create, view, and modify standard process flows.
On going	Cloud-hosted environments	The cloud-hosted environment is a tool that you can use to deploy and manage Microsoft Dynamics environments on Microsoft Azure.
On going	Configuration and data manager	Configuration and data manager lets you copy a configuration from one instance to another.
On going	Customization analysis	Customization analysis validates model files against best practices and provides a report of the potential areas for improvement.

Support	Issue search	Issue search helps you find the existing solutions and workarounds for known issues in Microsoft Dynamics products.
Support	Cloud-powered support	Cloud-powered support helps you manage support incidents.
Support	System diagnostics	System diagnostics helps administrators monitor the Microsoft Dynamics environments.
Support	Updates	The Updates page hosts the details about updates that are available for the environment.

Let's now learn some select tools of LCS in detail.

Foundation

The following are the key tools to laying down the foundation for your initiative in LCS. These are typically one-time setup and the structure remains the same throughout the lifecycle of the project while the data within could be updated/change.

Methodologies

Methodologies provide a tool that you can use to ensure more repeatable and predictable implementation projects.

The following are the salient features of a methodology in LCS:

- You can use one of our methodologies or create your own.
- By using a methodology, you can easily track and report on your progress.
- Always keep the objective of using best practices to simplify and standardize the implementation process in the adoption of your solution.
- Methodologies can be edited or appended.
- One should not change the methodology for implementation projects, as there could be severe consequences of changing methodology mid-flight and may require a lot of efforts to get it back on track.

- The methodology is super important when the customer is ready for production deployment. We need to identify the gold build. It is mandatory for an organization's user to sign off and complete the provisioning checklist. The user will also be added as the admin user in Dynamics 365 for Finance and Operations, Enterprise edition as an *admin*.

Let's see a sample visual of how a methodology looks in LCS:

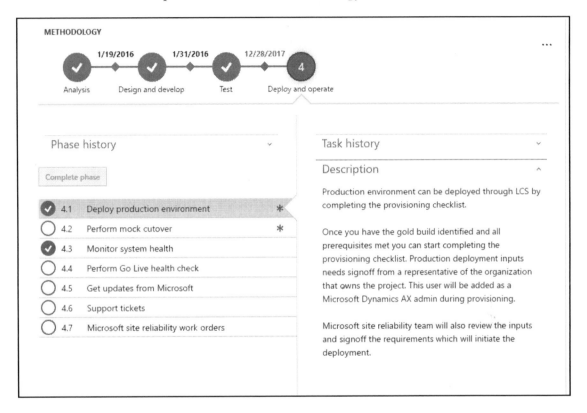

In a methodology, you can define a number of phases, phase-specific activities, descriptions, add references, add attachments, and so on.

Projects

Projects are the key organizers of your experience in LCS. Projects let you invite your partners to collaborate with you, and they also let you track the progress.

The following are the salient characteristics of a project in LCS:

- Each customer who purchases Dynamics 365 for Finance and Operations, Enterprise edition will receive one LCS implementation project. Customers can then add their partner/CSP/VAR as a user to those LCS projects.
- Based on the offer selected by the customer, the features in this project workspace will be enabled.
- Environments included in the offer will be deployed and managed by Microsoft.
- The Action center will guide you through the required actions that must be completed.
- A new methodology experience includes locked tasks as you progress through the implementation.
- A more complete trail specifying who completed each methodology phase and tasks.
- Milestones that can be used to track critical project dates.
- The organization that owns a project must maintain a valid service plan to keep the project active and responsible for all the charges related to the project.
- Partner users can see the implementation project for each customer using their credentials.
- Before kicking off, you should complete the required configuration for LCS for SharePoint and Visual Studio Team Services.

Project users

You can grant users various level access on an LCS project.

The following explores access levels and their purpose:

Role	Usage
Project owner	Members of this role have access to all the tools in LCS, can add other users in any role, and can delete the project
Environment manager	Members of this role have access to all the tools in LCS and can manage Cloud-hosted environments
Project team member	Members of this role have access to all the tools in LCS but can't manage Cloud-hosted environments
Project team member (prospect)	Members of this role have limited access to all the tools in an LCS project: • Prospects are users who have been added to a project, but who don't have an account in VOICE or an Azure AD account • You can identify that a user is a prospect because a prospect is listed as his or her organization
Operations user	Members of this role have access to the following tools in LCS: • System diagnostics • Issue search • Cloud-powered support • Updates • Cloud-hosted environments

Organization users

By default, membership in an LCS organization is controlled by organization membership in CustomerSource or PartnerSource. All users that are members of the CustomerSource or PartnerSource organization are added to LCS.

- You can also create organization users that are not affiliated with CustomerSource or PartnerSource
- Users can access organization-specific information, such as business process libraries and methodologies
- Organization users do not have access to specific projects until they have been invited to join them

SharePoint online library

When a SharePoint online site is configured to use in a LCS project, SharePoint can then be used to power all document management for that LCS project. In the SharePoint Online library, you can see the list of documents in the folder. The integration between LCS cloud services, and SharePoint uses OAuth user authentication.

Preview feature management

This is also known as beta feature management. The following are the salient characteristics of this feature:

- If you've been invited to try an LCS preview, you can enter a code or enable the preview here
- Public previews are available for any LCS user
- Private previews are available only to users and organizations that have been invited to participate
- To get involved in LCS previews, you can sign up for the Dynamics 365 for Finance and Operations, Enterprise edition feedback programs

Shared asset library

You can maintain a lot of assets in a common organization library for the purpose of reusability and productivity. The following are the shared asset types:

- Configuration
- Deployment
- Model store
- Model database
- Business database
- Localized financial report

Subscription estimator

This is the sizing tool and it uses a usage profiler, which is a data-gathering tool that helps you describe your projected or current usage of a Dynamics 365 for Finance and Operations, Enterprise edition implementation.

The usage profile that is generated can be used for various purposes, such as hardware sizing for production environment by Microsoft and support.

The usage profiler seeks information in the following broad three sections:

- Deployment details
- Instance characteristics
- Retail and commerce

Microsoft Dynamics Lifecycle Services subscription estimator provides an automated estimate of the subscription needed for your Dynamics 365 for Finance and Operations, Enterprise edition instance:

- It uses the user license details and the transaction count to infer the subscription needs
- There can be multiple versions of estimates and one of them can be marked as *Active*, which in turn is used by Microsoft for production sizing purpose support

Asset library

An asset library is a single repository to maintain all the artifacts related to your implementation of Dynamics 365 and the project in LCS.

There are several asset types that can be used to store, use, reuse, and deploy the following artifacts:

- Cortana intelligence application:
    - This is explained in detail in analytics topic in the later chapters
    - These are Microsoft-provided machine learning and recommendations related components, installed in your environment via the LCS asset library repository, which bring insights derived from the Cortana intelligence suite components using machine learning right within Dynamics 365
- Data package:
    - This is explained in detail in the data migration topic in later chapters
    - Data packages are particularly used in loading data using the LCS asset library repository into your Dynamics 365 environment
- Dynamics 365 for Finance and Operations, Enterprise edition database backup:
    - This procedure can only be used in non-production environments.
    - In this tool, a Microsoft Dynamics 365 for Finance and Operations, Enterprise edition database backup is uploaded as a file in the LCS asset library repository and then reimported in the same or another instance for quickly using the system
- GER configuration:
    - This is explained in detail in the analytics topic in later chapters.
    - This involves uploading and leveraging **Electronic Reporting (ER)** configuration into an asset library repository in Microsoft LCS and subsequently use in your Dynamics 365 environment
- Localized financial report:
    - Any country/region-specific localized solutions prepared by developers and ISVs can be created as a solution and added in the LCS repository, which could subsequently be used in other implementations by the partner/advisor owning it.
- Marketing asset:
    - Here, organizations can upload their logo of different sizes in the LCS asset library repository for subsequent use in other environments

- Model:
  - This is explained in detail in the development topic in later chapters
- Power BI report model:
  - This is explained in detail in the analytics `Chapter 10`, *Analytics, Business Intelligence and Reporting.*
- Software deployable package:
  - This is explained in detail in the development `Chapter 9`, *Building Customization.*
- BPM artifact:
  - Use this repository within the LCS asset library to manage and reuse your business process libraries
- Process data package:
  - This is explained in detail in the data migration `Chapter 6`, *Configuration and Data Management.*
- Solution package:
  - Here, one can obtain solution packages published from Microsoft to use it during your environment spun up time.

One can make a copy of an asset directly from the asset library. Also, one can ship a new version of any file in the asset library and provide release notes when you publish an asset. This is useful when you have assets that are published with your organization users.

Organization users can now get additional versions of the same file and check what has changed with each version from the release notes, before they download a specific version.

Ongoing

The following are the key tools in LCS for ongoing usage in your initiative. These tools are expected to be used frequently and, hence, the information within always keeps evolving.

Business process modeler

Business Process Modeler (BPM) lets you create, view, and modify standard process flows inside Microsoft Dynamics AX. One of the top goals for BPM is to standardize the process flows, its documentation, and its usage throughout the initiative.

One can achieve the following with BPM:

- Align Microsoft Dynamics 365 for Finance and Operations, Enterprise edition processes with industry-standard processes, as described by the **American Productivity and Quality Center (APQC)**
- Identify the fit and gaps between user requirements and the default functionality that Microsoft Dynamics 365 for Finance and Operations, Enterprise edition provides
- Use the synchronize option in the BPM library hierarchy with your VSTS project
- At present, this is a one-way sync from LCS to VSTS, which will keep your VSTS work items (epics, features, and so on) updated with any changes that are made in the LCS BPM library
- There are three kinds of library where BPM can be maintained:
  - *Global library*: Available to all LCS users
  - *Corporate library*: Available to all organization users
  - *Project library*: Available to users within the LCS project with appropriate access

The following image shows one such global library from Microsoft:

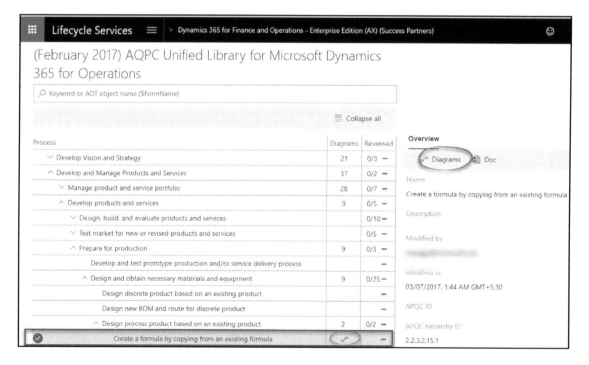

As shown in the preceding image, one can create and maintain the hierarchical flow of business processes and requirements by leveraging branching and segmenting.

Refer to `Chapter 5`, *Requirements, Business Process Analysis and Traceability* and `Chapter 6`, *Configuration and Data Management* for more details on LCS BPM.

 LCS BPM has a feature of getting synchronized with VSTS, where more detailed information, processing, and workflow can be implemented.

Let's now learn how to manage cloud-hosted environments using LCS in the next subsection.

Cloud-hosted environments

Cloud-hosted environment is a tool that you can use to deploy Microsoft Dynamics 365 for Finance and Operations, Enterprise edition environments on Microsoft Azure.

When you use cloud-hosted environments, you must select the type of Microsoft Dynamics AX environment to deploy, such as a demo, developer/test, or production environment. The following is from the LCS cloud-hosted environment screen, which depicts the environments and their types:

Based on your selection, the cloud-hosted environments tool provisions the appropriate number of **Virtual Machines** (**VMs**) in Azure.

These VMs have the components (and all their prerequisites) of Microsoft Dynamics 365 for Finance and Operations, Enterprise edition already installed on them.

You can get details of your deployment status, URL for Dynamics 365 for Finance and Operations, Enterprise edition, URL for retail Cloud POS, and local VM credentials along with domain accounts and system diagnostic information.

 Other than the production environment, customers interested in resizing their **Virtual Machine** (**VM**) once it has been deployed from the LCS can only do it from the Azure Portal.

Code upgrade

The code upgrade tool helps you plan your upgrade to the latest version of Microsoft Dynamics 365 for Finance and Operations, Enterprise edition by analyzing code artifacts from the prior versions of Finance and Operations or Dynamics AX 2012.

It can also be just run for estimations, so as to receive an analysis reports. When only the estimation is used, then the exported and upgraded models will not be checked in to Visual Studio Team Services and will not be available for download.

There are brief steps when upgrading from Dynamics AX 2012:

1. Create an upgrade analysis job (the task you are performing now).
2. Export your AX 2012 model store.
3. Zip (compress) the model store file.
4. Upload your compressed model store.
5. After the job has completed, download the metadata file, `UpgradedMetadata.zip`, or connect to the Visual Studio Team Services project containing the upgraded code. We expect Microsoft to release a data upgrade service as well for the previous versions.

Configuration and data manager

Configuration and data manager lets you copy a configuration from one instance of Microsoft Dynamics 365 for Finance and Operations, Enterprise edition to another.

You can copy from and to Dynamics 365 for Finance and Operations, Enterprise edition environments that meet the following criteria:

- They are managed as part of an LCS project
- They run on the data management framework in Dynamics 365 for Finance and Operations, Enterprise edition and can leverage data packages (containing entities)
- You can also create groups of data packages called **Process Data Packages** (**PDP**) and use them for all kinds of deployment to any environment in the LCS project being worked upon. Refer `Chapter 6`, *Configuration and Data Management* for more details.

Localization and translation

The Dynamics ERP regulatory alert submission service is designed to support the localization community in reporting changes in a country/region legislation, which impacts the Microsoft-supported localized country/region solution.

If there is an upcoming regulatory change in your Microsoft-supported country/region that you are aware of, you can now flag it to Microsoft by submitting a regulatory alert. The solution is based on a simple four-step wizard that will take you through the regulatory alert submission:

1. Searching for the alert or associated feature.
2. Associating business processes with the regulatory change.
3. Alert details.
4. Submission confirmation.

The Microsoft Dynamics 365 translation service is designed to improve the experience of the partners and customers when translating the Microsoft Dynamics product UI into existing and additional languages.

The following are some additional capabilities:

- The solution can also be used to translate custom features developed by partners
- The solution is based on the Microsoft Translator Hub and the Multilingual App Toolkit
- It provides customized machine translation as the starting point of the translation process, reducing the effort to post editing and review
- A major benefit of the solution is that Microsoft Linguistic Assets are made available through the Microsoft Translator Hub

Support

The following are the key tools in LCS for ongoing support. These tools are expected to be used frequently right after the go-live, while some can also be used for ongoing activities.

Issue search

Issue search helps you find existing solutions and workarounds for known issues in Dynamics 365 for Finance and Operations, Enterprise edition.

You can see which issues have been fixed, which issues remain open, and which issues have been resolved as unable to be fixed.

Support

This tool helps in managing various support incidents.

The support tool provides the following information in different tabs:

- **Manage incidents**: This is a single window to view all your support incidents raised with Microsoft from your organization across projects. These incidents are classified as premier and non-premier and is based on your support agreement with Microsoft.
- **Open work items**: This provides a list of the currently open work items.
- **Support issues**: The project team or business users can submit an issue from within the Dynamics 365 for Finance and Operations, Enterprise edition client or manually create an issue in the LCS. Issues can be investigated by customer or partner team and can also be raised to Microsoft.

- **Service request**: All service requests are raised with **DSE (Dynamics Service Engineer)** for any matter related to the production environment.
- **Hotfix request**: When business users encounter an issue while using the Dynamics 365 for Finance and Operations, Enterprise edition client, they can search to find whether Microsoft has published any hotfixes regarding the same issue. If so, the business user can submit a request for a hotfix, which will be available under this section. The system administrator can assign the request to the IT team for further evaluation.

> It is recommended that you rightly classify the severity of the issue when submitting to Microsoft, as they will ensure that you are on top of the issue and that you know the background well to help the support team quickly get on the same page; hence providing a better chance for an accurate and early resolution.

Work items

This is another view that shows all the open work items. These work items are possible on Visual Studio online services, which have to be configured to the LCS project.

The following are the two modes of work items usage in LCS:

- When you choose the storage location of LCS, then you can create new work items in LCS, but then, there is no VSTS integration.
- When you configure the VSTS integration in your LCS project, then you need to link it to a specific VSTS project. When you create work items in the linked VSTS project, then the work items will be seen in your LCS project/work items. You can open the work items from LCS by clicking on the ID link.

> Out of various types of work items, types bug or tasks created within VSTS are visible in LCS.

System diagnostics

System diagnostics help administrators monitor Microsoft Dynamics 365 for Finance and Operations, Enterprise edition environments:

- The dashboard provides a visual indication of the number of hosts in the selected environment that encountered errors when running rules and also displays the last five messages
- It also indicates whether any collector jobs have encountered errors while running

> Only production environments that are deployed through LCS in Microsoft Managed Subscription will be actively monitored by the Microsoft Service Engineering team. All other environments, such as the Sandbox environment, do not have the monitoring features turned on.

The following is a sample system diagnostics dashboard with sections giving information about the quick health of the environment, messages, jobs, detailed reports, and admin functions:

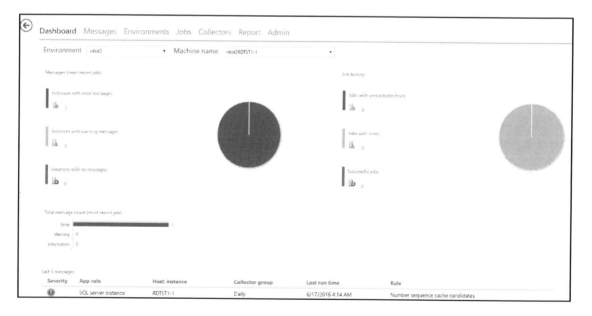

Updates

The updates page hosts the details about updates (application and binary) available for the Microsoft Dynamics 365 for Finance and Operations, Enterprise edition environment. It also provides access to groups of updates that can be used for slipstream installations for on-premise environments. The slipstream process involves installing Microsoft Dynamics 365 for Finance and Operations, Enterprise edition components, for example, cumulative updates, binary hotfixes, or service packs into a process, which is known as slipstreaming.

 Updates intended for slipstreaming can neither be installed by using the update installer nor can the updates intended for use with the update installer be slipstreamed.

Along with LCS, you will also need a lot of additional resources to be on top of, which we will elaborate and share in the next section.

Resources

We would like to share some resources, which every person using Microsoft Dynamics 365 should be aware of and always keep visiting:

- Wiki/help: `https://docs.microsoft.com/en-us/dynamics365/unified-operations/fin-and-ops/index`
- **Dynamics Learning Portal (DLP)** : `https://mbspartner.microsoft.com` (partners only)
- Roadmap: `https://roadmap.dynamics.com`
- Idea portal: `https://ideas.dynamics.com/ideas/`
- CustomerSource: `https://mbs.microsoft.com/customersource`
- PartnerSource: `https://mbs.microsoft.com/partnersource`

Summary

In this chapter, you learned about the importance of a methodology and the various choices of methodologies available. **Conference Room Pilot (CRP)** is clearly preferred and the recommended option, while organizations can adapt to any other methodology depending on the organization culture and project requirements.

We introduced important tools while embracing Dynamics 365, such as LCS. LCS has a plethora of tools to benefit from and derive value in your implementation. We expect Microsoft to enhance these tool's existing capabilities. We also expect new functionality additions to benefit customers and partners worldwide and to lay a strong foundation of successful adoption of Dynamics 365 for Finance and Operations, Enterprise edition (AX) as the platform of choice to run their businesses.

Understanding the architecture is critical to know how the system works. In the next chapter, you will learn about architecture and the various components of Dynamics 365 for Finance and Operations, Enterprise edition. You will also learn about deployment options, such as Cloud, Cloud + Edge, and local business data, different scenarios where one is desirable, recommendations, and comparison between them.

3
Architecture and Deployment

Enterprise resource planning software Dynamics 365 for Finance and Operations, Enterprise edition is a massive software application that supports global enterprises in providing information across all the functional units of a business entity. Understanding the architecture is critical to know how the system works.

Software architecture is fundamental to answer the following questions:

- How does the software application work?
- What different components are part of the software and how do they interact?
- Can software grow as business grows?
- What infrastructure do we need to deploy the software?
- How can a software application be deployed and managed?

In this chapter, you will learn about the architecture of Dynamics 365 for Finance and Operations, its various components, and the different deployment choices available for Microsoft Dynamics 365 for Finance and Operations.

Architecture

The Dynamics 365 for Finance and Operations architecture is completely overhauled from its predecessor, Dynamics AX 2012 R3. It is built for the cloud, to embrace the investment and innovation happening in the Microsoft Azure cloud. The Finance and Operations architecture is built for the cloud first and uses a modern user interface, integration, and web technologies. Dynamics 365 for Finance and Operations, Enterprise edition can be deployed on cloud, on-premises, or as a hybrid. Cloud deployment uses Microsoft Azure, and the production environment is fully managed by Microsoft, while on-premise deployments are deployed locally within a customer's data center.

Hybrid deployment is also called Cloud and Edge, where business-critical operations, such as retail, warehouse management, and so on, can be deployed across distributed on-premise environments and connected to the cloud for a single view of the business, cloud services, and disaster recovery.

Conceptual architecture

From the conceptual architecture perspective, all deployment options use the same application stack, clients, development environment, and application lifecycle management. The difference is primarily on the infrastructure, database, and identity provider. The following diagram represents a high-level conceptual architecture of Dynamics 365 for Finance and Operations, Enterprise edition:

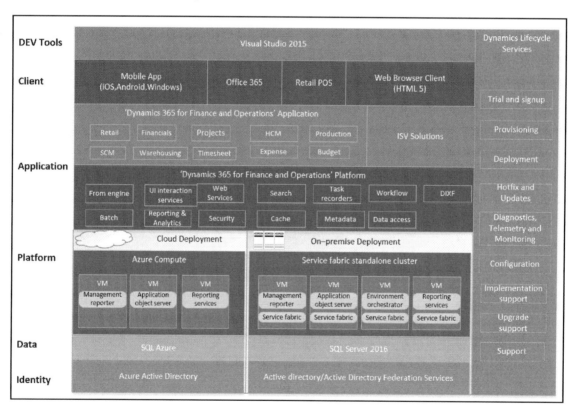

As shown in the preceding diagram, Dynamics 365 for Finance and Operations architecture can be divided into the following conceptual components:

- **Identity**: This component represents the identity and authentication management of Dynamics 365 for Finance and Operations. In cloud deployment, **Azure Active Directory** (**Azure AD**) is used for authentication, while on-premise deployment relies on on-premise **Active Directory Federation Services** (**AD FS**) for authentication.
- **Data/storage**: This is the data or storage layer, which represents the database used to store the core business configuration and transaction data. In cloud deployment, SQL Azure is used as the database. On-premise deployment uses Microsoft SQL Server 2016 Standard edition or Enterprise edition.
- **Platform**: This layer represents the compute, operating system, and applications to host the various components of Dynamics 365 for Finance and Operations. Cloud deployment uses many features of the Azure platform, such as virtual machine, Azure storage, networking, monitoring, and so on. On-premise deployment uses on-premise infrastructure and VMs to deploy the various components through the service fabric standalone cluster.
- **Application**: This layer in the architecture diagram represents the Dynamics 365 for Finance and Operations application components, metadata, and code. The core application components of Finance and Operations are the same, irrespective of the deployment choices.
- **Client**: This represents the various client components to access Dynamics 365 for Finance and Operations, such as the browser client, mobile app, and Office 365.
- **Development tools**: Visual studio is the exclusive development environment for a developer to extend the existing application logic or build new features.
- **Lifecycle services**: These manage the application's lifecycle, including deployment, monitoring, and support for the cloud, as well as on-premise deployments.

Now let's look at the deployment architecture of Dynamics 365 for Finance and Operations. Later in this chapter, we will explore the various components and architecture in detail.

Deployment architecture

Deployment architecture depicts the mapping of a conceptual architecture to a physical environment. The physical environment includes the computing nodes and services, and how they connect with each other to make the final environment. In this section, let's explore the deployment architecture of Dynamics 365 for Finance and Operations, Enterprise edition.

The cloud deployment architecture

The Dynamics 365 for Finance and Operations, Enterprise edition architecture is built for cloud-first, which is the recommended and preferred option of deployment. Cloud deployment uses Microsoft Azure, managed by Microsoft, as the cloud platform. The following diagram shows an example of the production environment deployment architecture:

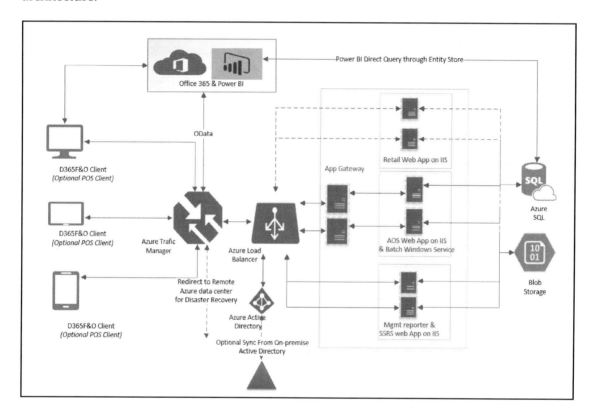

To understand the diagram, let's walk through the image from left to right and explore the various components and their roles:

- **Client devices**: These are the devices that use Finance and Operations through the web browser or mobile apps. The Office 365 and Power BI applications connect using OData.

- **Azure traffic manager**: This is used for DNS resolution and Azure region identification. It also redirects to remote Azure data centers in disaster recovery scenarios.

- **Azure load balancer**: This is used for VM-level load balancing--generally, round robin, but more custom solutions are possible.

- **Azure active directory**: This provides identity management and authentication. Optionally, you can use Azure sync to sync identities from your on-premise active directory.

- **App gateways**: These are used for application-level load balancing, essentially for session management between the client and server and mainly for AOS.

- **Application VMs:** These are deployed in the **HA (high availability)** mode (at least two in the availability set). Application VMs can be scaled out based on demand. There are separate VMs for AOS, retail sever (optional), and management reporter and reporting services. AOS is deployed as a web app on IIS and Windows services for batch processing. Management reporter, reporting services, and retail servers are also deployed on the IIS as web apps.

- **Data layer**: All databases are deployed on SQL Azure. Blob storage is used to stores files.

 This architecture diagram is just an example to help you understand the architecture; your actual deployment design will vary according to your resources and requirements.

The on-premise deployment architecture

The on-premise deployment option uses Finance and Operations components running on the premises, leveraging service fabric standalone clusters. The following diagram shows an example of the on-premise deployment architecture with the minimum recommended nodes for Dynamics 365 for Finance and Operations, Enterprise edition:

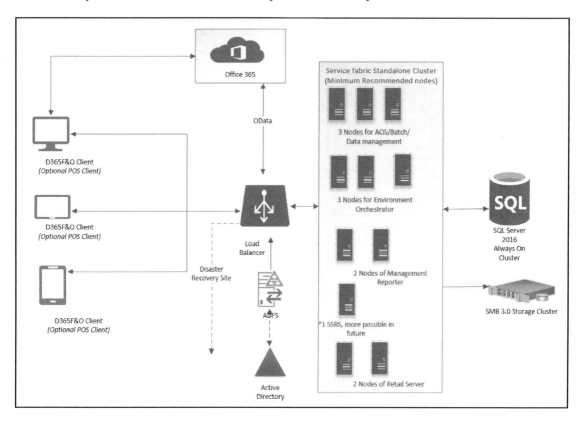

Let's again walk through the preceding image from left to right and explore the various components:

- **Client devices**: Similar to the cloud environment, various devices use a web browser or mobile application to access Dynamics 365 for Finance and Operation, Enterprise edition. Office 365 uses OData for communication.
- **Load balancer**: The network load balancer is used for balancing the load between application nodes and redirecting the disaster recovery scenario.

- **ADFS and AD**: **Active Directory Federation Services (ADFS)** is used along with the on-premise active directory for authentication.
- **Application VMs**: In on-premise deployment, all the core components of finance and operations are deployed using the service fabric standalone cluster. In addition to the regular application VMs, another set of VMs is needed for on-premise environment management from LCS.
- **Database layer:** All databases are created on Microsoft SQL Server 2016 Standard edition or Enterprise edition. **Server Message Block (SMB)** 3.0 storage cluster stores unstructured data on the AOS servers.

 This architecture diagram is just an example to understand the architecture; your actual deployment design will vary according to your resources and requirements.
At the time of writing this book, the Power BI integration was not available for on-premise deployments. In the future, there may be a possibility of enabling the Power BI through data synchronization to cloud.

On-premise deployment was made available for Dynamics 365 for Finance and Operations, Enterprise edition in June 2017. At the time of writing this book, many features were not supported or needed to be configured differently from cloud deployments.

 For the latest details on the on-premise deployment option, follow
`https://docs.microsoft.com/en-us/dynamics365/unified-operations/`
`dev-itpro/deployment/on-premises-deployment-landing-page.`

Application components and architecture

In the previous section, we explored the conceptual and deployment architecture of Dynamics 365 for Finance and Operations, Enterprise edition. To understand the various components within the architecture, let's go through each component in the architecture separately in this section.

Identity

Dynamics 365 for Finance and Operations cloud deployment uses Azure AD for identity management and authentication. Microsoft Azure AD is a modern, cloud-based service that provides identity management and access control capabilities for your cloud applications. You can use **Azure AD Connect** to integrate and synchronize with an on-premise Windows active directory and provide the **Single Sign On (SSO)** functionality to the user and devices. Azure active directory not only powers the identity and access management for Dynamics 365 but also supports many other SaaS-based web applications, such as Office 365, NetSuite, ServiceNow, Salesforce, Workday, and many more third-party web applications. The following diagram shows the high-level capabilities of Azure AD:

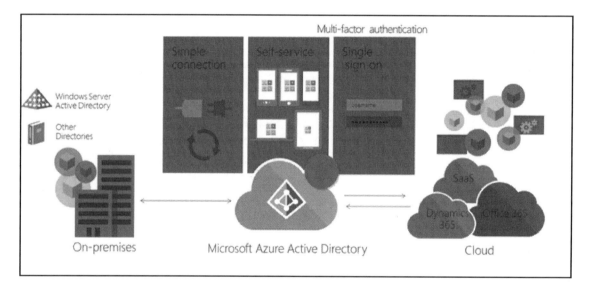

Cloud deployment of Dynamics 365 for Finance and Operations uses Azure AD and **SAML 2.0 (Security Assertion Markup Language)** protocol for the authentication and authorization process. The following diagram depicts in simple steps how this happens:

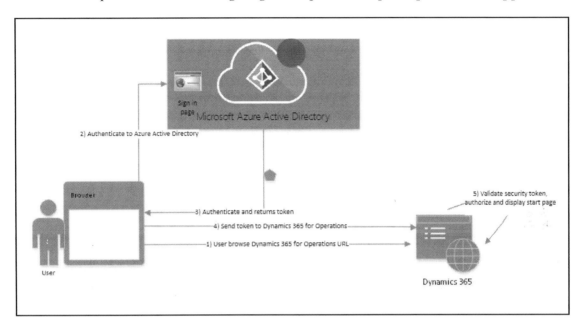

As the diagram shows, the **User** logs on to Dynamics 365 for Finance and Operations, Enterprise edition using a **Browser** (step 1) and gets redirected to the Azure AD login page for authentication (step 2) . The user logs in to Azure AD using the user ID and password. Azure AD authenticates the user, generates the SAML 2.0 token and redirects to Dynamics 365 for Finance and Operations, Enterprise edition with security tokens, (step 3 and 4). In the end, Dynamics 365 for Finance and Operations validates the security token, authorizes the user (if the user is registered as a valid user in the application) and displays the start page.

The on-premise deployment option uses ADFS for authentication and active directory for identity management. The following diagram shows the authentication flow in on-premise deployment:

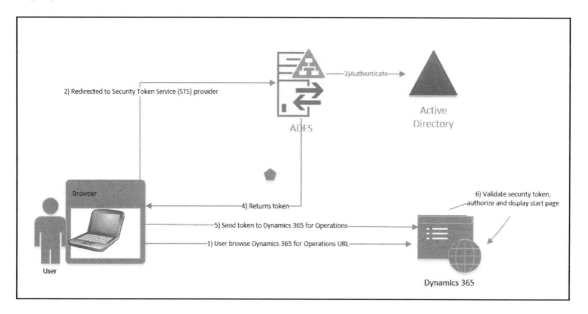

As shown in the diagram, the authentication flow for on-premise deployment is similar to cloud deployment. The only difference is that for the cloud, Azure AD is used as STS and identity provider, whereas for on-premise deployment, ADFS is used as the STS provider and AD as the identity provider.

 A **security token service (STS)** is a software-based identity provider responsible for issuing security tokens as part of a claims-based identity system.

Data layer

Dynamics 365 for Finance and Operations, Enterprise edition uses Azure SQL or SQL Server 2016 for the data layer. Separate databases are used for primary transactions, reporting services, management reporter, and Power BI reporting.

The following diagram shows the different databases used in Dynamics 365 for Finance and Operations, Enterprise edition and their purposes. As shown in the diagram, the primary read and write workload of Dynamics 365 for Operation can either use Azure SQL or SQL server, depending on the customer deployment model. Cloud deployment uses Azure SQL as the primary database, while for on-premise, SQL Server 2016 is used.

Cloud deployment also uses blob storage for scenarios involving file upload or download and document databases for document handling within the application. To improve the performance, Dynamics 365 for Finance and Operations, Enterprise edition automatically redirects some read-only workload to secondary databases. Examples of such scenarios are fact boxes on the list page and counters on the workspaces:

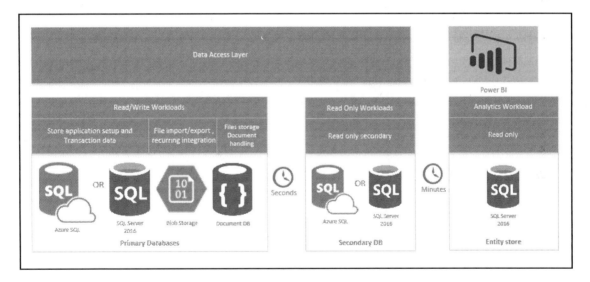

Platform

Dynamics 365 for Finance and Operations comprises multiple applications, such as application object server, retail server, SQL server reporting services, and management reporter. Let's explore these components:

- **Application Object Servers (AOS)**: This provides the ability to run the Finance and Operations application functionality in client, batch, and import/export scenarios.
- **Retail Server:** This provides stateless services and business logic for Retail Modern Point of Sale (MPOS) and e-commerce clients.
- **Management Reporter (MR):** This provides the financial reporting functionality and also known as Financial Reports.
- **SQL Server Reporting Services (SSRS):** This provides the document reporting functionality.

In cloud deployment, these components are deployed and run on Azure compute VMs. The following diagram shows a logical view of the VMs deployed in the cloud deployment model:

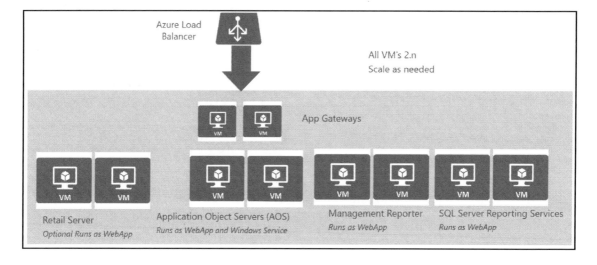

In the local business data or on-premise deployment, all the application components are deployed using **Microsoft Service Fabric Standalone Clusters** on the customer data center.

Service fabric is a next-generation Microsoft middleware platform for building and managing enterprise-class high-scale applications. Service fabric standalone clusters can be deployed on any computer that runs a Windows server.

On-premise deployment needs another component called **Environment Orchestrator** to enable the on-premise environment management from LCS. The following diagram shows the logical architecture of on-premise deployment:

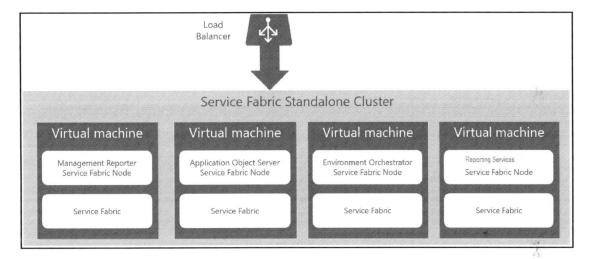

At the time of writing this book, retail server is not supported in on-premise deployments.

Application

The Dynamics 365 for Finance and Operations application layer is primarily represented by application runtime, known as **Application Object Server (AOS)**. AOS runs as an ASP.NET web application hosted on **Internet Information Services (IIS)**. AOS has all the core kernel components (security, metadata, and data access), forms engine, UI interaction service, web services endpoints, and so on. Asynchronous batch processing capability and data management is provided by a Windows service running on each application server. The following diagram shows the key components of the server and how they are stacked together:

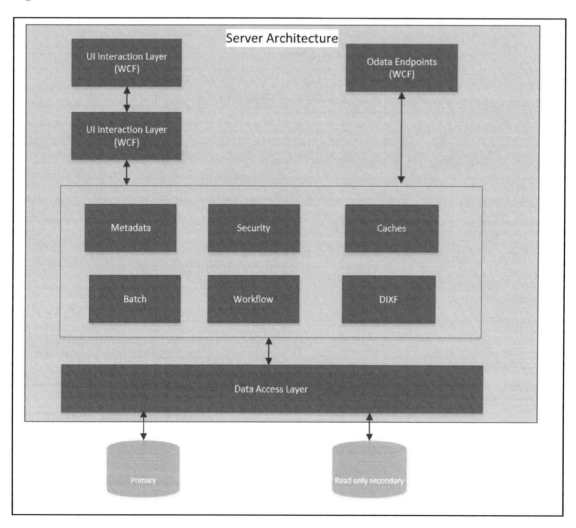

The Dynamics 365 for Finance and Operations, Enterprise edition application stack is divided into the following distinct models and further divided into multiple packages:

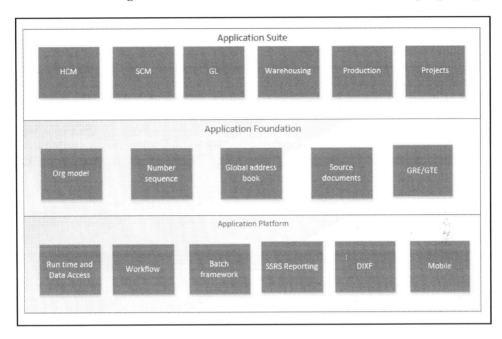

As shown in the image, the following are three models representing the application stack:

- **Application platform**: This is the lowest-level model and contains application code, handling the core application functionalities, such as runtime and data access, workflow, batch framework, SSRS reporting , **Data import/export framework (DIXF)**, task recorder, and mobile framework.
- **Application foundation**: This contains shared application code used by the different modules in the application, such as number sequence, global address book, source document format, generic report engine, generic tax engine, and so on.
- **Application suite**: This is the top-level model containing the code of the basic application functionality for each module. Customers, partners, and ISV can extend the application suite to add additional functionality to fulfill their unique business requirements. Application suite started as a monolithic big model containing the entire application area; however, probably over time, this will get divided into multiple models to create independent applications out of Dynamics 365 for Finance and Operations.

Splitting the application code stack into multiple models provides many benefits, including modular code, faster compile time, and better servicing models. More details about the models and packages are available in `Chapter 9`, *Building Customization* in this book.

Client

User experience is fundamental to the success and adoption of ERP systems. If an ERP application is not easy and pleasant to use, the end user starts showing resistance to using the ERP system and starts using legacy tools and processes. An intuitive and enjoyable user experience naturally increases productivity. Dynamics 365 for Finance and Operations, Enterprise edition comes with a completely revamped and immersive user interface to meet the modern expectations of design and usability. These clients are browser-based HTML 5 client, a mobile app, and integration with Office 365 to increase productivity and usability for the end users.

Browser client

The primary client for Dynamics 365 is the web browser. Dynamics 365 for Finance and Operations, Enterprise edition supports many browsers, such as Internet Explorer, Microsoft Edge, Google Chrome, and Safari. Dynamics 365 for Finance and Operation can be used across platforms and devices.

The following are the key highlights of the browser client:

- Use of pure web technologies: HTML 5, CSS, and JavaScript
- All communication is HTTPS, using the RESTful protocol in the JSON data format
- All code runs on the server within the context of the ASP.NET web app

From an architecture point of view, the following diagram shows how the browser and the application server interact when the user interacts with Dynamics 365 for Finance and Operations, Enterprise edition in a browser:

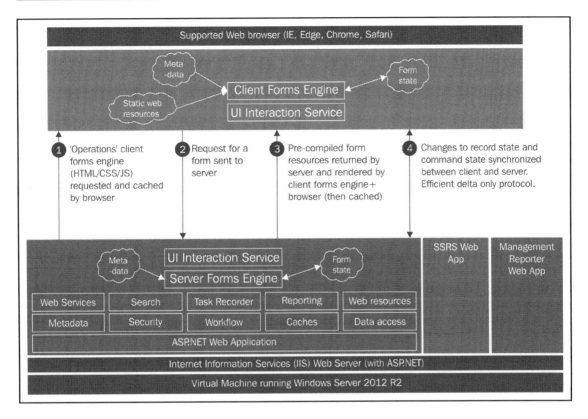

The following steps describe the interaction between the browser and the application server as shown in the preceding image:

1. As the very first step, when the user browses the application page using the browser, the user gets authenticated and redirected to the home page of Dynamics 365 for Finance and Operations, Enterprise edition. If the user is using Dynamics 365 for Finance and Operations, Enterprise edition for the first time, then the application form engine is requested and cached by the browser.

2. When the user navigates to a form within Dynamics 365 for Finance and Operations, Enterprise edition, the browser sends the form request to the server.

3. In response to the form request, the server returns precompiled form resources. Form resources are rendered by browser and client form engine and then cached locally by the browser.

4. Now, the changes made by the user on the form, such as changing the data, clicking a button, and so on, are synchronized between the client and the server using delta changes.

Mobile app

In the last few years, mobile has grown so fast that it's now the leading digital platform. Users are spending more time on mobile devices than on their personal computers. Business applications are also impacted with this trend. Employees need mobile apps to create and submit their timesheet and expenses, managers need apps to approve workflow requests on the go, sales reps need customer information and can create orders on the go when they are visiting the customers. Dynamics 365 for Finance and Operations, Enterprise edition includes support for mobile phone apps on Android and iOS devices.

The following are the key highlights of the mobile app for Dynamics 365 for Finance and Operations, Enterprise edition:

- **Offline capability**: You can view, edit, and operate the mobile app when your device is connected to the network and while your mobile phone is completely offline. If a user creates or updates data while his or her device isn't connected to the Finance and Operations server, temporary records are created in the local cache. When your device reestablishes a network connection, your offline data operations are automatically synchronized.
- **Build and deploy**: IT admins can build and publish mobile workspaces as per the organization's need. The app leverages your existing code, business logic, and security configuration. IT admins can easily design mobile workspaces using the point-and-click workspace designer that comes built in with the Dynamics 365 for Finance and Operations, Enterprise edition web client.
- **Business logic extensibility**: IT admins can optimize the offline capabilities of workspaces by utilizing the business logic extensibility framework. Using this, you can provide additional business logic and render support by adding a JavaScript file with the application workspace metadata.

The following screenshot provides an overview of the Dynamics 365 for Finance and Operations mobile application user interface:

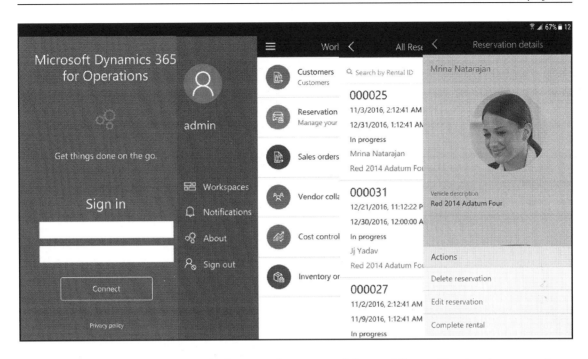

The following diagram shows the basic architecture of the mobile application framework:

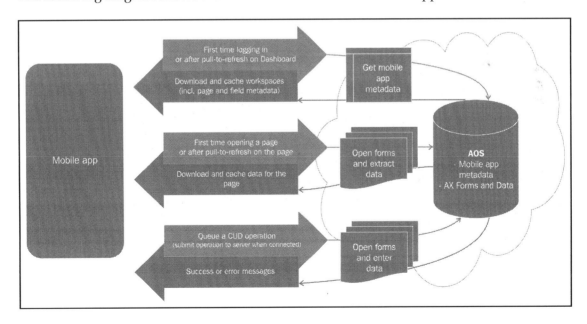

As shown in the diagram, mobile app metadata, forms, and data are all stored on the application object server. When the user logs in for the first time or pulls to refresh the dashboard, the mobile app requests the metadata and downloads and caches the workspaces and pages. When the user opens the page or pulls to refresh the data on the page, the mobile app opens the form, downloads the data for the page, and caches it. Any operation, such as editing the data or taking an action that results in a create, update, or delete operation, goes into the queue and is subsequently executed on the AOS, with the result synchronized.

Office 365

The office integration capabilities of Microsoft Dynamics 365 for Finance and Operations, Enterprise edition enables end users to interact with the operations data in their favorite office application, such as Excel and Microsoft Word. In Excel, the Microsoft Dynamics Office addin allows users to export, edit, and publish data back to the Finance and Operations application. In Word, the Microsoft Dynamics Office addin allows users to build templates and upload those templates to the Finance and Operations application. A user can then trigger document generation to populate Dynamics 365 data to word, which can be used for light reporting.

The Microsoft Dynamics Office addin is a lightweight Office web add-on available for free in the Office store. The Office add-on is built using the Office web JS API and HTML, and uses OData to interact with the data entities of Dynamics 365 for Finance and Operations, Enterprise edition.

The following diagram shows the architecture of the Dynamics 365 for Finance and Operations, Enterprise edition integration with Office 365:

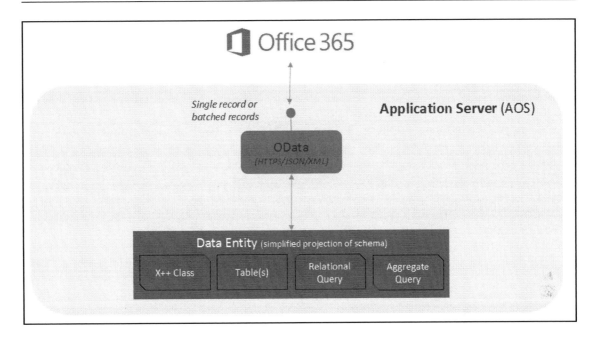

The following diagram represents the interaction between Dynamics 365 for Finance and Operations, Enterprise edition and the Office addin when open in Excel:

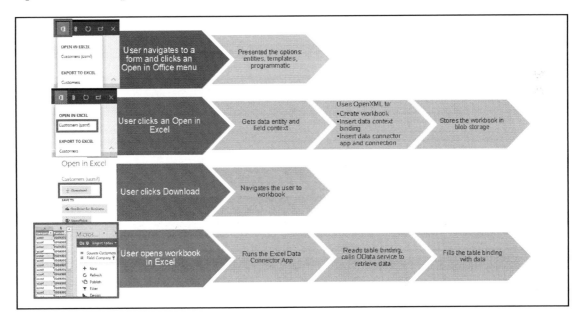

As shown in the diagram, the Excel addin scenario starts when the user navigates to a form and clicks on the **Open in Office** menu. The user is presented with the options of the available entities, templates, and any programmatically added integrations. Then, the user selects the entity and clicks **Open in Excel**; in this step, the system gets the data entity and the field context, creates a workbook, inserts the data context, and inserts the connector manifest and the server URL. The workbook created is stored in a temporary Azure blob storage, and the user is presented with the option to **Download** the file to the local filesystem or save to the cloud, such as One Drive for business or SharePoint online. When the user downloads the file and opens the Excel workbook, Excel runs the data connector app, makes a connection to the server URL, reads the table binding, calls the OData service to retrieve the data, and finally, fills the table binding with data. All interactions with the Excel addin scenario use the current user login and, hence, the security context. Users can only read or update data that they have access to.

Lifecycle Services

Lifecycle Services (**LCS**) is one of the most important components of the Dynamics 365 for Finance and Operations, Enterprise edition architecture. LCS is a Microsoft Azure-based collaboration portal that provides a unifying, collaborative environment along with a set of regularly updated services that help you manage the application lifecycle of your Microsoft Dynamics 365 for Finance and Operations, Enterprise edition implementations.

The following diagram shows the various services supported by LCS during the implementation, upgrade, and support phases of Dynamics 365 for Finance and Operations, Enterprise edition:

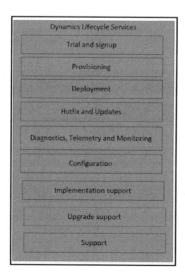

As is clearly evident, LCS is used throughout the lifecycle of the project. You will learn about the different tools available in detail throughout this book.

The application lifecycle management for on-premise deployments is also orchestrated through LCS. Customers can use LCS to help manage their on-premise deployments. The following diagram shows the on-premise ALM process through LCS:

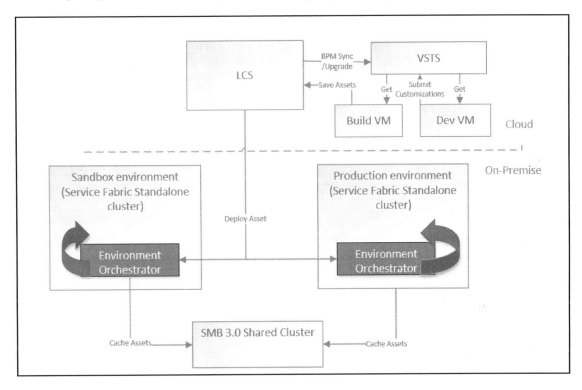

As shown in the diagram, similar to cloud deployment, LCS can be used to synchronize the LCS project artifacts to VSTS. The developer can use the one box cloud machine or already downloaded machines to get the latest code in their development environment. Once done, the code is checked in the VSTS. The cloud build environment can pull the latest code and generate the deployable artifacts that can be uploaded to the LCS asset library. The on-premise, production, or sandbox environment can be serviced directly through LCS with the help of the environment orchestrator within the service fabric standalone cluster node.

For more details on LCS, refer to `Chapter 2`, *Implementation Methodology and Tools*.

Let's now explore the development architecture in the next subsection.

Development architecture

ERP applications are built for generic industry requirements, and most of the customers implementing an ERP system need some level of customization application to satisfy their unique business requirements. The Microsoft Dynamics 365 for Finance and Operation development environment is completely different from its previous version; it uses Visual Studio as the only IDE for development. The following diagram shows the development environment architecture:

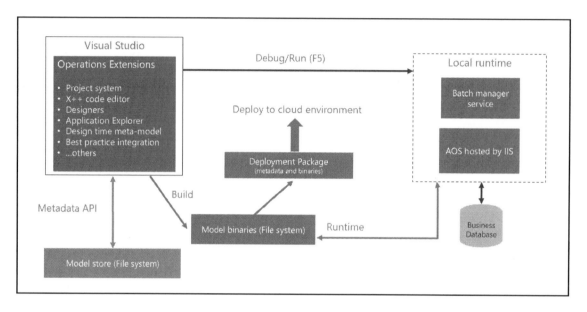

As shown in the diagram, in Visual Studio, **Operations Extensions** provide the developer, application explorer, X++ code editor, project system, UI designer, debugger, and other tools to extend the existing functionalities and add new functionalities. Visual Studio is also used to debug and create a deployable package to promote the application code to test and production environment. In Dynamics 365 for Finance and Operations, Enterprise edition, X++ is a 100% managed language running in the .NET CLR. The compiler is rewritten entirely and compiles directly to .NET assemblies. Now, in Dynamics 365 for Finance and Operations, Enterprise edition, the source code is stored in the development VM filesystem as XML files and used by the metadata API of the Visual Studio extension for editing and design experience. The developer builds the application that compiles the source to .NET CIL (DLL) files. The following diagram represents the code, design time and run time experience in Dynamics 365 for Finance and Operations, Enterprise edition:

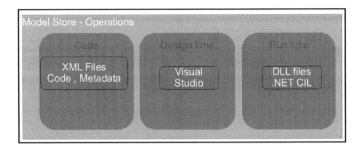

Those who are familiar with the previous version can understand how different this architecture is from it. In the previous version, MorphX was used as the development IDE, which was built as part of the Dynamics AX Windows client. Certain development scenarios, such as SSRS report and enterprise portal development, required Visual Studio for development. In Dynamics AX 2012, the metadata (source code) and the runtime code was stored in the SQL server database. All AX X++ code is compiled into an AX 2012 intermediate format called **P-Code** and used by the client and the server. In addition, all the classes and tables are compiled into .NET CIL, and are used by the batch framework and some other scenarios.

The following diagram shows **Model Store** in Dynamics AX 2012 R3:

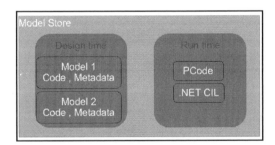

We will discuss more about the development environment, concepts, and practices in Chapter 9, *Building Customization*.

Integration architecture

Dynamics 365 for Finance and Operations, Enterprise edition supports the modern HTTP-based RESTful model of integration, along with recurring integration for high volume, asynchronous integration models. New integration framework is based on the OData 4.0 protocol and supports the JSON format for data exchange. **JavaScript Object Notation (JSON)** is a lightweight data-interchange format. It is easy for humans to read and write. It is easy for machines to parse and generate.

Integration in Dynamics 365 for Finance and Operations is based on data management platform and built on earlier version's **Data Import/Export framework (DIXF)**, which serves multiple purposes, such as integration, data migration, configuration management, and analytics. Dynamics 365 for Finance and Operations also supports the custom services concept which was also available in the earlier version, Dynamics AX 2012. A custom service is basically X++ business logic that can be declared as a service and consumed by external applications.

The following diagram shows the conceptual architecture of integration architecture in Dynamics 365 for Finance and Operations, Enterprise edition:

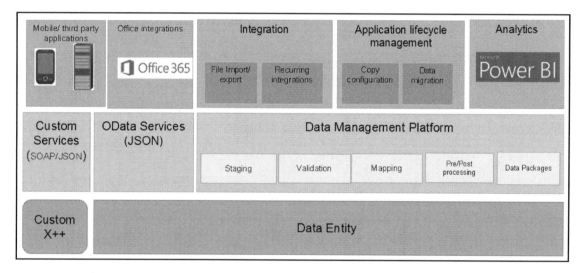

Dynamics 365 Data Integration is another integration framework primarily used to integrate a Dynamics 365 family of products, such as sales, project service automation, field services, and finance and operations. This framework is based on the common data services platform and is flexible for customization to support third-party integration on the cloud.

Integration for business applications is a big topic and cannot be covered in a couple of paragraphs. We will learn more integration architecture, concepts, and best practices in Chapter 8, *Integration Planning and Design*.

Security architecture

An ERP system provides unified business functions to organizations by integrating data and processes from different departments, such as human resources, accounts receivable, accounts payable, inventory management, general ledger, and so on. Since the ERP system stores all the company data, ERP security is extremely important. Dynamics 365 for Finance and Operations, Enterprise edition provides a comprehensive security model to secure application access and defines security policy for business users using security roles and data security policies.

The following diagram provides a high-level view of the security architecture used in Dynamics 365 for Finance and Operations, Enterprise edition:

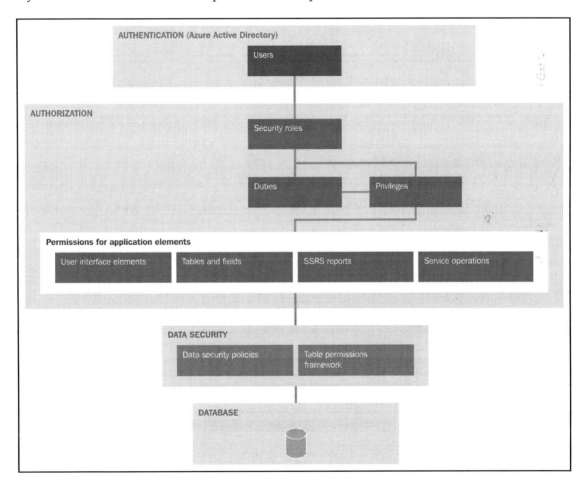

As shown in the image, there are three components of the security architecture:

- **Authentication**: As discussed earlier in this chapter, Azure AD is used for the authentication process in Dynamics 365 for Finance and Operations, Enterprise edition. If the user is not authenticated, the connection to application will be closed.
- **Authorization**: Authorization is the control of the application access. Once the user is authenticated, the Finance and Operations application determines what the user can see based on the security roles he or she is assigned. Security roles comprise duties and privileges which are designed to secure individual user interface elements, tables and fields, reports, and service operations. The privileges defined in the application also define the access levels, such as delete, read, and write. Based on the access level, the application element access is controlled for the user at runtime.
- **Data security**: Data security is used to deny access to tables, fields, and rows in the database. An extensible data security framework provides the ability to filter data based on the user context. The table permission framework provides the ability for AOS servers to enforce permissions on certain tables.

Deployment options

Whether your organization is ready to embrace the power and ease of the cloud or still prefers on-premise applications due to connectivity, data sovereignty, CAPEX versus OPEX costs, or any other reason, Dynamics 365 for Finance and Operations, Enterprise edition has all the scenarios covered. Microsoft Dynamics 365 for Finance and Operations can be deployed on Azure Cloud, completely offline on-premise (local business data), or as a hybrid model (Cloud and Edge). To maximize the benefit and power of the cloud, cloud deployment is the preferred and recommended option.

Cloud

The cloud deployment option enables the deployment of Dynamics 365 for Finance and Operations, Enterprise edition on the Microsoft Azure Cloud platform. There has been an unprecedented adoption of cloud ERP systems by mid-sized and large organizations. Cloud deployment is the preferred and recommended option, as Microsoft is committed to its cloud-first approach in business applications and continues to invest more in cloud services.

The following are the key highlights of cloud deployment:

- Fully managed by Microsoft Cloud service
- Subscription pricing--pay per user per month
- System of intelligence
- Scale out as needed with the help of Microsoft's support team
- ExpressRoute as an add-on

ExpressRoute lets customers connect their on-premise infrastructure to Azure data centers using a dedicated, private connection that's highly available, highly reliable, has low latency, and is supported with a published 99.95% financially-backed SLA.

The following image describes the idea of a cloud deployment model, where the application as well as the configuration and customization, telemetry and diagnostics, and business data are all in the cloud. Microsoft is a data trustee and manages the environments. The customer and partner do not have direct access to the production infrastructure but can access ALM, telemetry, and diagnostics data through LCS. The customer and partner have full access to the development, build, and sandbox environment and can log in to the environment using a remote desktop:

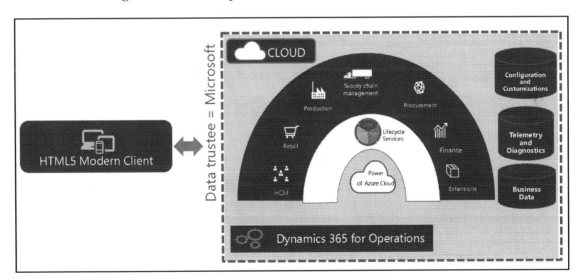

Specific scenarios where cloud deployments are desirable are as follows:

- An organization desires to move their operations to the cloud completely to save on-premise infrastructure cost and maintenance
- An organization has already been using Office 365 or Dynamics 365 products, such as CRM tools, and wants an integrated view
- You'd like to innovate faster and utilize the power of the cloud with Microsoft cloud services, such as Power BI, Cortana intelligence, and so on

Cloud and Edge or hybrid deployment

Cloud and Edge, or hybrid deployment, is not a self-contained on-premise deployment like local business data. In this deployment model, components will be deployed both on the cloud and on the premises, and are designed to work together and complement each other. The following image shows conceptual architecture of the cloud and edge deployment model:

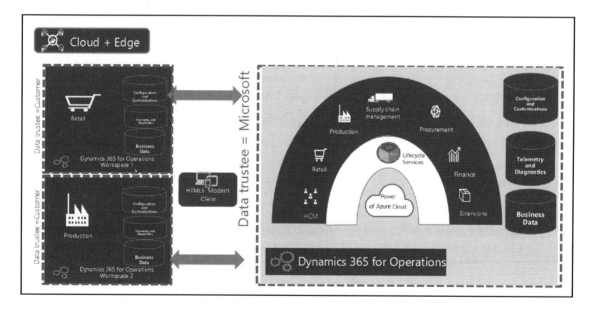

The Cloud and Edge deployment model starts with cloud components deployed on Azure to provide enterprise-level functionalities such as complete enterprise view, business intelligence, and disaster recovery. In addition to cloud deployment, some operations, such as retail and manufacturing, can be deployed on the customer's infrastructure for business continuity or integration with local systems. These local components are called *my workspace*. Local workspace stores their code, configuration, and telemetry data locally and periodically synchronizes with the cloud to provide enterprise data view. It is also possible to use the hybrid model to deploy Dynamics 365 for Finance and Operations, Enterprise edition in a fully distributed model, where a company or operations can live on the cloud and multiple on-premise locations at the same time. For example, the company headquarters can operate on the cloud and access full enterprise view while different warehouse operations can be deployed on on-premise servers in different data centers. This distributed environment will all be invisible to the end user, as both the on-premises and cloud components extend the same functionalities and user interface.

The following are the key highlights of the Cloud and Edge deployment model:

- Cloud — MS managed
- Edge — customer managed
- Multiple local compute and storage workplaces for retail, shop floor, and warehouse while utilizing the cloud for scale, master data management, and data aggregation
- Local data residency in addition to cloud

Specific scenarios where hybrid configuration could be desirable are as follows:

- Retailers can have a local store server on the premises so that they can continue to process orders if the internet is down
- Manufacturing companies that have multiple plants can maximize the system performance by having users connect to local hardware
- Distribution companies that may want the control of having their warehousing operations on the premises
- Operations in countries or locations where internet latency is a major problem
- Operations in countries that have data sovereignty laws where data must originate in-country, as opposed to in a foreign country data center or in the cloud

In these cases, Dynamics 365 Finance and Operations will be able to run on hardware that is local to that entity. The transactions will happen on the local hardware, and will then replicate to the cloud.

The Cloud and Edge scenario will provide the ability to manage and to control the entire environment through LCS. This includes the built-in telemetry and other components that assist with the performance diagnostics and other management tools.

The following are the major highlights of the Cloud and Edge deployment model:

- Deployment on the cloud provides single view and disaster recovery
- Deploys a part of the application on the premises (retail, warehouse, and shop floor)
- Supports distributed environment

 At the time of writing this book, the Cloud and Edge deployment is only available for retail scenarios. For the latest information, availability, and features, visit the Microsoft documentation and roadmap website.

Local business data or on-premises

Some organizations do not want to store their data on infrastructure they don't fully control. Local business data deployment is a choice for them. Local business data deployment is a deployment model where the key components of Dynamics 365 for Finance and Operations, Enterprise edition are deployed on the customer's local data center. This model is suitable for customers who are not ready for the cloud journey due to regulatory reasons or their existing data center investments.

As explained earlier in this chapter, local business data deployment still uses LCS for deployment and management of Dynamics 365 for Finance and Operations, Enterprise edition. However, there is no business data processing outside the customer's or their partner's data center. In this model, the customer/partner is responsible for managing the infrastructure and disaster recovery. Power BI or cloud intelligence is optional for local business data, as these options need business data in the cloud. Customers will have an option to enable it by allowing the business data to be replicated in the cloud. The following diagram represents a local business data deployment model:

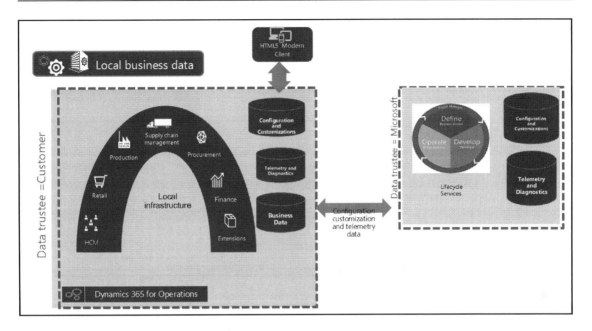

As shown in the diagram, local business data means that the finance and operations application deployment is limited to the customer data center. LCS in the cloud is still used for deployment and management, where the configuration, customization, and telemetry data is synchronized to the cloud to enable management and diagnostics.

The following are the key highlights of local business data deployment:

- Disconnected data centers
- Local data residency
- Capitalize HW investments
- Single instance only

The following are the key components that enable you to host your solution on the premises:

- Azure Service Fabric:
    - Microsoft Azure Service Fabric standalone clusters deployed on Windows 2016 server
    - SMB 3.0 cluster (**Server Message Block**)
- Azure Active Directory (AAD):
    - Authentication for LCS
    - Authentication for VSTS
- OS:
    - Windows 2016 server (standard or data center)
    - Virtual machines running on Hyper-V
- SQL:
    - 64 bit only version
    - SQL 2016 Standard/Enterprise
    - Always ON cluster
    - Bandwidth: minimum 100 MBps with AOS
    - SAN (storage area network optimized for OLTP throughputs)
    - SAN IOPS: minimum 2,000 **input/output operations per second (IOPS)**
    - Cores: recommended minimum 8 cores for production in dedicated mode
    - RAM: recommended minimum 24 GB for production
    - Hard disk should be **solid-state drive (SSD)**
    - Virtualization
- Local windows server active directory:
    - **Active Directory Domain Services (AD DS)**
    - **Active Directory Federation Services (AD FS)** 3.0

- LCS:
  - Application management
  - Machine deployment
  - Code deployment
  - Servicing operations
  - Environment orchestrator
  - Primary fabric service requiring at least three VMs

- AOS:
  - Should be co-located with SQL
  - Bandwidth: minimum 50 KBps per user
  - Latency:
    - minimum < 250–300ms for clients
    - < 1ms in LAN only with SQL
  - Cores: standard box – 4 to 24 cores
  - RAM: minimum 16 GB per AOS instance
  - Virtualization
  - Typical AOS-to-SQL core ratio 3:1 for the primary SQL Server

- Others
  - Development experience continues to be the same as in cloud deployments through 1-box VHDs, which may need Microsoft Remote Desktop and Visual Studio licenses
  - MR/SSRS (local)
  - Web client (able to access intranet IIS websites)

 We recommend you always get the latest information from these links:
https://docs.microsoft.com/en-us/dynamics365/unified-operations/
dev-itpro/deployment/setup-deploy-on-premises-environments
https://docs.microsoft.com/en-us/dynamics365/unified-operations/
dev-itpro/deployment/on-premises-deployment-landing-page

Let's now compare the deployment options that will help you choose the best fit for your business.

Comparing deployment options

The following table (taken from the Microsoft announcement on Feb 2017 located at `https://community.dynamics.com/b/msftdynamicsblog/archive/2017/02/23/the-right-cloud-option-for-your-business`) compares all three deployment options in terms of use cases, compute and data residency, data trustee, capabilities, and business intelligence options:

Cloud Scenario	Full cloud	Cloud and Edge	Local business data
Use-case scenarios	Fully managed by Microsoft cloud service Systems of Intelligence Planned multi Instance federation Elastic scale out	Cloud – MS managed, Edge – customer managed Multiple local compute and storage workplaces for retail, shop floor and warehouse while utilizing cloud for scale, master data mgmt., data aggregation Local data residency in addition to cloud	Disconnected data center Local data residency Capitalize HW investments Single instance only
Compute and data residency	Cloud	Cloud and customer or partner infrastructure	Customer or partner infrastructure
Data Trustee	Microsoft	Microsoft and Customer	Customer
Application management	Fully managed by Microsoft Customer access to ALM and telemetry via LCS	Cloud managed by Microsoft, Edge managed by customer or partner with Cloud-based ALM and telemetry via LCS	Infrastructure managed by customer or partner with Cloud-based ALM and telemetry via LCS
Cloud capabilities	HA and DR included Sandbox environments Cloud-based intelligence	Data Federation and Master Data Management HA and DR included sandbox environments Cloud-based intelligence	Automated deployment intelligence as optional Cloud-based add-on
Intelligence	Cloud-based	Cloud-based	Optional cloud add-on

Continuous updates and health monitoring	Cloud-based, LCS	Cloud-based, LCS	Cloud-based, LCS
Planned availability	Available	Availability: Q4 CY2017	Availability: Q2 CY2017

Summary

In this chapter, we started with understanding the architecture of Dynamics 365 for Finance and Operations. We covered the conceptual architecture, various components, their roles, and how they function. Dynamics 365 for Finance and Operations embraces modern architecture built for cloud-first deployment. New architecture, when deployed in the cloud, uses Azure AD for the identity model and Azure SQL as the database, and the application components get deployed using Azure VMs. On-premise deployment uses AD FS for authentication, SQL Server 2016 for database, and Service Fabric Standalone Cluster to deploy application components. In the new architecture, Application Object Server (AOS) is hosted on IIS and batch operations run as a Windows service. Application logic is now modular and separated into application platform, application foundation, and application suite.

Dynamics 365 for Finance and Operations clients now comprises of the modern HTML 5-based web client and mobile app and has seamless integration with Office 365. It uses an exclusively new development platform on Visual Studio. LCS is used to manage the cloud as well as the on-premise deployment application lifecycle--from project inception to upgrade.

You also learned about three deployment choices available: Cloud, Cloud and Edge, and local business data. The cloud deployment option is the preferred and recommended option, while the other options can be useful for the organization having reservations in moving to the cloud due to regulatory or other challenges.

In the next chapter, you will lean about project initiation and management for implementing Dynamics 365 for Finance and Operations.

4
Project Initiation and Kickoff

In the previous chapter, you learned about the architecture of and the deployment options in Microsoft Dynamics 365 for Finance and Operations, Enterprise edition (AX).

In this chapter, we'll share the importance and details of conducting project initiation, with the help of the following topics:

- The need for a solid project start
- Project team composition
- The backbone of the project
- The ground rules for day-to-day operations
- The kickoff meeting
- Project Initiation and LCS
- The project deliverables in the CRP methodology
- Best practices in project initiation

The need for a strong project start

A project is in place for something to be achieved, and any initiative in ERP adoption is considered a major undertaking. Hence, such initiatives should not be treated as mere IT programs but as organizational initiatives.

A strong project start is imperative in laying down the foundation for assured success. One can ensure a strong start by mixing in all the key ingredients:

- Vision for transformation
- Executive buy-in
- Talent acquisition

The definition of a strong start is important and may need to be personalized as per the size and complexity of the project. In essence, when project goals are committed from top to bottom and the vision is accepted by all the stakeholders of the project, it is considered to be a strong start. Often, this is just like laying down the seeds of a plant and watering them with commitment. While detailed planning will happen shortly, emphasis needs to be given to preplanning.

Business drivers and organizational goals often trigger the conceptualization of an initiative. Use these levers to preplan for the project and have a high-level of execution throughout the process.

You can tell that a project is ready to start when the project initiation checklist is ready. We recommend that the checklist contains the following:

- Vision statement:
    - This is super important and should be written in a business language, in such a way that any person outside the project should also be able to read it and understand what the project aims to achieve
    - A project vision statement should always be tangible and achievable
- Executive sponsorship
- Benefits
- A high-level timeline envisioned for going live
- Constraints and assumptions called out upfront and validated
- Identification of advisors and partners
- Budgetary approvals

Project team composition

The formula for any project's success is to involve the right talent. A team working towards a common goal is a must, and each member who is on board with the project must be clear on the objectives of the project.

Each team member must be trained in a matrix management style so as to get the best from them, as this form of organizational structure fosters collaboration unlike any other. Not just Dynamics 365, but any ERP project has so many moving parts that unless the team works unitedly, success can't be guaranteed.

Remember that no single cross-functional team is alike, as it is influenced by individual personalities, strengths, and weaknesses, coupled with the unique requirements of each initiative. This is what makes every Dynamics 365 implementation unique; hence, it is important for the project sponsor and the project manager to play the role of a binder to foster strong team dynamics.

The following is a typical project team structure based on our experiences while implementing Dynamics 365 solutions to leverage the CRP methodology. As ERP projects are usually large-scale initiatives, the support of external consulting partners and advisors is needed to form the right team for success. As described in the following diagram, there are a number of full-time or part-time internal (client) roles as well as advisor/consulting partner roles highlighted:

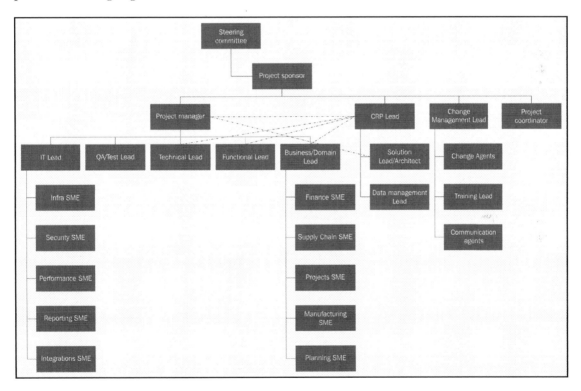

As shown in the preceding diagram, both sides of members need to function as one team, and hence, it typically becomes a matrix organization reporting with lots of dotted, as well as direct, reporting responsibility.

We'll now share our knowledge on a complete team composition, comprising a group and/or an individual, as follows:

- **Steering committee**:

    - These are the owners in providing resources, securing the funding, and liaising with the executive management/board of the organization
    - The role typically involves management representatives from the key departments of an organization
    - The committee is expected to execute executive-level leadership, keeping the larger vision in perspective
    - The committee needs to make policy decisions as necessary to ensure the success of the project

- **Project sponsor**:

    - This role acts as a champion and gives the much-needed thrust in order to be able to meet the project's goals and objectives
    - A project sponsor needs to be ahead of all the project activities and is a single point for all the decisions needed for the project
    - A project sponsor acts as a liaison to the steering committee and also leads such meetings

- **Project manager**:

    - The project manager is responsible for the overall management and implementation of the solution throughout its lifecycle
    - The project manager leads the project planning activities and manages the execution of projects according to plan
    - He/she manages relationships with stakeholders and keeps them informed of the progress and issues
    - He/she is the driving force for managing the expectations from all project deliverables
    - He/she is the motivator of the team, and enables and empowers the team members to deliver their best
    - He/she is responsible for creating and maintaining the project plan
    - He/she manages and protects against scope creep
    - He/she should always baseline the project plan in line with the objectives, changing conditions, and actuals

- He/she manages the financial aspects of the project, ensuring accurate budgeting and estimates to the actual variance
- He/she prepares the contingency plans and proactively works to identify triggering events for any issues/risk, and also comes up with an initial mitigation plan
- The project manager is the single point of contact for sign off-related activities
- He/she is the knowledge champion of the project management methodology, standards, tools, processes, and procedures

- **Business lead:**

  - This is an internal role and mostly comprises business experts, process owners, or **SMEs (Subject Matter Experts)**
  - Business leads are a central point of contact for a specific business process, and they need to carry end-to-end responsibility for the process
  - They are responsible for translating the business needs into processes and requirement specifications
  - They ensure that all the current (as-is) and future (to-be) processes are incorporated in the solution scope
  - A business lead is the owner of an end-to-end business process

- **CRP lead:**

  - This is a cross-functional role involving knowledge of project management methodologies and the commitment to drive the project to success
  - CRP leads are responsible for defining, planning, tracking, and managing every identified pilot
  - They participate in the project planning activities and lead the execution of the pilot
  - They manage relationships with project stakeholders, keeping them informed of the progress, issues, and deliverables in a pilot
  - They are the owners of the business blueprint

- **Advisor and partner**:

    - These are external knowledge experts in the solution, whom we generally refer to as value experts
    - They need to lead by example and carry multiple roles (viz. architects, consultants, and so on)
    - They are the key link in enabling business transformation initiatives
    - They are the owners of the solution blueprint
    - They lead strategic discussions with stakeholders on matters of systems, business processes, and requirements

- **Change management lead**:

    - Change management leads are the owners of all the change management initiatives that spin off when implementing/adapting the Dynamics 365 solutions
    - They chair the **Organizational Change Management (OCM)** discussion, and they provide advice for and direction in managing the changes arising from the project
    - They assist the project manager and the CRP lead in identifying potential risks, and they create plans to mitigate the risks in plan execution
    - They need to proactively identify new processes and changes to the existing business processes, and communicate these changes well through proper training

- **IT lead**:

    - IT lead is usually an information technology role, involving the customer personnel
    - The role supports all IT-related enablers in project execution
    - The IT lead develops and reviews the technological scope
    - IT leads bring in the technical direction and guidance
    - They provide system and technical expertise to the project team

Once you have a project team composed of the aforementioned roles, you have laid down a solid foundation for the success of your project. However, the preceding recommendations need to be mashed up as per the project's and organization's needs. We have seen exceptions to the preceding team structure and would like to call out the top two reasons for exceptions:

- Based on the project size, type, and complexity, a single person may perform more than one role. For larger initiatives, a dedicated **project management office (PMO)** may also be formed, which enables the coordination of meetings, travel, activity collection, and project status distribution.
- Large enterprises also set up something called service desk, which is typically an IT function that supports several IT operating processes, depending on the nature of the task. Also, if there are multiple initiatives, then each initiative can be treated as a project, which necessitates the need of the dedicated role of a program manager.

 ERP implementation is a long ride; hence, you must implement measures so as to have continuity in all the key resources, from the beginning to end.

The backbone of a project

Every initiative needs to have a backbone structure, which keeps things together. The project charter and project plan are amongst the top contributors to driving the project and keeping it together.

In this section, we will share insights into the project charter and project plan.

Project charter

The project charter is the foundation on which the success of a project depends. It must be complete and made as a formal document. All the initial conceptual planning that triggers an initiative is expected to be taken as the key input.

Project initiation being the early stage, the project contributors/participants suggested in the earlier section must brainstorm, innovate, and commit in this formal document.

The following are the salient features of a project charter:

- It should clearly articulate and describe the project objectives in a **SMART (Specific, Measurable, Achievable, Repeatable, and Time bound)** format
- It should form a solid agreement between the sponsors and the project management team
- This formal document should give the project manager the authority to manage the project
- It should define the types of resources that will be needed across project activities
- It should empower the OCM lead to drive the business process changes
- This document should be able to give a top-level view of the initiative in focus and list out all projects that are expected to be spun out of it
- A project charter should define a high-level scope of the initiative
- All critical success factors of accomplishing the goals must be called out, including the key milestones and target dates
- This document is typically prepared by the project sponsors, along with the stakeholders involved in delivering the project
- In a project charter, one must define a rough order of magnitude estimate for completing the project with some buffer as agreed with project stakeholders.
- It must mention the approved funding for the project and contingencies, if any
- The selection of the project delivery process, that is, methodology, assumptions, constraints, known risks, and identified issues, along with the other key elements, must be suggested as guidelines of the project charter

 A project charter should simply be seen as a map for everything that is expected to be achieved in the initiative and the direction for achieving the same.

Often, a project initiation document is used along with a project charter to act as a level between the project charter and the project plan.

In larger initiatives, a project scope document is also prepared, which lays down the exact description of requirements and deliverables. This formal requirement document, scoped for an initiative along with the project charter, forms the basis for developing a project plan.

Project plan

A project plan is a road map document on how to achieve the objectives of the initiative as described in the project charter.

 What needs to be accomplished should be in the project charter.
How the goals will be achieved should be in the project plan.

A project plan must facilitate a concise and effective communication. This is important, as it ensures that all the stakeholders are on the same page as to where their project stands at any point in time. A project plan is also a measurement to define outcomes, timelines, activities, resources, and commitments.

Any stakeholder at any point in time should be able to use the project plan and know what to expect by using the following fundamental questions:

- **Why**: The goals and reason for this initiative, typically coming from the project charter
- **How**: The list of all the activities needed to accomplish the project's goals
- **What**: The work expected to be performed in a specific activity
- **Who**: The person/team responsible for the individual work
- **When**: In a project timeline, when the work is expected to be completed

Let's take a look at some of the salient features of a project plan to implement Dynamics 365:

- The project implementation methodology must be selected, as recommended in the project charter.
- The project plan must always have detailed requirements, covering all the business processes as per the project goals. This could be based on a scope document, also known as **Statement of Work (SOW)** or contract, if prepared before the project plan.
- The project plan must define the **Work Breakdown Structure (WBS)**, which identifies all the work that needs to be done to complete the project. Structuring the work into logical components and subcomponents is an important aspect in WBS. The work definition should be at such a level of detail that it could be used to assign an individual.
- The project plan must list the resources that need to contribute to the project. All internal and external resources must be maintained in the project plan

- It should depict a schedule, laying down all the scope items with their projected start and end dates, effort, and the duration needed. This is also where responsibilities are assigned. Always ensure and follow the **Responsible, Accountable, Consulted, Sign Off, Informed (RACSI)** matrix for responsibility assignment. A schedule is never complete until all the resources necessary to complete the project have been committed or assigned.

- The project plan should always keep the critical path in check. A critical path is a set of activities in a path with the least slack and the longest duration. Activities that lie along the critical path cannot be delayed without delaying the finish time for the entire project. Hence, close monitoring and proactive measures are needed to ensure the timely attainment of project goals. You can use the critical path method to analyze the activities that have the least amount of scheduling flexibility.

- A project must be a living document and, hence, must be periodically updated with any changes in the due course of the project timeline.

- Each individual activity should also carry an estimate so as to know the cost to complete the activity. This forms the basis of a project budget by summarizing the cost estimates for all the activities in a project plan. Top-down budgeting involves allocating the overall cost estimates to individual work items in order to establish a cost baseline for measuring the project performance.

- A project plan should always be a perfect balance of the following three constraints in managing the scope:
  - Quality
  - Budget
  - Cost

- A project plan must comprise of the following sub-plans for effective management:
  - **Communication plan**: This is mostly a policy-driven approach for providing the project status information to the stakeholders. The plan should formally define who should be given what specific information and when the information should be delivered. We recommend that you also outline how such information should be disseminated and the form of communication matching the purpose: email, websites, printed reports, presentations, and so on.
  - **Risk management plan**: Risks are impediments to project success. This plan is intended to cover all the potential risks and issues, as well as suggest corrective options. Having a risk assessment matrix fosters the effectiveness of such a plan. Always maintain a log for **Risk, Assumption, Issue and Dependency (RAID)**.

- **Quality and acceptance plan**: This plan enables securing the acceptance of the deliverables produced by the project from the required stakeholders (both internal and external). Identify the external dependencies, as these may directly or indirectly impact the project plan and hence may need to be kept in close check.
- **Change management plan**: A project plan must always incorporate all the key decisions due to which any activity gets impacted. **Change request (CR)** should also be captured in the due course of the project and be updated in the project plan after baselining it. Multiple levels of approval may not be a bad idea (for example, approvals for estimation, approvals for implementation, and so on). Often, the change itself may not be big, but its impact on the overall project may be huge. The impact on the testing and training aspects needs to be evaluated carefully in addition to the actual design and development. Understand the impact of timing of the change, as it is crucial; the later the change in the project lifecycle, the more costly and widespread impact it may have.

- Project plans must form the basis of all the project reporting requirements:
    - The point-in-time position
    - Dashboard reporting for project sponsors and the executive committee:
        - This should cover the overall progress in percentage
        - Phase-wise completion percentage
    - Financials:
        - Project earned value
        - Current actual cost (AC)
        - Burn rate (the rate at which the project budget is being spent)
        - Estimate to complete (ETC): *ETC = Budget - Actual Cost*
        - Estimate at completion (EAC): The final forecasted value of the project when it is completed
        - *EAC = actual costs (AC) + estimate to complete (ETC)*
        - Budget
        - Actuals (variance to budget)

- Detailed reporting for project stakeholders:
  - Activity-wise status for the phase in progress
  - The overall state of the project
  - Key risks and issues

The Microsoft project is a popular tool that can be used to prepare and maintain a project plan. The following screenshot is a snippet of a project plan based on the CRP methodology, containing milestones, timelines, tasks, duration, a gantt chart, and several other informative insights:

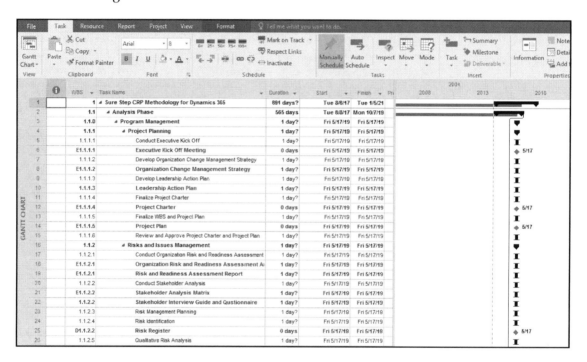

 Even though the project manager has the overall responsibility for developing and maintaining a project plan, a good plan cannot be prepared without the participation of the project team members.

A project plan must follow the established guidelines and standards and should always be baselined for all evaluation and reporting purposes.

FastTrack for Dynamics 365

We recommend that you make the most of your investment in the Microsoft Dynamics 365 platform by signing up for the customer success service from Microsoft, known as *FastTrack for Dynamics 365*.

This service is intended to smoothen your project implementation by giving guidance on best practices and answering your how-to-do questions from Microsoft engineering resources, committed to making your experience with Dynamics 365 a success.

For more details on FastTrack, please visit `https://docs.microsoft.com/en-us/dynamics365/unified-operations/fin-and-ops/get-started/fasttrack-dynamics-365-overview`.

Ground rules for day-to-day operations

Ground rules are policies and guidelines that are to be made by the project group and intended to help individual members. They must be clear, consistent, agreed-to, and followed by the team members. The purpose of ground rules is to adhere to the agreed style of working, which directly impacts the project's success.

We have seen that ground rules add value to the overall team communication, participation, cooperation, and support, as these are meant to address the behavioral aspects of project delivery.

The following are some of the top areas where ground rules are seen effective and, hence, should be created:

- Team meetings
  - For example, the ground rule for stand up meetings could be just highlighting in brief the key accomplishments and challenges per track/lead

- Communication
  - Verbal communications are a must and soft skills are important traits to have for the project team members. However, sharing relevant information with the impacted stakeholders in a formal mode is recommended as a ground rule

- Team culture

- Key decisions
    - A ground rule in communication could be to document all the key decisions in a common repository, available to the concerned project stakeholders
- Logistics
    - Ground rules for in-person workshops and virtual meetings
- Terminologies and abbreviations
    - Team members must agree on any kind of abbreviations and terminologies and host the list in a team site accessible to all.
    - This ensures less assumption in communication.
- Proactive management of risks and issues
    - Every team member must take up the ownership of bring up issues and risk proactively and as well as potential ways of reducing/solving it.
    - Risk and issues brings in a lot unknowns and lesser the unknowns in a project, higher would be the chance of achieving success timely.
- Vacation and time off
    - A ground rule in project time off could be to seek leave approval from the project manager for any leaves more than a week, and approval should be at least be two months in advance
- Workload/priority conflicts
    - The single most factor which could derail any project.
    - Work prioritization ensure efficiency, stronger collaboration within and outside team and helps in bringing stakeholders on the same page.

While a number of ground rules can be created, we recommend that you ensure agreement and commitment from the stakeholders before formalizing a rule.

Kickoff meeting

Every project must have a kickoff meeting, and it is about setting expectations, and clearly calling out and communicating goals. You must involve executives from all sides (partner and customer) in a kickoff meeting. The following line is very true:

Successful projects start with a great kickoff meeting.

We would like to share our knowledge by outlining the key requirements for a successful kickoff meeting:

- Review the goals with the key stakeholders and ensure that you have the goals defined in the order of priority.
- Review the project goals and charter. Define and get commitment on how success is going to be measured.
- Getting team commitment is a key.
- Review the project plan in detail. Review the project milestones and deliverables, validate the team structure, roles, and responsibilities fitment with the resources, and emphasize the implementation methodology and the steps to success.
- Brainstorm and seek the team members' acceptance of ground rules. Communication and logistics are super important.
- Carry out the project communication plan and the risk management approach.
- Review the change control process.
- Ensure that all team members attend the kickoff meeting in person.
- For a geographically spread team, you may schedule a web conference or conduct another one for remote members.
- Optionally, tools that are going to be leveraged can also be included in the kickoff meeting.

 Kickoff meetings should be simple and thorough, and should enable team members to feel empowered, motivated, enthusiastic, energized, and focused. Kickoff meetings should be conducted at a common place for better alignment and commitment.

Project initiation and LCS

All deployment choices must go through a series of steps, guidelines, and tools from Microsoft leveraging LCS.

In LCS, you start by setting up a new project yourself via an invitation from Microsoft, or you can create one for your organization. The ability to create an implementation project in LCS is provided by Microsoft only. However, a project can be set up by yourself or your partner/advisor for learning, testing, demonstration, and so on.

Please refer to the following screenshot showing various options in LCS project creation:

- Prospective presales
- Migrate, create solution and learn
- Implementation

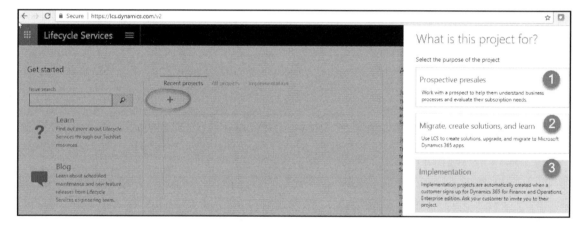

In LCS, projects are the key organizers and lay down the foundation for your goals. It is here that the methodology connection happens, and the rest of the execution follows this methodology using phases and tasks as your project phases, activities, and milestones.

The following screenshot shows a form where you have to select from various options to set up a project in LCS:

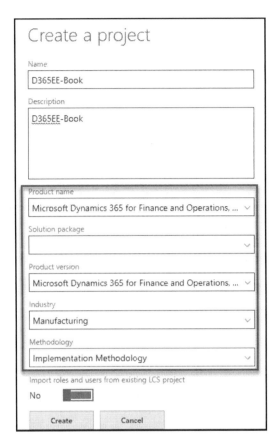

 Note that you can create your own methodology for a non-implementation project.

For an implementation project, you can only make limited changes to the existing phases and tasks provided by Microsoft; however, you can add as many phases and tasks as you'd like to within them.

A project contributor (be it from the customer side or the partner side) must complete the mandatory steps outlined in the implementation methodology to gain access to the production environment.

The following is a sample visual for a project and its implementation methodology in LCS:

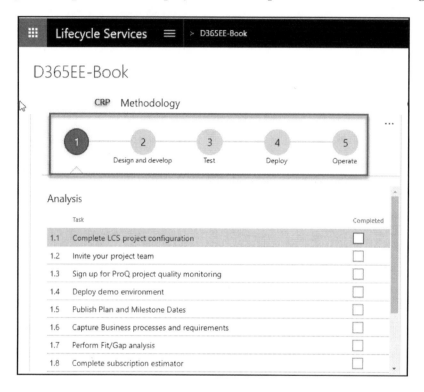

Before a phase can be marked as complete, you must complete the specified mandatory tasks and their dependent tasks.

 For more details on LCS and setting up a project, please visit `https://docs.microsoft.com/en-us/dynamics365/unified-operations/dev-itpro/lifecycle-services/lcs-works-lcs`.

Once the required project requisites are defined in LCS methodology, it is going to be helpful for team members to understand expected deliverables at various stages. Typically deliverables are common in a type of methodology being followed and we'll share these deliverables and best practices keeping CRP methodology in focus.

SharePoint online

Managing documents in a SharePoint library is very convenient, and leveraging the same with your implementation methodology in LCS is a great combination. LCS provides the capability of SharePoint online integration with an LCS project:

1. To set up a SharePoint online site in an LCS project, go to the **Project settings** tile.
2. On the **Project settings** page, click the **SharePoint Online library** tab.
3. Enter the **SharePoint Online site** URL belonging to your Office 365 tenant and then click **Next**.

Clicking **Next** would open a screen as the following shows the URL of your SharePoint online site.

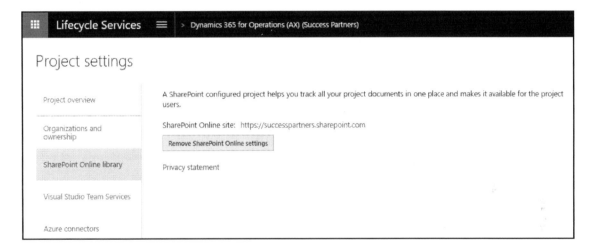

The preceding visual shows LCS project settings screen with tab on SharePoint online library. Here one needs assign your SharePoint online site to integrate with LCS so as to keep your LCS documents in sync with it.

4. Once the SharePoint online site URL is accepted by LCS, you are now ready to upload documents to any step in the LCS methodology.

5. To upload a document, select a task to which you want to upload the document, select the folder on SharePoint online library, and then click **Attach document**, as follows:

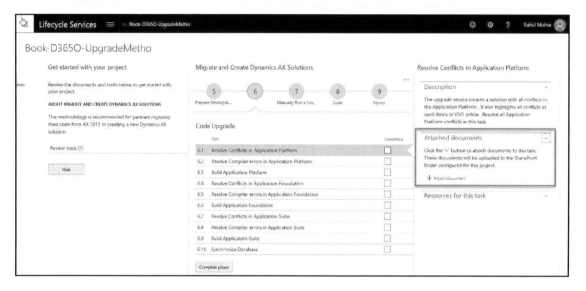

6. Browse to the document and then upload it.
7. The project team members, while working on the LCS methodology task, can now download the document.
8. If the document is no longer relevant to the step, click **Detach** to remove the link between the document and the step.

9. You can also verify the uploaded documents by traversing to a tile on the LCS project dashboard and selecting your SharePoint online library, as shown in the following screenshot:

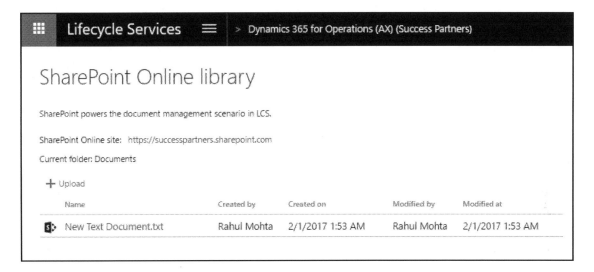

Project deliverables in the CRP methodology

A project is successful when the expected outcome is achieved, which is measured by the deliverables. The knowledge of which deliverables are needed in which phase of the project is crucial.

Every phase must have a milestone before you hand it over to the next phase, and its achievement should be measured by the deliverables that resulted in the phase.

Hence, we are showing a diagram as well as calling out a number of key deliverables across phases in your Dynamics 365 implementation, as follows:

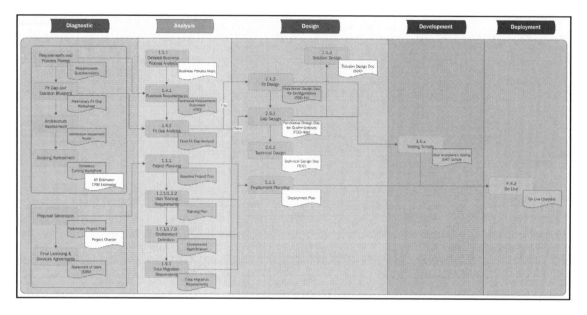

The preceding diagram is from Microsoft Sure Step online, depicting the phases in a CRP approach and the key milestones along with their deliverables. It documents in diagnostics the phase spans, project charter, project plan, SOW, and so on.

Let's now learn the deliverables in conjunction with the CRP methodology and their key constituents across phases.

The planning phase

In the planning phase of the project, the implementation team should address the following milestones:

- Project charter
- SOW (statement of work)/contract
- Project plan:
    - Communication plan
    - Test plan
    - Training plan
    - Data migration plan

- Cutover plan
- Risk and issue matrix
- Acceptance criteria
- Ground rules

Once the planning activities are completed, the scope of the project should be covered in the definition phase.

The business requirement definition phase

In the definition phase of the project, the implementation team should address the following milestones:

- The business scenarios and processes in a hierarchical format
- End-to-end process flows
- Use cases
- **Requirements Traceability Matrix (RTM)**
- As-is business flows
- To-be business flows
- Solution blueprint (the big picture)

After defining the scope, the implementation team should analyze each requirement in the analysis phase.

The solution analysis phase

In the analysis phase of the project, the implementation team should address the following milestones:

- Fit gap analysis
- Workarounds and customization options
- Build versus buy evaluation
- The **SWOT** (**Strength, Weakness, Opportunities, and Threats**) analysis for workarounds and customizations/enhancements

Along with the analysis, the overall design of the solution gets started and continues in detail in the design phase.

The solution design phase

In the design phase of the project, the implementation team should address the following milestones:

- Out-of-the-box capabilities as fitment
- Functional and technical designs for any gaps in the present solution
- Test scripts spanning:
    - End-to-end test scenarios for overall solution acceptance
    - End-to-end for a business process area
    - At least one test script per requirement
- Future-state solution blueprint
- Key decision matrix

After designing the solution, one should configure the representative capabilities in the configure phase.

The configure/preview/prototype phase

In the configure phase of the project, the implementation team should address the following milestones:

- A representative configuration of the business flow in Dynamics 365
- Sample data migration
- Demonstration scripts and videos
- High-level hands-on exercises

After the acceptance of the prototype, any gaps, interfaces, reports, and so on can be undertaken in the development phase.

The development phase

In the development phase of the project, the implementation team should address the following milestones:

- Development artifacts:
    - **ER (entity relationship)**
    - Code

- Designs
- White boardings

There are some nuances in the development phase based on the methodology selected. For example, when using the waterfall methodology, the emphasis is on the overall design and then the actual development commences when the individual technical designs are ready. In the agile approach, the sprint determines the workload in development and the churn is expected to be done quicker.

After developing the solution, it is now ready for testing by the implementation team in the testing phase.

The testing and acceptance phase

In the testing phase of the project, the implementation team should address the following:

- Test plan
- Test scenarios
- Test cases
- Issue logs

After testing the solution, it is now ready for training the end users in the training phase.

The training phase

In the training phase of the project, the implementation team should address the following milestones:

- Training manuals
- User/task guides

After the training phase, the solution is now ready to Go Live.

The Go Live phase

In the Go Live phase of the project, the implementation team should address the following milestones:

- Cutover checklist
- Go Live readiness:
    - Environment
    - Access
    - Communication mailers

After a successful Go Live, it is important to continue the journey and keep reaping benefits from the business platform while keeping it healthy.

The support phase

In the support phase of the project, the implementation team should address the following milestones:

- Support/sustenance plan
- Team spanning varied levels support needs
- Enhancement initiatives
- Good-to-have business needs from RTM
- Issue portal
- Ongoing training, roll out initiatives, and others

You should treat the aforementioned phases as a starting point, and we recommend that you leverage the CRP methodology concepts, PMI, and other useful resources to come up with your project-specific deliverables and milestones.

Best practices in project initiation

Always remember that every project is unique; the objectives of each project vary, and so do the challenges.

Based on our experiences, the following are the recommended best practices that need to be evaluated for every project and its goals for effectiveness:

- Identification of the right stakeholders before project kickoff, and keeping them up to date. You must have written and verbal commitments from all the stakeholders towards meeting the objectives of the project and their contribution. You should also have a lot of team building exercises through the duration of the project, as it facilitates the team members working more closely together.
- Ensure that your project charter has the following mentioned in detail:
  - The charter must be a formal document prepared from inputs from the key stakeholders. The project charter is not a legally binding document; hence, it is a great place for all stakeholders to openly contribute.
  - The objectives of the project must be explicitly mentioned in detail, in a clear and concise format. The goals should be quantifiable, realistic, time-bound, and should not contain any ambiguous elements. Using the SMART approach is very helpful to craft the project objectives.
  - The project charter must always be approved/signed off by the appropriate authority and should be easily accessible to all the stakeholders in a collaborative work space. The extent of details in a project charter to be shared with individuals may vary and should be factored in during sharing/access.
  - Get the executive buy-in towards the business transformation initiative. Seek executive support in early communications in the project to create the much-needed excitement and commitment from all the other stakeholders. Get the change management lead on board at the start of the project, as implementing Dynamics 365 impacts the existing business processes. To accelerate the implementation and ensure that the right approach and best practices are leveraged, make sure that an experienced, knowledgeable expert/advisor is on board.

- For internal customer team members, always have a dedicated core team that would be working full time on the project. The core team should bring in the business process expertise from the customer side, and often, they are the SMEs as well. Getting part-time involvement is going to be a challenge going forward and slows down the whole initiative.

- For other internal team members (non-core team members), ensure that their work-life balance is planned in advance and expectations are set early. Some team members may see a spike in their average daily work, as they will now be doing more than one job. They would need to balance their existing daily job with implementation activities and any other additional role taken up in the project.

- Identifying a dedicated CRP/project leader is vital for a smooth journey. Strong communication, ability to handle ambiguity, commitment, passion, and so on, are some of the attributes that you should seek in your CRP leader.

- Avoid false starts. If any key information regarding the project is yet to be finalized, such as the project charter is not complete, the project goals are incomplete, the project manager is not identified, the CRP leader is not identified, the right stakeholders are not identified, or the funding not approved, then one should wait until all of these key attributes are clear to start the project.

- Prepare a resource-onboarding checklist, covering all the information related to access, VPN, environments, SharePoint, distribution lists, and so on. Every resource should have his/her own dedicated account. There should never be a sharing of accounts/passwords, and no generic accounts, such as user1, user2, and so on, should be used.

- Have a published and centralized project calendar accessible to all the stakeholders. Each stakeholder should keep the calendar LIVE with their vacation plans, time offs, unavailability, and so on.

- Always have a key decision matrix/log throughout the project, as these decisions can alter the path and progress of the project. They also act as a knowledge repository. Leverage a user-friendly collaboration tool to maintain all the project artifacts, deliverables, sign offs, and so on.

There could be a number of CRPs based on the nature of initiative and the goals to attain. It could be a pure business transformation or a functional, technical, or project-driven need, and one must tailor-fit the standards and processes accordingly.

Summary

In this chapter you learned about the need for a solid project start and how important it is to lay down the foundation for success early on. The key ingredients to be successful includes forming the right team composition, laying down the ground rules (for behavioral aspects), and outlining the goals in the project charter.

The key deliverable (and a living document) is a project plan, which must always be kept in sync with the latest activities, using the baselining approach, to predict the future set of activities and milestones.

In the next chapter, we explore requirements, business processes, analyses, traceability, solution design, and other topics focusing on the scope of the project.

5
Requirements, Business Process Analysis, and Traceability

In the previous chapter, you learned the building blocks of a project by defining a project charter and a project plan. The next step is to build the foundation of your implementation project by collecting requirements, its analysis and fit-gap. Following are the key objectives of the requirement gathering or analysis phase of the project:

- Understanding the customer business process and goals
- Define the project scope
- Identify the fit and gaps
- Develop the solution blueprint

In this chapter, we will explore requirements, processes, and solution blueprints, emphasizing their need and various other moving parts in managing the scope for your project.

Following are the topics that will be covered in this chapter:

- Requirements scoping
- Hierarchy of business processes and subprocesses
- LCS Business process modeler and VSTS
- Requirement gathering techniques
- Requirements Traceability Matrix (RTM)
- Requirement segmentation and ownership

- Analysis of requirements
- Solution blueprint
- Key decision logs
- Best practices in managing requirements

Requirements scoping

Where can we start to collect and document requirements? What kind of requirements need to be collected? How do we ensure that all the requirements are collected?

You might be wondering about the previous questions, which are common for all ERP implementations. For a successful project, laying down a strong foundation right from the start is needed and collecting accurate and documented requirements is one such activity.

Often, even before engaging a solutions partner/advisor, organizations internally come up with a requirements list for their business transformation. The size of the organization, the businesses involved in the transformation, and the future state goals, all play a significant role in driving requirements, and it is a project in itself. In any implementation methodology, exhaustive requirement collection and analysis is a must to be successful.

 Often, organizations engage external firms and advisors to support them in the requirements gathering, as this is like defining the goal of your journey.

The focus of requirements collections should cover all the aspects of the existing business processes as well as the future state business processes. The whole requirement gathering and understanding process is a highly scientific approach that needs niche expertise and the ability to give attention to details.

Hierarchy of business processes and subprocesses

There must always be an explicit link between business processes and the requirements.

It should start at a high level for the coverage perspective, but the requirements must be collected in detail. Asking the five Ws is always a good idea to ensure that enough details are collected.

Five Ws: *Why, What, Where, Who,* and *When*
When solution envisioning is performed, another crucial question, *How,* gets answered.

All the business processes that will be part of the initiative and each of their subprocesses must be considered for preparing the requirements list. There should never be a requirement without being linked to one or many processes; alternatively, there should not be any process/subprocess that does not have any requirements. Any such situation, wherein a requirement does not belong to any business process should be validated with the out-of-scope criterion and accordingly addressed by the change control board.

We recommend that you follow a hierarchical approach while gathering and documenting requirements. The following visual represents one such approach and depicts the goal leading to the business process, that, in turn, leads to a subprocess and, ultimately, the requirement:

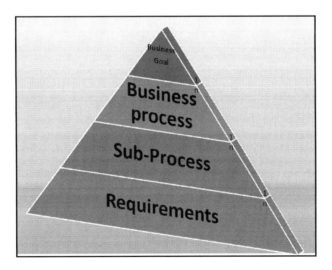

The hierarchical way of recording requirements is a proven approach to orient and structure requirement gathering process and ensure the each requirements downstream usage. Systematic success warrants manageability of the project scope and, hence, a hierarchy. The project benefits when the stakeholders can clearly understand the big picture as well as the activity-level details. Empowering team members with scope clarity is a solid foundation for collaboration and achievement of goals.

Laying the foundation using a hierarchical approach, we'll now explain the elements involved in achieving it.

Business goals

This is the highest-level view of the project in existence. This is the big picture for anyone within or outside the project to know what the project is going to achieve at a high level. As explained in the earlier chapters, project goals are defined in the project charter and the approach to achieving these goals is defined using the project plan.

A quick mathematical expression for viewing a project top-bottom is as follows:

- 1 goal : n business processes
- 1 business process : n subprocesses
- 1 subprocess : n requirements

Business process

A business process is a collection of related, structural activities/requirements with interconnection among them, and which can be represented in a flowchart comprising decision points and dependencies.

For more details, refer to `https://en.wikipedia.org/wiki/Business_process`.

Many organizations follow the industry-specific nomenclature of business processes:

- **Record to report**: This domain describes the process of managing financial and ledger information for any organization
- **Order to cash**: This domain describes the process of receiving and processing customer sales and its entire lifecycle till their payment

- **Procure to pay**: This domain describes the process of ordering and processing vendor invoices and its entire lifecycle till payment settlement
- **Plan to produce**: This domain describes the process of creating and building products/services and its entire chain from demand to supply

Business processes are best described using flows and visuals and have several uses, such as training, testing, solution acceptance, and so on. Each business process comprises one or many subprocesses in the functional domain.

Suggested in the following visual are the set of business processes as per generic industry nomenclature:

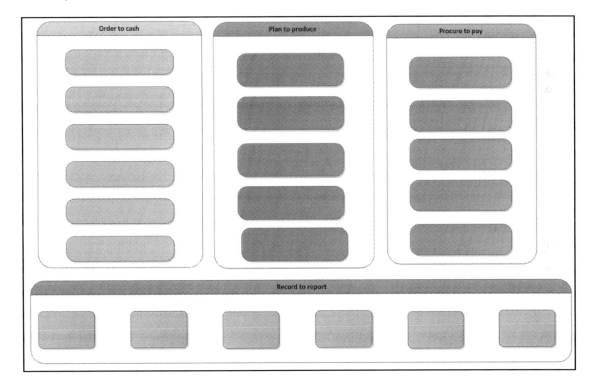

 Always leverage industry-specific business processes to gain uniformity and consistency.

As an example, order to cash processes may cover lead generation, prospect identification, opportunity creation and management, order management, order fulfillment, order returns, and so on.

Refer to the following links for more details:

```
https://en.wikipedia.org/wiki/Order_to_cash
https://en.wikipedia.org/wiki/Procure-to-pay
```

Once you have identified and documented all the business processes of the project visually, the next step is to define their subprocesses.

Sub-processes

A sub-process is a level in a business process for each individual business process function. Detailing of business functions starts from this level. It comprises one or many connected requirements to be able to perform a particular set of activities.

Sub-processes help in visualizing inter-dependencies within a business process and have links to other processes.

Each sub-process must constitute all the grouped functions within it. For example, in order to cash a business process, the following sub-processes should typically be covered:

- Order intake
- Order processing
- Order release and credit checks
- Product and service sales
- Pricing and term agreements
- Consignments
- Picking, packing, and shipping
- Customer invoicing
- Customer payments
- Intercompany documents
- Returns

The selection of grouped results/subprocesses varies per customer and should always be tailor-made to fit into their business model.

Sub-processes are well documented in visual tools such as Microsoft Visio. The following diagram depicts a sample sub-process with swim lanes showing the involved departments/roles and their inter-dependencies:

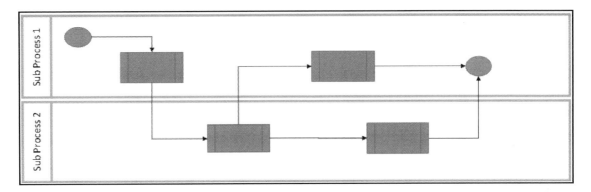

 Always get a happy path of an end-to-end business scenario for every initiative. This will enable all the people to connect the dots to the big picture of the project, and this happy path process will be utilized at various milestones, for example, testing, training, and so on.

A sub-process could be dedicated to a single functional area or it could be a cross-functional area as well. Some may go a level deeper than the requirements to the activity level, the decision for which depends on the type, complexity, and nature of initiative. Essentially, in process-flow documentation, there should be a clear definition and depiction of information flow with inputs, outputs, decision points, and roles involved.

Let's now deep dive into requirements in the next section.

Requirements

A requirement is a series of activities/steps within a subprocess. Often, organizations may leverage use case scenarios to explain the requirements clearly. Typically, a use case is a pattern of behavior and a sequence of related activities. Every organization must keep a goal of collecting the requirements as structured as possible, as it smooths out the rest of the project activities, thereby securing success.

Our recommendations on requirement attributes crucial in a Dynamics 365 implementation are as follows:

- Business processes and requirements should contain detailed information about the business needs.
- Each requirement is typically expected to be executed by one person.
- Requirements could be shared and reused in multiple subprocesses.
- In the CRP methodology, it's beneficial to have the business blueprint, business processes, and subprocesses, all prepared before the start of the initiative.
- All the requirements can be collected at the start, or they can be collected as per the CRP pilot to accomplish
- The documentation of requirements in detail is a must, and various techniques can be leveraged
- Typically, an RTM should be leveraged, which hosts the laundry list of requirements and is used for tracking, linking to activities, and deliverables in a project.
- Ensure that each requirement can be tested and a positive test can be performed on it.
- Requirements should be defined with the **Specific, Measurable, Achievable, Realistic, Timebound (SMART)** principle.

There are several factors to be considered while preparing process flows; based on our experience, we recommend the following factors to leverage while preparing them:

- **Related**: Document all the related flow that directly or indirectly impacts the business process in focus.
- **Well-structured**: Always bring in a systematic approach of documentation and start with the various inputs and triggers for a process flow.
- **Uniform**: Ensure consistency and uniformity across the flows.
- **Consistent**: There may be several team members who may be documenting such process flows and details, and it helps to prepare a guideline and an outline for the entire project to follow.
- **Clear and unambiguous**: Business understanding may be complete right away in one session and so must the process flow documentation. Consider preparing the base flow of the process first, ensuring absolute clarity and no ambiguity or assumptions.

There are a lot of tools available for managing business processes and requirements; however, we recommend that you leverage LCS **Business Process Modeler** (**BPM**) along with **Visual Studio Team Services** (**VSTS**) to manage these more effectively in the context of Microsoft Dynamics 365 for Finance and Operations, Enterprise edition (AX).

Let's now learn how LCS BPM can be leveraged to manage your entire set of processes and requirements in the next section.

LCS Business process modeler and VSTS

You may be wondering where and which tool to use to capture detailed information about business processes and requirements. While traditionally Excel, SharePoint, **Team Foundation Services** (**TFS**), and various other tools were being leveraged, there came a need to have a tool that would facilitate this information capture quickly and with high productivity. The place for such a tool has been filled with BPM in LCS.

It's easy to manage your business process, subprocess, and requirements in LCS BPM and use them throughout the implementation and after implementation. Based on our experience, the following are the top level steps involved in utilizing LCS BPM in your implementation:

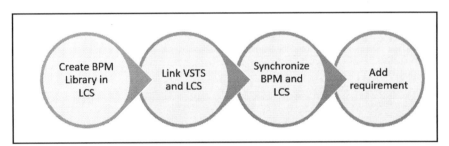

As shown in the preceding image, using LCS, you can create business processes specific to your implementation project. The next step is to set up the VSTS project and link it with VSTS. You can further synchronize the BPM with LCS and then add the requirements. Synchronization with VSTS provides a collaborative environment for further planning and tracking work throughout the lifecycle of the project. In the following subsections, let's take a deeper look into the BPM library and the VSTS integration and synchronization features in LCS.

Business process modeler

The BPM tool comes with a set of public libraries, enabling you to leverage them as a reference, or you can create a new one from scratch. Often, advisors/partners would come up with their existing business process libraries as a starting point and modify them according to your industry and organization needs.

By using the BPM, you can achieve the following goals:

- Standardize the process flows and business requirements maintained as a library
- Ability to align the Microsoft Dynamics 365 for Finance and Operations, Enterprise edition processes with industry standard processes, as described by the **American Productivity and Quality Center (APQC)**
- Prepare a hierarchy of business processes and their associated requirements, all under one repository

You can view the three types of libraries in BPM, as follows:

- **Global libraries**: These are available from Microsoft, and can be used as a starting point to build your own
- **Corporate libraries**: These are libraries owned by your organization for any organization user to leverage
- **Project libraries**: These are available to users within the LCS project with appropriate access

Following visual shows the various libraries accessible in your LCS project:

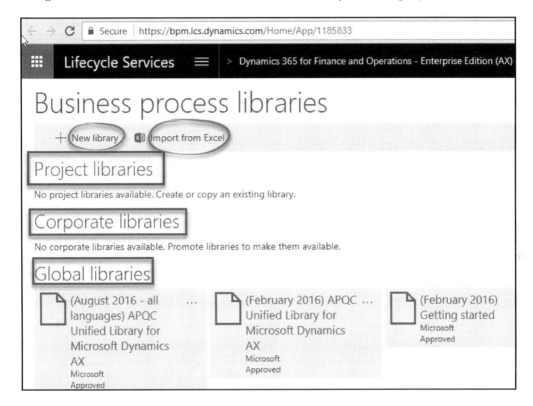

Microsoft regularly updates LCS and released a new interface for BPM that is used throughout this book.

Following visual is of a global library from Microsoft, leveraging an APQC cross-industry business model:

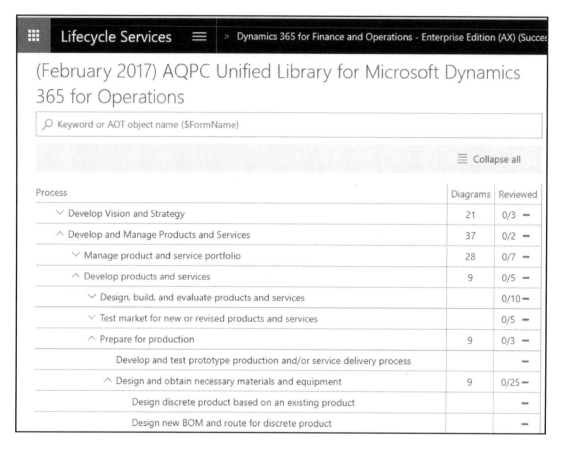

The preceding library is divided into three sections, as follows:

- **Core view**: Here you can edit, review, and combine your hierarchy with the configuration and data manager tool.
- **Process hierarchy**: Here you can view/build your business process and requirements hierarchy.
- **Process details**: Here you maintain more information for a specific reference/line in the hierarchy and include details such as countries applicable, industry applicable, and so on. Identify the fit and gaps between user requirements and the default functionality that Microsoft Dynamics 365 for Finance and Operations, Enterprise edition provides.

APQC stand for American Productivity and Quality Center, a recognized non-profit organization working in benchmarking, best practices, process and performance improvement, and knowledge management. APQC works with its member organizations to identify best practices, discover effective methods of improvement, broadly disseminate findings, and connect individuals with one another and provide the knowledge, training, and tools they need to succeed.

You can create a new BPM library in the following ways:

- **Copy the existing libraries and modify them**: You can copy libraries provided by Microsoft or your organization and modify them to suit your project-specific processes.
- **Create a new library from scratch**: You can create a new library from scratch by either adding steps one by one or importing as an Excel file. You can also import and add steps from the existing libraries accessible in your LCS project.
- **Import from Excel**: Use the **Import from Excel** button, which opens a dialog, as shown in the following image. **Download template**, prepare your library in Excel, and then import it back to create your BPM library:

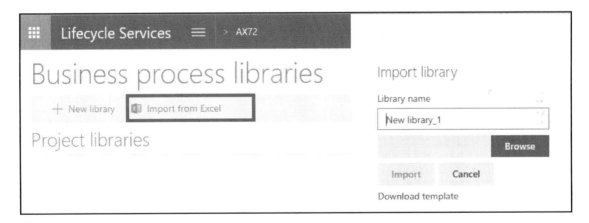

Let's now create a new library from scratch and learn the steps involved in it. Click on the **Create library** button. A new dialog box will open, where you can enter your library name and click **OK** to create the library. Once the library is created, you can open the library. A new library will have two default processes created. You can rename those processes and then add additional processes as children or siblings, as shown in the following image:

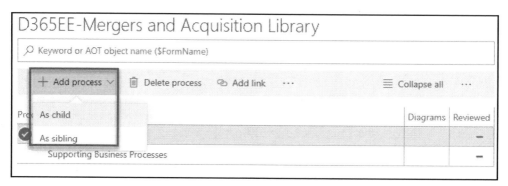

There is also an option to import from other available BPM libraries, which can be the fastest way to build your library. The following image shows an example of importing the **'Deliver Products and Services'** process and its sub-process from the APQC library:

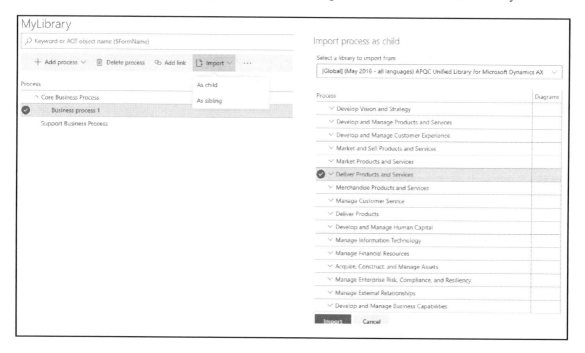

We recommend you build your processes and subprocesses in BPM and then add requirements within that structure. This ensures completeness of business processes as per the project objectives. Adding requirements within subprocesses could be done, either in BPM or it could also be done via VSTS. To add requirements, navigate to the subprocess node in the BPM hierarchy, and on the right-hand side, go to the **Requirements** tab as shown in the following screenshot:

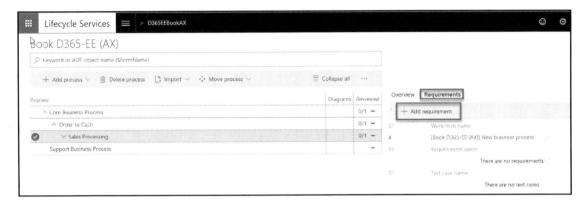

As shown in the preceding screenshot, there is an **Add requirement** button, which can be used to create requirements at this node.

 Remember that the Requirement level in BPM is supposed to be mapped to the requirement work item in VSTS in the LCS project settings.

While adding a requirement, you can specify a title, detailed description, and the initial assessment, whether it is a fit or a gap type and if unsure at the time of creating the requirement, just leave it as **Not assessed**, which is the default value.

The following is a visual of the requirement popup screen depicting the fields:

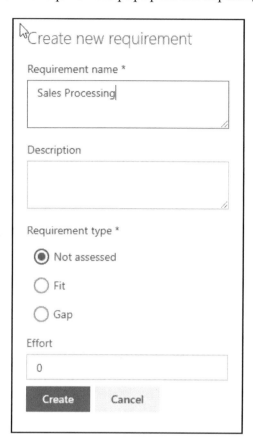

If requirements are not maintained using LCS BPM in a hierarchical format, then it would become tough to manage them as a flat list, thereby adding cost and tenure to the overall project, along with a lot of risks.

In addition to creating and importing the process, you can delete a process, create linked processes, rearrange them by moving up or down, and move them as a sibling or child.

You can also add additional information to process nodes. The following tables highlights additional information that you can add to the process node:

Properties	Description
Description	Add a detailed description of the process
Keywords	Add keywords that can be used for an easier search
Links	Link external links; you can use a link to provide external documentation for related processes
Industries	You can select one or more applicable industries where a particular business process is applicable
Countries	If you are working with a multicountry implementation, it is not uncommon to have country-specific business processes. You can select one or more countries where the business process is applicable.
Activity diagram	You can associate an activity diagram with a business process. Activity diagrams are used to describe how a business process or task is completed in a proposed software solution. There are three types of activity diagrams: • **Task recordings**: You can upload the business processes task recording to automatically generate activity diagrams and process steps • **Microsoft Visio**: You can associate a business process with a Visio diagram by manually uploading a Visio file • **User-defined**: You can manually create flowcharts as a BPM activity diagram

Following screenshot is an activity diagram for a business process; this diagram can be edited and updated with elements from the left, and saved and published:

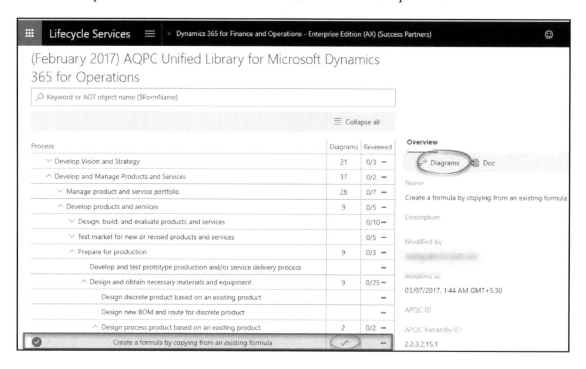

You can create process-specific flowcharts or import a Visio diagram after clicking on the **Diagrams** button, as highlighted in the preceding screenshot.

To see the action pane in the diagram, you need to right click on the canvas to see the toolbar at the bottom with the options of **Edit**, **Save**, **Export**, and **Gap list** as shown here:

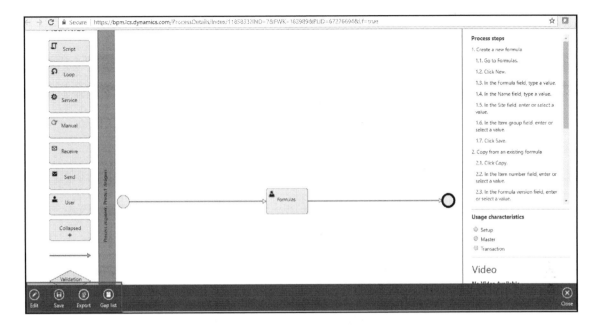

Once your business processes are complete, you can export a business process node as a Microsoft Word document and use it as a training manual in the later phases of the project.

Clearly, the BPM tool helps you easily define and manage your business processes and requirements during the analysis phase of the project. Integration with VSTS and in-product help take it to the next level, where you can utilize these business process in the later phases of the project.

With LCS being a cloud service, Microsoft releases new features and enhancements on a monthly basis. To know the latest features and capabilities, follow the *What's new* documentation of LCS on the Microsoft official documentation site at `https://docs.microsoft.com/en-us/ dynamics365/unified-operations/dev-itpro/lifecycle-services/ whats-new-lcs`.

Managing the business hierarchy in LCS has one more advantage: its out of box synchronization with VSTS. Here, you can synchronize the LCS BPM library hierarchy with your VSTS project as a one-time push, and from there on, maintain all project delivery-related information in VSTS.

With your BPM library defined, let's now configure your VSTS account with the LCS project in the next section.

Visual Studio Team Services (VSTS)

VSTS stands for **Visual Studio Team services** and is also known as **Visual Studio Online (VSO)**. It's a single collaboration platform to manage all the aspects of your project, including planning, execution/delivery, and support.

The top two benefits of leveraging VSTS with Dynamics 365 for Finance and Operations, Enterprise edition and LCS are as follows:

- **Application Lifecycle Management** (**ALM**): Management of business processes and requirements in LCS, using the same for delivery in VSTS
- **Continuous delivery**: Seamless code and data movement across environments/projects

To connect and manage your BPM library artifacts in VSTS, the LCS project must be linked to VSTS. If your project team has already deployed a DEV/build environment using the LCS project, your LCS project is most probably already linked to VSTS. You can utilize VSTS capabilities to manage all configurations, data, business, integrations, reporting, or any other requirement in your Dynamics 365 implementation.

Let's now learn the steps involved in setting up your LCS project and VSTS as per following:

1. Log in to `https://www.visualstudio.com/` and create a new VSTS account, as follows:

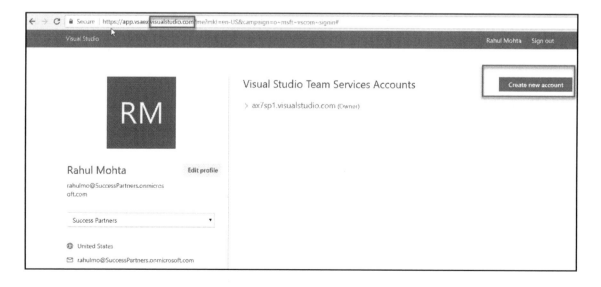

2. Create a new VSTS project to be hosted in that account:

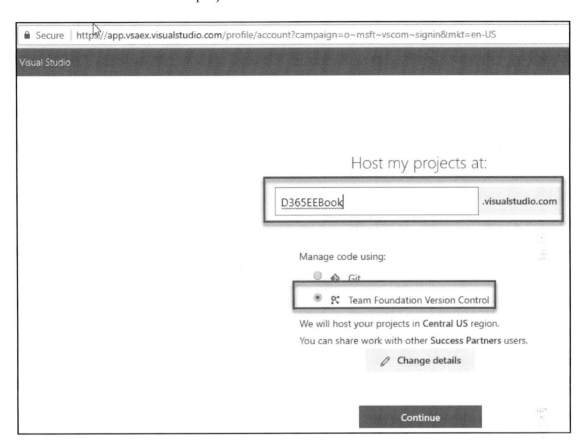

3. Verify whether the new project is created in VSTS:

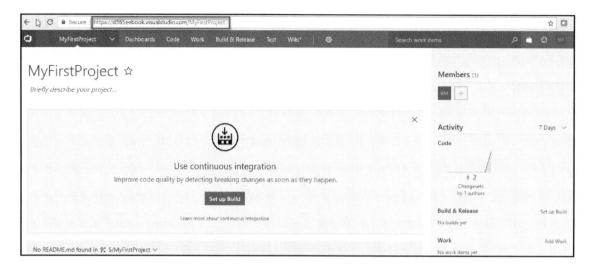

4. *Link LCS project with VSTS*: The LCS project needs to be connected to the VSTS account and project from the project settings. Go to the section for VSTS and click on the **Setup Visual Studio Team Services** button to set up the LCS and VSTS project link:

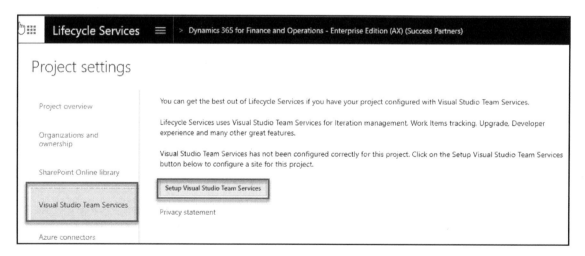

5. In order for the LCS to access the VSTS account, it needs to be provided with a personal access token, which can be accessed from VSTS **Security** settings:

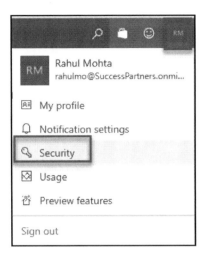

6. You can create a token valid for a fixed duration as per the options in VSTS, for as shown here:

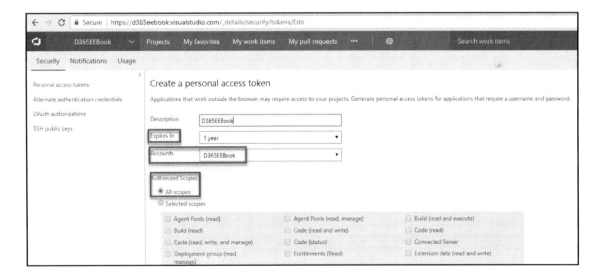

7. This token should be copied and pasted in the LCS BPM - VSTS screen, along with your VSTS account URL:

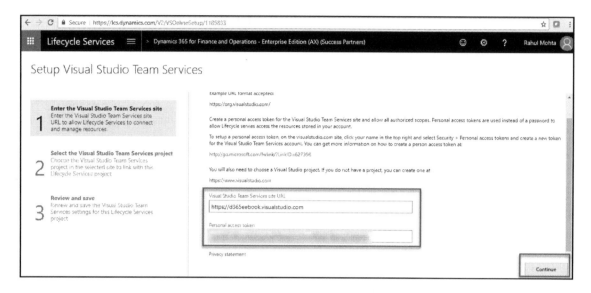

8. Once you click on **Continue**, the LCS will be allowed to access the projects in this account, and you need to select one of the projects from VSTS:

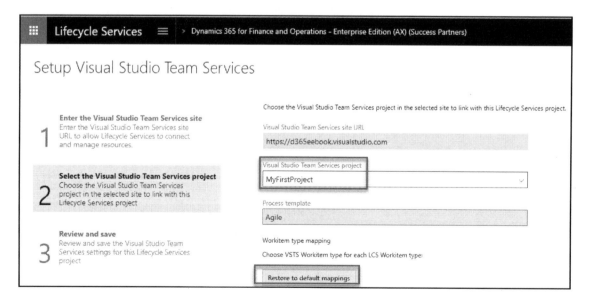

9. After selecting the project, the work items mapping can be selected by clicking on **Restore to default mappings**. These work items can be changed between BPM and LCS.

10. Associate VSTS work item types with LCS items based on the process template used in the VSTS project:

11. For the **Capability Maturity Model Integration (CMMI)** process template, the following is a mapping of work items:

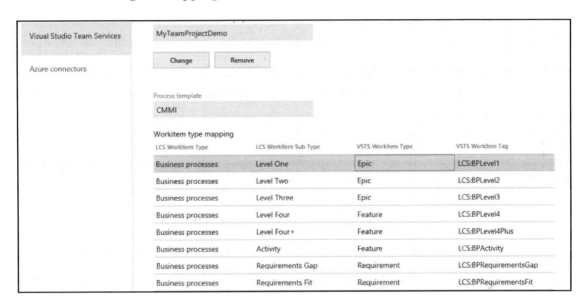

Visual Studio Team Services — MyTeamProjectDemo

[Change] [Remove]

Azure connectors

Process template
CMMI

Workitem type mapping

LCS Workitem Type	LCS Workitem Sub Type	VSTS Workitem Type	VSTS Workitem Tag
Business processes	Level One	Epic	LCS:BPLevel1
Business processes	Level Two	Epic	LCS:BPLevel2
Business processes	Level Three	Epic	LCS:BPLevel3
Business processes	Level Four	Feature	LCS:BPLevel4
Business processes	Level Four+	Feature	LCS:BPLevel4Plus
Business processes	Activity	Feature	LCS:BPActivity
Business processes	Requirements Gap	Requirement	LCS:BPRequirementsGap
Business processes	Requirements Fit	Requirement	LCS:BPRequirementsFit

12. For **Agile** process template, the following is a mapping of work items:

Process template		
Agile		
Workitem type mapping		
LCS Workitem Type	LCS Workitem Sub Type	VSTS Workitem Type
Business processes	Level One	Epic
Business processes	Level Two	Epic
Business processes	Level Three	Epic
Business processes	Level Four	Epic
Business processes	Level Four+	Epic
Business processes	Activity	Feature
Business processes	Requirements	User Story
Risks		Issue
Issues		Issue
Change Requests		Issue
Functional Design Docu...		Task
Technical Design Docum...		Task
Development Deliverable		User Story
Development Tasks		Task
Development Tasks	Upgrade Tasks	Task
Test Cases		Test Case
Test Tasks		Task
Bugs		Bug
Operate Issues	Monitoring alerts	Task
Operate Issues	Support Issues	Task

13. Once the VSTS project process template is selected and the work item mapped, you can turn on the synchronization from LCS BPM to the VSTS project backlog.

14. Use the backlog capability to keep items in the correct order and connected to the right things and to keep items in your backlog linked to epics or scenarios you're using to drive your business.

As per the mapping done in LCS project settings, the levels of BPM are reflected as *features* and *stories* in VSTS.

15. Here are some acronyms used in VSTS :
      - **Epic**: This is a virtual package which can span across releases and that allows you to group features.
      - **Feature**: This is a simple explanation of business needs.
      - **Stories**: This explains features in more detail, based on several constraints and conditions.

Let's now learn how to synchronize BPM with VSTS, and how it looks like on both sides in the next section.

BPM and VSTS sync

You can synchronize the BPM library hierarchy into your VSTS project, as a hierarchy of work items (Epics, Features, …and so on.) by clicking on the **VSTS sync** option:

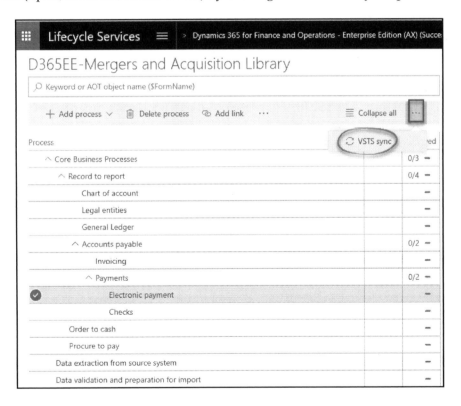

This is a limited two-way sync from LCS to VSTS that will keep your VSTS work items updated with any changes that are made to the LCS BPM library. Only when the requirements are added to the right level can VSTS be synchronized with BPM.

Once the work items are synchronized, you will notice a new **Requirement** tab visible to your work item in BPM, showing the VSTS requirements ID:

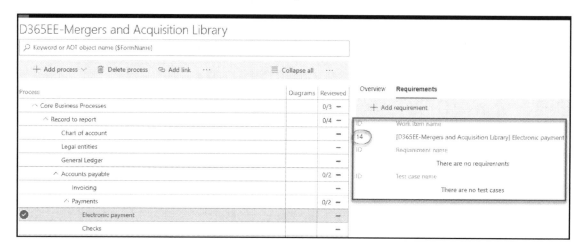

 Hyperlinks in the BPM work item directly open the work item in VSTS.

Inside VSTS, the sync work items can easily be seen under the work section of the project and under the **Backlog** features:

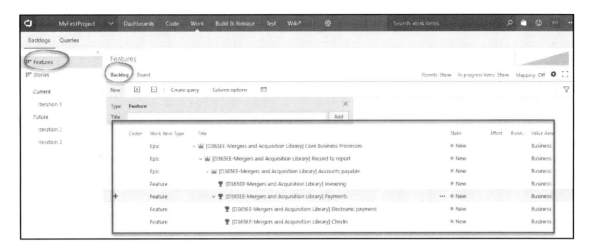

Once the work item is available in VSTS, you can perform all the necessary steps and actions to update it with additional information, links, documents, and so on, and use them for various purposes throughout the project (such as reporting, tracking, status, planning, and so on). The following is a sample BPM library work item being edited in VSTS:

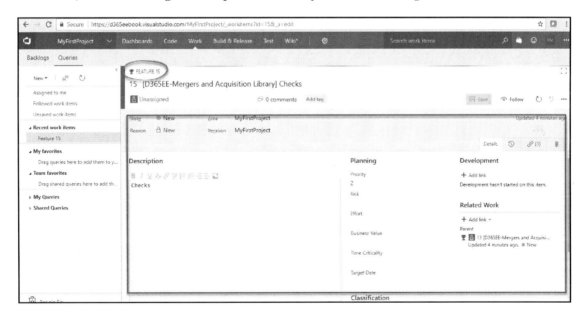

Note the acronyms and their relationship between VSTS and BPM:

- 1 (LCS) Project : n (VSTS) Epics
- 1 (VSTS) Epic : n (VSTS) Features
- 1 (VSTS) Feature : n (VSTS) Stories
- 1 (VSTS) Story : 1 LCS BPM (requirement)

Continuous reporting and VSTS

Are you wondering how you can get the right insights with so much information involved? We recommend you leverage the VSTS content pack for Power BI to gain insights into your team projects with automatically built dashboards and reports that are available quickly.

 For more details refer to `https://powerbi.microsoft.com/en-us/documentation/powerbi-content-pack-visual-studio`.

Having understood the background on creating business processes and requirements in BPM, let's now learn the various techniques to collect and analyze them.

Requirement gathering techniques

Achievement of requirements is the reason a project exists. You must always ensure a lot of due diligence in capturing, maintaining, and using requirements to drive the project towards success.

In the CRP methodology, you must conduct several workshops focusing on requirements collection, understanding validation, and the solution approach.

How good the requirements are depends on how they were collected; the purpose and technique of gathering requirements is a significant contributor. Based on our experiences, we recommend that you leverage a technique that uses the following three verbs:

- Listen
- Lead
- Negotiate

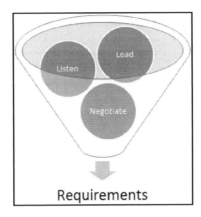

You can use any technique that facilitates information collection and understanding the process based on industry- and customer-specific situation; however, the verbs; listen, lead, and negotiate, are expected to be leveraged one way or the other.

Listen

As a first step in requirement gathering phase, you must listen to the customer on what they need/want to accomplish.

If you are a customer, you must ensure you convey all the business requirements to your Dynamics 365 solution advisor/partner/consultant. The business process owners are among the best to communicate requirements.

 Some clients may seek external professional help with companies specializing in **Business Process Reengineering (BPR)** or the likes of the *Big 5* consulting firms.

For any Dynamics 365 implementation, we recommend the following tools to make listening smoother:

- Questionnaire
- *As-is* business processes
- Calculations and examples
- Existing templates and formats
- A walkthrough of the existing system

Prepare questionnaires to collect information and have the business SMEs fill it out. At this stage, you are giving them the opportunity to provide you details of what the business needs and provide you their view of requirements.

The questionnaire should be tailored for the client by the domain, functional area, and role. If you are an implementation partner/advisor, you should use industry templates, the business process libraries in LCS, and any other tool that provides a good starting point for questionnaires.

You will have to tailor them considering the client's business, scope, and requirements based on the proposal and the client's organization structure. Always make a note of your understanding.

The quality of your questions makes a difference in requirements understanding and collection. Ask the process owners/SMEs to explain the entire process, and after it's over, ask open-ended questions--for example, what would you like to have in the new system?

A thorough understanding of your business process is important for your advisor/partner. We recommended that they prepare well in advance. Doing detailed homework will help leverage their knowledge about the topic and also in gaining the customer's confidence. It also reduces the chances of missing any areas during discovery and the time the customer has to spend on explaining the process to you.

The following is our expectations from a solution advisor and implementation partner/consultant, as part of this process:

- Seek/get examples of complex calculations (for example, revenue deferrals, royalties, commission, pricing calculations).
- Seek all the possible scenarios and the factors that influences the outcomes.
- Understand the current business process flows (*as-is* processes) thoroughly.
- Ask for any work instructions or operations manuals to document their current process, to help in understanding the current business process.
- Ensure that all present and expected interfaces are well-documented with a clear handover criteria, and clear success and exceptions factors. Integrations are important in a modern hybrid environment, wherein business applications must always exchange information with other best-of-breed systems to ensure the expected goals of an organization.
- Get samples of the reports, especially external facing documents (invoices). Sometimes customer invoices can become a project by themselves (checks, customer statements, packing slips, shipping labels, and so on, as applicable).
- Schedule an existing system walkthrough, especially for areas that are unique for the customers business.

- Take screenshots and document the *as-is* as well as the *to-be* process.
- Clarify if there are any changes to the existing processes and provide recommendation for changes to be made in the processes.
- When working on global projects, ensure that the SMEs from different locales come up with unified processes and share their requirements, which may be unique.

With the listening process complete, it's time for the solution owners to take a lead in the requirement gathering phase.

Lead

Upon collecting information from the customer in detail, it's time to analyze and come up with your understanding of what they need. Document all the open questions you want to discuss further to get ready to lead the discussions about requirements. It's a must to understand the requirements in depth, and this can be easily achieved by engaging the customer and asking the right questions.

We recommend to seek future state (*to-be*) business process and sub-processes in flow charts and detailed requirements from client and get started with existing (*as-is)* business processes.

In the leading process, we expect the solution advisor and implementation partner/consultant to be on top of the following activities:

- Seek the business process flow in detail and ask for a walk through.
- Get the business rules defined at various decision points in the flow chart.
- Validate the completeness of requirements coverage, dependencies, and business rules.
- Understand and document the pain areas and ask questions to clarify if you have any doubts.
- Never assume a requirement; always get it validated
- Avoid discussions about solutions in the requirements meetings; this will dilute the purpose of the requirements workshop.
- Avoid spending time discussing the out-of-scope areas until the client has approved the change order.
- Project derailment happens when scope creeps are allowed.

- It is in the interest of the customer and external stakeholders of the project to keep the requirements/scope in check.
- Capture the details of reporting, security, integration, and data migration along with the other requirements discussions.
- Non-functional requirements play a key role in shaping project success.
- Avoid using Dynamics terminologies or acronyms (for example, posting profile, value models, and so on, during CRP discussions).
- Usage of short forms early in the discussion activity should be avoided, as these may prolong or confuse the stakeholders' understanding, as they may be unaware of such terminologies or acronyms.
- Once the requirements have been heard and you have led the discussion, it's time to strike a balance between business and project goals and constraints.

Upon listening to and leading the business conversations, it is time to get back to your drawing board to work out all the solution capabilities available as per the project scope and accordingly initiate the next activity of negotiating, as described in the next subsection.

Negotiate

This technique in requirements workshops is also known as solution brainstorming in CRP methodology. You may use knowledge in industry best practices to push back on requirements that do not add value to the business.

As part of this negotiation, you need to provide insights into why a specific feature is not needed anymore, what is the replacement as part of the new process. Also, always seek and negotiate the necessity and impact of requirements. Knowing this, enables the project delivery team to prioritize the activities.

Often, requirements come from *how* it works in the current system (it does not always mean how it should work). Even worse is the fact that challenges/bugs in the current system become requirements for implementation in Dynamics 365. Consultants accept these as requirements and provide custom solutions. Understand what problem you are trying to solve and get to the bottom of the issue and then brainstorm the solution using the artifacts and information collected.

 Finding the bottom of the issue is also known as **Root Cause Analysis (RCA)**.

Use the power of w*hy*. *Why do you do this as part of your process?* Often, when you get to the *why*, it is due to the current limitation and it can expose a requirement that is not adding value. In most cases, customization is a convenient way of providing solutions as an analyst--you are just taking the solution from the existing system and pushing your work to the developers in terms of customization.

Here is an example of requirements for which you should push back: we had a customer requirement to post an out-of-balance general journal entry. Dynamics 365 for Finance and Operations, Enterprise edition doesn't support it. The reason users were asking for this to be a requirement was because the previous system had a bug that would post an out-of-balance entry in certain scenarios and then accountants had to use this *feature* to correct it.

Requirements are always needed and they keep coming back; hence, you should document them in your RTM and **Business Requirements Document** (BRD). As the list of requirements in a typical Dynamics 365 implementation is long, we recommend that you segment them rightly and have a clearly defined owner.

Requirements Traceability Matrix (RTM)

In Dynamics 365 implementations, there are many business processes involved containing several scenarios and potentially many requirements per scenario. Also, there exists some relationship/connection among the requirements. In order to closely manage these many-to-many requirements relationships, formulating the comprehensive network of requirements for a process is a must for project success.

One easy way of remembering could be this definition: RTM is a single repository/document that collects all the requirements, their relationship with other requirements, their role in business processes, all pertinent information related to solution, development, and Go Live.

It is one live matrix that should be kept up to date throughout the life cycle of project and is often used by the project manager to re-baseline the project plan as needed.

We would like to suggest an end-to-end goal of requirements collection, analysis, and closure with the following diagram:

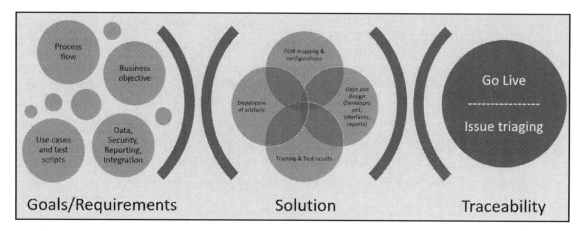

The preceding diagram shows the goals described as requirements belonging to a process/subprocess and influencing the solution analysis.

Solution acceptance becomes easier when an RTM is used. Also, stakeholders can validate and confirm whether each identified requirement meets the solution being delivered, leveraging the RTM and solution artifacts.

Let's now learn how to collect, define, and scope the requirements in your initiative in the next section.

Requirement segmentation and ownership

During requirement gathering, an important aspect is to rightly classify it. Classification plays a vital role in the lifecycle of a requirement and how it gets addressed downstream. An accurate classification of requirements helps project stakeholders to use it adeptly and see it from various sides.

We recommend that you use the following techniques for classifying requirements and tailor-fit them based on the size, complexity, and business situation of your Dynamics 365 project:

- Ask the question **WHAT**:
    - What kind of requirement is this? For example, functional process oriented, non-functional security, decision making, and so on
    - Impact on business (must-have or good to have)

- Ask the question **WHY**:
    - This classification is oriented to weigh the importance of a requirement
    - Recommended usage values: must-have, good to have

- Ask the question **WHEN**:
    - This classification is oriented to know when the requirement is needed so that it can be taken for solution and deployment planning in the CRP

- Ask the question **WHERE**:
    - This classification is oriented to gather and learn all the dependencies a requirement in focus has over other requirements

- Ask the question **WHO**:
    - This classification is oriented to always ensure that there is an owner of the requirement
    - Usually, ownership is by subprocesses, and all the requirements within the process should inherit it
    - There should be at least four owner types for every requirement, as follows:
        - Business owner/SME
        - Project core team owner from customer
        - Project core team owner from advisor/partner
        - Technical owner

- Ask the question **HOW**:
    - This classification is solution-oriented, and if a solution that was already committed or agreed upon is available, then it should get captured as well

There are a number of details that goes into a requirement, and hence, analysis is an important activity that may overlap or happen right after requirement collection.

When collecting details and classifying, watch out for loops and ensure that ambiguity, if any, is validated with the right owner. Also, ensure that all potential scenarios/outcomes of the requirement are collected along with the exceptions.

Segmentation of requirements with the definition of an owner is important to assist in analyzing the requirements effectively.

Let's now explore typical areas of collecting requirements while implementing Microsoft Dynamics 365 for Finance and Operations, Enterprise edition (AX) and their representative sections, as follows:

Type	Sub type	Requirement area
Generic/foundation	Generic/foundation	This includes collecting requirements about the companies involved, business verticals/industries involved, countries, sites, locations, solution instances, and so on
Functional	Finance and accounting	This includes collecting requirements about general ledgers with a chart of accounts, financial reports, financial dimensions, posting rules, currencies, country-specific taxation and compliance, financial periods, month end, fiscal close, accounts payable, accounts receivable, invoicing and payments, fixed assets, bank, cash flow, electronic payments, budgeting, allocation, provisions, and so on
Functional	Supply chain and distribution	This includes collecting requirements about products and their lifecycle, engineering change management, bill of material or formula management, stock keep units, sales order processing, purchase order processing, warehousing and transportation, returns, inventory management, inventory costing, customer service, **Maintenance, Repair, and Operations (MRO)**, and so on

Functional	Manufacturing and planning	This includes collecting requirements about production processing and control, scheduling, resources management, quality control and assurance, demand planning, forecasting, and so on
Functional	Projects	This includes collecting requirements about contract management, professional services, project management, project types and their accounting, project budget, grants, and so on
Functional	Human resources	This includes collecting requirements about talent/workforce management, leave management, skill management and training, payroll, and so on
Functional	Mobile workforce	This includes collecting requirements about time sheet management, expense management, self-servicing, and so on.
Non-functional	Security	This includes collecting requirements about business function and security roles, user interface-based security, data-dependent security, policy-based security, read only versus transactional security, and so on
Non-functional	Data migration	This includes collecting requirements about configurations, master data, data volume, data validations, migration from other systems, open transactions, historical and closed transactions, and so on
Non-functional	Data warehousing and reporting	This includes collecting requirements about single source of truth reporting across systems, day-to-day reporting, analytical reporting, dashboard, interactive information exploration, and so on
Non-functional	Integration	Middle-ware and integration, **Electronic Data Interchange (EDI)**, workflow, and so on
Industry-specific business needs	Specifics	Industry-specific requirements

The preceding table is just a representative sample of what to expect in requirement gathering. The scale, depth, and coverage varies from customer to customer and industry to industry, so you must ensure that all the requirements related to the contract/scope are well-captured and classified.

After collecting and segmenting the requirements across various areas, let's now analyze these requirements and capture the entire process in RTM, to be used throughout the initiative.

Analysis of requirements

Requirement analysis is supposed to be done by experts of the Dynamics 365 solution. The expert could be external advisors/partners or internal team members and should bring in the much needed experience with solution guiding options.

Customers must push their advisors/partners/consultants to seek solution options, both in the form of workarounds and in the form of customizations or extensions when a requirement can't be met with out-of-the-box capabilities. Even when requirements are envisioned to be met out of the box, their mapping must be documented and should be validated during the learning/prototyping phase in the CRP approach.

When a requirement can't be achieved with out-of-the-box capabilities in a Dynamics 365 solution, then the solution analysis stage starts. Poor analysis will add more time, effort, and cost to the project. Every time you get a requirement that needs customization, try to think how the other Dynamics 365 customers are using it. Ask why Microsoft (the principal) did not build the feature, and you will find pointers to push back.

When a requirement is a must-have and is legitimate enough to break a process, then the customization route should be taken in. Care must be taken not to customize the Dynamics 365 solution beyond 50% of the core functionality, as it would be similar to the situation of a magician who has several balls to juggle at the same time. You should certainly try to avoid such a conundrum.

We recommend the following steps to be performed when analyzing the requirement bearing the gap:

- Classification and the impact of gap:
    - Here, the extent of gap from a customization perspective should be captured.
    - Some usage examples are simple, medium, and complex.

- The impact of a gap is essentially two fold: impact to other business processes and requirements, and impact to the overall solution. Both the impacts should be well thought of and documented for the solution planning.
- Ensure that you capture both the extent and impact, as they are like two sides of the same coin.
- Both are needed to evaluate the solution options, feasibility, acceptance criteria, and other highly influential elements of a project's success.

- Workaround analysis:
    - Before any customization is taken up for brainstorming, ensure that the solution owner has exhausted all possible workarounds to solving the gap.
    - When possible, look for multiple workarounds, come with a SWOT analysis, and jointly discuss in a project.
    - When an approach is seen as a major decision, it is recommended that you use a key decision log along with updates to the requirement.
    - After careful evaluation of all workarounds, when no alternative exists, then solution brainstorming for customizing the solution should be taken up.
    - Often, when thinking of solutions, there are situations when the solution may not be comprehensive enough.
    - You should capture all risks, issues, and potential side effects along with the customization approach.
    - It is recommended that you always get the right stakeholder buy in for all the major gaps with their solution propositions.

- Ballpark estimates for customization:
    - Preparing estimates for customization could be done at the time of customization envisioning or, subsequently, upon finalizing the customization approach.
    - Estimation techniques are out of the scope for this book; however, you should always explore the best-recommended estimate techniques applicable to your project.
    - The available partner solution assessment for gaps by checking Microsoft AppSource to search all solution providers and their capabilities. For more details, refer to `https://appsource.microsoft.com`.

- When customization was the only resort, look for the estimates, extent, and impact of the gap to ascertain if it makes sense to get a ready-made solution addressing all or most of the gaps.
- Build or buy decision for gaps:
    - Based on the estimate, complexity, and the comfort level of the partner solution versus in-house capabilities of customizing the solution, you should be able to make the decision of make or buy.
    - Similar situations may still have a varied effect on decision making, and hence, it is advised that you always evaluate every project undertaken in the Dynamics 365 world.

Having analyzed the gap and with the solution options zeroed in, it is time to build the entire solution proposal from bottom up.

Solution blueprint

Solution blueprint is the ultimate visual in a project. It's a midway checkpoint, the acceptance of which means that the project now changes its phase from assessment to building. A solution blueprint is always best when represented in an end-to-end flow diagram showing all the solution elements that are envisioned and agreed to be leveraged from here on.

A typical business blueprint must cover everything that the business is going to leverage in their future state operations. The solution blueprint is now the central-most important element when making any key decision and adjusting scope, and going forward, it will be leveraged in almost all the deliverables in the project.

All project stakeholders should have access to it, must have a voice to suggest optimizations, and must be involved in accepting the solution blueprint.

A much detailed document called the **Solution Design Document (SDD)** is also recommended for in-depth documentation of the solution details, using the solution blueprint as the foundation.

Following diagram is a sample solution blueprint spanning all business processes, tools, legacy applications, and top sub-processes:

We, as solution advisors, often take the preceding solution blueprint one step forward and align the Dynamics 365 terminology, leveraging the fit-gap analysis of requirements.

We recommend a checklist for a typical solution blueprint, as follows:

- Are all the business processes and sub-processes covered?
- Are all the requirements (functional and non-functional) addressed?
- Has any other solution being used in the solution matrix been depicted and documented?
- Are all the interfaces specified?
- Are all the solution elements or apps specified?
- Are all the pilots or phases in a CRP covered?
- Is a supporting SDD prepared?

Arriving at the solution blueprint is a long process, and during this journey, there are several decisions made in the project, which leads to our next topic of maintaining a key decision log.

While preparing the solution blueprint and during the requirements analysis, decisions are often to be taken. We recommend to leverage a key decision log to register them, which is explained in the next section.

Key decision log

Based on our experience, one of the top reasons that causes a lot of issues in project delivery is the availability and usage of a key decision log. This is one binding matrix that can streamline communications and expectations, and bring in a lot of delivery efficiency.

Once the solution blueprint and the solution design document are prepared, people seldom go back to the original requirement, that is, the **Business Requirement Document** (BRD), situation, use cases, and exceptions to understand, or people seldom recall what had happened and triggered a particular approach. Hence, it is crucial to always maintain a key decision log that is easily accessible to all the relevant project stakeholders.

Any decision that could alter the course of the project and impact its objectives must be documented. Also, the circumstances of taking the decision should also be noted, as this would complete the entire story for the decision. A decision may impact one or more requirements, and hence, all the impacted processes must be mentioned in the key decision as well. This will enable the various owners of the project to participate in the impact analysis and, hence, the decision making process.

Best practices in managing requirements

Based on our experiences, we have the following recommendations in managing requirements:

- A business transformation initiative is not a destination; it is rather a journey that must constantly evolve. Hence, one must always keep the requirements up to date. This includes key decisions made in a process/requirement, and it should be easily available in RTM.
- Always capture the requirements in a SMART format. It should not have abstract details.
- Never assume any requirement; always get it validated. Validation is the best when documented and signed off.
- Requirements change over time and how you handle such changes decides the fate of the project. Scope management and change request should be the key levers for a project manager/CRP lead.

- Requirement collection and documentation is a zero-sum game; both the parties (on the business and solution sides) should participate well and the RTM should be a living document that is easily accessible, simple to understand, and that can be leveraged throughout the lifespan of project.

 If you can tell and trace the life of a requirement, then it is a strong foundation for success. This traceability can subsequently be referenced in all business documents, and it empowers the change management initiative and, ultimately, project success.

Summary

In this chapter, we explored scoping, defining requirements, and RTM, along with their connection with business processes and subprocesses. While some implementations may consider a requirement document a good enough artifact to continue on the project, we have seen that with a structured approach to documenting requirements, maintaining its traceability ensures that the entire project team is bonded more closely to the goals, and hence, there is a greater chance of achieving success.

While sharing insights on various requirement gathering techniques, we highlighted the need to listen well, lead the discussion, and negotiate the must-have requirements. The answer to fundamental questions (*why*, *what*, *when*, *where*, *who*, and *how*) and requirement ownership ensures that a proper analysis is performed. This leads to the right selection of the solution mapping, approaches, **Independent Software Vendor** (**ISV**) solutions, enhancements, and so on, thereby leading to the preparation of the solution blueprint, which is the backbone of the project.

The key deliverables from this chapter that we expect you to address are RTM (comprising business processes and requirements), solution blueprint, and key decisions captured in a log.

In the next chapter, we will cover effectively addressing configurations and data management by defining strategies and planning for them. You will also learn about golden configuration, various data management techniques, data cleansing, and quality validation recommendations.

We will cover the key topics from a solution perspective on data entities and data packages, LCS--configuration and data manager, **Process Data Packages** (**PDP**), and VSTS.

6
Configuration and Data Management

In the previous chapter, you learned about the importance of requirements, business processes, solution blueprints, and requirement traceability.

Data is an important facet in any initiative and is often the most complex and underestimated area in ERP implementations. Effective management of data can be achieved with the help of right scoping, tool selection, techniques for migration, validation, and well defined acceptance criteria. In every implementation project, following are two primary segments which a project team needs to address in their data activities and planning:

- **Configuration data**: Configuration means setting up the base data and parameters to enable your functionalities, such as financial, supply chain, taxation, project management, and so on. Managing these configurations is an important task, as it is mostly driven by the key decisions in your solution and project.
- **Data migration**: Data migration is the task of migrating data from the existing legacy system to new ERP system. Typically, it includes master data such as customers, vendors, and products, and open transactions such as opening balances, open AR, open AP, open orders, on-hand inventory, and so on.

In this chapter, we'll explore configuration management and data migration, which play a vital role in the implementation of Microsoft Dynamics 365 Finance and Operations. We will be covering the following topics in this chapter:

- Strategies for managing configuration and data migration
- Configuration management

- Data migration management
- The data management framework
- Data management scenarios
- Best practices for managing configurations and data migration

Strategies for managing configuration and data migration

Consistencies from systems are received when they have the right configuration and data. Both of them have a lifecycle to be managed and need to be continuously optimized at every phase of the initiative. These elements persist beyond just the attainment of project goals, as they are used until the systems are in use.

ERPs need a strong framework and policy for managing the configuration and data, as these inputs play a significant role in getting the output from solutions used in an organization's business transformation initiative. Both configuration and data are better managed when there are tools that make management easier. Dynamics 365 for Finance and Operations gives customers and partners the much-needed tooling to effectively manage them.

There is a direct link between execution and success: *planning*. A well-planned project sets it up for assured success. Planning makes the rest of the project activities and deliverables easier and allows stakeholders to know what, when, and from whom to expect. In planning, ownership is an important attribute as it helps in making implementation more accountable and predictable.

Both configuration and data migration need thorough planning. In the absence of a good plan for any of the two, chaos would prevail and may bring the project to a halt.

 Hence, it is important to facilitate a scoping exercise with the project team and remember that every record that needs to be migrated comes at a cost; the question is not whether it can be done but should rather be whether is it worth it.

Let's now learn about configuration and data migration planning and management in the next section.

Configuration management

Planning is a stepping stone to success. It is needed for both managing the configuration and for data migration, and there are some common factors that can be used for the purpose. Configuration means setting up the base data and parameters to enable your functionalities, such as finance, supply chain, taxation, project management, and so on. Managing these configurations is an important task, as these are mostly driven by the key decisions in your solution and project.

The following diagram shows the various phases of the configuration management lifecycle:

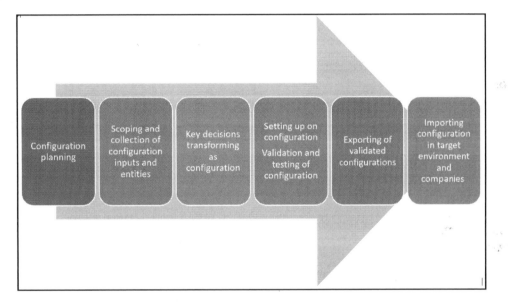

Configuration planning

Configuration planning is the identification of all the configurations required for your implementation. These configurations cover parameters, key master data, and the reference/supporting data across modules.

Most configuration requirements are known from the solution design phase and finalized with the sign-off of the functional and technical design specifications. The first step towards configuration planning is to identify the modules and functional areas that need be to be configured.

Implementation teams typically build a repository of all the configurations in Excel files, which are then imported to the relevant environments. This is expected to be done with proper version control and should clearly segment the validated configurations as well as all the incremental configurations that are expected to be created or updated. We recommend that you leverage the following key considerations in your configuration planning:

- Create a list of configurations that are needed for the project, and identify and assign the resources responsible for configuration. As a part of this list, identify the cross-functional module configuration and add the secondary responsible resources.
- Build a list of environment-specific configurations. Some of the configurations, such as links between applications talking to each other, need to have different values in different environments. For example, you need to ensure that the test instance of Dynamics 365 for Finance and Operations, Enterprise edition (AX) is pointing to the test instance of the shipping solutions and that the payment gateways are configured in the test mode.
- Try as much as possible to automate the changes to configurations and their movement across environments to avoid the risk of human errors.
- Maintain a list of company-specific configurations. When you are planning global rollouts, define a global template and maintain a list of configurations that need to be revisited for every company.
- Create a configuration template to collect data for the setup of each module, and describe the purpose of configuration and its usage for tracking purposes.

Let's now learn about the various environments used in configuration management, especially the golden configuration environment, in the next section.

The golden configuration environment

Let's now learn the environmental factors in configuration planning, as for configurations, there are several environments that are typically involved. One of the biggest challenges that an implementation team faces is moving the configuration from one environment to another. If configurations keep changing in every environment, it becomes more difficult to manage them. Similar to code promotion and release management across environments, configuration changes need to be tracked through a change control process across environments to ensure that you are testing with a consistent set of configurations.

The following diagram shows the various environments typically needed in a CRP approach:

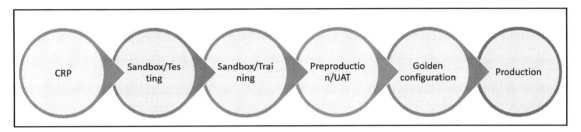

The objective is to keep track of all the configuration changes and make sure that they make it to the final cut in the production environment. While all environments are important and have a purpose, the golden environment is a special one and should always be pristine (without any transactions). As part of the configuration management process, once configurations are accepted/tested/approved in the test environment, they should be moved to a golden environment. This golden environment can also be turned into a production environment, or the data can be copied over to the production environment using the data management platform or one-time database restore. The golden environment is usually the starting point for various environments, for example, UAT, training, preproduction, and so on.

The advantages of golden environment are as follows:

- Single environment for controlling all configuration related information.
- Base environment to set up other tools for initial solution validation.
- Template environment to spun other environment thereby reducing chances of any configuration changes or data corruption which could directly impact testing or any other related activity.

The one factor that you should remember is to keep the code base of the golden configuration with the latest approved code base for production so as to keep this environment in sync with the latest updates.

Let's now summarize all the activities involved in configuration planning:

- It should leverage industry-best practices that are relevant to the customer organization for configuring your Dynamics 365 solution.
- It should define and document what all constitute configuration.
- One should identify the environments to manage the configuration and data.

- In the project plan, one should define the acceptance criteria for golden configuration that are user-accepted, tested, and ready to move to production.
- For repeatable and assured success, keep the project goals in context and use them as reference.
- Configurations evolve over time; hence, proper versioning should be maintained:
    - Your Dynamics 365 solution, based on the business objectives, may need to be baselined for an initial configuration
    - All intermediate versions should be well thought of, and key decisions should be captured and tested before marking them ready for production usage
- Identify and leverage the tools provided by Microsoft. We recommend that you leverage the tools offered by Microsoft to save the cost of your implementation initiative and to make a positive impact on the **returns on investment** (**ROI**).
- The data exchange with Microsoft Dynamics 365 for Finance and Operations, Enterprise edition (AX) happens via data entities and it is important to map them with the business needs and migration requirements:
    - This will help us know whether the entities are all available out of the box or some need to be built.
    - Also, by knowing these entities, you can start planning your sequence of loading and leverage the same during the actual migration
- It is often difficult to perfect the configuration, data dependencies, and their sequencing in any implementation. Hence, one should build and leverage a reusable library of configuration and data templates. Reusability brings in predictability and accuracy, and you need not start from scratch all the time; rather, you could just use a template and build the delta (data) on top of it.
- Also, a strategy for the building blocks of configuration is needed. This helps in manageability and the controlled movement of configurations.

Configurations are the base elements that help tailor solutions to exactly suit the business/project need. Some configurations are non-reversible; hence, utmost care must be taken when arriving at such decisions. Experts in solution can help you to accurately plan for the right configuration without much rework.

A lot of advisors and partners are creating their own industry-specific configuration templates and offerings for Microsoft Dynamics 365 solutions, which should be explored by customers and other partners in their implementation to maximize their returns on investment and get off to a great starting point.

With configuration explained in detail, let's now learn about planning related to data migration in the next section.

Data migration management

Similar to configuration management, data migration is an important activity in a project. By data migration, we mean the data that you need to migrate from the legacy system, such as master data and opening balances. Data is needed for any kind of task and has multiple attributes. Hence, to ensure that it is managed and utilized well, we need to undergo a systematic approach. In the context of implementing a Dynamics 365 solution, we are focusing on overall data management and would like to share a visual for an end-to-end understanding of all the activities involved in planning for data:

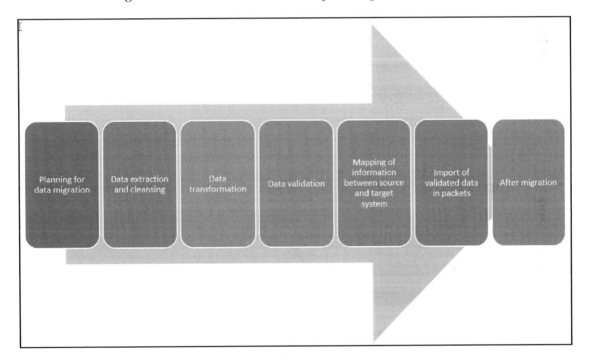

The full suite of activities involved in data migration is as follows:

- **Planning for data migration**: Involves planning the scope, tools, techniques, volume, and environment
- **Data extraction and cleansing**: Cleansing is a business function; however, milestones and dates must be well planned and baked in the data migration plan

- **Data transformation**: Seek and agree on the transformation requirements and rules
- **Data validation**: Maintain a checklist of validation criteria for the business for extracted data
- **Mapping of information between the source and target systems**: This mapping is per entity level; for example, customer entity can span account related information, contacts, address, and so on. One must ensure to have find a home for entity information to be exchange at the field level including any transformation needs on the data.
- **Import of validated data in packets**: Maintain a log of what all data and which all records have been extracted, cleaned, validated, and migrated
- **After migration**: Always confirm with the business about data accuracy and completeness

To be successful, involve business users and data experts right from the start of the project. Based on the size, complexity, and nature of the customer business, you may also need to include a data governance strategy in data migration planning.

Data migration may just seem like a one-time activity of moving data from the source to the Dynamics 365 solution, but it goes through the same lifecycle as that of any other requirements in a project. Planning for data migration is a must in order for us to be able to systematically identify and execute a number of activities spread over time with multiple stakeholders. It also eases out potential unknowns and makes it easier to know what to expect next.

 We recommend that you start negotiations from point zero so as to condense huge data migration needs to a minimum of only what is a must. For example, when discussing customer transactions, start the discussion to bring only open records for active customers and not all the historical transactions.

Scoping

Rightsizing the scope is amongst the first steps towards a successful initiative. The scope must be well-documented and agreed upon by all the relevant stakeholders to ensure smooth and accurate data migration.

Often, implementation teams either do not consider data migration at all or have unreasonable expectations regarding the data migration requirements.

Even if the original sales proposal has explicit data migration requirements that have been identified, many of the project team members and stakeholders may not be aware of what was specified or may not agree to the mentioned scope.

We recommend that you always have a dedicated data scoping activity planned, which should give an opportunity to both the sides to be on the same page and leave very little room for any assumptions. This scoping activity can be achieved by checking on the following set of questions:

- **What all is needed to keep the business running efficiently?**

  Define the business goals with this question in mind, and then approach the issue of what information needs to be migrated to meet these goals or what solutions can be provided to meet the goals without migrating the data. For example, a customer may say, I need to be able to collect my receivables and run aging for customers—this is the business goal. This means that you only need to migrate Open AR for the customers along with the due date.

- **Is there an alternative to bringing the existing data over?** Reporting out-of-legacy systems or data warehouses and defining a manual process, if it is going to be used only for inquiries over a short period of time, are some potential alternatives.

- **How much of the data present in the legacy systems is up to date, validated, and good for future use?**

  Do you want the new system to have the same issues that you are trying to solve in the current system?

- **How many records are involved or what is the volume of data migration to accurately pinpoint the tool and technique for loading?**

  Ensure that the ballpark numbers of record counts are defined for each area during scoping (for example, 4 million products, 200,000 customers, 2000 open orders, and so on). This will help you select the right tools.

- **How often will you be asked to retrieve this data?**

  Usually, the activity of configuration and data migration is an iterative exercise, and hence, the need to leverage/build reusable capabilities to address this iterative nature.

Identify and document the business needs clearly and accurately with examples where possible. You can avoid the cascading effect and carve out the critical pieces of data that you need frequently in order to limit the scope. For example, just migrating the open balance of each customer invoice rather than trying to bring the complete line item detail requires less effort. If a customer service needs the invoice line detail to research a customer issue that happens once a month on an average, the detail generally would not be worth the effort of trying to migrate it.

Part of data migration planning process involves educating business stakeholders about cost of migration and focus on migrating information which would enable better business decisions, better servicing of customers and information insight. In principle, one should avoid migrating historical transactions, such as posted sales invoices, posted purchase orders, individual general ledger transactions, inventory transactions history, and so on.

The effort to clean and transform data is a humongous task and an expensive proposition. Certainly, historical transactions are needed for various purposes such as compliance, regulatory requirements, business analysis, customer support, and so on. However, there are other solutions available as alternatives for migrating all the legacy data. These solutions/tools can be selected based on the size of the data set, transformation requirements, and storage and access needs. Here are some common tools that we have used for our customers for historical transaction insights:

- Leverage an existing or new data warehouse to meet the reporting/analysis requirements, and extract and store the historical information from the legacy system into Cubes or SQL tabular format.
- Storing data on the cloud, such as Azure SQL, and then showing them in reports (SSRS).
- A shared folder or a SharePoint site to store the extracted files from the source system in various formats, such as Excel, CSV, PDF, and so on.
- Set the security of the legacy system to read-only and do historical lookups there. Make sure that support contracts and an exit strategy are part of any discussion regarding this option so that the customer is not paying for multiple systems indefinitely. This is a good option for a stable legacy system where support is still available (without paying a hefty annual support price) and also helps ease the transaction for the legacy system support vendor.

If none of the preceding fits into your solution design and customer requirements, then you can consider creating a new SQL database as an exact replica of the legacy data tables and pull in the data without having to do a mapping or cleansing process. As part of the business intelligence and analytics planning, you should factor in this new SQL database along with your new ERP database to combine and deliver reports involving historical transactions.

Common data migration areas

In any implementation, there are a quite a number of common business areas that need to be migrated. Let's explore some of these business areas along with our recommendation for their scoping.

The following table is an example that you can use as a starting point to help validate the decisions to be agreed upon in a data migration requirements session:

Functional area	Guidance for scoping
General ledger history	• Prior years' history: periodic balances for 2 years • Current year—till date, periodic balances
Customers	• All the active customers (and addresses) • Has performed a transaction in the last 18 months, has an open balance, or has open sales orders
Vendors	• All the active vendors (and addresses) • Has performed a transaction in the last 18 months, has an open balance, or has open purchase orders
Products and prices	• All the active products and prices • Products have been created in the last six months, there is stock in hand, the product has open purchase, sales, or production orders, or the product was sold in the last 12 months • Prices: All the active and future prices for customers and vendors • Trade agreements and sales/purchase agreements in Dynamics 365 for Finance and Operations terminology
Open AP	• Migrate all the open documents: invoices, payments, and debit notes • **Key fields**: Vendor ID, open amount, description, due date, invoice number, document number, document date (original invoice date), method of payment, PO/reference, or any other information that you need in order to pay the vendor • You should be able to run vendor aging and pay the vendors (1099 reporting considerations)

Open AR	• Migrate all open documents: invoices, payments, and credit notes • **Key fields**: Customer ID, open amount, description, invoice number, original date, due date, method of payment, customer PO number, and reference to sales order number • You should be able to run customer/AR aging and collect payments from the customers
Inventory (On Hand)	• Migrate in-hand inventory for each product by dimensions • Are your product's numbers changing (this would mean changing labels in the warehouse)? • Cost for each lot and dates for batch numbers • Review the impact on inventory costing
Open Orders	• Open sales orders and open purchase orders—orders that are not yet delivered • Discuss the returns (you may need to refer to the old system for a short period of time) • Orders that are delivered but yet not invoiced
Bank Balances	• The last-reconciled balance • Unreconciled transactions
Fixed Assets	• **The active assets**: Assets that are in possession and in the books • **Key values**: Fixed asset number, acquisition price, accumulated depreciation till date, remaining periods, acquisition date/put-in-service date, date depreciation last run, serial number, assigned to, dimensions, and so on

Planning

Data is both qualitative and quantitative in nature; hence, your data migration strategy should include a concrete and measurable success definition to determine when a migration can be considered complete. With solid planning done for configuration and data management, you should now explore all the available techniques to assist in accomplishing the plan.

We'll now suggest the key activities to factor in your data migration plan/strategy, as follows:

- Collect the requirements for data migration with measurable factors
- Identify all the data elements/entities and their sources
- Understand and keep in perspective the target solution/system schema
- Develop a governance strategy for leadership and direction
- Define data quality and integrity parameters
- Identify all the data validations and rules
- Identify and assign an owner for every type of data
- Define data conversion needs (if any)
- Agree on a data cleansing approach
- Collect data volumes per entity
- Identify when full data loads are needed and when incremental approach needs to be taken
- Identify all the post data migration checkpoints
- Identify and leverage the tools provided by Microsoft/principal

Let's now consider a list of items to factor in for your data migration plan:

- **Environment**: You need to plan for an environment to run the data migrations iteratively. You don't want the test environment to be messed with every week while the data migration team is still trying to stabilize the data migration processes.
- **Cycles**: You need a plan for multiple cycles of data migration that are a few weeks apart. This allows time to validate the data, fix issues, and improve the performance of the migration processes.
- **Resources**: Business resources will be required to help extract and validate the data for each cycle. They may be needed to help cleanse the data if you run into issues from the legacy data. IT resources will be required to extract, import, and validate the data.
- **Training**: It is a good idea to train and utilize dedicated resources in the data conversion process, as it is an iterative process, and to have experienced resources focus on improving the process based on the feedback received from data validation.
- **Verification**: Data quality in the source system has a huge impact on the number of data migration iterations that you have to perform during tests.

- **Testing**: Complete a full data migration prior to starting system integration testing, UAT, and training. These migrations should be performed by following the data migration process documentation, and the time for each step needs to be recorded. As a part of this process, have the migrated data validated by the business prior to starting the tests in these environments.
- **Automation**: Come up with iterative/automated processes, including data extraction from legacy systems. This makes the cycle time for data migration shorter, improves the quality, and provides consistent results. For extraction, you may be lucky to get away with the reports that the business uses. For example, if a business uses a detailed **Accounts Receivable** (**AR**) aging report, you can use that report as an input for migration rather than building a separate job for data extraction.
- **Teamwork**: The team should record the timing for each process and arrange dependencies and processes that can be run in parallel.
- **Communication**: Document the migration process end to end--from data extraction and intermediate validation to migration (the development team that writes the code should not be the one executing it). With a documented process, you can engage more team members to execute the repetitive data migration processes.

The next step after planning is a smooth and spot-on execution, which is explained in the next section.

Execution

There is no single technique in managing data which can be leveraged all the time in a typical Dynamics 365 implementation. Discipline, ownership, and a process for master data governance are critical success factors for the sustainability of a system. Data management is not a one-time affair and, hence, should always be closely monitored, optimized, and executed as per plan. **Extract, Transform, and Load** (**ETL**) is amongst the most common approaches in data migration planning, and you will be using it in one way or the other, no matter which solution/application is in focus.

The following steps are involved in ETL technique:

- Identify all the source systems as per the data migration requirements
- Build data templates to extract information from the source system:
    - When volumes are high, you can leverage an SQL database as a common repository to extract the information

- For smaller data and configurations, you can directly leverage Excel as the mechanism
  - For larger data sets, you should leverage the data entity framework
- Prepare for data export from the source system into the staging places
- Perform data cleansing and validation activities:
  - System validations and automation should be leveraged wherever you can generalize a rule for validation and cleansing, and use it to make the staging data in a format that can be imported to the target system
  - When some human decision is involved, then introduce manual checkpoints for data validations in the staging system, for example, mandatory data, data types, data length, and so on.
  - Leverage the tools available in the Dynamics 365 solution to import data

Let's now learn the select data mapping and transformation considerations:

- **Cleanest data**: If the data is stored at multiple places in a legacy system, you should pick the cleanest one to extract a copy from. Consider the update timings in the source and add dependencies in the go-live plan to get the source data updated, prior to starting the extraction.
- **Business rules in transformation**: Define and validate the field mapping between the legacy systems and Dynamics 365 for Finance and Operations, Enterprise edition (AX) along with any transformations that need to happen between the extraction and the import process. Define rules in the target system or in the source systems (for example, bad addresses, phone numbers, and so on) to enable automation and transformation as much as possible.

 Identify the areas that need data cleansing earlier in the planning stage so that these cleansing efforts can start early and the data sets can be made ready well ahead of time.

Leveraging the aforementioned techniques, let's now evaluate the various tools and see how we can benefit from them.

Data management tools

Dynamics 365 for Finance and Operations provides a comprehensive functionality within the application and LCS to manage the configuration and data migration process. Best practices from a systems' perspective are already baked into them, and hence, using these tools should be included in planning.

We are focusing on the tools available in Microsoft for Dynamics 365 for Finance and Operations, Enterprise edition at the time of writing this book. Some of the capabilities shown in this section were introduced with the July 2017 release, with Platform update 9 of Dynamics 365 for Finance and Operations, Enterprise edition. Functionalities may be different in other application and platform versions.

In Dynamics 365 for Finance and Operations, the implementation team can use various tools and frameworks for data management. The following image shows the different tools and frameworks available for data management in Dynamics 365 for Finance and Operations:

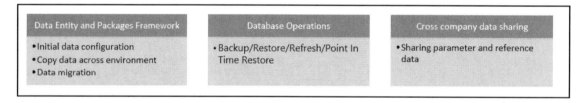

The data entity and packages framework is the primary and most useful tool to handle the various data management scenarios. This tool helps the implementation team to perform the initial data configuration, manage configuration data within the environment, copy the configuration across environments, and migrate the data from legacy systems. Database operations, such as backup, restore, and point-in-time restore, are another set of tools that can be used to quickly set up a new environment and to even move your final golden configuration environment to production for the first time. The cross-company data sharing tool can be used in an implementation scenario where multiple legal entities are involved in sharing common parameters and reference data, for easier and effective data management.

Now that we have introduced you to the various tool sets, let's explore these tool sets in detail in the subsequent sections.

The data management framework

The data management framework in Dynamics 365 for Finance and Operations, Enterprise edition is based on **Data Import/Export Framework (DIXF)**. This tool, along with the other tools in LCS, helps the customers and partners to quickly set up their initial environment from blank data, manage the configuration data throughout the lifecycle of the project, plan and execute data migration, and move the data from one to another environment.

There are several tools and concepts that constitute the overall data management platform in Dynamics 365 for Finance and Operations. Some of these tools are within the Finance and Operations application while the others are available in LCS. Let's learn about these tools and concepts and how they can be used for various data management scenarios.

Data management concepts

Let's first understand the various concepts used within the data management framework, as it forms the core element that is used in any data-related activity.

The data management workspace

The data management workspace in finance and operations provides a single entry point for the data administrator to configure, plan, export, import, and monitor data projects. The data management workspace is available in the Finance and Operations, system administration area, or from the dashboard.

The following screenshot shows the data management workspace in Dynamics 365 for Finance and Operations:

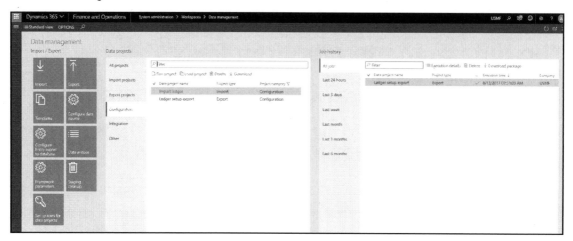

The data management workspace has several functions that can be be used to import data, export data, export entities to an external Azure SQL database, get list of data entities, set up roles, and facilitate other useful capabilities and views to quickly manage your data flow.

Data entities

Data entities provide a conceptual abstraction and encapsulation of the underlying table schema that represent the data concepts and functionalities. Data entities are the foundation bricks of a data management platform and serve many other purposes, such as integration, analytics, and office integration.

> For more details on data entities, refer to the Chapter 8, *Integration Planning and Design* in this book. You can also refer to the Microsoft documentation at https://docs.microsoft.com/en-us/dynamics365/ unified-operations/dev-itpro/data-entities/data-entities.

From a data management perspective, data entities enables scenarios for configuration data provisioning and data migration, as shown in the following image:

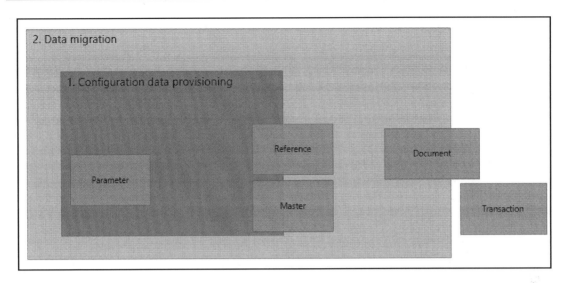

As shown in the preceding image, activities related to setting up a company, its parameters, and select reference and master data are within the boundary of the configuration data provisioning, where a number of tools are available to select from.

The migration of open documents, master data, and supporting data could also be done using tools in LCS or using data management within Dynamics 365 for Finance and Operations, Enterprise edition.

For more details on data management, refer to `Chapter 3`, *Architecture and Deployment* and `Chapter 8`, *Integration Planning and Design*.

Configuration data templates

Configuration data templates are predefined lists of entities for each module area that can be used in a data project. You can create, view, and modify these templates by using the template page in the data management workspace. The **Template** page in the Data management workspace provides tools that let you create a template of entities. Similar to exporting data projects, you can create data templates by adding one entity at a time or adding multiple entities. You can also use the **Open in Excel** button to open the contents of the grid in a Microsoft Excel workbook. Modify the entities as you require and then use **Publish** to upload the changes back into Dynamics 365 for Finance and Operations. You can also use any existing data projects to create a template.

Default data templates

Templates makes it easier to jump start your data activities and Microsoft has released predefined templates to help you create configuration data projects. The templates will be sequenced so that the data that the entities generate will be processed in the correct sequence. These predefined templates are also designed to maintain the correct sequence when more than one template is added to the same data project.

In the July 2017 update of Dynamics 365 for Finance and Operations, Enterprise edition, you can get these data templates by using the **Load default templates** button. The future goal is to provide these templates through LCS.

Many default templates include entities for master data as well as customers, vendors, released products, and so on. These entities are included with a proper sequencing of the entities. The following screenshot shows a sample list:

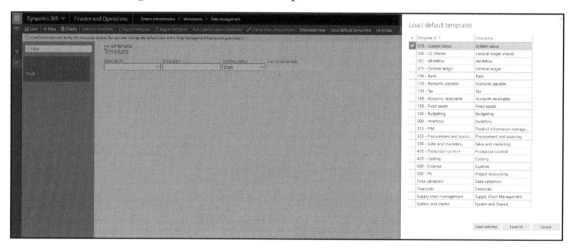

For more details on data templates and their sequencing, refer to `https://docs.microsoft.com/en-us/dynamics365/unified-operations/dev-itpro/data-entities/configuration-data-templates`.

Data templates are reusable artifacts and are used to create data projects quickly, as explained in the next subsection.

Configuration data project

A data project or configuration data project contains configured data entities, their source data format (Excel, CSV, and XML), mapping, and default processing options (execution sequence or dependency). Configuration data packages are created by using the data import and export projects in the **Data management** workspace. Data projects support the following scenarios:

- **Export of configurations**: Create configurations of entities and use the data management framework to export them to a package
- **Import of configurations**: Upload a configuration package and use the data management framework to import the package

To export data packages, you simply click on the **Export** tile in the data management workspace, which opens the configuration data project page, as shown in the following screenshot. You can name the project and add entities to create the data project:

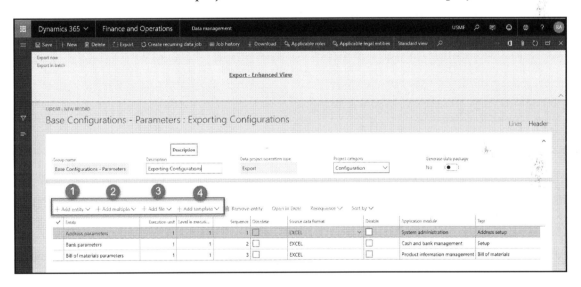

As shown earlier, in the enhanced view there are a number of ways that can be leveraged to add data entities in your export data project, as follows:

- **Add one entity**: Enter the first part of the name of the entity until it appears in the lookup.
- **Add multiple entities**: Enter any part of the entity name, use the lookup for the module, enter any part of the tag name, or use the lookup for the entity category to show a list of entities. Press **Tab** to move the focus away from the **Lookup** field and activate the filter. In the grid, select the entities to add.
- **Add a file:** Browse to a file that contains a name that matches the name of an entity and a file name extension that matches the file name extension that is in your data sources.
- **Add a template:** Select from a list of templates that you've loaded in your instance.
- **Open in Excel:** Another option is open in Excel to edit and publish it back.

After you have added the list of entities in your configuration and sequenced them, you can click on the **Export** button to export the data project and create a data package. During the export, you can see the execution history of the data project, as follows:

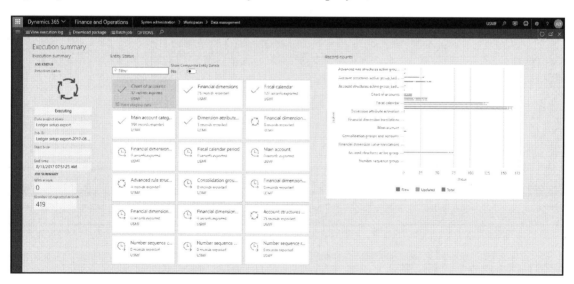

After the export is completed, you can download the packages locally by clicking the **Download Package** button.

Once the configurations are exported in a data package, they can be imported in another company or environment. The following screenshot shows the setup of such an import type:

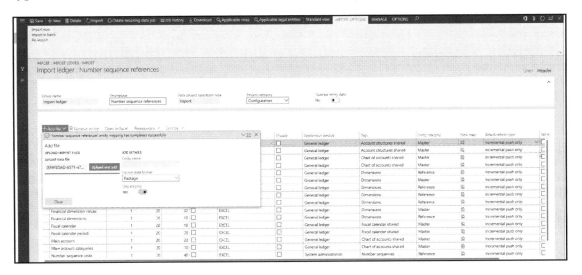

As you learned, exporting a data project generates the output as a data package, which we will be explaining in the next section.

Data packages

A data package typically consists of one to many data entities. A typical data package consists of a group of entities for a particular task, process, or function. For example, the data entities that are required for general ledger setup may be part of one data package. The format of a data package is a compressed file that contains a package manifest, a package header, and any additional files for the included data entities.

The following screenshot shows the content of a sample data package containing sample configuration data for the data validation checklist process:

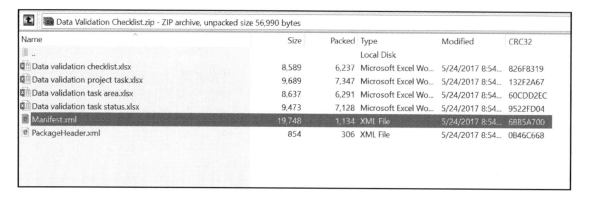

In a typical implementation scenario, when you start to set up the initial configuration data, you create data packages with entities containing standard business data, sample data, and entities without any data. You can then decompress the package, use data spreadsheets to collect the business data, and compress them to create the final data package. You can import this data package in your environment to complete the initial set of configurations.

Data packages can be directly imported using the **data management** workspace or uploaded to the LCS asset library and applied to the same or another environment through the data configuration manager. These concepts are covered in the next subsection.

LCS Project | Asset library | Data packages

Once the data packages are downloaded from your initial configuration environment and the data is finalized, you can upload these data packages to your LCS project library. As shown in the following screenshot, the LCS asset library can be used as a repository for the data packages:

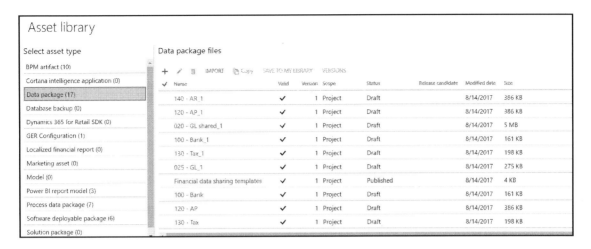

The following are the key features of data packages in the LCS asset library:

- **Upload new data packages**: You can use the + button to create new data packages and upload the data package file.
- **Save it in your shared asset library**: Similar to the other asset types in LCS, you can save the data package as a shared asset. A shared asset can be imported into other projects within your organization.
- **Import**: Using the import option in the **Asset library** project, you can import the assets shared with you. While importing the assets, you can see all the data project assets shared within your organization or shared by Microsoft. To get the shared data package, simply select the data package and click on the **Pick** button to import the data package to your project asset library.
- **Maintain version**: You can use the LCS asset library to manage the different versions of the asset file. You can also see the previous versions and pick a previous version to import it back if needed.

Configuration data packages

To reduce the implementation time, Microsoft releases multiple base data packages that you can used as a starting seed for your implementation projects. These packages contain the elements that are required in each module/area in order to meet the minimum requirements. For advanced business processes, you may have to add more entities to the list of packages.

The configuration data packages are available in LCS in **Asset library | Data packages** and can be imported into your implementation project data package asset. These data packages contain configuration entity spreadsheets based on the best practices data from Microsoft, which can be used to create an initial golden environment.

The entity spreadsheets include three types of data:

- **Business data**: The spreadsheet contains standard business data for a sample mid-sized company, combining the best practices and business standards to be used as a starting point for your initial configuration.
- **Sample data**: The spreadsheet contains data that can be used as an example for business-specific data. This data can be imported and used as an example, but it is expected to be changed in the spreadsheets itself, before loading it.
- **No data**: These spreadsheet don't contain any data. Several areas of the product are unique to each business and its business practices; hence, these spreadsheets must be reviewed and updated as per the organization's needs.

Data entities in configuration data packages are sequenced appropriately to guarantee a successful single-click import of the data, thereby ensuring data dependencies. These configuration data packages are great starting points to accelerate the configuration of your solution on Microsoft Dynamics 365 for Finance and Operations, Enterprise edition.

Refer to this link for detailed information on configuration data packages and package listing with their entities and content in the spreadsheets:
`https://docs.microsoft.com/en-us/dynamics365/unified-operations/dev-itpro/data-entities/configuration-data-packages?toc=dynamics365/unified-operations/fin-and-ops/toc.json#data-packages-system`

LCS -- configuration and data manager

Configuration and data manager is a tool in the LCS that helps you apply data packages to your Dynamics 365 for Finance and Operation environment.

The following screenshot shows the configuration and data manager tool in LCS:

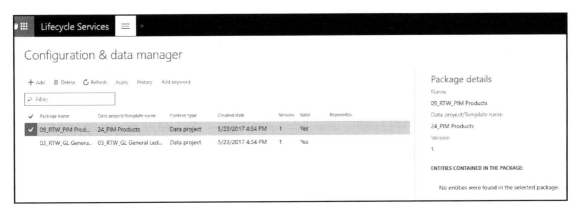

The configuration and data manager tool shows all validated data packages available in the project asset library. Using **Configuration & data manager**, you can select one or more data projects and click **Apply**. This opens up a dialog where you can select the environment and a legal entity, and click **OK**. This will apply the selected data packages to your environment.

When applying multiple data packages, you can choose to apply concurrently or sequentially, based on the dependencies, as shown in the following screenshot:

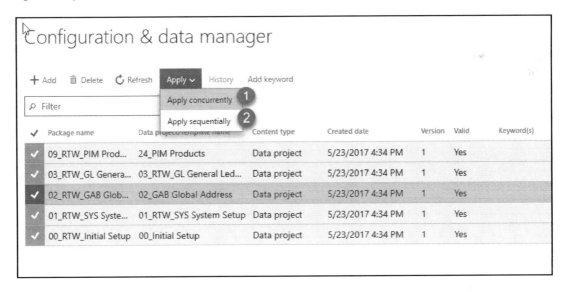

Once the consumption of the data package is over, you can see the status in three ways:

- In LCS, select a data package and click **History** to review its status
- The information shown as part of the status is: target environment, company, package name, start and end times, status by data entity, and the overall status of the data package
- To see the details of any errors that occurred, one needs to sign in to the target environment and see it in the data management workspace job history

Process data packages

Process data packages, also known as **PDPs**, are a collection of data packages arranged in a specified order to load them in a target environment. PDP consolidates data packages into a unified bundle. The PDP is then used to configure a business process or a group of business processes in one business process library.

Here are some select features of PDP and its configuration:

- PDPs can be used from within LCS only
- As shown in the following screenshot, you can create/import PDP only in the project-specific asset library in LCS:

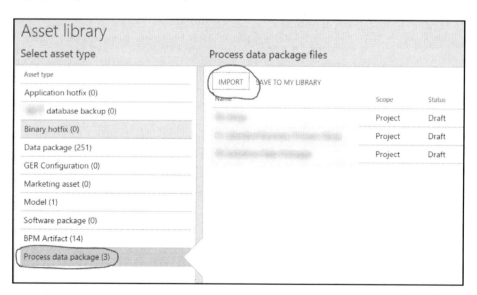

- PDP needs to be linked to the business process nodes in a business process modeler

- The processing/consumption of PDP is done using the following steps:
  - First, PDPs are created and associated with a BPM library
  - Next, one or more data packages are added from the LCS asset library
  - Next, one or more nodes are selected to associate the PDP with BPM nodes
  - Lastly, the dependency is set on the data packages

Following is a visual of consuming **PDP (Process data package)** showing the three step approached on the left, with **BPM (Business process modeler)** in the centre and details of a selected process to the right.

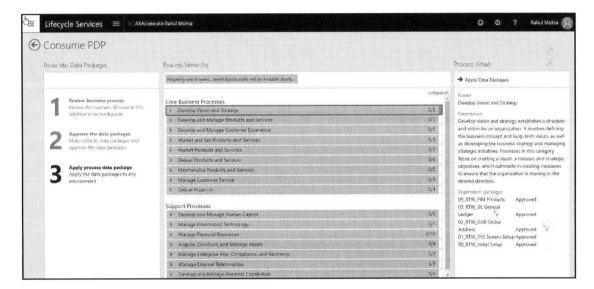

- To consume a PDP, you need to complete the BPM review of a business process and then apply the required configuration and data for implementing the business process to the Dynamics 365 for Finance and Operations, Enterprise edition environment
- You should open **Business process modeler** from the LCS tools list and assign the PDP to its respective business process, as shown earlier, and click on **Consume PDP**
- Once the approval of a business process and PDP is done, then during deployment, a target environment and legal entity can be specified

From our personal experience, PDP can be used in implementation projects; however, the data management framework is mostly used directly to seed the environments. PDP is helpful for quickly provisioning environments for demo purposes.

How these concepts come together

As you learnt in the preceding sections and chapters, managing the data and configuration is highly important and Microsoft has provided a lot of tools to leverage. However, the right selection of these tools, fitting the purpose, is needed and must be done carefully. Let's give you an end-to-end visual of all the tools and elements that can be used to manage the data and configuration in your implemenation and beyond.

The following diagram shows the information flow and the tools leveraged within Dynamics 365 for Finance and Operations, Enterprise edition as well as LCS:

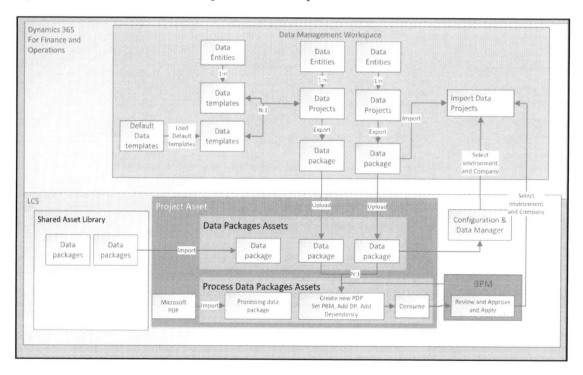

The sequence of activities within Dynamics 365 for Finance and Operations, Enterprise edition to manage the data and configurations starts with the identification and creation of data entities. Once the data entity and its related entities are identified, they can be grouped together in a data package, where the dependencies can also be assigned. These data packages are built using a data project.

For an implementation initiative, when you need to start from ground zero, the identification of these entities could be time consuming. This activity can be avoided using the default data templates provided by Microsoft or by creating your own data templates. These templates are meant to be reused to create data projects, whether you need to load the information in the same environment or another environment.

While the full suite of data and configuration activities can be done entirely in Dynamics 365 for Finance and Operations, Enterprise edition, Microsoft has provided more tools in LCS. These tools in LCS primarily start with data packages. These are the same data packages created in Dynamics 365 for Finance and Operations, Enterprise edition that could be added in the LCS asset library and used to import the data and configuration in an environment.

One can directly execute these data packages in LCS, or combine them and sequence them in a PDP, and apply to an environment using the configuration and data manager. One can also leverage the predefined templates from Microsoft, available as configuration data packages, which could be downloaded and updated with customer-specific information/data and uploaded back in LCS to be applied to an environment. These configuration data templates could also be directly processed in Dynamics 365 for Finance and Operations, Enterprise edition using the data management framework.

Database operations

There are occasions when, instead of working on a particular data or configuration, you may need to work on the entire database. Such scenarios could come up while creating a new environment and seeding it with the data from the golden environment, or while requesting Microsoft to use the database of the golden environment and populate production for the first time.

One must acknowledge the differences in the database platform when using Azure SQL and SQL on the premises. The process involves the following information flow when moving the database from Azure SQL to Microsoft SQL Server (on-premise):

Copy from Azure SQL to SQL Server	Copy from SQL Server to a production Azure SQL
Create a duplicate of the source database.	Create a copy of the source database.
Run a SQL Server script to prepare the database.	Run a script to prepare the database.
Export the database from the Azure SQL database.	Export the database from SQL Server.
Import the database to SQL Server 2016.	Import the database into an Azure SQL database.
Run a SQL script to update the database.	Run a script to update the database.
Update enviornment specific information and any encryption information	Update enviornment specific information and any encryption information
Synchronize database and restart services	Synchronize database and restart services

As shown in the preceding image, there are some common steps in the database export and import process, and it leverages BACPAC (SQL backup files) files.

For more details, refer to the following links:

https://docs.microsoft.com/en-us/dynamics365/unified-operations/
dev-itpro/database/copy-database-from-sql-server-to-azure-sql

https://docs.microsoft.com/en-us/dynamics365/unified-operations/
dev-itpro/database/copy-database-from-azure-sql-to-sql-server

LCS has tools for initiating database operations, such as backup, restore, and so on, using the support request that we explained in Chapter 2, *Implementation Methodology and Tools*. We have seen on the Microsoft Dynamics roadmap a self-service capability that Microsoft intends to provide to customers and partners to empower them to leverage this step on their own instead of contacting the Microsoft operations team every time. These database operations include promoting a golden configuration to production, refreshing the sandbox from production data, and a database point-in-time restore for your environment.

Cross-company data sharing

Cross-company sharing is a mechanism for sharing reference and group data among companies in finance and operations deployment. This feature simplifies the master data management for customers with multiple legal entities. For example, if your implementation project is dealing with multiple legal entities but some setup and parameter data is common across the legal entities, you can use this feature to share the data. When a particular table is added to a master data sharing policy and the applicable legal entities are mapped, the data in the underlying tables get synchronized over to the other legal entities seamlessly. The business user does not have to worry about maintaining this setup data in multiple legal entities. One can simply create, update, or delete these records in one company, and the system instantly synchronizes the changes to all the other applicable legal entities. Currently, this feature only supports configuration (such as parameter tables) and group tables (methods of payment, payment terms, customer groups, and so on).

 Detailed documentation is available on Microsoft's official documentation site: `https://docs.microsoft.com/en-us/dynamics365/operations/dev-itpro/sysadmin/cross-company-data-sharing`

Data management scenarios

These are some typical data management scenarios a project goes through. Let's explore the tools and processes to use in each scenario.

Initial configuration in a blank environment

We recommend that you leverage the data management framework within Microsoft Dynamics 365 for Finance and Operations, Enterprise edition and start with the base data packages released from Microsoft. We typically download them, extract the data files, fit them to the customer's business needs, and then load them in the initial environment.

Many partners and ISVs are investing in creating industry-specific data packages that they intend to use repeatably in various implementation scenarios. These data packages can also be used to seed the initial configuration environment.

Once you have applied the base data packages, you can save them as data templates. You can also load the default template provided by Microsoft. You can add and remove entities, according to your requirements, and maintain the data template for creating future data projects.

Data migration from legacy systems

After your initial Dynamics 365 for Finance and Operations environment is configured, it is time to perform data migration from the legacy system. The following diagram depicts the data migration process that can be used in your implementation project:

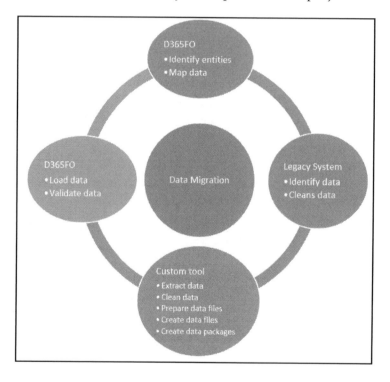

As shown in the preceding diagram, data migration activities start from identifying data entities in Dynamics 365 for Finance and Operations and the corresponding data in your legacy system. Once the data elements are identified, you need to work on mapping these data elements. Data templates in Finance and Operations can be used to define the mapping rules and default values. Often, the data in a legacy system is not in a very clean state and you do not want to bring unnecessary data to your new system. If possible, clean or filter such data in the legacy system.

For large data migration scenarios, you may need custom or ETL tools for data extraction and data cleansing. You can use these tools to create data files and data packages as needed for Dynamics 365 for Finance and Operations. Once the data packages are prepared, you can load and validate the data in Dynamics 365 for Finance and Operations, Enterprise edition.

Data migration is usually not a one-time process; it needs to be repeated multiple times to get to a clean state. Repeat the process multiple times in the development environment and every other environment, such as training, testing, and UAT, to catch any errors.

 If you are migrating to Finance and Operations from a previous version of Dynamics AX, such as AX 2009, Microsoft has already built a data migration tool, which can be leveraged to plan and execute data migration. For more details, visit the `Chapter 14`, *Update, Upgrade, and Migration*, where the data migration process from Dynamics AX 2009 is covered in detail.

Remember that for production to go live, data migration activities usually need to be performed during system downtime. Apart from a successful run, another aspect that you may have to manage is the total time to run the data migration activities. This time must be measured and optimized to fit your overall downtime window.

Copy the company configuration within an existing environment

Microsoft is expected to release a company-copy capability in Dynamics 365 for Finance and Operations, Enterprise edition (AX), which is a going to benefit configuration activities a lot by defining the template company. This template company's data can be copied over to new legal entities using the company copy feature.

Refer to this link for more details:
`https://roadmap.dynamics.com`

This approach is useful for projects going live in multiple phases, where a global template is created and used across different legal entities.

For more information on configuration copying across companies, refer to `https://docs.microsoft.com/en-us/dynamics365/unified-operations/dev-itpro/data-entities/copy-configuration`.

Until such a tool is available, you can create a data template spanning an entire set of configurations and master data and use it to export and import data in the same environment or other environments. As per the business needs, you may also create another template or package to address open transactions, such as open purchase orders, open sales orders, and so on.

Copy data between environments

If your golden environment is already ready, and the data and import processes are validated, then we recommend that you use the database copy functionality to seed any other environment, including production.

For any incremental data load, you may directly utilize data management tools such as data entities or data packages within Microsoft Dynamics 365 for Finance and Operations, Enterprise edition.

There is another option of leveraging the LCS and data packages to load; however, for a controlled process with approvals, this activity is recommended to be done directly within the application.

Ad hoc data loading

If you have to process any new load or import/export data for a new data entity, then you can directly process it by quickly creating a data project using a data entity or data package and use it for loading the information in the application.

Best practices in managing configurations and data migration

We would like to share our knowledge and best practices in configuration and data migration:

- Always have a configuration management and data migration plan:
    - The solution advisor/partner and customer business owner are both required to play an active role
- Always baseline the configuration whenever it is to be deployed in production:
    - Be it a full configuration set or delta, it must be tested with all the potential use cases and the test result should be baselined
- Collaboration tools should be leveraged as a repository with track changes enabled for traceability
- There is a lot of decision making that happens in configurations and data migration, and it should always be updated in the key decision matrix
- Align your configuration and data migration plans with the implementation methodology
- Ensure sign offs on business requirements towards data migration
- Always ensure that you have a golden environment in your plan and use it to seed the other environments
- Keep multiple data migration strategies for the following:
    - Initial system load
    - Key configuration masters
    - Business-specific master data
    - Open transactions
    - Regular and cut-over time
- The migrated data must always be verified, tested, and accepted as part of system acceptance
- Ensure that the mapping and transformation logic is tested for sample data before running full fledged for all data:
    - Always try and keep the transformation as simple as possible with very few conversions
- The data to be imported is always reviewed, validated, and cleansed by the business before being imported

- Do not forget the sequencing of data load; this is one activity that can bring in a lot of rework if not managed carefully
- When taking key decisions on configurations and data migration, ensure that they are taken up in the **change control board** (**CCB**) for their validation/approval
- Never run short of documentation and tracking, as these activities evolve with time
- Always ensure that the naming conventions are defined for the configuration and data migration elements, and are used consistently throughout the project
- Conduct human and system data integrity checks post data migration

 Configuration and data migration are like icebergs in an implementation initiative. They may look simple at first sight, but deserve a lot more attention.

Summary

In this chapter you learned how to best manage configuration and data. The strategies suggested for managing configuration and data are based on our experience, and they lay a strong foundation for configuration and planning, including migration. It is super important to have the right data management strategy, as it has a direct impact on everyone who's going to use the system, on decision making, on driving daily operations, and on achieving the project objectives. As there are a number of data management techniques and tools, it is highly important to select the right one to effectively manage your configuration and data in Microsoft Dynamics 365 for Finance and Operations, Enterprise edition. Understanding the solution capabilities of data entities and their usage in the solution directly, as well as through LCS using data packages and PDP, are must-haves in your configuration and data planning.

With the growth of LCS, it has become imperative to leverage capabilities such as data packages, BPM, PDP, and other key tools to ensure faster and higher ROI, and on-time delivery/go-live of your project. Though it may look optional, we strongly recommend that every implementation leverage the VSTS to manage your project task, design documents, code, build, and various other key artifacts, along with SharePoint online as a shared document repository.

From the next chapter onwards, we will explore how to best address the various design patterns, key deliverables, and development approaches. We will start with the key design documents, that is, the functional design document, the solution design document (which is also known as the big picture), and the technical design document, based on the latest architecture stack of Dynamics 365 for Finance and Operations, Enterprise edition. We will also cover resources such as AppSource for your ISV solutions evaluation and selection. We will discuss the recommended features in Dynamics 365 for Finance and Operations, Enterprise edition to leverage, so as to avoid customizations.

7
Functional and Technical Design

The solution design process begins once the analysis phase has been completed. By now, the project plan is ready, the requirements document has been signed off, the **Conference Room Pilot** (**CRP**) has been completed, and the fit-gap exercise has been completed and documented as part of the analysis phase. In the fit-gap exercise, if the team has decided on using some ISV solution to fill the gaps, then you may need to evaluate the best ISV solution. For any other gaps, the implementation team needs to document the overall solution and produce the functional and technical design documents to address the gaps through customization and extension. However, before starting on writing design documents, a functional and technical consultant also needs to know the common features that can be used to fill the gaps or complement the solution design they are proposing.

In this chapter, we will cover the following topics:

- Finding the right app for your business needs
- Common features
- The functional design document
- The solution design document
- The technical design document

Finding the right app for your business needs

After the business requirements are identified and the fit-gap analysis is done, one important decision the project team has to make is whether to build the required customizations or buy an existing solution to bridge the solution gap. During the fit-gap analysis, you can use the LCS BPM libraries and add your requirements associated with the business process. You can specify whether the requirement is a fit or gap, and you can also specify a high-level estimation. You can then use the LCS BPM library to view all the processes and gaps to identify the areas that require ISV solutions.

There are a great many ISV solutions available in the Dynamics 365 ecosystem that can help you bridge the gap between the standard product and the required industry-specific functionality. Usually, if someone already has a solution that has been used by multiple customers, it will be less risky than developing your own solution--you don't want to reinvent the wheel.

Solution architects and the technical and functional teams need to act as the customer's advocate in choosing ISV solutions. Getting the right ISV solution is important for your success.

The introduction of Microsoft AppSource has made it super easy to find the right ISV solution. As shown in the following image, simply visit `https://appsource.microsoft.com`, refine your search by category, industry, and product, and you'll get a list of ISV solutions available as per your criteria. You can sign up for a trial or contact the provider directly through the portal to get the process started:

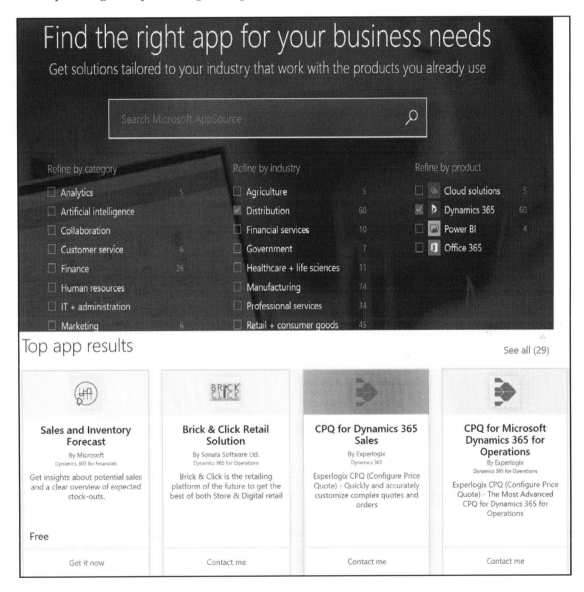

Before choosing ISV solutions

It is indeed easy to find all the ISV solutions available as per your requirements. However, before choosing an ISV solution, consider the following points:

- *Build versus buy analysis*: Sometimes, going with an ISV solution may look like a quick win. However, it comes with a cost. When evaluating the cost of the ISV solution, you must consider the total cost of ownership and not just the cost of licensing. Others may include code merging, support, training, and so on. High-level estimation on the original requirements and gaps can help you evaluate the cost of building these customizations yourself and compare that with the cost of an ISV solution in the long run.

- *Benefits and percentage of fit*: Understand all the benefits that the ISV product has to offer and identify the percentage of fit that you have with the requirements. If you still have to customize for more than 20-30 percent of the scenarios, you may be better off building the whole solution by yourself.

- *Readiness of the current version*: It is very important to see a demo of the current version of the product (that is, the version you are planning to use) or to understand how close the ISV is to delivering the solution for the version that you will implement. Try to defer the decision to buy an ISV solution until the product is functional for the version you need.

- *Product roadmap*: Understand the product roadmap and features. Make sure that these deadlines are mentioned as part of the contract. For example, ISV currently provides tax calculations only for the US. However, Canada is on the roadmap. Make sure that you understand the deadlines for Canada and have those documented as part of the contract to ensure that your project doesn't suffer due to delays from ISV. Also, review the roadmap for the upcoming cumulative updates.

- *Dynamics 365 for Finance and Operations, Enterprise edition roadmap*: Be aware of any new functionality that Microsoft is working on for new releases. You can find the features that Microsoft is already working on in the Dynamics roadmap portal (`https://roadmap.dynamics.com/`). Will these features supplant the ISV solution? How easy would it be to upgrade your solution and take advantage of the new features? Would it be more cost-effective? How will it affect the business if you wait for the new features versus if you do a temporary customization or implement the ISV solution?

- *Architectural review*: Have detailed architectural reviews done by the solution architect or technical architect on the team as part of the evaluation to ensure that there are no architectural gaps and that the solution is scalable.

- *References*: If you don't have an existing relationship with the ISV, ask for customer references and have a discussion with the references prior to making a decision.

- *Company size and support*: Evaluate the ISV solution provider's size, their financial strength, and any risk associated with the long-term support of the product.

 If there are a lot more features included in the ISV solution than the customer may ever need, it may not be the best fit.

After selecting the partner

Consider the following after partner selection:

- If possible, try to reduce the dependency as much as possible. Have a single partner/advisor who manages ISV and the development partners.
- Get the budget approved and have all the invoices billed through the partner. This way, the customer doesn't have to deal with multiple parties.
- Share your project plan with the ISV partner and align their delivery dates according to your schedule. Update your project plan to include the key ISV deliverables.
- Have them attend weekly meetings for status updates (if they are working in parallel on building the solution).
- Plan the code and configuration changes from ISV that must be incorporated into your development and other environments.

Common pitfalls

Consider the following to avoid the common pitfalls during ISV selection:

- You don't want to involve too many ISV solutions as part of the overall solution. It will increase the dependencies for upgrades and take away time from your core implementation team in managing conflicts and testing.
- Each ISV solution being envisioned in the overall solution design should have a minimum or no overlayering.

Common features

During the fit-gap analysis sessions, the consultant and the product experts should try to find workarounds for every possible gap. Utilize the LCS BPM library to identify the common business processes and best practices. There are many common features in finance and operations, applicable to any module. These features, if carefully examined, can address many gaps. In this section, we will briefly cover some of these common features.

 The intent for the overview of the common features in this chapter is to use these features as possible workarounds to avoid customization or use them as part of your custom solution to provide a consistent user experience.

Personalization

Customization is often requested by business users to simply hide, move, or rename fields displayed on the forms. These types of customizations can be avoided with a powerful personalization feature.

With personalization, a user can change how certain UI elements are displayed in his/her version of Finance and Operations to best serve his/her needs. It is possible to personalize a page and share it with other users by simply exporting the personalized page and asking the other users to navigate to the personalized page and import the personalization file that you've created. If a user has admin privileges, they can also manage personalizations for other users. While the user can make the screens morph the way it suits them to help their productivity, these personalization changes do not impact other users or the underlying code base. The following image shows how users can manage the personalization in Dynamics 365 for Finance and Operations, Enterprise edition:

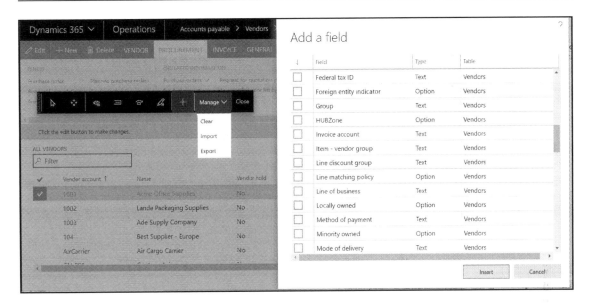

To learn in detail about the personalization feature, visit the following URL:
`https://docs.microsoft.com/en-us/dynamics365/operations/get-started/personalize-user-experience`

Office integration

Office integration is another great feature in Dynamics 365 for Finance and Operations, Enterprise edition that can cut down many customization requests related to user productivity. The Excel Data Connector addin makes Excel a seamless part of the user experience within the user interface. The application uses data entities and OData services to interact with Office addins and to provide the ability of exporting static data available on the page and doing template-based export. Moreover, you can modify the data in Excel and push it back.

The **Open in Microsoft Office** menu is available on any page that has a data source, as shown in the following screenshot:

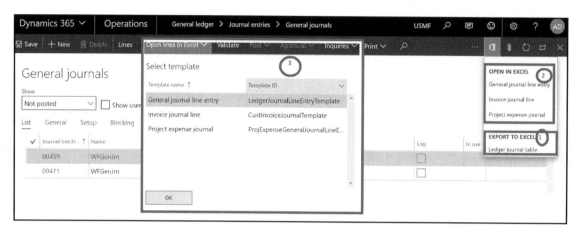

As shown in the preceding image, the **Open in Microsoft Office** menu provides three types of options:

1. **Export to Excel:** These options are automatically added to all the visible grids on the page. These options are static exports of data from a grid.

2. **Open in Excel:** These options are automatically added to the data entities and entity-based templates that share the same root data source as the current page. These options make it easier to read data in Excel and publish the data changes back to Finance and Operations application using OData services.

3. **Open lines in Excel:** These are the options that are added by code using the export API. These options can be custom-generated exports or custom template exports.

Excel integration can be used as an option to fill the gaps related to data import/export and ad hoc reporting done by business users. You can also use these features by building data entities for the custom features that you build as part of your solution. The following link provides in-depth coverage of the concept, features, and how you can extend the solution to add open lines in Excel:

https://docs.microsoft.com/en-us/dynamics365/operations/dev-itpro/office-integration/office-integration

Document management

The **document management feature** (also known as **document handling**) enables users to attach documents to a particular transaction or a master data record in Dynamics 365 for Finance and Operations, Enterprise edition. It can be used to attach supporting documents, such as an invoice copy received from a vendor, purchase order quotes, contracts, and so on. Different document types can be created and configured to be used across solution areas. Normally, separate document types are created for use by departments, as you can limit who can see the notes by the document type. You can save the notes and print them on output documents, such as purchase orders, packing slips, and invoices. The files that are attached can be viewed using the **Attachment** option on the Finance and Operations screen.

For sophisticated needs, for example, if you are using **Optical Character Recognition** (**OCR**) to capture the vendor invoices, a side-by-side attachment viewer is available on exception handling forms, pending invoices, and journal inquiries. The following image shows the side-by-side document view of vendor invoices:

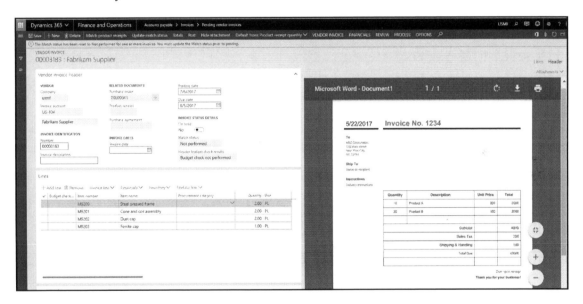

 You can utilize these document management capabilities in your custom solution easily to deliver a consistent user experience and increase productivity.

Workspaces

Workspaces are activity-oriented pages that are designed to increase the user's productivity. Workspace provides information that answers most of the targeted user's activity-related questions and allows the user to initiate more frequent tasks. As shown in the following screenshot, a workspace usually contains tiles (displaying counters or KPIs to answer a set of questions), a set of relevant lists, and action buttons (to initiate activities), graphs, charts, or Power BI dashboards, and a set of links to pages that are important but not frequently used for this activity:

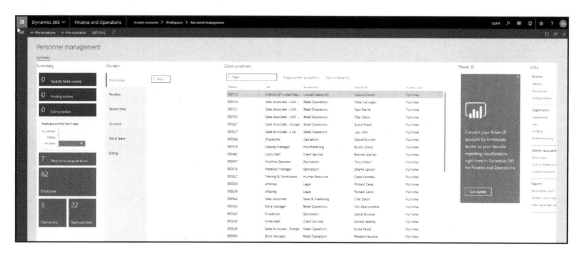

The best part is that you can create a new workspace, add counters, list pages and links, and add power BI dashboards without writing a single line of code, all using the personalization feature. While creating custom solutions, you should always consider how business users are going to use the system, what common questions they usually have, and what their most frequent actions are. You can combine all these into a single page by creating a workspace.

Electronic reporting

Electronic reporting (**ER**) is a tool that you can use to configure the formats for electronic documents in accordance with the legal requirements of various countries/regions. ER simplifies the creation, maintenance, and upgradation of electronic document formats by enabling business users to create these reports through configuration. Because you configure formats, not code, the processes of creating and adjusting formats for electronic documents are faster and easier.

The ER engine has the following capabilities:

- It represents a single common tool for electronic reporting in different domains and replaces more than 20 different engines that do some type of electronic reporting for Microsoft Dynamics 365 for Finance and Operations, Enterprise edition.
- It makes a report's format insulated from the current Dynamics 365 for Finance and Operations, Enterprise edition implementation.
- It supports the creation of a custom format that is based on an original format. It includes capabilities for automatically upgrading the customized format when changes to the original format occur because localization/customization requirements are introduced.
- It becomes the primary standard tool to support the localization requirements in electronic reporting, both for Microsoft and for Microsoft partners.
- It supports the ability to distribute formats to partners and customers through Microsoft Dynamics **Lifecycle Services (LCS)**.

Many requirements that need customization through code, for example, bank file export/import, remittance report, and so on, can now be delivered through configuration using the ER model. Electronic reporting can support a range of functions in Dynamics 365 for Finance and Operations, Enterprise edition, including the following:

- Financial auditing
- Tax reporting
- Electronic invoicing
- Payment formats

The best part is that in most cases, you do not have to create these formats from scratch; Microsoft has already delivered the base version of an electronic report format and will continuously provide updates through LCS. The partners or customers can utilize the base model and create their own version, as per their requirements.

For more details, follow the direct link to read more about electronic reporting:
https://docs.microsoft.com/en-us/dynamics365/operations/dev-itpro/analytics/general-electronic-reporting

Tax engine

Similar to electronic reporting, Microsoft is introducing a **tax engine** (TE) to set up and calculate taxes from a code-based approach to configuration. The new tax engine is highly configurable and lets business users, functional consultants, and power users configure tax rules that determine tax applicability, tax calculation, posting, and settlement, based on the legal and business requirements. The tax engine covers the following functional scopes:

Functional area	Scope
Tax administration	• Tax registration • Tax authority • Tax-related information on master data • Tax invoice and voucher numbering
Tax applicability	• The application scope of a tax • Applying taxes on transactions
Tax calculation	• Determination of tax basis and tax rate • Calculation and distribution of tax amount
Tax accounting	• Accounting treatment of the calculation and distributed tax amounts
Tax documentation	• Tax invoice
Tax settlement	• Output tax and input tax assessment • Tax adjustment • Tax payment, carry forward, and refund
Tax return	• Tax inquiries • Tax report • Filing and e-filing

Just like electronic reporting, the tax engine feature can be leveraged to implement tax-related requirements through configuration.

Batch framework

The batch framework provides an asynchronous, server-based batch processing environment that can process tasks across multiple instances of the **Application Object Server (AOS)**. Any transaction that needs to be executed in an asynchronous way can run using the batch framework. Performance scaling of volume-intensive transactions or actions to be performed periodically are the typical uses of batch jobs, for example, invoicing shipped orders every 15 minutes, daily export of positive pay files, and inventory recalculation or close process.

In batch jobs, tasks are created to perform the necessary actions, and these tasks can be multithreaded to fully utilize the available resources. You can also create dependencies between batch tasks. For example, when you want products to be imported before importing the product pricing information. To achieve this, you can setup product pricing import task to run only when product import job is completed successfully. Other usage of batch jobs include workflow execution, recurring data export/import, scheduling reports execution, and so on.

Workflows

Workflows are the mechanisms by which business rules and approval processes are implemented in the solution. You can direct certain transactions for approvals using workflows. Some examples of documents for which built-in workflows can be set up are AP invoice journals, purchase requisitions, expense reports, budget planning processes, general journals, customer payments, free text invoices, and so on.

The usage of workflows includes the following:

- Assigning a transaction for review
- Assigning a transaction for approval
- Automation of a business step
- Conditional decisions on business data, which the next steps are dependent upon
- Multiple levels of approvals
- Approval type selection, such as based on role, based on position, managerial hierarchy, and so on
- Workflows can be delegated and/or escalated after a certain time frame

Always keep the workflow implementation as simple as possible. Many organizations move from paper or manual approval processes into systematic workflows and come up with complex rules. It becomes difficult to build and maintain such workflows as organizational changes occur, and eventually, these workflows are abandoned.

Database logging

The database log is a feature that helps in auditing. It keeps track of the changes made by users. You can enable *track* on specific actions, such as insert, delete, and update. For updates, you can turn on the tracking for specific fields. It keeps track of who created or modified the record and when. In the case of updates, you can see the previous value and the new value.

This is typically used in areas where audit tracking is required, such as credit limit updates. Standard reports are available for reviewing any changes made.

If changes are made directly in SQL through updates, these will not be visible to AOS and will not be available in the database log. It is one of the many reasons why the ERP data should not be directly modified in the SQL database.

Mobile application

Mobile application is another common application that can be utilized for requirements where you need to serve a mobile workforce. The Dynamics 365 for Finance and Operations mobile app can work even in the offline mode and automatically synchronize when connected to the internet. The best part is that as an IT admin, you can build and publish mobile workspaces as per the organization's needs. The app leverages your existing code, business logic, and security configuration. You can easily design mobile workspaces using the point-and-click workspace designer that comes built in with the web client of Dynamics 365 for Finance and Operations, Enterprise edition. You can further optimize the offline capabilities of workspaces by utilizing the extensibility framework for business logic. Using this, you can provide additional business logic and rendering support by adding a JavaScript file with the application workspace metadata.

Microsoft has already shipped and is continuously shipping several common-use, out-of-box mobile workspaces; however, you can further extend or create new mobile workspaces as per your specific requirements.

Common Data Services, Microsoft Flow, and PowerApps

Common Data Services (CDS), Flow, and PowerApps are another set of solutions that can play a big role in your custom solution design. As you may already know, CDS is the Microsoft Azure–based business application platform that enables you to easily build and extend applications with your business data. Using Microsoft Flow and many other connectors, you can bring data from multiple data sources, including Finance and Operations and other Dynamics 365 family applications. On top of this data, you can build modern low-code Apps using PowerApp or CDS SDK.

In an implementation project, you can explore whether requirements could be best-suited to be a PowerApp using CDS platform. Typically, the applications that you build using CDS and PowerApp are last-mile applications that are not fundamental parts of the ERP system but are either managed in spreadsheets or different third-party systems. Using CDS and PowerApps, you can build these applications very quickly and integrate them easily with Finance and Operations. You can also embed the PowerApps applications within the Dynamics 365 application as control, which provides the ability to access PowerApps within the Finance and Operations user interface. The following are some scenarios we think will be best-suited to be developed using the CDS platform to cover last-mile scenarios and to integrate business processes.

 Independent solutions having a low dependency -- for example, a service desk app that can be used by employees to request products or services, and once it is approved by managers, it can go and create purchase orders in the application.

A solution that requires data from multiple sources, such as sales, operations, and social media data. For example, an app for sales persons who go on the field to manage collections and need to pull data related to the customer from operations, sales, and social media to understand the full picture of the customer before meeting.

Sophisticated solutions utilizing the power of Azure cloud infrastructure, such as Azure machine learning and Azure IoT, along with data from Dynamics 365 for Finance and Operations, Enterprise edition. For example, a plant management system for the manufacturing industry that collects IoT data related to machines used at the production site. The app can provide sophisticated functionalities that are specifically related to the plant management system; however, it can also pull operations data, such as machine details, purchase order, supplier and warranty details, and so on.

The functional design document

In the previous section, you learned how to provide solutions for the identified feature gaps by using ISV solutions or utilizing some of the common features and tools available. The next step is to start the design process for the requirement gaps that still do not have a home in the overall solution. The **functional design documentation** (**FDD**) describes the features of the desired customizations. The document can include things such as flowcharts, screenshots, wire frames, and so on. At a minimum, an FDD will contain an organized list of requirements that can be used for development, testing, and client sign off. Before going further with the details of why functional design is important, what it should cover, and best practices, let's first learn about the process of the fit-gap review session, which is critical before moving forward with writing an FDD.

The fit-gap review session

The fit-gap document is the primary input document to write the FDD. It is very important to review the fit-gap document in detail before starting with the FDD. The following are a few pointers to take note of when conducting a successful fit-gap review session:

- The fit-gap review session should involve the functional and technical solution architects, project manager, and customer **subject matter experts** (**SMEs**).
- It is important to remember that this is a fit-gap session, so the fit should also be analyzed. Any degree of customization identified in the fit should be recorded.
- Often, you may find gaps listed that aren't really gaps, as the solution can handle the requirement. The review session should discuss each requirement in detail and discuss all possible alternate solutions.
- All gaps should be recorded and assigned a unique number. The Microsoft LCS business modeler tool enables you to document your business processes and record gaps.
- Take a detailed look at how the gaps are going to be addressed. Outline the testing/review process for customizations/extensions and how the testing will be administered.
- By focusing on these topics, you will soon learn where the team stands with regard to the appropriate documentation and its approach to the customization or extension process.

Why write FDD?

Now, let's gets back to the functional design document. Why is it necessary and what purpose does it serve? Functional design documents help developers, testers, and customers to understand the customizations in detail. Following are key benefits of functional design documents:

- FDDs help the development team to understand the feature and provide a clear scope and definition of what to develop. Function design documents streamline the development process. The development team working on the feature has a clear understanding and answers of all their functionality related questions to start development. Since this document is approved by the customer, the developers only develop customizations/extensions that are approved.
- FDDs help the testing team to understand the feature under development and to develop a test plan around it.
- FDDs provide the customer with a clear vision and definition of the feature being developed. Also, it helps the entire project team to be able to visualize and see the solution much before it is built.
- FDDs provide the baseline of the training documentation for the application support team and business users.

Project management aspects of design

The following are a few pointers for project managers to consider during the design phase of the project:

- The fit-gap analysis, requirements analysis, and the project plan need to be signed off to start the functional design phase. You can break them up into areas and start early if you have specific areas signed off.
- Make the team put together the overall functional architecture and the flow across applications, and review with the respective stakeholders.

- Start with the functional design for areas on which the rest of the solution has a dependency. For example, customer, product masters, and so on, are important for the downstream supply chain, invoicing processes, and others.
- Dedicate resources for large, complex functional areas early on. Also, make sure to have dedicated time from business users.
- Based on the fit-gap analysis, the implementation team, along with solution advisors, should prepare a plan of approach to address the key gaps.
- Divide responsibilities by area and try to have smaller FDDs created for each area. This will help manage them better.
- While the FDD work is in progress, assign the development and QA teams for each functional area. Engage them in reviewing the functional design, and support the respective business analysts early on.
- You need to plan for multiple iterations and reviews. Functional designs are very crucial. Upfront reviews can save a lot of development hours and rework, while also increasing the overall quality of the deliverables.
- Identify all the cross-functional requirements; the solution architect should lead them to suitable designs.

Cross-functional reviews are very important in larger projects. Have recurrent meetings every week or twice a week (as needed) to review the functional designs with all the functional team members together. Prioritize the reviews for foundation items, such as customer-master and product-master changes, which will impact other functional areas.

Cross-functional reviews will help improve the solutions (the rest of the team may have inputs on doing the same thing in a better way or with less customization). Also, more importantly, you will be forcing the team to review each other's designs by pulling them together into a room.

Engage business SMEs early on for reviews (set up a design walkthrough, provide deadlines for getting feedback, and seek a sign off for each of the functional designs).

Depending upon the complexity, involve SMEs external to the project for an independent review and recommendations. For example, when you start auditing the financial results of the company, your accounting practices will automatically improve as people know that they are going to be audited.

Things to know before writing an FDD

FDDs speak the application language and terminology, so business analysts writing the functional design documents must understand the Dynamics 365 for Finance and Operations, Enterprise edition application and functionality. A lack of product knowledge and understanding can keep the documents at a high level, pushing the design aspects to the developers, which deviates from the purpose of the documents.

Always ensure that all the key decisions made during the design time are recorded in the key decision log and signed off from the project team. Recommended areas where key decisions are mostly taken are as follows:

- Financials
- Inventory costing
- Adjustments
- Integrations
- Reporting

Also, all assumptions should be documented and validated with the concerned stakeholders to ensure a solution built to purpose.

Microsoft Dynamics Sure Step provided good templates to write FDDs. Create your own version with the sections relevant to your project and have the team follow the template.

Always have one or many requirements in the **Requirements Traceability Matrix (RTM)** corresponding to the functional design document. RTM is a foundational element in ERP implementations, as it ensures consistent delivery against contract and business requirements.

Feasibility analysis

In recent announcements, Microsoft has made it very clear that the Dynamics 365 for Finance and Operations, Enterprise edition application cannot be customized in the same way as it used to be done in the past. Currently, there are two approaches available for customizing Operations: overlayering and extensions. Overlayering allows the customers and partners to change the code that Microsoft has shipped as part of the core application. Extension is a new development model where the developer can utilize events and hooks within the application code to include additional functionalities without impacting the Microsoft code. As is obvious, overlayering is easy and provides great flexibility but comes at a huge cost at the time of upgrade and also prevents customers from utilizing the continuous updates and innovation that Microsoft is bringing to the product. With the third platform update, Microsoft has already hard-sealed the platform and foundation models, which means that you cannot overlay those models. The application model, which is the last model, is going to be hard-sealed after the Spring 2018 release. What this means from a solution design perspective is that unlike earlier versions, there will be a scenario when a requirement cannot be customized. To make sure that your custom solution is feasible, consider the following points:

- There could be a customization requirement, which may not be possible to be developed through extensions.
- If there are no options available in the product to extend the requested functionality, find a workaround or take Microsoft feedback. Ultimately, if it's not feasible, say no to the customer.
- If you think your requirement is common, suggest the same to Microsoft using the idea portal; it might become a part of the core product in future releases.
- Also check the Microsoft roadmap to see upcoming features and if those can fill the gap.

Extension capabilities in Dynamics 365 for Finance and Operations are being improved with every platform release. The latest one is method wrapping or chain of command; this allows extending the logic of public and protected methods without the need to use event handlers. Follow Microsoft's official documentation page to know more about exensibility:

https://docs.microsoft.com/en-us/dynamics365/unified-operations/
dev-itpro/extensibility/extensibility-home-page

Dos and don'ts

The following are some dos and don'ts while writing FDDs:

- Do not repurpose the fields to avoid customization. You will end up causing unforeseen issues down the road or blocking any future use of the functionality related to the field.
- Keep the architecture simple and easy to follow. The more complexity you add to the solution, the more difficult it will be to implement and support.
- Try to reduce the duplication of data in multiple places; avoid unnecessary/ complex integrations.
- Design the solutions around standard functionality, without touching the core system. For example, if the customer wants to automate the creation of allocation journals based on the allocation rules defined in the general ledger module, as a functional consultant, I will design a separate customization that will extend the functionality of the core Finance and Operations allocation process rather than changing standard forms and features.

The solution design document

A **solution design document** (**SDD**) includes information about the elements of the overall solution, including Dynamics 365 for Finance and Operations, Enterprise edition standard features (fits), gaps, and integrations. It is important to get the entire solution depicted in a pictorial representation. The business process modeler in LCS is a great tool with which to put together the solution design document.

Overview and objectives

Solution design documents are primarily referred to by the core team members of the implementation team. The following are the key objectives of solution design documentation:

- The details of the business flow in the future solution, based on Microsoft Dynamics 365 for Finance and Operations, Enterprise edition
- Solution validation
- A single point of reference for future value additions, issues, and troubleshooting
- Documenting in the high level
- Business and solution flow diagrams

Guidelines for solution design documents

Solution design is a solution binder and puts together all the aspects of the solution. The following are suggested coverage areas that a solution design should comprise:

1. There should be an end-to-end pictorial flow of the entire business process by function, for example, one end-to-end flow diagram for the supply chain, one end-to-end flow diagram for financials, and likewise for the other business functions.

2. The end-to-end flow must have starting/entry points, ending/closure points, and handover to other process diagrams.

3. All the decision points that can bring in additional business scenarios should be included.

4. There should be steps that are manual or automated.

5. The roles expected to perform the function in Microsoft Dynamics in a swimlane view should be present.

6. Key security and integration solution components should be included.

7. All the artifacts and configurations that will be needed to deploy the solution in production should be included.

8. The SDD must be able to convey the entire set of business processes in scope for the project. These may include, but are not limited to, the following:
   - Record to report
   - Order to cash
   - Procure to pay
   - Plan to inventory
   - Others

   Also, it must contain the core processes that enable the previously mentioned processes, as follows:

   - Legal entity
   - Number sequences
   - Languages
   - Users
   - Countries involved
   - Systems involved

9. The key takeaway from SDD is that the core implementation team (especially customer members) is on board with the overall solution flow and design.

10. The solution design document is a highly important artifact in implementing Dynamics 365; it is your single point of reference to know anything about the solution. In simple words, an SDD connects all the dots together. We consider an SDD as the key to your solution for all future enhancements and upgrades, and it should be baselined after each major decision/release.

The technical design document

After the functional design document is completed and signed off, the development team needs to start writing a technical design document. A **technical design document** (TDD) includes information about the programmatic approach of how a particular requirement will be implemented. This section covers the objectives, guidelines, preparation, execution, and expected outcome of TDDs.

Overview and objectives

TDDs are prepared primarily by the developer for the final development. They are also used by the testing team to write detailed test cases. The following are the key objectives of technical design documentation:

- The details of application architecture and design goals
- Data validation
- Documentation of the code (high-level)
- Data flow diagrams

Guidelines for the technical design document

Technical design is about planning the solution and putting together a skeleton of the technical solution. Putting together good design documentation will help you save development rework and improve the quality of code by allowing you to think through several facets of the solution before you start coding. TDD speaks the language of applications and, often, the code and technology, in order to achieve the solution. It is incumbent on the solution architect and technical leads writing the TDD to have expert knowledge about the system, design patterns, limitations, and the recommended customization approach. Consider the following guidelines when writing TDDs:

- Follow the Microsoft roadmap as to where the overall solution is headed--for example, the application suite will be discontinued after Spring 2018, which means that we should use extensions and not overlayering
- Utilize the standard solution frameworks as much as possible and extend if required
- Be cognizant of the cloud-first solution approach; consider the Edge and on-premise scenarios in your custom solution
- Consider recommendations and best practices when designing a solution

Preparation

Consider the following before you start writing TDDs:

- The technical design typically starts after the sign off of the functional design. It can also start early for a functional area where the requirements are clear.
- Engage the technical lead early on during functional designing to understand the functional requirements and flow.
- Plan brainstorming sessions among the team to discuss different solution ideas.
- Plan separate technical specs for integrations and data migration.
- Plan communications within the team to handle cross-functional designs.

Execution

Consider the following when writing TDDs:

- **Process flow**: Depict the overall process flow for the functional area so that it is clear to the developer what the final outcome is and how to reach it.
- **UI and usability**: Keep in mind the users and processes that will be using the new forms. Is it the workers on the floor or a person in the accounting department? Is it a repetitive function, such as shipping sales orders or invoicing POs, or is it a batch process, such as invoicing sales orders? Use familiar UI patterns, considering the users of the functionality.
- **Scalability of the solution**: Think about how the solution can be scalable, that is, more controlled by parameters and data instead of code. Having it controlled by parameters will help you in global environments. For example, you can turn off the functionality for companies that don't want to use it. Also, should you have an issue in production with a recently released functionality, you can have the option of turning it off by using parameters.
- **Apply generic design patterns**: Utilize solution ideas and frameworks offered within the product. The goal is not to rewrite the product; you are just extending its capability for business use. Follow the design patterns of the standard pages for custom pages.
- **Performance**: Identify the volume of transactions in the current production and the anticipated growth in the next few years. The solution should consider the performance requirement early on. Design a prototype and generate sample data to test the performance.
- **Exception handling**: Identify exceptional scenarios and document them. Build enough controls to avoid mistakes by users (you don't want to leave flaws that would let users hurt themselves). On the other hand, you don't want to spend too much time on building an extremely idiot-proof system.
- **Security**: Consider the security aspects as part of the technical design.
- **Review**: Review the technical design solution ideas with the solution architect and functional leads for their input on a periodic basis in order to incorporate feedback.
- **Brainstorm**: There are multiple ways to solve a problem--discussions and brainstorming lead to the identification of the best possible one.

Outcome

Expect the following as the outcomes of TDDs:

- Technical designs have been signed off by the technical solution architect
- The development team has a good understanding of what needs to be built and how to build it

 Large projects have multiple CRPs and they could run in parallel. We recommend that you leverage the Requirements Traceability Matrix (RTM) to keep a track of all the design artifacts, decisions, releases, and so on, for a systematic approach to implementation delivery and support.

Summary

In this chapter, we reviewed the design aspect of an implementation project. After the requirement document is signed off and the fit-gap process is completed, the consultant starts the design documentation process. We started the chapter with topic finding the right app for your business needs and discussed the of evaluation, selection criteria, and engagement of ISVs solutions on the project. There are many common features that can fill the gaps further or complement your custom solution design; we went through them briefly to understand how you can use them in your solution design. We concluded with the functional and technical aspects of the design, primarily around the generation of functional, solution, and technical design documents.

In the next chapter, you will learn another key aspect of the design process, that is, configuration management.

8

Integration Planning and Design

ERP is in the middle of the ecosystem of business facing applications, and Microsoft Dynamics 365 for Finance and Operations will need to directly or indirectly integrate with other applications. Accuracy and timely update of this information is very important for business success and growth. It is important to ensure that the technical analysts and developers in your project are familiar with integration technologies, so that they can support the design process and identify the best integration solution for your project. This chapter is about integration planning, understanding integration technologies, and integration design/development.

In this chapter, the following topics are covered:

- Integration architecture
- Basic integration concepts
- Integration tools, midleware, and scenarios
- Dynamics 365 data integrator
- Integration planning
- Integration design and development
- Best practices and recommendations

Integration architecture

As enterprises move toward using more and more specialized applications rather than having an ERP do everything for them, you need a robust framework and strategy to manage integrations within the ERP system. Dynamics 365 for Finance and Operations, Enterprise edition provides robust frameworks and functionalities to integrate with third-party applications using modern techniques. Integration framework is completely changed in Dynamics 365 for Operation from the earlier version. In the previous versions, **Application Integration Framework (AIF)** was the main integration platform of integration with third-party applications. AIF used SOAP-based XML technology and had the following drawbacks:

- SOAP message exchanges are bulky and not suitable for cloud-based integration
- The AIF framework has performance overhead
- The duplication of business logic due to different frameworks for integration (AIF) and data management (DIXF)

Dynamics 365 for Finance and Operations, Enterprise edition supports the modern HTTP-based RESTful model of integration, along with recurring integration for high-volume asynchronous integration models. The new integration framework is based on the OData 4.0 protocol and supports the JSON format for data exchange.

The following diagram shows the conceptual architecture of integration architecture in Dynamics 365 for Finance and Operations, Enterprise edition:

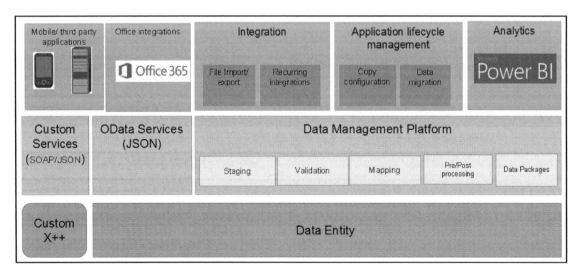

As shown, data entities are the key components of integration frameworks in Dynamics 365 for Finance and Operations, Enterprise edition, and serve multiple integration scenarios through data management platforms and OData endpoints. The other integration option is **Custom X++** classes, which lights up custom services with the SOAP and JSON endpoints.

To understand integration architecture in Dynamics 365 for Finance and Operations, Enterprise edition, let's take a deep dive to know some of the basic integration concepts and how they are related to Finance and Operations.

Basic integration concepts

To understand the integration concepts in Dynamics 365 for Finance and Operations, Enterprise edition better, it is important to know the basic web integration concepts first. In this section, we will learn the basic web concepts, such as RESTful APIs, SOAP, OData, JSON, and OAuth.

RESTful APIs

Representational State Transfer (REST) is an architecture style that relies on six guiding constraints: stateless, client-server, cacheable, layered system, code on demand (optional), and uniform interface. Web server APIs that adhere to the REST architecture are called RESTful APIs.

Many modern internet applications, such as Microsoft Azure, Twitter, LinkedIn, Google, Paypal, and Amazon, use RESTful architecture style in their APIs, which allows easy integration over HTTP communication protocol. The primary reason RESTful APIs are useful in cloud and web applications is because the calls are stateless. This means each requests or interactions are independent, there can be nothing saved that has to be remembered by the next request also any request can be directed to any instance of a component.

A RESTful API explicitly takes advantage of HTTP methodologies. They use GET to retrieve a resource, PUT to update a resource, POST to create that resource, and DELETE to remove it. A resource can be an object, file, or a table row in a database. HTTP-based RESTful APIs are defined by the following key aspects:

- **Base URL:** Such as `http://YourDynamics365ForOperationsURL/data/`
- **Media type:** Such as application/JSON and application/XML
- **Standard HTTP methods:** Such as GET, PUT, POST, and DELETE

SOAP

Simple Object Access Protocol (SOAP) is a specification for exchanging structured information for web service implementation. SOAP uses XML as a message format and relies on application layer protocol, such as HTTP, TCP, and SMTP, for message transmission and negotiation. SOAP defines a message format based on envelop, header, and body. All request and response messages must be serialized into this message format.

The following diagram shows the structure of the SOAP message:

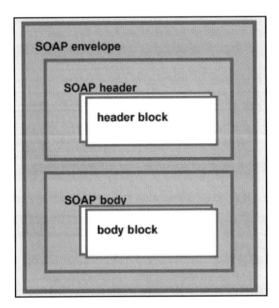

A SOAP message always starts with an envelop that contains the mandatory SOAP header block and SOAP body block. SOAP header contains the application-related information, such as message ID and soap action. The SOAP body block contains the actual message intended for the recipient.

Dynamics AX 2012 AIF uses SOAP over NETTCP and HTTP protocol. When an AIF integration port is deployed on the AOS, it uses the NETTCP protocol, and to use it over the HTTP port, it needs to be deployed on an **Internet Information Service (IIS)**.

SOAP versus REST

There is always discussion among integration experts with regards to which one is better: SOAP or REST. How do they compare? The following bullet points highlight some of the comparisons between SOAP and REST:

- SOAP is a protocol and REST is an architectural style
- SOAP defines standards to be strictly followed, REST does not define too many standards like SOAP
- SOAP requires more bandwidth and resources than REST
- SOAP defines its own security; RESTful web services inherit security measures from the underlying transport layer
- SOAP permits the XML data format only; REST permits different data formats, such as plain text, HTML, XML, and JSON

In summary, REST is lighter and simpler for integration, especially with cloud web applications, and hence, it makes sense for Dynamics 365 for Finance and Operations, Enterprise edition to adopt RESTful services.

JSON

JavaScript Object Notation (JSON) is a lightweight data-interchange format. JSON is self describing and easy for humans to read and write. It is the most commonly used data format in the web and RESTful web services.

The following is a simple example of the JSON format, describing customer group data containing two customer groups with customer group IDs of 10 and 20, with the additional Description and PaymentTermId fields:

```
{
  "CustomerGroupId":"10",
  "Description":"Wholesales customers",
  "PaymentTermId":"Net30"
},
{
  "CustomerGroupId":"20",
  "Description":"Retail customers",
  "PaymentTermId":"Receipt"
}
```

Another little complex example of the JSON data format describing personal details is shown here. The following example represents personal details, including address, phone number, and children and spouse details. As stated earlier, it's easily readable by humans, and at the same time, lighter and easy to parse by a computer program. These characteristics make JSON the preferred data type for web and cloud applications:

```
{
  "firstName": "John",
  "lastName": "Smith",
  "isAlive": true,
  "age": 25,
  "address": {
    "streetAddress": "21 2nd Street",
    "city": "New York",
    "state": "NY",
    "postalCode": "10021-3100"
  },
  "phoneNumbers": [
    {
      "type": "home",
      "number": "212 555-1234"
    },
    {
      "type": "office",
      "number": "646 555-4567"
    },
    {
      "type": "mobile",
      "number": "123 456-7890"
    }
  ],
  "children": [],
  "spouse": null
}
```

OData

OData stands for **Open Data Protocol**, which is an open protocol that enables the creation of REST-based data services, which allow resources to be published and edited by web clients using simple HTTP messages. The OData protocol was initially developed by Microsoft in 2007 and is now a standardized protocol of the OASIS OData technical committee. Dynamics 365 for Finance and Operations, Enterprise edition supports Odata v4 with the JSON data type, and supports complete **CRUD (create, read, update, and delete)** operations.

OData provides the following benefits:

- It lets developers interact with data using RESTful web services
- It provides a simple and uniform way to share data in a discoverable fashion
- It enables broad integration across products
- It enables integration using the HTTP protocol stack

For more information about OData, refer to the following web links:

Topic	Link
OData standards	`http://www.odata.org/documentation/`
OData introduction	`https://msdn.microsoft.com/en-us/library/dd541188.aspx`
OData by example	`http://www.odata.org/odata-services/`

OAuth

OAuth is a modern authentication standard used by many popular web applications such as Facebook, Twitter, LinkedIn, and Google. OAuth is an open standard for token-based authorization and authentication on the internet. It provides client applications a secure, delegated access to server resources on behalf of a resource owner. It specifies a process for resource owners to authorize third-party access to their server resources without sharing their credentials. OAuth was first released and used by Twitter in 2007, and the latest version of OAuth is OAuth 2.0.

In Dynamics 365 for Finance and Operations, Enterprise edition OData services, JSON-based custom service, and REST metadata service use OAuth 2.0 for authentication. This diagram shows authentication using OAuth 2.0 flow:

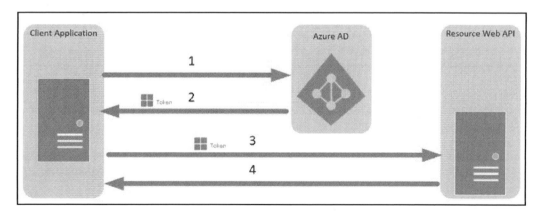

As illustrated, the OAuth authentication flow starts with the **Client Application** requesting a token from the identity provider, such as **Azure AD**. The identity provider authenticates the client application and returns the token to the calling application. The **Client Application** then presents the access token to the Dynamics 365 for Finance and Operations, Enterprise edition resources.

Integration concepts in Dynamics 365 for Finance and Operations, Enterprise edition

In the preceding section, we understood the basic integration concepts used in modern cloud- and web-based applications. Microsoft Dynamics 365 for Finance and Operations, Enterprise edition uses these concepts as part of the core integration architecture. On a high level, there are primarily four key integration components, namely data entities, OData services, custom services, and recurring integrations. In this section, we will explore these components, concepts, and terminologies in detail, and we will also explore how to use these technologies while building integration solutions in your implementation projects.

Data entities

Data entities are the most important concept for integration in Dynamics 365 for Finance and Operations, Enterprise edition. In Dynamics 365 for Finance and Operations, Enterprise edition, data entities are first class citizens, and it enables data management, data migration, OData integration, Office integration, and Power BI integration.

What is a data entity?

A data entity is an abstraction over underlying tables, and a simplified projection of the schema, which is more conceptual in nature than the physical tables underneath. All business logic resides in the entity or in the underlying tables. Entities can expose both relational as well as aggregate data.

To summarize, data entities provide
conceptual abstraction and encapsulation (denormalized view) of the underlying table schema to represent key data concepts and functionalities.

The following diagram shows the current normalized model for customer data in Dynamics 365 for Finance and Operations and the corresponding denormalized customer entity:

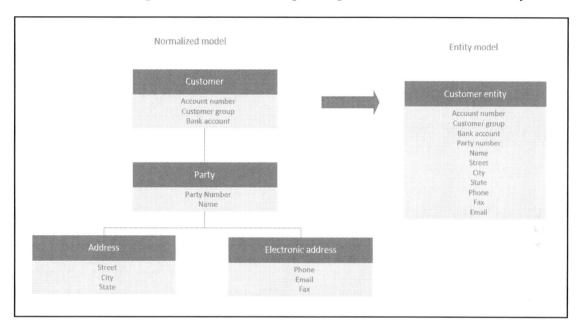

Listed here are the key highlights of data entities in Dynamics 365 for Finance and Operations, Enterprise edition:

- First-class citizen and defined as metadata objects
- In the database layer, data entities are represented as updatable views
- Serves multiple purposes such as OData services, recurring integrations, Office integration, data management, and Power BI

OData services

In Dynamics 365 for Finance and Operations, Enterprise edition, OData services are the primary integration method. The OData REST endpoint exposes all the data entities that are marked as public. The **IsPublic** design-level property is all that it needs to determine whether the data entity needs to be exposed as the OData endpoint.

The following screenshot shows `CustCustomerEntity` in Visual Studio, marked with the **IsPublic** property to **Yes** to expose the entity as the OData endpoint:

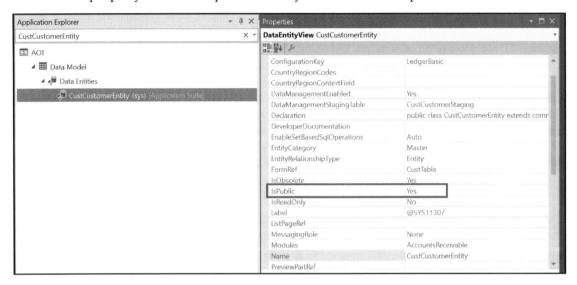

Dynamics 365 for Finance and Operations, Enterprise edition ships more than two thousand data entities out of the box, which includes more than 1,500 public data entities.

The list of data entities is growing with every major release of Dynamics 365 for Finance and Operations, Enterprise edition to cover missing areas and new functionalities and integration points.

In addition to the out-of-the-box data entities, customers and partners can easily extend the existing data entities or create new data entities as per their data management and integration requirements.

An entity marked with the **IsPublic** property to **Yes** is automatically available as an OData endpoint and can be consumed for various tools and purposes, such as third-party client applications for integration, Microsoft Office for data export/import, Power BI for analytics, or any other client applications that can consume OData feeds.

In the next section, let's explore how to query, browse, and consume Dynamics 365 for Finance and Operations, Enterprise edition's OData services.

Querying or browsing an OData endpoint

If you want to know what OData endpoints are available in your Finance and Operations environment, or want to query a specific entity to get the data, you can simply browse using a web browser. OData provides a simple query format to browse the resources using a web browser. The following table describes a few basic query formats to access OData resources and entity data:

URL	Description
`[Your Organization Root URL]/data/`	Get a list of data entities
`[Your Organization Root URL]/data/Customers`	Get a list of all the customers
`[Your Organization Root URL]/data/Customers?$top=3`	Get a list of the first three customer records
`[Your Organization Root URL]/data/Customers?$select=FirstName,LastName`	Get a list of all the customers, but show only the first name and last name properties
`[Your Organization Root URL]/data/Customers?$format=json`	Get a list of all the customers in a JSON format that can be used to interact with JavaScript clients

The OData protocol supports many advanced filtering and querying options on entities such as `$filter`, `$count`, `$orderby`, `$skip`, `$top`, `$expand`, and `$select`. Many built-in operators are available to `$filter` data, such as equals, not equals, greater than or equal, less than, less than or equal, and, or, not, addition, subtraction, multiplication, and division.

For complete details about filter and query syntax and its capabilities, follow the official OData URL--http://docs.oasis-open.org/odata/odata/v4.0/errata02/os/complete/part2-url-conventions/odata-v4.0-errata02-os-part2-url-conventions-complete.html#_Toc406398092.

Consuming OData services

It's good that you can browse the OData services using a browser and evaluate the response; however, real-life integration is always system to system, running in the background. Let's try to understand how these real-life integrations can be built using Dynamics 365 for Finance and Operations, Enterprise edition's OData services.

OData services can be consumed by client application in two ways:

- Using the pure HTTP communication model, where you build URLs, build request messages, parse and handle responses, and do error handling. Doing all this from scratch can be complicated and unnecessary.
- Using the already available libraries; there are various libraries and tools available to encapsulate OData HTTP communication in different programming languages.

The following table features many such OData libraries for various development platforms, such as .NET, Java, and JavaScript:

Library	Platform	Description
OData client for .NET	.NET	LINQ-enabled client API for issuing OData queries and consuming OData JSON payloads
Simple.OData.Client	.NET	A multiplatform OData client library supporting .NET 4.x, Windows Store, Windows Phone 8, Silverlight 5, iOS, and Android
SDL OData frameworks	JAVA	Open source Scala/Java-based SDL OData framework that aligns with the v4 specifications
Apache Olingo	JAVA	Apache Olingo is a Java library that implements the OData
ODataJS beta	JavaScript	The Apache Olingo **OData Client for JavaScript (ODataJS)** is a library written in JavaScript that enables browser-based frontend applications to easily use the OData protocol for communication with application servers

The OData official website page--http://www.odata.org/libraries/--features many more libraries, including documentation and download links.

Now, let's explore how we can use the OData client for the .NET library to build a client application using the C# programming language, and consume Finance and Operations OData services. The following figure describes high-level steps that a developer needs to go through to consume OData service endpoints:

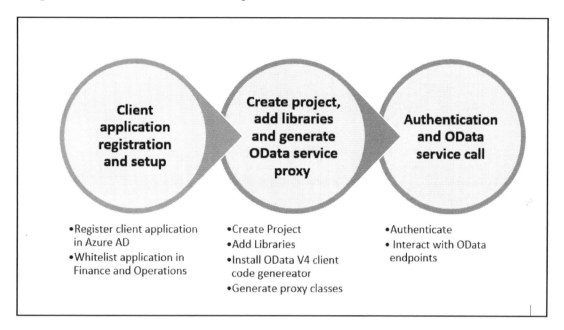

As shown, consuming OData endpoints can be explained by three activities. Let's try to explore this as we go further.

Client application registration and setup

To consume Dynamics 365 for Finance and Operations, Enterprise edition's OData services, the client application needs to know the following:

- **OData service endpoint URI**: Your Dynamics 365 for Finance and Operations, Enterprise edition base URL; for example, if your development environment is XYZIncDEV, your base URL will be `https://XYZINCDEV.cloudax.dynamics.com`

- **Authentication details**: Your Azure AAD organization tenant ID, such as `XYZInc.com`, and credentials for connection

OData Services in Dynamics 365 for Finance and Operations uses the OAuth 2.0 authentication model, as described earlier in the chapter. Client application can either use a valid Finance and Operations user ID and password, or use the service-to-service authentication model. In cloud deployment, the service-to-service authentication model is the recommended option as you do not have to store the real username and password in the client application.

To use service-to-service authentication, a client application must first be registered under your organization Azure active directory and given the appropriate permissions. When an application is registered in Azure AAD, you will get the application ID and also, security keys. The application ID and keys can be used by the client application to obtain an authentication token.

The following diagram shows various screen captures from Microsoft Azure to depict the steps to create and set up the Azure client application:

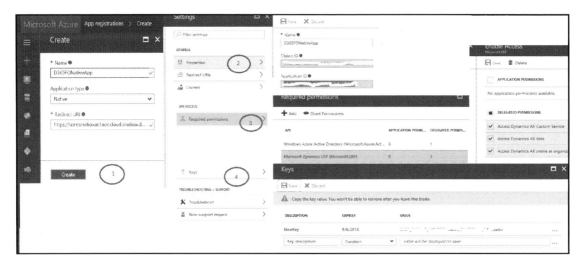

Here are the steps to create and set up the Azure client application:

1. Register a new native application under your organization's Azure AD. Once you create the application, you can get the **Application ID** under the application's **General properties**.

2. Next, you need to set the required permissions for the new application; for that, you need to **Add** permission, select **Microsoft Dynamics ERP (MicrosoftERP)**, and enable all permissions. Lastly, click on the **Keys** and select **DESCRIPTION** of your keys and the duration to get the key **VALUE**. Note down **Application ID** and key value, which will be needed to be configured in your client application for authentication.

3. Then, white-list **Application ID** in Finance and Operations, and map it to a valid application user for authorization. The following screen shows a visual of the mapping application ID with Finance and Operations user:

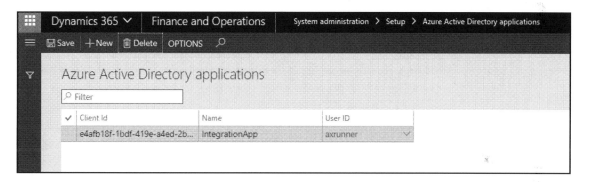

Setup is available under **System administration** | **Setup** | **Azure Active Directory applications**.

Creating a project, adding libraries, and generating an OData service proxy

Once you are done with the application registration process and have collected all the details, you are ready to create your client application. In this example, we will create a console C# application to interact with Dynamics 365 for Finance and Operations OData services. The given steps describe how to create the client application:

1. **Create the C# console application**: To start, use Visual Studio to create a C# console project. In Visual Studio, click on **File | New | Project....** In the new project dialog, use the Visual C# template, select Console Application, and enter the name as `D365FO_ODataServiceClient`.

2. **Add reference libraries**: To authenticate and consume Finance and Operations OData services, you need at least the following two library packages. You can use the NuGet package manager in Visual Studio to install these libraries in your project and add references:

   - **Microsoft.IdentityModel.Clients.ActiveDirectory**: This package contains the binaries of the **Active Directory Authentication Library** (**ADAL**). ADAL provides a .NET standard class library with easy-to-use authentication functionality for your .NET client.
   - **Microsoft.OData.Client**: This library provides a LINQ-enabled client API for issuing OData queries and consuming OData JSON payloads.

3. **Add OData v4 client code generator**: This is the Visual Studio extension from Microsoft to generate OData entity proxy classes for your OData entities. If you do not have this extension already installed, you can download and install this template from Visual Studio **Marketplace**. After you download and install the tool, you can add the OData client to the project. This will create a file with an extension of `tt` (text template). Then, you need to update the `MetadataDocumentUri` string value in the `tt` file to your OData metadata endpoint. The next diagram illustrates the steps to add the OData Client `tt` file and update the `MetadataDocumentURI` in Visual Studio:

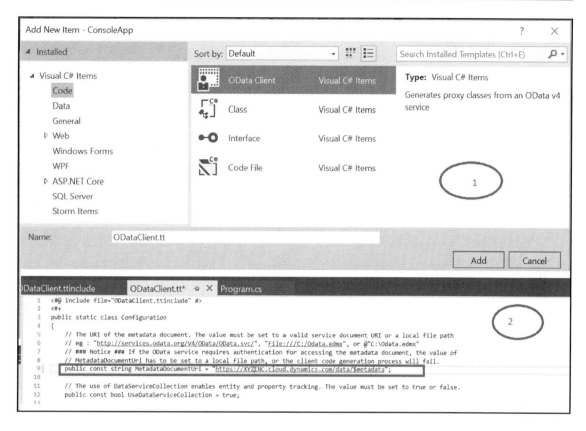

Once the metadata endpoint URL is updated, right-click on the `tt` file and choose to **Run custom tool**. This will read the metadata and build proxy classes for all OData services. This step generates a library containing all your OData services and their operations with the name like `<YourProjectNameSpace>.Microsoft.Dynamics.DataEntities`.

Once the required packages are added to your project and the entity proxy is generated, next step is to implement the code to authenticate and consume OData entities. Let's explore the code sample next.

Authentication and OData service call

OData Service call will need an authorization token passed as a header on the service request. Using ADAL library, retrieve the authentication token from the Azure Active directory. Using generated proxy classes, you can instantiate the data entity objects, set properties, and call methods to interact with the OData endpoint. The following sample code shows how to build the OData endpoint context, attach the authentication header, create a new customer group, and then read and print customer groups on console:

```
using D365FO_ODataServiceClient.Microsoft.Dynamics.DataEntities;
using Microsoft.IdentityModel.Clients.ActiveDirectory;
using Microsoft.OData.Client;
using System;
using System.Linq;
namespace D365FO_ODataServiceClient
{
    class Program
    {
        static void Main(string[] args)
        {
            //Part 1 - Set Variables (Replace the variables values with
              your
            //environment URI)
            const string UriString =
                "https://XYZINCDEVENV.cloudax.dynamics.com";
            const string ADTenant = "https://login.windows.net/XYZINC.com";
            const string ADClntAppId = "YourAPPID";
            const string ADClntSecret = "AppSecret";
            // Part 2. Create context
            Uri oDataUri = new Uri(UriString + "/data", UriKind.Absolute);
            Resources context = new Resources(oDataUri);
            //Part 3. Set Authorization Header
            context.SendingRequest2 += new
                    EventHandler<SendingRequest2EventArgs>
            (delegate (object sender, SendingRequest2EventArgs e)
            {
                var authContext = new AuthenticationContext(ADTenant);
                var cred = new ClientCredential(ADClntAppId, ADClntSecret);
                var result = authContext.AcquireTokenAsync(UriString,
                                            cred).Result;
                e.RequestMessage.SetHeader("Authorization",
                            result.CreateAuthorizationHeader());
            });
            // Part 4: Create data in Operations - create Customer
              group -create
            //entity object
            CustomerGroup customerGroup = new CustomerGroup();
```

```
//create collection and set context
DataServiceCollection<CustomerGroup> custGroupCollection
    = new DataServiceCollection<CustomerGroup>(context);
// add to collection
custGroupCollection.Add(customerGroup);
// Set properties
customerGroup.CustomerGroupId = new
            Random().Next(1000).ToString("000");
customerGroup.Description = "Brand new group";
customerGroup.DataAreaId = "USMF";
// save changes
context.SaveChanges(SaveChangesOptions.PostOnlySetProperties |
        SaveChangesOptions.BatchWithSingleChangeset);
//Part 5. Reading data from Operations
DataServiceQuery<CustomerGroup> usmfCustomerGroup;
usmfCustomerGroup = context.CustomerGroups
        .AddQueryOption("$filter", "dataAreaId eq 'USMF'")
        .AddQueryOption("cross-company", "true");
foreach (var custGroup in usmfCustomerGroup)
{
    Console.WriteLine("Name:{0} {1}",
            custGroup.CustomerGroupId,
            custGroup.DataAreaId);
}
Console.ReadLine();
            }
        }
    }
```

The preceding code can be understood in five parts:

- **Part 1**: Configure your Dynamics 365 for Finance and Operations base URI, active directory tenant, and authentication details
- **Part 2**: OData Service context is created using OData endpoint URI
- **Part 3**: Trigger an OData service request, acquire an authentication token using AAD tenant and credentials, and set the authorization header to the request
- **Part 4:** Create a new customer group record, instantiate the `CustomerGroup` entity, create data collection and set context, add the entity to the collection, set the properties, and call the `context.SaveChanges()` method to save the new customer group changes to the Finance and Operations database
- **Part 5**: Use LINQ expression to instantiate and query the `CustomerGroup` OData service, and print the ID and company as output

The mentioned steps and sample code are high-level steps to understand the integration concept and does not cover exception handling. To compile and execute this code, you must use your development environment and follow the steps as described in this section (registering application, creating console application, registering the assemblies, adding and generating template code, and finally, replacing the variables in the code). The Microsoft product team has developed more sophisticated examples, which are available on GitHub. The sample code can be downloaded from `https://github.com/Microsoft/Dynamics-AX-Integration`.

Custom services

Custom services are programming models through which a developer can convert the X++ business logic to a service. Using this model, any existing X++ code can be exposed as a custom service simply by adding an attribute. There are standard attributes that can be set on the data contract class and methods to automatically serialize and deserialize data that is sent and received.

In Dynamics 365 for Finance and Operations, Enterprise edition, custom service programming model supports SOAP and JSON endpoints. Custom service model was available in the previous version--Dynamics AX 2012. The following are the key changes to custom services in Dynamics 365 for Finance and Operations, Enterprise edition from the previous version:

1. Inbound port and outbound port no longer exist to manually deploy custom services, but you must add custom services to service groups that are automatically deployed.
2. Custom services are always deployed on two endpoints; the following table shows endpoint URIs:

Type	Endpoint URI
SOAP endpoint	`https://<host_uri>/soap/Services/<service_group_name>`
JSON endpoint	`https://<host_uri>/api/Services/<service_group_name>/<service_group_service_name>/<operation_name>`

Most of the custom services available out of the box in Dynamics 365 for Finance and Operations, Enterprise edition are system services utilized for internal application processes or integration with various components, such as DIXF, retail, warehouse web application. There are various functional services available, for example, `FormLetter` services and `financialDimensions` services, which can be used for third-party integration scenarios.

The given bullet points summarize the custom services programming concepts in the Dynamics 365 for Finance and Operations, Enterprise edition application:

- Custom services are based on the data contract defined by developers, and the service contract can be controlled
- The existing business logic can be utilized and exposed as a service
- Custom services are good for simple requirements, which are not otherwise easy to achieve using data entities
- Custom services are best suited for an action triggered by third-party applications, such as PO receiving/posting and packing slips

Recurring integrations

It is a very common and important integration practice in ERP systems to handle high-volume integration in asynchronous patterns. Dynamics 365 for Finance and Operation, Enterprise edition provides the ability to configure export or import of data in files using the recurring integration pattern. The recurring integration pattern is based on the data entities concept, with additional capabilities such as different file format, transformation, and RESTful API to export and import data.

The following figure shows the recurring integration conceptual architecture in Dynamics 365 for Finance and Operations, Enterprise edition:

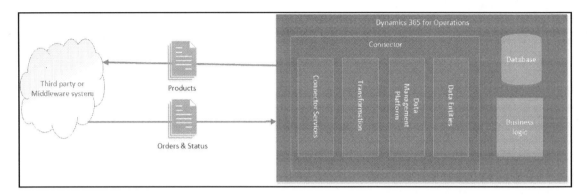

As depicted, recurring integration is based on the data entity and data management framework. Recurring integration also provides support for XSL transform for XML files. Connection Services provide RESTful OData services for third-party applications to submit an inbound message, get the status of the import job, retrieve outbound data, and acknowledge the retrieval of the messages.

The following diagram describes the process of setting up and consuming the recurring integration using RESTful services:

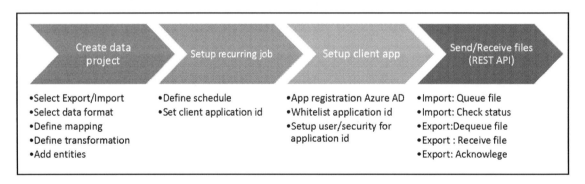

As highlighted in the preceding diagram, the next heading describes steps to set up recurring integration using Dynamics 365 for Finance and Operations, Enterprise edition:

1. **Set up data projects**: In order to set up recurring integration, we need to first set up data projects. This step involves creating the data project by adding the required data entities for the integration for import or export, selecting the source file format, and defining mapping and transformation. The following screenshot shows an example of creating data projects to export sales order details in the XML format:

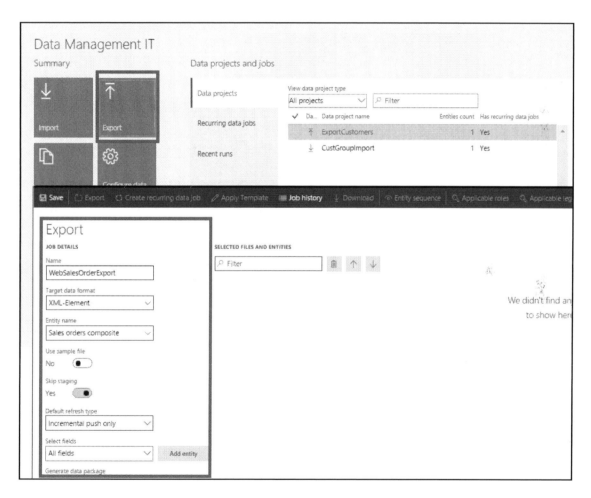

2. **Set up recurring job**: A data project can be converted into a recurring job by defining the recurrence and consumer application ID for the data project. Recurrence setup basically schedules a batch job to run the export/import process as per a defined schedule. The following screenshot highlights the steps to create a recurring job from data projects. As shown here, to create a recurring data job, users simply create the data project and then click on the **Create recurring data jobs** button to give a name to recurring job. Then, click on the **Set processing recurrence** button to set up the schedule, add client **application ID** and click on the **OK** button:

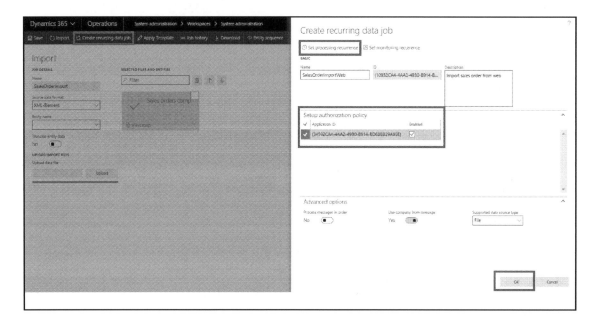

3. **Set up client application**: The next step is to set up client application. The integration REST API uses the OAuth 2.0 authentication model, as described earlier in the chapter. Before the integrating client application can consume this endpoint, an client application must be registered in Microsoft Azure AD and given appropriate permission to Dynamics 365 for Finance and Operations, Enterprise edition. When an application is registered in Azure AD, you will get an application ID and can also generate keys. The application key generated needs to be white-listed in Dynamics 365 for Finance and Operations, Enterprise edition and mapped to a valid application user. Azure application ID also needs to be configured on the recurring data job. The next screenshot shows the setup form in Dynamics 365 for Finance and Operations, Enterprise edition to add Azure AD application and define user mapping:

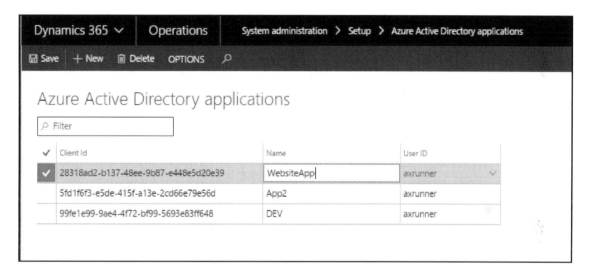

4. **Send/receive file (REST API)**: Once the preceding setup is completed, the client application can use the integration RESTful APIs to send and receive messages. The given table describes the integration APIs that are available for recurring integration:

Type	Operation	Description	Actions
Import	Enqueue	Submit the files for import	**Method**: HTTP POST **Relative URI**: `api/connector/enqueue/<activity id>?entity=<entity name>` **Body**: Pass data as memory stream **Response**: Task ID
Import	Status	Get the status of import operations	**Method**: GET **Relative URI**: `api/connector/jobstatus/<task id>` **Response**: Status code
Export	Dequeue	Get the files content for export activity	**Method**: GET **Relating URI**: `api/connector/dequeue/<activity id>` **Response**: Data package download URL
Export	Ack	Acknowledge the dequeue operation	**Method**: GET **Relative URI**: `api/connector/ack/<activity id>` **Response**: HTTP status

Either you decide to use synchronous OData services or asynchronous integration pattern using recurring integration; there are various ways you can consume these RESTful services in your integration. In many cases, you may need middleware tools to provide end-to-end integration between Dynamics 365 for Finance and Operations, Enterprise edition and your integrating application. In the next section, we will learn some of middleware tools and scenarios where you can use them.

Integration tools, midleware, and scenarios

In the earlier topics, we learned various integration concepts and technologies applicable to Dynamics 365 for Finance and Operations, Enterprise edition. Using RESTful APIs and OData service, any third-party application can directly integrate with Finance and Operations. However, system-to-system integration is not a preferred option as it leads to direct dependency between systems. Also, if your operation is deployed on the cloud and integrating application is on-premise, you have to use some middleware or integration broker applications. Many organizations have already invested in many such middleware applications, such as BizTalk server or Enterprise service bus. There are several other middleware integration tools that can be used to integrate Dynamics 365 for Finance and Operations, Enterprise edition with third-party applications. In this section, we will discuss some of these tools, along with different integration scenarios where these tools can be useful.

The following are some of the common tools and technologies that can be used with Dynamics 365 for Finance and Operations, Enterprise edition to provide end-to-end integration:

- **Third-party applications**: Using OData services as RESTful APIs HTTP protocol, any third-party application with appropriate access to Finance and Operations application can directly perform CRUD operations. Integrating application, in this scenario, can either use pure HTTP request response model or client libraries to consume OData services as per their preference. An example of such integration is frontend web application, when order is submitted on the website and sales orders are created in Dynamics 365 for Finance and Operations, Enterprise edition.

  The following table provides suitable recommendation when direct OData services are best suited:

Scenarios	Real time/recurring	Volume	Frequency
Integration with external web application	Real time	Low	Ad hoc

- **Custom daemon tools**: According to Wikipedia, daemon is a computer program that runs as a background process, rather than being under the direct control of an interactive user. Many organizations that do not want to spend money on third-party middleware applications to establish the integration between your third-party application and Dynamics 365 for Finance and Operations create a custom tool using .NET or any language of their choice and set it as the background deamon process. The tool can provide a bridge between your third-party application and Dynamics 365 for Finance and Operations. An example of such a tool is already developed by Microsoft for recurring integration pattern and is available on GitHub at `https://github.com/Microsoft/Dynamics-AX-Integration`.

The following table provides suitable recommendation as to when direct OData services are best suited:

Scenarios	Real time/recurring	Volume	Frequency
On-premise middleware	Recurring	Low to medium	Ad hoc

 It is important to note that error handling, logging, and scalability are important features of any such applications, and the responsibility lies on you.

- **BizTalk server:** Microsoft BizTalk Server (or simply BizTalk) is a middleware system that connects applications across your enterprise. BizTalk Server is one of the top integration broker or middleware system to integrate enterprise applications. It provides advance integration scenarios with in-built adapters, message orchestration, mapping and monitoring, and administration capabilities. The latest version of BizTalk server 2016 has added bidirection integration with cloud application via Logic app:

Scenarios	Real time/recurring	Volume	Frequency
On-premise middleware	Both	Medium to high	Regular

If your organization already uses BizTalk server, this might be a good option to consider as middleware. The BizTalk server is a massive application and requires significant investment if you do not already have it in your organization; for low to medium volume ad hoc integrations, you might be better off using custom daemon tools or Logic apps.

- **Logic apps**: Logic apps is cloud-based, fully managed **iPaaS (integration Platform as a Service)**, which provides a way to simplify and implement scalable integrations solution in the cloud. Logic apps provides a visual designer to model and automate your process as a series of steps known as a workflow. There are many connectors across the cloud and on-premises to quickly integrate across services and protocols.

For more advanced integration scenarios, Logic apps comes with Enterprise Integration Pack connectors. This allows you to easily include validation, transformation, and message exchange through industry-standard protocols, including AS2, X12, and EDIFACT. You can also secure messages with both encryption and digital signatures.

Using on-premises data gateway with Logic apps, you can connect to your on-premise resources that includes SQL server, BizTalk server, filesystem, DB2, Oracle database SAP application server, SAP message server, and many more.

Logic apps is the recommended option for integrating Dynamics 365 for Finance and Operations, Enterprise edition cloud version with third-party systems. Dynamics 365 for Finance and Operations, Enterprise edition OData services connector is available on Logic Apps, which can be used for CRUD on data entities exposed as OData Services. Dynamics 365 for Finance and Operations, Enterprise edition trigger and recurring integration connectors are under development and should be available soon. However, you can still use Logic apps for recurring integration scenario by simply using generic HTTP connector and RESTful recurring integration APIs.

The following screenshot shows Logic app designer, using a simple example to read the filesystem using on-premise data gateway, and using HTTP connector to post the file content to Finance and Operations RESTful services and finally, moving the file into the processed folder:

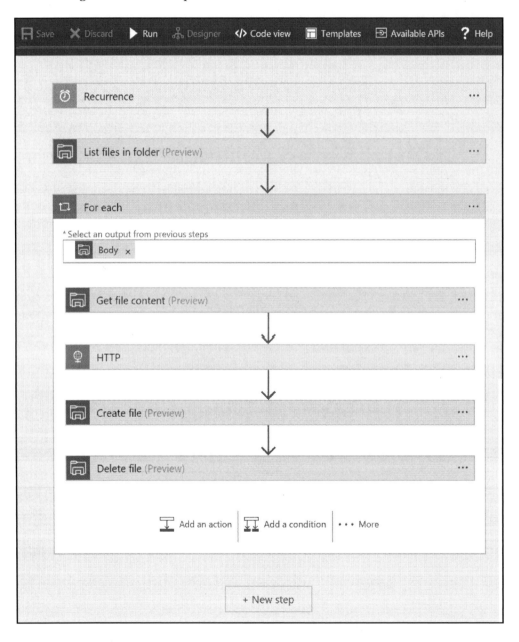

Logic apps has these advantages:

- Scalability
- Manageability
- Guaranteed delivery
- Error handling
- Real time alerts

The following table highlights the recommended scenarios to use Logic app:

Scenarios	Real time/recurring	Volume	Frequency
• EDI integration • Integration with SaaS applications • Integration with on-premise application	Both	Medium to high	Regular

- **Microsoft flow:** Microsoft Flow is built on top of Logic apps and has the same workflow designer and connector experience. Flows is designed for any office worker to perform simple integrations or designing a simple document workflow without going through developers or IT. Subscription of flow uses is included as part of enterprise licensing plan at no additional cost.

The next figure shows a Microsoft Flow template to move rows from Microsoft Excel to Dynamics 365 for Finance and Operations, Enterprise edition vendors entity. Users can simply set recurrence and credential details and get the integration established:

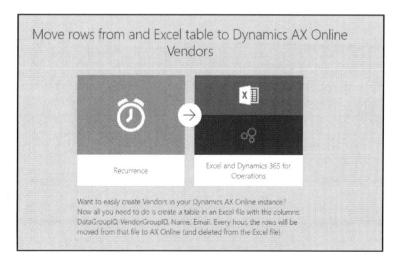

This tables highlights the recommended scenarios to use flow:

Scenarios	Real time/recurring	Volume	Frequency
• Simple integration with SaaS applications • Document workflow and notifications	Both	Low	Ad hoc

- **Common data services**: Common data services is the core component of integration model between Dynamics 365 application such as Sales, and Finance and Operations. The new integration model is based on integration templates and connections. Microsoft out of the box ships integration templates to integrate Dynamics 365 family applications. In addition to out-of-the-box templates, customer or partners can customize the existing templates or build new ones to enable new integration capabilities and integrate other enterprise applications. More details about CDS integrator can be found in the next section of this chapter:

Scenarios	Real time/recurring	Volume	Frequency
• Integration between enterprise applications example, CRM, and Finance and Operations	Recurring	High	Regular

- **QuartzAX: QuartzAX** is a tool developed by the Microsoft product team to assist customers and partners in utilizing recurring integration pattern with on-premise filesystem. QuartzAX is easy to configure and use, but lacks advance integration capabilities such as scalability, monitoring, and alerts. This tool can be useful for small-to-medium size implementation projects to quickly build recurring integration using on-premise filesystem.

This table highlights the scenarios and use case for QuartzAX tool:

Scenarios	Real time/recurring	Volume	Frequency
• Recurring integration using on-premise filesystem	Recurring	Medium	Regular

Dynamics 365 data integrator

Microsoft Dynamics 365 offering combines CRM and ERP services into a single offering, with a promise that these individual applications are *Intelligent applications that work smarter together*. The following diagram shows Microsoft vision of how different applications under Dynamics 365 will be integrated:

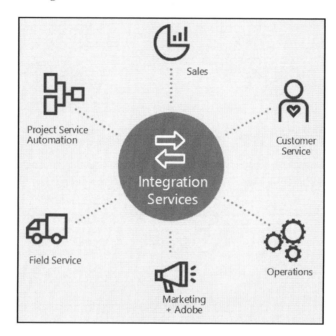

As shown, a common platform serves as an integration service between various applications. These integrations will enable breaking down silos of data, enable collaboration, automate workflows, and unify the business front office and back office applications. With the help of these integrations, a business user in Dynamics 365 for Sales who initiated the quote will be able to see the order status and fulfillment details without leaving the sales system he always uses.

The Dynamics 365 Data Integration feature enables the flow of data between Dynamics 365 for Sales, Dynamics 365 for Finance and Operations, and other products through **Common Data Service**. In this section, we will explore this very integration architecture and various planned applications and scenarios, which will have out-of-the-box integration with Finance and Operations.

Integration architecture

Dynamics 365 data integrator architecture leverages the strengths of the individual Dynamics 365 components and connects them via Common Data Service. The solution provides powerful integration with a flexible solution and simplification of the integration process, without dependency on third-party solutions.

The following diagram represents the high-level architecture of Dynamics 365 data integrator using common data services:

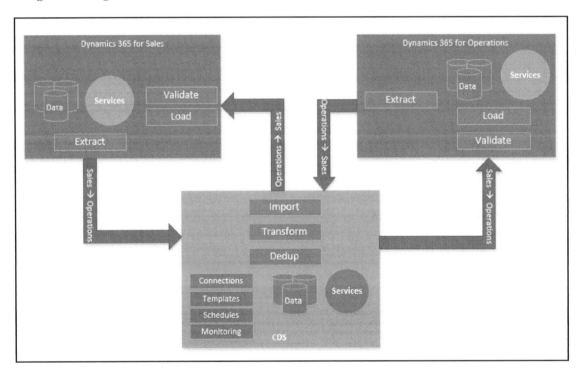

As illustrated, common data services serve as the core of this integration architecture and provide capability to define the connection between application, integration templates, and schedule and monitoring capabilities. Individual Dynamics 365 applications (Sales and Finance and Operations, Enterprise edition in this example) provide application capability to export, validate, and import the business data.

Setting up data integration

Setting up data integration between Dynamics 365 products is done through PowerApp. Data Integrator is available as a tab under PowerApp admin and can be accessed through `https://admin.powerapps.com/dataintegration`. The following screenshot shows the data integrator home page under PowerApp **Admin center**:

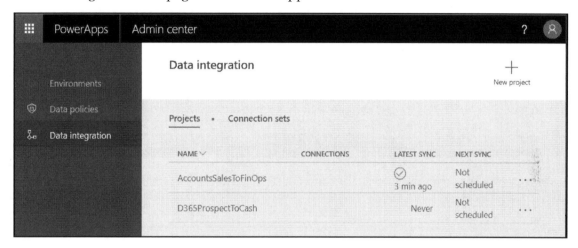

As shown, the **Data integration** home page provides a simple view of all the projects, connection sets, and **LATEST SYNC** history.

Now, let's explore various concepts, along with the process to set up integration projects using data integrator. Let's see the high-level steps to set up your integration project:

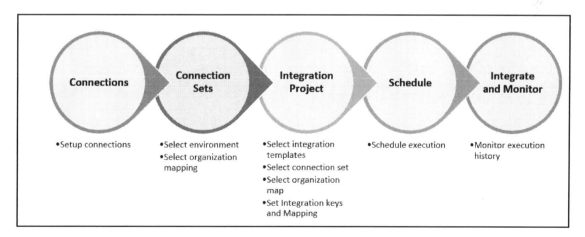

As illustrated, as an example, you can set up integration between Dynamics 365 for Sales, and Finance and Operations simply, by performing the following steps.

Connections

The very first step to set up data integration is to create connection. Connections provide the ability to define and manage connections to Dynamics 365 individual applications. These connections, once defined, are later used during data extraction and import. Connections are stored in a Common Data Service environment. When you create a connection on the PowerApps site, you are not connecting to a specific instance of your target system. This just stores your credentials with a target system. The following screenshot shows the connection details in the PowerApp environment:

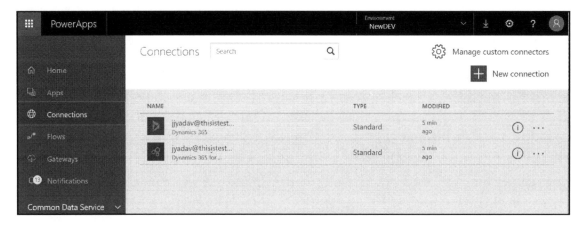

To create a new connection, log in to `https://web.powerapps.com`, select a CDS environment where you have administrative privilege, and simply click on new connection and search for the product you want to connect and authenticate using your credentials. Any connection you create in the CDS environment where you have administrative privilege will be available when setting up integration project.

Connection sets

Once you create the connection sets in the CDS, the next step is to create a connection set. Connection sets are a collection of two more connections and organization mapping information that can be reused among projects. Connection sets are also artifacts where you select environment. You may create separate connection sets for development environment and production environment and use them accordingly on your project.

Other key information connection sets store is organization unit mapping. These are mappings between the Finance and Operations legal entity (or company) and the Common Data Service organizations and sales organization or business units. You can store multiple organization mappings in a connection set. Later on, when you use a connection set, you will choose which specific organization mapping you want for a given project.

The following screenshot shows how to create a new connection set:

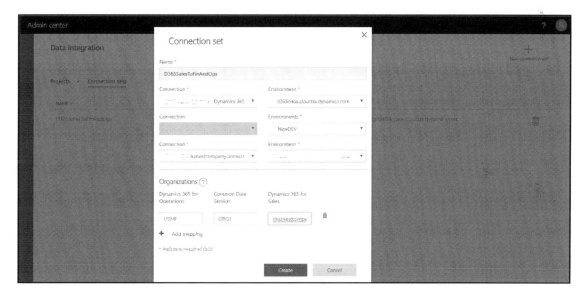

As depicted, to create connection set, go to PowerApps **Admin center**, click on the **Connection sets** tab, and then click on the **New Connection set** button. This will open a new dialog form where you can give your connection set a name, select environment, provide organization mapping, and click on the **Create** button.

Integration keys

Sometimes, unique keys in the Entities are represented by system IDs, such as System GUID or RecIds; while integrating such entities, these values need to be replaced with business key values. **Integration keys** are the keys the data integrator uses to join entities to replace system IDs with business key values. Data Integrator has the ability to automatically discover the business key for a related table. If not, you will need to identify the business key in the related table as part of the connection set your project is using in the **Integration keys** tab. When connection sets are first created, this tab is empty. When you create project and task and add entities, integration keys will appear in a list on the connection set as part of the integration key tab. Similar to a connection group, you define integration key once and can use it on one or more projects.

Projects

Projects are key artifacts for data integration and enable data flow between connecting applications.

Once you have created the connection sets, you can create Data integration project using the **New Project** button on the **Projects** tab. This will open a form wizard, as follows:

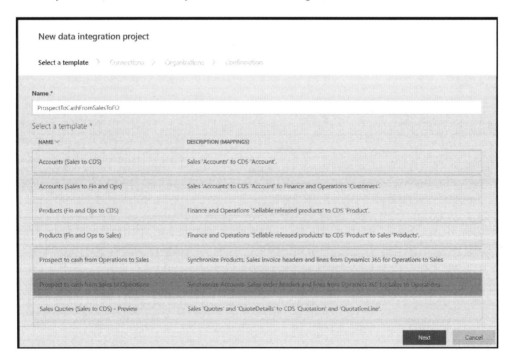

As shown, the first step on the project creation wizard is to give it a name and then select an integration template. Integration template defines data entities and field mapping to achieve specific integration scenario between two applications. Depending on the requirement, partners and customers can customize the template or create a new template to achieve specific integration scenarios. The advantage of having template-driven integration solutions is that partner or customer can use the existing templates or add an additional template to create a new integration between third-party and Dynamics Applications.

Next, you select the connection set and organizations map that you created earlier and finally, provide your consent to create the project. This screenshot shows the final project:

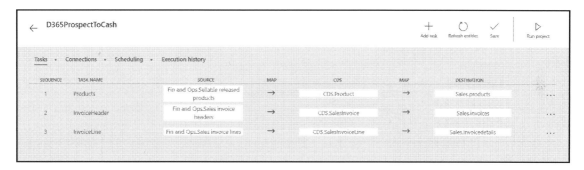

As shown, a project is list of one or more task and each task has mapping between a source entity and a Common Data Service entity, and then, optionally, a mapping between the Common Data Service entity and a destination entity. Mappings indicate which fields map to which other fields. Mapping can also have transformation logic, default values, and value maps. Each task is run in the order in which it appears in the project.

Integration templates provided by Microsoft have predefined entity and mapping between them. You can customize these mappings according to your integration requirement and save the changes as a new template.

Schedules

Once the project is created, you can run the project manually or define schedule for specific integration. Integration schedule will control how frequently the data between integrating application will be synchronized. To create schedule, simply click on the scheduling tab and define and save the schedule, as shown in the following screenshot:

Integrating and monitoring

Integration projects are not easy, and there will be scenarios when integration may fail due to various reasons. Monitoring capability is important for any integration platform. The Dynamics 365 integration platform has robust monitoring capabilities to identify any integration failure and the ability to identify the reason for failure. The following screenshot shows the monitoring capabilities under the **Execution history** tab of the integration projects:

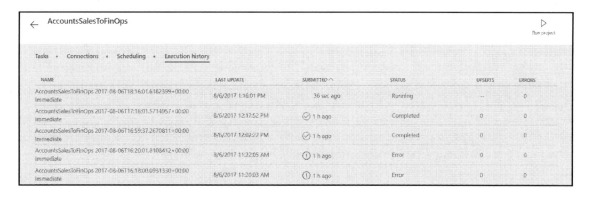

Benefits of CDS data integration

The idea of integrating front office (CRM System) and back office (ERP) system out of the box is, probably for the first time, perceived and done by any Software vendor, and it is unique. Listed here are key benefits of this integration model for the overall Dynamics 365 ecosystem:

- **Easy access to data through the power of Dynamics 365 Common Data Service**: The solution leverages the power of Azure Public Cloud and combined data via Dynamics 365 Common Data Service. This enables business users to access, visualize, share, and modify the unified data for various business processes.

- **Fast implementation**: Integration between different ERP systems has traditionally been known for its rigidity, complexity, and slow deployment and implementation. This integration approach is changing the game in this area by providing prepackaged integration templates. The templates provide a out-of-the-box experience, including synchronization. In addition to an intelligent and easy-to-use setup experience, it is optimized to quickly adjust integration settings for your data structure and business needs.

- **Enhanced systems and flexible setup**: The integration comes with a rich solution to optimize the experience and allow for complex process flows between Dynamics 365 systems.

Scenarios focus

Microsoft Dynamics 365 integration will be focused on specific business scenarios that start in one application and end in another application. Microsoft has already planned out different scenarios, for which they will be delivering out of the box integration solution. One of the first scenarios that Microsoft is currently focused on delivering is the **prospect to cash** scenario. Prospect to cash scenario involves Dynamics 365 for Sales and Dynamics 365 for Finance and Operations, Enterprise edition. The following diagram represents the data flow between Sales and Operations as part of this integration scenario:

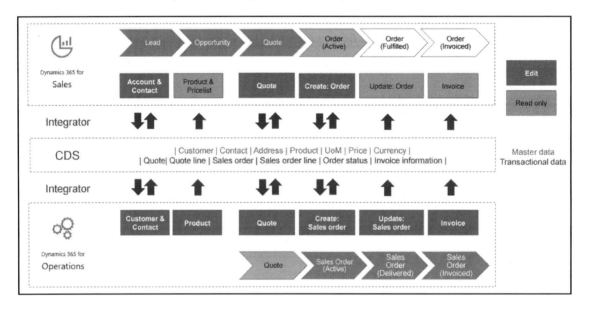

As shown, prospect to cash scenario will synchronize the following business data entities as part of this integration:

- Maintain accounts in Dynamics 365 for Sales and sync them to Dynamics 365 for Finance and Operations, Enterprise edition as customers.
- Maintain contacts in Dynamics 365 for Sales and sync them to Dynamics 365 for Finance and Operations, Enterprise edition.

- Maintain products in Dynamics 365 for Finance and Operations, Enterprise edition and sync them to Dynamics 365 for Sales.
- Create quotes in Dynamics 365 for Sales and sync them to Dynamics 365 for Finance and Operations, Enterprise edition.
- Generate sales orders in Dynamics 365 for Sales for the existing products and sync them to Dynamics 365 for Finance and Operations, Enterprise edition.
- Generate invoices in Dynamics 365 for Finance and Operations, Enterprise edition and sync them to Dynamics 365 for Sales.

Various other scenarios with relation to Dynamics 365 for Finance and Operations, Enterprise edition, are currently under planning and development, and one can expect many more in the near future:

- **Project service to project accounting**: This scenario will integrate Dynamics 365 Project Services with Dynamics 365 for Finance and Operations, Enterprise edition project accounting. At the moment, there are not much details around what this integration scenario will cover, but one can imagine customer project getting created in project service automation and synchronizing to Dynamics 365 for Finance and Operations, Enterprise edition for project for further processing and customer billing.
- **Field service to service management**: This scenario will integrate Dynamics 365 for Field Service with Dynamics 365 for Finance and Operations, Enterprise edition Service management module. In this scenario you can expect, product and inventory information to be synchronized from Dynamics 365 for Finance and Operations, Enterprise edition to Field services application; scheduled work order being created in field service application and synchronized in Dynamics 365 for Finance and Operations, Enterprise edition. Time and material is consumed by performing job on the site, being able to synchronize it to Dynamics 365 for inventory consumption and accounting.

At the time of writing, Only integration scenarios publicly release was prospect to cash, and the others are still in the conceptualization and development phase within Microsoft. The final solution can be different from what is stated here. For more details on the concept and solution, follow the data integrator page on the documentation site at `https://docs.microsoft.com/en-us/common-data-service/entity-reference/dynamics-365-integration`.

Integration planning

Planning is an important part of any data integration effort. Data integration planning requires identifying integration scenarios and the high-level requirements of integration. This topic covers common integration scenarios and the common questions to be asked for gathering integration requirements.

Integration scenarios

Every project is different, and integration requirements will vary depending on the scope and needs of the specific project. However, there are some common areas where most of the businesses have processes that require integration. The following table shows the common integration points and possible scenarios:

Integrations	Possible scenarios
Customers	Customers need to be maintained in the CRM system, which needs to be synced with the ERP system.
Sales orders	Integrating web orders with the ERP system that includes delivery notification, invoicing, and payments or with customer systems directly (for example, EDI integration).
Product and inventory (on hand)	Receiving product data from a PLM system. Sending the product-and-inventory-on-hand data to external systems or customers, for example, e-commerce, Amazon, Marketplace, and so on.
Price list	Sending product price list to external systems or customers. For example, e-commerce, marketplace and so on.
Sales tax	Sales tax integration with sales tax solutions (to calculate the sales tax based on the product, customer, ship to, price, and other relevant parameters).

Purchase orders	Purchase order, including ASN and AP invoice, integration with the vendor systems.
Employee and positions	Receiving employee and reporting relationship from the HR system or sending employee information to the payroll or expense systems.
Chart of accounts and financial dimensions	Sending the chart of account and financial dimension data to other internal systems such as the payroll system, expense system, and others.
Exchange rates	Downloading daily exchange rates from exchange rate providers, such as Oanda.
Payment integration with banks	Sending AP payments such as check, ACH, and wire to the banking systems or automating bank reconciliations.
GL integration	Importing GL journal entries occurring outside of Finance and Operations system, such as expense, payroll, loan accounting systems, or other divisions using a different accounting system (acquisitions).

Integration requirements

In a typical integration scenario, the implementation team works with the business users, internal IT, and in some cases, representatives of the applications identified for integration to determine the requirements in detail. The following questions must be answered and documented in order to have a successful integration solution. Often, the answers to these questions are not clear-cut and will require modeling of the different scenarios to develop the best solution. That being said, starting this process early on in the project is the key:

Questions	Example values	Effects on design
What type of data needs to be integrated?	Sales orders, purchase orders, and so on	This will help you determine whether you can use any existing data entities or need to create a new one.
What kind of integration type will the other applications support?	XML, web services, and flat file	This will help you determine the technology to use.

What is the availability of the systems that are being integrated? What are the requirements of real-time data exchanges?	Asynchronous or synchronous	This will help you determine the integration technology and configuration requirements.
Is the integration based on the pull model or the push model?	Pull, push, and eventdriven	This will help you determine the technology and configuration of the exchange event.
What is the volume of transactions?	Number of transactions (daily, weekly, monthly, and yearly)	This will help you determine the scale of integration, suitable integration technology, and deployment options.
What will be the frequency of data exchange?	Timing per second, minute, and hour	This information helps you determine how to configure the integration solution.
What business rules are associated with the data?	Sequence of events and exception handling	This will help you determine the customization requirement for the document exchange.
Does the data need to be transformed? Will the transformations be performed before data is sent or when data is received?	Extent of transformation-- field level mapping, value mapping, and flat file to XML or vice versa	This will help you determine which integration configuration and transformations need to be used.
Is the external system an in-house system or an external trading partner?	Security and encryption requirements	This will help you determine how the users and security need be configured.

Synchronous or asynchronous

One of the key decisions to be made is whether integration should be real time (synchronous) or asynchronous. The following table analyzes both the messaging approaches and describes the scenarios when one should be selected over the other:

Type	Pros	Cons	Good for	Examples
Synchronous	Fail-safe communication Error/exception handling	Tight coupling between systems Block sender until receiver is finished Network dependency must be available	Transaction processing across multiple systems	Mobile app/handheld for PO receiving, SO picking, Inventory onhand, and so on.
Asynchronous	Decoupled systems Does not block sender Network need not be available Messages can be queued	Reliability Error/exception handling	Publish and subscribe Request reply Conversation	General ledger, sales order, purchase orders, and master data integrations.

Asynchronous messaging architectures have proven to be the best strategy for an enterprise integration because they allow for a loosely-coupled solution that overcomes the limitations of a remote communication, such as latency and unreliability. The issues of reliability and exception handling in asynchronous messaging can be overcome by utilizing recurring integration acknowledgement, status check, and logging features in the Microsoft Dynamics 365 for Finance and Operations, Enterprise edition.

Integration design and development

Once they have all the detailed integration requirements, an integration specialist works with business analysts, developers, and system administrators to create a detailed design. The following topics in this section explain the process of designing an integration solution.

Developing a high-level conceptual design

Developing a high-level conceptual design diagram is important to explain the different integration points and directions. The following diagram shows an example of a conceptual integration design between Dynamics 365 for Finance and Operations, Enterprise edition and a B2B e-commerce applications:

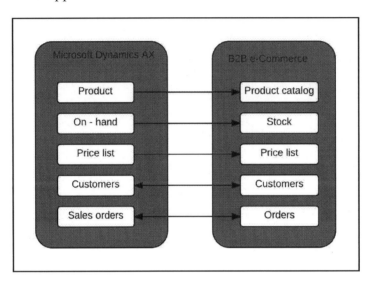

Selecting the right integration technology

It is important to select the best-suited integration technology for each of the identified integration requirements. The earlier section describes the different integration technologies and tools with recommendations on their use cases. Depending on the requirements for each integration, different technologies can be used. The following table explains the integration points shown earlier and the recommended integration technologies:

Integration point	Description	Recommended solution
Product	Products and attributes will be stored in operations and synced nightly with an e-commerce application as a flat file.	Reccuring integration to on-premise flat file or common data services to synchronize product master.

Product on-hand	Product on-hand needs to be shared with the e-commerce application in real time.	RESTful Odata Services
Price list	The price list will be mastered in Finance and Operations and will be updated on the e-commerce application on a nightly basis as a flat file.	Reccuring integration to on-premise flat file or common data services
Customers	The customer can be created or updated either on the e-commerce website (such as address) or updated in Finance and Operations (such as credit limit), and synced in both the systems.	Common Data Service integration model
Sales orders	Sales orders will be created in the e-commerce application and created or updated to Finance and Operations. Sales order status updates such as shipment confirmation, invoices, and payment application need to be synced to the web application.	Reccuring integration via RESTful APIs using Logic app or common data services

Defining field mapping

Defining field-level mapping for each integration point includes data type, field length, applicable values, and validation logic for each field. This mapping helps you identify mapping requirement between the system to address any data type, field length, and restrictions. The ensuing table shows customer integration between Finance and Operations, Enterprise edition and an e-commerce application as an example:

AX Field name	Data type	Requirement	Default value	E-Commerce Field	Description
CustTable.AccountNum	NVARCHAR(20)	Mandatory	Number sequence	Account.Id	Unique identifier for the customer record
CustTable.CustGroup	NVARCHAR(10)	Mandatory	Web	NA	Define customer group
DirPartyPostalAddress.PostalAddress	NVARCHAR(250)	Optional		Account.PostalAddress	Stores the customer's address

Developing, configuring, and testing

The next step is to do the required development, configuration, and testing of the integration. The following are some helpful tips for developing integration solution:

- Utilize the existing code and functionalities for integration; extend as needed.
- Keep the message format generic as far as possible so that the same integration point can be used with other applications, if needed. Use the XSLT transformation or other transformation tools to transform the messages in an appropriate system schema.
- Build an error handling and notification mechanism to monitor the failure. Keep a closed loop; there should be a mechanism to notify other applications of the success or failure of message processing.
- Develop the test data and a unit test scenario; perform unit testing before end-to-end integration testing.
- Develop test simulation, if possible, for system testing. This can save a lot of time during the end-to-end testing.
- Perform load testing by generating a large set of data. Many a times, integration solution fails on the production load as the development or test environment does not have sufficient data to simulate the production load.
- Prepare a test plan including the positive and negative scenarios. Test all exceptions and boundary scenarios. Also, test the end-to-end business process on integration data to avoid any fallback impact in the production environment.
- Develop a security and deployment plan for integration solutions and test deployment and security in the test environment before moving to production.

Best practices and recommendations

Here are a few considerations to keep in mind while designing your integration solution for Dynamics 365 for Finance and Operations, Enterprise edition:

- Simplify the overall architecture and try to reduce the number of integrations between applications wherever possible. It is one of the areas that cause recurring issues in production.
- Clearly define the master system for each data element, even though you may have it stored at multiple places. In some cases, this may have to be defined at the field level. For example, a customer master is stored in CRM and Finance and Operations as well. CRM might be the master for all the customer information except credit limit.

- Ideally, you should avoid duplication of data across multiple systems, although in some cases you cannot avoid it for business reasons or for systems to work. For example, customer records are required in both the CRM system and operations. However, you can opt not to integrate the CRM-centric customer information that may not be needed in operations.
- Understand and document business SLAs for each integration; think through the impact in extreme situations.

One of my customers had the inventory getting refreshed into their e-commerce system every two minutes. It was okay until the Black Friday weekend. During that 2-minute window, they oversold a product that was being sold below its cost (they only wanted to get rid of the on-hand stock). However, the customer ended up buying more to fulfill the additional orders that were received due to the delays in inventory updates. It is important to understand SLAs and the business impact while designing integrations.

Summary

In this chapter, we learned about the tools and techniques for integration planning and design. We started with the integration architecture and learned how integration architecture for Dynamics 365 for Finance and Operations, Enterprise edition is completely changed. Data entities are at the center of integration architecture and support RESTful OData services and recurring integrations. We learned various modern basic integration concepts, such as RESTful, SOAP, JSON, OData, OAuth, how these concepts are utilized within Dynamics 365 for Finance and Operations, Enterprise edition, and how they can be utilized for various integration scenarios. Microsoft Dynamics 365 applications are intelligent applications that work smarter together, and we learned how these applications will be connected together using a new integration platform built on top of Common Data Service. Then, we learned different integration scenarios and tools such as BizTalk server, Azure Logic app, Flow, CDS, and how they can help achieve end-to-end integration with cloud and on-premise system. Subsequently, we learned how important integration planning is in an ERP implementation project, and how to approach integration design and development with real-life integration examples. At the end, we learned about the common industry best practices and recommendations related to integration planning.

In the next chapter, we will cover another important phase of the ERP project development. We will learn how Dynamics 365 for Finance and Operations, Enterprise edition can be customized and extended for specific business scenarios, including common recommendations and best practices.

9
Building Customizations

Customization is one of the most debated topics in ERP implementation. A majority of the customers have intentions to implement the ERP system without any customization. However, when a project team starts gathering the requirements and doing fit-gap analysis, one or more customizations are inevitable. Dynamics 365 for Finance and Operations, Enterprise edition provides a broad variety of technologies and tool sets for developers to build additional solutions and functionalities. These tools not only enable the customer and the partners to customize the end product in order to meet the business requirements in a specific project but also help **Independent Software Vendors (ISVs)** to build industry specific vertical solutions for a larger ecosystem. In this chapter, we will learn about the development process and tools in Dynamics 365 for Finance and Operations, Enterprise edition. We will cover the following topics in this chapter:

- Architecture and concepts
- Development environment
- Development planning
- Development process
- Build and continuous updates
- Guidelines and best practices

In this architecture, we will explore the things that you need to know before starting the development, for example, development environment, tools, technical concepts, and build and versioning strategies. In development planning, you will learn about setting up the basic rules and guidelines before the development starts. In the development process, we will walk you through the development process, frameworks, and best practices. In the build and continuous update section, we will explore the automated build and deployment processes. In the end, we will discuss some common best practices and guidelines applicable in the development phase.

Architecture and concepts

As we learned earlier in `Chapter 3`, *Architecture and Deployment*, development experience and architecture has completely changed and been modernized in Dynamics 365 for Finance and Operations, Enterprise edition, as compared to the earlier version, Dynamics AX 2012. Many new concepts have been introduced and many have been changed. In this section, we will explore these new and changed development concepts in detail.

Programming language

The X++ language remains the vehicle for a developing application code for Dynamics 365 for Finance and Operations, Enterprise edition. Those who don't know what X++ is, it is a native programming language used in the development of Dynamics 365 for Finance and Operations, Enterprise edition since the beginning of the product known as Axapta.

X++ is an object-oriented language with similarities to C# and provides SQL-like constructs for data selection and manipulation. In Microsoft Dynamics 365
for Finance and Operations, Enterprise edition, the X++ programming language has been modernized to achieve the following:

- Better consistency with other managed languages such as C#
- Better integration with the managed stack (CIL)
- Some cleanup--fewer quirks and badly defined areas

Let's understand the changes in the X++ programming language in the following subsections.

Compile exclusively in .NET CIL

In Microsoft Dynamics 365 for Finance and Operations, Enterprise edition, X++ is a first-class citizen in the .NET world. The X++ compiler is rewritten and compiles the source code exclusively as .NET CIL. There are important benefits to X++ code running exclusively as .NET CIL, as follows:

- CIL runs much faster in most scenarios. You can expect significant performance improvements in the cases where complex algorithms are executed.
- You can now easily write application logic in other .NET languages such as C#.
- AX **.NET Business Connector** or managed proxies are no longer needed; you can simply add assembly reference in X++ code.
- CIL can be operated on by the many .NET tools.

Language enhancements

Along with making X++ completely compile in CIL, several language enhancements and constructs have been added to get X++ closer to C#. The following code summarizes some of the new enhancements in X++:

```
//using keyword for referencing - just like C#
using coll = System.Collections;
using System.CodeDom;
class MyMainClass
{
  // Declare variables and instantiate them in the class declaration
  // granular field access mark them public, private or protected.
  //static, constant and read only member variables
  static int loop;
  private const int constValue = 4;
  public readonly str readOnlyValue = "ReadOnly";
  CodeComment comment = new CodeComment("Print something");
  // static constructor using TypeNew keyword
  static void TypeNew()
  {
    loop = 4;
  }
  public static void main(Args _args)
  {
    MyMainClass mainClass = new MyMainClass();
    mainClass.myMethod();
  }
  public void myMethod()
  {
    coll.ArrayList arrayList = new coll.ArrayList();
    // Const or readonly variables change- generate compile error
    // constValue = 5;
    //readOnlyValue = "I want to change this but i cant";
    try
    {
      info(comment.Text);
      //use var keyword
      for (var i = 1; i <= loop; i++)
      {
        arrayList.Add(i);
        if (i == 3)
        {
          throw error("Catch me.");
        }
      }
    }
    catch
```

```
    {
      error("something happened in try.");
    }
    // Finaly keyword
    finally
    {
      info(strFmt("Error happened at %1", arrayList.Count));
    }
  }
  /*Output
  Print something
  Catch me.
  something happen in try.
  Error happened at 3
  */
}
```

The preceding code highlights the following new concepts and keywords in the X++ programming language:

- **The using keyword**: Similar to C#, now you can use the `using` keyword to reference assemblies. The preceding code shows two different ways of how you can use the `using` keyword.

- **Instantiate variables in class declaration**: As shown in the code, now you can instantiate variables in the class declaration.

- **Static constructor and member fields**: You can now declare member fields as static and create static constructors using the keyword `TypeNew`. In the example code, an earlier static constructor is used to initialize the value of the variable loop.

- **Const and read-only member fields**: Now you can declare member field as `const` or `readonly`. Attempting to change these fields throws compile errors. Similar to C#, Const are static by default and must have a value at compilation time. The ReadOnly field must have a set value, by the time constructor is evaluated and the instance is created.

- **Granular field access**: Now a field can explicitly be marked as private/protected/public. Default is protected.

- **The var keyword**: Similar to C#, now you can use var keyword in X++. The code example earlier shows `i` in the `for` loop declared using the `var` keyword.

- **Declare anywhere/smaller scope**: Now X++ allows you to declare variables in a smaller scope. The preceding code demonstrates this concept where the variable `i` is declared in the scope of the `for` loop.

- **The finally keyword:** You can now use the `finally` keyword along with the `try...catch` statements; the `finally` block is always executed.

 To learn more about these additions, check out the following link: https://docs.microsoft.com/en-us/dynamics365/operations/dev-itpro/dev-tools/programming-language-support.

Unit of compilation

Another important change you will notice in X++ is about the unit of compilation. In Dynamics 365 for Finance and Operations, the X++ compilation unit is now the same as for the other .NET languages such as C#. If any method in a model element (class, form, query, and so on) fails to compile, the whole compilation fails. In the previous version of Microsoft Dynamics AX , you could change a method code and compile that method successfully, which means that if the compilation of a class found an error in one method of the class, the methods that did compile correctly were still runnable. However, at runtime, if the non-compiled method is used, it will throw an error.

Compiler and tooling

Since there is no more p-code in Finance and Operations now, and the code compiles exclusively in .NET CIL, the following tools that worked with p-code are now obsolete and have been removed and replaced by .NET tools:

Tools in the previous version of Dynamics AX	New replacement tools
The X++ compiler that generated p-code.	New compiler which generate .NET CIL
The special compiler that inputted p-code and generated .NET CIL.	Not needed anymore
The run time interpreter of p-code and its deterministic garbage collector.	Not needed anymore
The Dynamics AX Debugger.	Visual studio debugger
The Dynamics AX Code Profiler.	Not needed anymore
The AX .NET Business Connector.	Not needed anymore

Integrated development environment (IDE)

Integrated development environment (IDE), the tool that you use to develop application code and metadata, has changed completely in Dynamics 365 for Finance and Operations, Enterprise edition.

Development IDE in Dynamics 365 for Finance and Operations, Enterprise edition

In the new version, Visual Studio is the exclusive integrated development environment with modern tooling using .NET components, and it completely replaces the MorphX development environment. The X++ language is fully integrated into the Visual Studio environment. You can use the code editor in Microsoft Visual Studio to write the X++ code for your applications. As you write your X++ code, you will see the familiar features of the Visual Studio code editor. For example, IntelliSense is displayed to help you write the code. You can also navigate to methods and classes in the code editor by using the navigation drop-down menus at the top of the code editor window. Other features, such as collapsible sections, are also available. The design experience, such as designing a UI element, is also integrated with Visual Studio. You can open the element designer that corresponds to the current X++ source code by right-clicking in the code editor and then selecting **Open Designer**.

Visual Studio is an exclusive development environment for Dynamics 365 for Finance and Operations.

The following screenshot shows the operations development environment in Visual Studio:

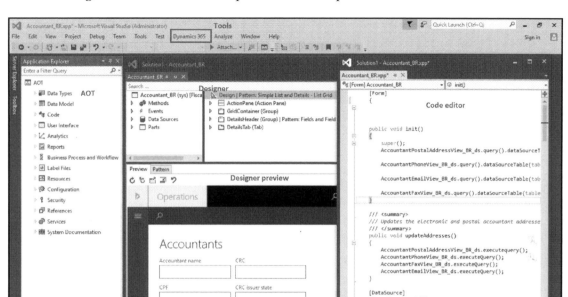

The preceding user interface shows a combination of views to show various relevant interfaces together on one screen. Normally, a code editor or designer is present in the middle section, and the right section has **Solution Explorer** or team explorer view.

As shown in the preceding screenshot, Visual Studio provides a complete new experience of designing and writing code within the Visual Studio environment. On the left, a familiar application object tree displays the application elements. Form designer can be used to design the form element, which also includes real-time preview control to display how the control will appear on the page, as shown in the middle. On the right is the code editor to write the business logic. Debugging the X++ code, displaying a form, or running a report is integrated with the Visual Studio debug (*F5, Ctrl-F5*) experience. All other development tools, such as cross reference, best practices checks, and so on, are replaced with a .NET-based tooling and are available under Dynamics 365 on the top toolbar.

It it important to note that the Dynamics 365 development environment in Visual Studio is enabled by the extension of Microsoft Dynamics 365 for Finance and Operations, Enterprise edition. The easiest way to get the extension and tools is to use cloud development VM or download the VHD on the premises.

Development IDE in Dynamics AX 2012

Earlier in Dynamics AX 2012, the IDE was called MorphX, which is built as part of the AX Windows client. It includes tools for designing, editing, compiling, and debugging code in Microsoft Dynamics AX. Certain development scenarios, such as SSRS reports and enterprise portal development, required Visual Studio for development. In AX 2012, the development environment was tightly coupled with the runtime environment **Application Object Server (AOS)** and database. The source code, as well as the compiled code, was stored in the SQL server database as a model store.

The following screenshot shows the MorphX development environment in Dynamics AX 2012:

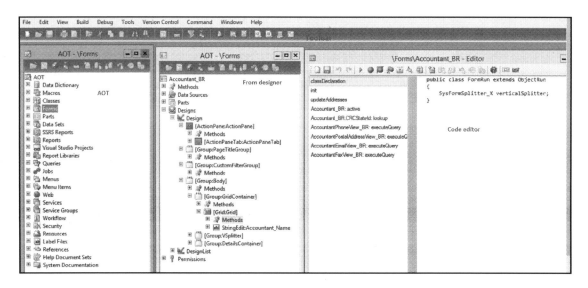

As shown in the screenshot, on the left, the **Application Object Tree (AOT)** represents all the metadata and code in the tree structure. You can design forms using the form designer, as shown in the the middle. The code can be written using the code editor, as shown in the right window. On the top, you have all the other tools available in the toolbar.

Development environment architecture

As shown in the following diagram, the development environment architecture is powered by the Visual Studio extension called Unified Operations. This extension provides the developer, application explorer, X++ code editor, project system, UI designer, debugger, and others tools to extend the existing functionalities and add new functionalities. The source code is stored on the development machine file system as XML files and is used by the metadata API of the Visual Studio extension for editing and design experience. Use the familiar build process developer to build the solution and to create binary assembly files and other deployment artifacts. The X++ debugging experience is integrated with the *F5*/Run function, which uses the local runtime environment to provide debug experience. Another important change in development is that the development tools are completely decoupled from any running environment, which means that unlike the earlier versions, you don't need an active application server to write your code:

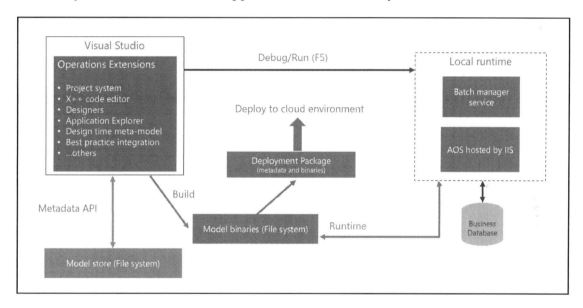

A new development environment changes the way customization and development was done in the earlier versions. The following are the key advantages of using Visual Studio as the development environment for operations:

1. Visual Studio is the most popular integrated development environment and the Finance and Operations development tooling can reap benefits for continuous investment and innovations.

2. X++ becomes a managed language within Visual Studio; the programming language X++ itself gets closer to C#, incorporating more and more familiar syntax from C#.

3. Easier than ever to on board the .NET resources to customize and extend Dynamics 365 for Finance and Operations, Enterprise edition with familiar tooling, programming concepts, and increased interoperability with managed languages.

Programming concepts

The Dynamics 365 for Finance and Operations, Enterprise edition development platform has gone through complete overhaul and modernization. Several new programming concepts are introduced. To better understand the overall development model, you must understand some of these basic concepts first.

Layer system

People familiar with the earlier versions of Dynamics AX may already know about the layer system. The layer system, in essence, is used to manage the application elements in a predefined order. The USR layer is the highest layer and the SYS is the lowest layer. The following table shows all the layers and the corresponding use:

Layer	Used by	Description
USR	Customer/partner	The user layer is for user modifications, such as reports.
CUS	Customer/partner	The customer layer is for modifications that are specific to a company.
VAR	Partner	**Value Added Resellers (VAR)** can make modifications or new developments to the VAR layer, as specified by the customers or as a strategy of creating an industry-specific solution.
ISV	ISV solution	When an **Independent Software Vendor (ISV)** creates his/her own solution, their modifications are saved in the ISV layer.
SLN	ISV	The solution layer is used by distributors to implement vertical partner solutions.
GLS	Microsoft	Country-specific localization layer.

FPK	Microsoft	The FPK layer is an application object patch layer reserved by Microsoft for future patching or other updates. **Note**: The FPK layer is no longer used in operations, as Microsoft directly ships patches in the SYS layer.
SYS	Microsoft	The standard application is implemented at the lowest level, the SYS layer. The application objects in the standard application can never be deleted.

As shown in the preceding table, Microsoft ships code in the lower layers. Technically, when an element is overlayered in a higher layer, the higher layer makes a copy of the lower layer and then you can modify or add additional code in the higher layer. When the application is compiled, only the top-most layer of an application element is used.

 The layer system is only applicable to the overlayering customization concept, which we will walkthrough shortly in this section.

The layer system will probably become less relevant, specially when all the source code delivered by Microsoft is hard sealed for overlayering. The concept may still be relevant for ISV solutions if they wish to support the overlayering concept. Later in this chapter, we have more details about the overlayering and extension programing model and Microsoft roadmap around eliminating overlayering.

Models

A model is a group of elements, such as metadata and source files that typically constitutes the solution. A model is a design-time concept and typically represents a solution area, for example, the general ledger model and project model. A model always belongs to a package.

A model concept was also available in Dynamics AX 2012. In Dynamics AX 2012, you can create one or more models in a layer. All the models are stored in a database.

Packages

Packages are new concept introduced in Microsoft Dynamics 365 for Finance and Operations, Enterprise edition. Package in Finance and Operations is essentially a deployment and compilation unit of one or more models. On the disk a package is a set of folders, consisting of XML files representing the objects. From the compilation and deployment point a package as a whole translates 1:1 as an assembly (DLL). Packages can have references to other packages, just like .NET assemblies can reference each other. One or more packages combine into a deployable package, that is, a unit of deployment.

Packages and models on the disk

Packages and models are stored as set of folders on Microsoft Dynamics 365 for Finance and Operations, Enterprise edition application server. The following image represents the folder structure:

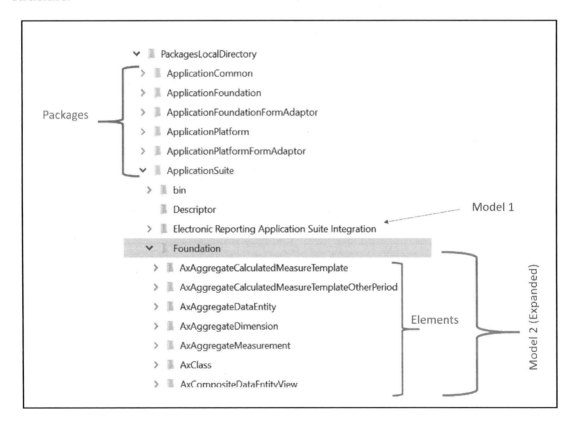

As shown in the diagram, `PackagesLocalDirectory` (called model store) is root folder which contains the individual packages for example `ApplicationCommon`, `ApplicationFoundation`, `ApplicationSuite`, and so on. Each package can contain one or more models; for example `ApplicationSuite` package contains multiple models `Electronic Reporting Application Suite Integration` and `Foundation`. Each model contains folders containing metadata elements and code.

Models and packages in Visual Studio

In Visual studio models and packages are represented in the **Application Explorer**. You can switch to model view by right clicking on the main node **AOT** and selecting model view. The following screenshot shows the model view of **Application Explorer**. As shown in the screenshot, all the models are represented as tree structures in the model view. Package names are displayed in the parenthesis for each model:

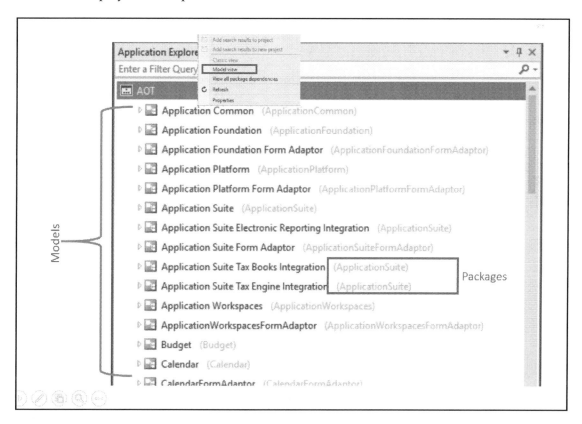

As highlighted in preceding visual, Application Suite Tax Books Integration, Application Suite Tax Engine Integration are two model part of ApplicationSuite package.

Overlayering

Customization using overlayering is similar to customization concept used in the earlier version of Dynamics AX. In Microsoft Dynamics 365 for Finance and Operations, Enterprise edition you can only override an element in the same package where it is originally created. You also have to use higher layer than the original layer of the element. For example, if you want to override an element created by Microsoft in `ApplicationSuite` package which is in **SYS** layer, you have to create a model in `ApplicationSuite` package and select higher layer such as **CUS or USR** to override the elements.

When you customize using overlayering original code element is copied over in model you are working on and you are technical changing that copy of code. As evident, when Microsoft release a fix or feature update and if this element is changed, now there could be conflict because you have changed the copy of that element in a higher layer. In the past several major releases Microsoft has been trying to define these code elements as granular as possible to minimize the impact of the conflict. But no matter how granular they are there will be some degree of code conflict if they are changed. These code conflict needs to be manually resolved to uptake any bug fixes or new features.

Other problem with customization using overlayering is, since it can be done in the same package where object was originally created, the entire package needs to be re-compiled and re-distributed.

The following image shows the concept of customization using overlayering. As shown in the following example the `ApplicationSuite` model is overlayered by *ISV1* and *ISV2* in ISV layer and then customer overlayered in layer CUS. All these models will compile into a single assembly. If the same object is changed by ISV and customer, the CUS layer customization wins:

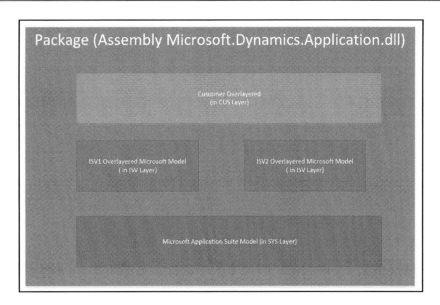

Extensions

Extensions is new concept to do customization in Dynamics 365 for Finance and Operations, Enterprise edition. An extension enables you to add functionality to existing code. The extension development approach is the best practice approach as it puts your customizations in a separate assembly that does not touch the standard application at all.

Extension models have several advantages, including:

- **Application lifecycle management (ALM)**: Extension models simplify and improve the performance of deployments, builds, test automation and delivery to customers.
- **Design time performance**: Building your model or project doesn't require you to recompile the entire application.
- **Servicing**: In the cloud, Microsoft can install, patch, upgrade, and change internal APIs without affecting your customizations.
- **Upgrades**: Unlike overlayering, extensions reduce the cost of upgrading to a new version, as this approach eliminates costly code and metadata conflicts.

The following image shows customization through extension:

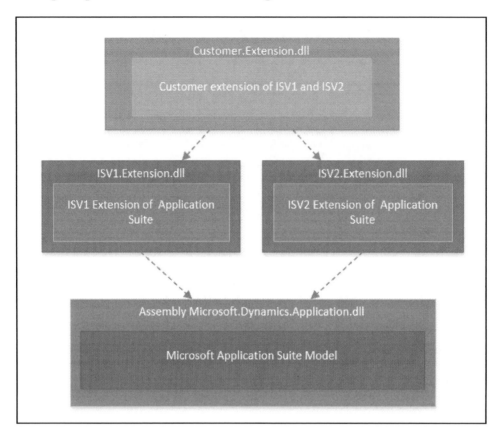

Model sealing and roadmap

As we learned that there are two approaches of customization in Dynamics 365 for Finance and Operations, Enterprise edition, however Microsoft is going to restrict overlayering and allow only extension for customization. Reason is very obvious, being in the cloud Microsoft wants to enable continuous update and want to get Dynamics 365 for Finance and Operations, Enterprise edition closer to SaaS offering. By eliminating the overlayering in the models which Microsoft ships as part of the project, Microsoft will be able to deliver application hot fixes and new feature updates and customer can uptake those features and hotfixes with very little or no effort.

The following diagram represents the goal and objective of sealing the model for overlayering:

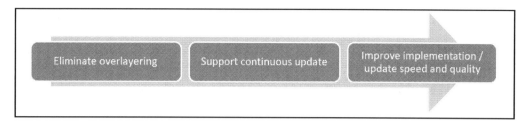

To eliminate overlayering, the following two new concepts are introduced in the product model:

- **Soft seal**: If a model is soft sealed, you will get compile time warning on overlayer of that model. You can still build the solution and use it but it's a warning to get prepared to replace your overlayered code with extensions.
- **Hard seal**: If a model is hard sealed, overlayering not allowed at design time and/or during implementation configuration. After Nov 2016 release, platform and foundation layers are hard sealed which means you can not overlayer those models.

The following image shows the roadmap shared by the product team on sealing the remaining models:

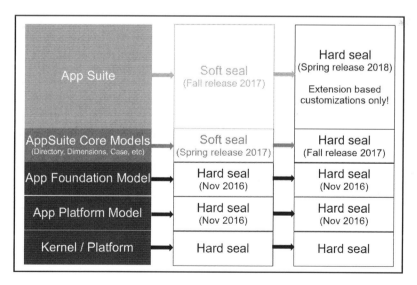

As shown in the diagram, application platform and application foundation models are already hard sealed with Nov 2016 updates. Application suite core models such as directory, dimension, case, and so on will be Soft sealed by Spring release of 2017 and hard sealed in Fall release 2017. Application suite which is the biggest model and contain most of the application functionality will be soft sealed by Fall release 2017 and hard sealed in spring release of 2018. This means if you use Spring release of 2018, you will not be able to overlayer any code shipped by Microsoft. Only option to customize is through extensions.

Development environment

After you understand the architecture and technical concept behind development environment in Dynamics 365 for Finance and Operations, Enterprise edition, it is time to iterate and build solution as per your requirement. Before the development phase of the project starts, you need to set up the development environment, version control strategy and a few ground rules, such as coding standards, the naming convention to be followed, and the code review process. In this section, we will walk through these topics in brief to understand what they mean.

The version control

Keeping track of the code is critical to good development practices. Visual studio team service (formally known as Visual Studio Online or VSO) is the version control system supported for Finance and Operations. VSTS includes source control, work item tracking, build and reporting services. VSTS build server can be used to build releases from specific elements stored in its source control system. Visual Studio's code analysis, test tools, and code coverage elements can be used to validate build before it is deemed fit for release.

VSTS is tightly integrated with LCS and can be used throughout the life cycle of the project. For example, all requirement gaps created in LCS BPM library can be converted into work item in VSTS. Build environment also uses VSTS to build solution and create deployable package. LCS code upgrade tool utilize VSTS integration to perform automated source code management. Post production support tools are integrated with VSTS as well, where an support request created by user can automatically create VSTS work item.

Branching strategies

Before starting development, the solution architect should also decide on the right branching strategy for VSTS, which can be useful in the following scenarios:

- When a stable version is needed for testing while the development work continues in the other areas.
- When multiple development teams are working on a set of features that are independent, but each team also depends on the features developed by the other teams. You need to isolate the risk of the changes made by each team and yet, you will finally need to merge all the features together into one product.
- When the implementation is being carried out in multiple phases, one phase that is in production may need continuous support but the team may be working on the next phase.

The following are some popular branching strategies typically used in the operations projects:

- **The main only strategy**: This is the simplest and most basic branching methodology where one branch is created and all the developers check in the changes to the main branch. The build machine can be used to create a build out of the main branch to be released for testing and later, for the production environment. The following image shows only the main branching strategy:

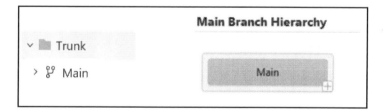

- **The development and main branching strategy**: The development and main branching strategy introduces one or more development branches from the main, which enables the concurrent development of the next release, multiple projects running in parallel, experimentation, or bug fixes in an isolated development branch. The following image shows the **Main** and **Dev** branching strategy:

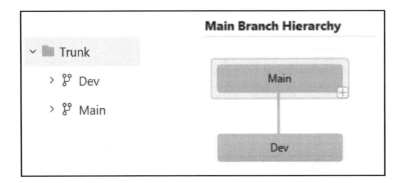

- **Development, main and release**: If you expect to be performing emergency break fixes outside of your normal release schedule, create a release branch. The release branch represents the code that exists in production. The following image shows the branching strategy with release:

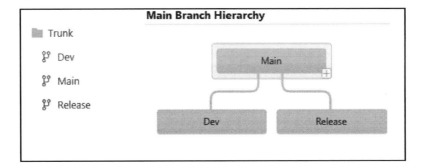

- **Development, main and multiple release**: If you are ISV, developing vertical solutions and want to manage and support multiple version of your solutions, you can create multiple release branch to service specific product version. The following image shows the multiple-release strategy:

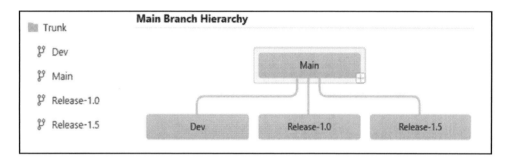

Keep branching strategy simple! Start small, expand later.

The development machines

In Dynamics 365 for Finance and Operations, Enterprise edition, development is done on a pre-configured one box VMs. These VMs have pre-installed Visual Studio, Dynamics, and SQL server; and integrated to ease development.

For development, you will need one development machine for each developer. Depending on the scope and complexity of your project and the number of developers working on it, you may need multiple development VMs. Along with machines for developers, you will need one build machine to build solution and create deployable packages. Build machine can also execute best practice check, unit test and automated regression test at part of the build process.

The following image shows a typical development topology:

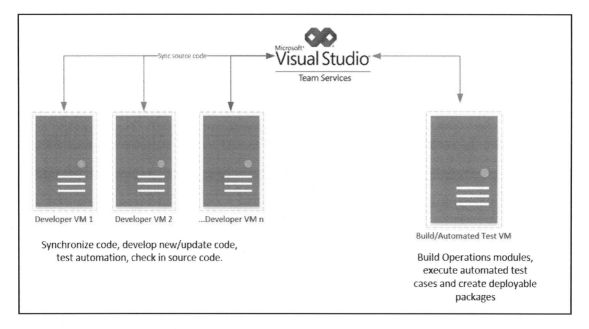

As shown in the diagram multiple developer VM used by developer to synchronize the source code, create/update code, create automated test cases and check in the code. Build VM is used to compile source code, execute automated test cases and create deployable packages. Cloud-based VSTS, links developer VM's for source control and build automation functions.

Now let's see how these VMs can be deployed, there are two options: Cloud VMs and on-premises VMs available via a downloadable VHD. Depending on your situation, you can use a combination of on premise VMs and cloud VMs for development.

Here, we point out some obvious scenarios of when to use on-premise and cloud:

- On-premise dev VMs are cost effective if you already have the hardware, IT infrastructure, and Windows server licenses to support it.
- Use cloud VMs to scale out when projects require additional resources for a limited period of time. It is more cost effective than planning for worst-case capacity on-premise.
- Connect all VMs (on-premise and cloud VMs) to VSTS for version control.

Cloud development environment

Before you can deploy developer topology using LCS, you need to link your LCS project with **Visual Studio Team Services** (**VSTS**) profile. When you deploy dev/test topology, you can select one or more developer VMS and one **Build** VM. In this deployment, the **Developer** VM is configured with workspace mapping to develop against a VSTS project. The **Build** VM is auto-configured with the build agent/controller to build modules VSTS project and to execute automated tests with external endpoint for validation. The following screenshot, shows a simple workflow to deploy DEV and build machines using LCS:

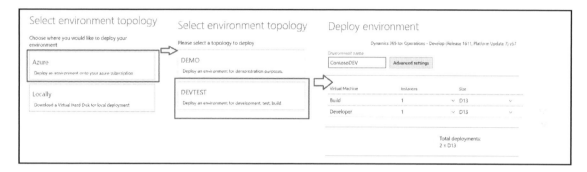

By default, each development environment you try to provision will by default a build env, if you have already deployed a build environment.you can skip the build environment by setting the number of instances to 0.

Note that LCS implementation projects only allow you to manage environments provisioned by Microsoft in their Azure subscription and demo environments. This means that if you don't want to pay 24/7 for development environments on Azure then you need to provision them to your own Azure subscription from a non-implementation LCS project.

Local development environment

To use development environment on-premise, you can download the VHD file and then create virtual machine using virtualization software such as hyper-V or VMWare. These VM's are similar to cloud VM and contain, complete install of Microsoft Dynamics 365 for Finance and Operations, Enterprise edition, Visual Studio and SQL server. To get started with development using these VM's simply do the following:

- Start these VMs and login using user name: `builtin\Administrator` Password: `pass@word1`
- Provision admin user within Operations using `AdminUserProvisioning` tool.
- Sing in to Visual Studio and map your local workspace to develop against the VSTS project.
- If you have more than one downloaded VMs to do development, you must rename them to work with VSTS.
- Optionally you can use manual steps to add these VM's into your domain and also connect to LCS.

Application explorer

Application explorer is main entry point to browse and interact with the elements in the model store that define the applications. If you are familiar with previous version Dynamics AX 2012, Application Explorer corresponds to the AOT. To open the application explorer, in Finance and Operations Developer VMs, in Visual Studio click on the **View** menu and then click **Application Explorer**. Application Explorer is used to view elements, view code, find references to a selected element, and add elements to a project. To create, design, edit, and build model elements, you must use a project.

Application explorer views

There are two views of **Application Explorer**. First view called *classic* view which displays all elements from all models grouped according to type. Second called *model* view displays each model separately and when you expand a particular model, it displays elements from that model grouped according to type.

The following illustration shows both classic and model views of the application explorer in Visual Studio. To switch between the views, you can right click on **AOT** and switch between the views:

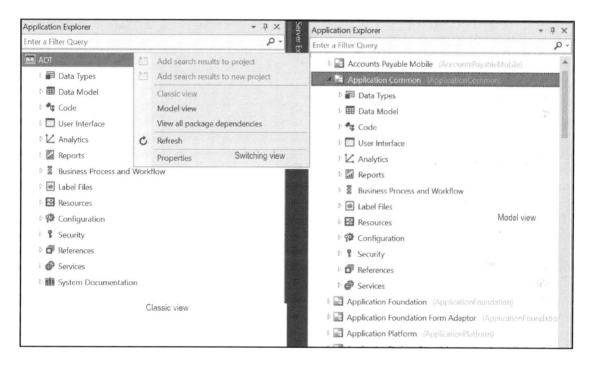

Filtering application explorer

Application explorer provides ability to filter the application element based on various criteria and queries. This makes it easier to find specific elements you are looking to explore or modify. To do a simple search just type the text that you want to filter by and hit *Enter*. For example, if you want to filter by text `custTable`, simply type `custTable` in search bar and hit *Enter*, it will filter and show all elements where element names contains `custTable`, as shown in the following screenshot:

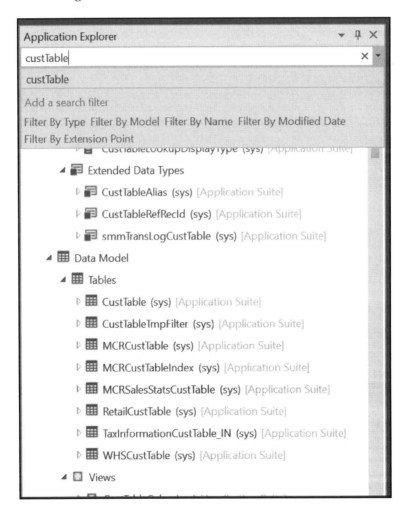

As shown in the preceding screenshot, there are various other filter options which you can add to your filter criteria to refine the search result. To get to those options click the drop-down arrow at the end of the search bar. If you click this arrow, you will see a list of filter options that you can use to refine the filter:

- Filter by type
- Filter by model
- Filter by name
- Filter by modified date
- Filter by extension point

After filtering the elements, you can add them into current project or create new project and add them. To clear the filter, you can click on the clear button (**x**) at the end of the search bar.

Working with elements

To work with specific elements in application explorer, find or search the specific element and then right click on the selection to see the action you can perform. The following screenshot shows the action available on the CustTable form element:

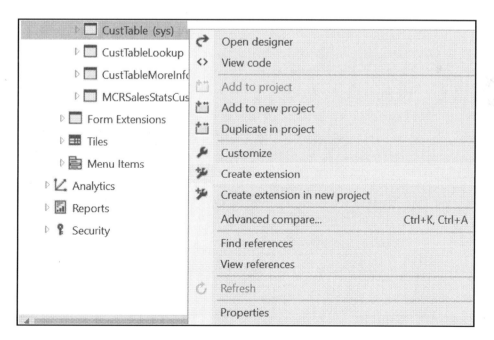

The actions that are available to perform on an element depend on the elements that you've selected. The following are some of the common actions that you can perform for elements in the application explorer:

Actions	Description
Open in designer	Open the element designer to view the object in element type designer. To be able to edit the object in designer, objects must be added in the project first.
View code	Open the element in code editor, where you can view edit the code.
Add to project	Add the element to current project. You can only add element to project if the project belong to same model as the element.
Add to new project	Create a new project and add the element to the project.
Duplicate in the project	Create a copy of the selected element and add to current project.
Customize	When you click **Customize**, a new customization model element file is created and is added to your project. This uses overlayering method of customization. The model that you're using for your current project must be in the same package as the selected element, and it must belong to a higher layer than the element that you want to customize.
Create extension	Create an extension for the element. A new extension model element (.extension) is added to the current project in **Solution Explorer**. This is the preferred way to work with existing elements.
Create extension in new project	Create an extension for the element as part of a new project. You define the new project when the **New Project** dialog box opens.
Find references	Find all of the X++ code and other elements that reference the selected element.
View references	Create a diagram that shows the other elements that reference the selected element.
Refresh	Update the metadata of application element selected.
Properties	Open the property sheet for selected element.
Compare	Compare the element with the different version of the same element from a source code control repository or file on the disk.

Apart from these common actions, some elements have unique commands that let you perform actions for that type of element. For example, table and classes elements have **hierarchy tool** that generate a diagram to display the class or table hierarchy. Table also has command **Open table browser**, which can be used to display data in table as a list in the program.

Tools addins for Visual Studio

Several great tools have been added to Microsoft Visual Studio to support development. However, there will always be additional tools to meet specific requirements. To make it easier to add these additional tools, an **Addins** infrastructure has been provided for developers. The additional tools are available in two places:

- The **Addins** submenu on the Dynamics 365 menu
- The **Addins** submenu on the shortcut menu in the element designer

The following screenshot shows **Addins** available in Visual Studio:

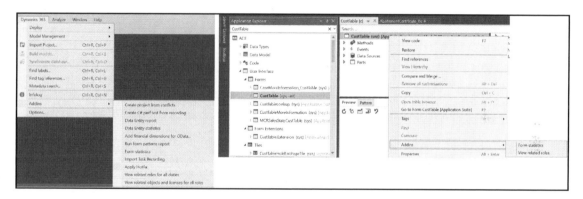

To make it easier to create your own addins, you can select the **Dynamics Developer Tools Addin** project type when you create a new project in Visual Studio. This project type has the infrastructure that is required to implement an add-in.

Creating a new model to start customization

To start development in Microsoft Dynamics 365 for Finance and Operations, Enterprise edition you need to create a model. To create a new model, open Visual Studio in Finance and Operations development environment and click on **Dynamics 365** menu in the toolbar and select **Model Management** and then click on **Create model....** This opens up a wizard to create the model. The following screenshot shows the process of creating a model:

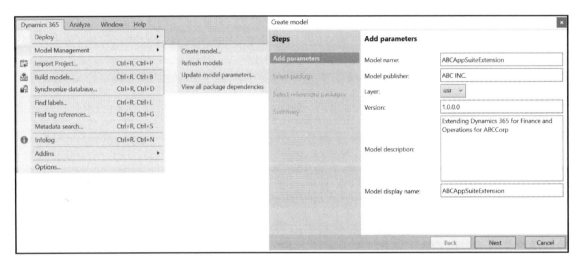

First step in the model creation process is to provide model name, publisher, layer, description of the model and model display name as shown in the preceding screenshot.

Next step is to decide on type of model, you can create two types of models:

- **A model that is deployed in its own package**: You can use this type of model to create new model elements, and extend the metadata and business logic of referenced models. You can select the referenced models at the time of creating model in Visual Studio. This type of model is compiled into its own assembly and binaries, and will simplify and reduce the cost of upgrades, deployment, and application lifecycle management in general.

- **A model that is a part of an existing package**: To create customization using overlayering, you need to create model in the existing package.

The following screenshot shows the two options described earlier:

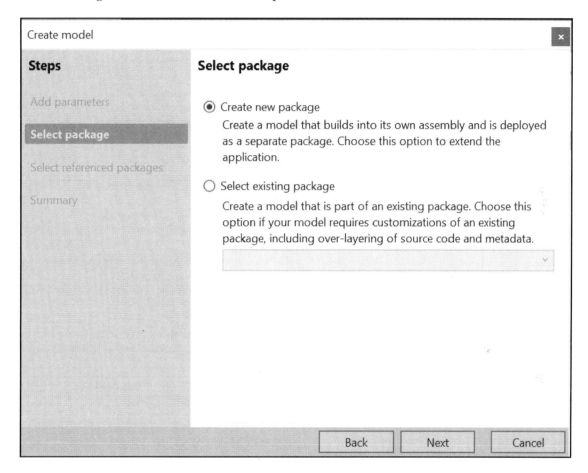

If you wish to do customization using extension approach, you select option **Create new package** and click **Next**. Next step will be to **Select reference packages** and click **Next** to get to summary page. On the **Summary** page, validate the information and click **Finish** to create the model that is shown in the following screenshot:

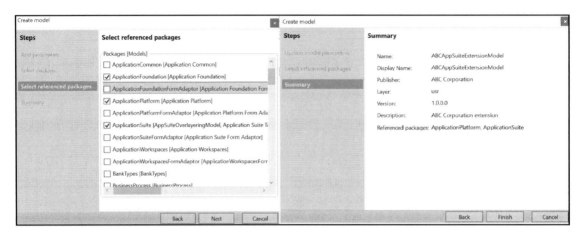

If you wish to do customization using the overlayering package, you select the option **Select existing packages** and choose the package from the drop down and click **Next** to go to **Summary** page. The following screenshot shows an example of creating a model for overlayering **ApplicationSuite**:

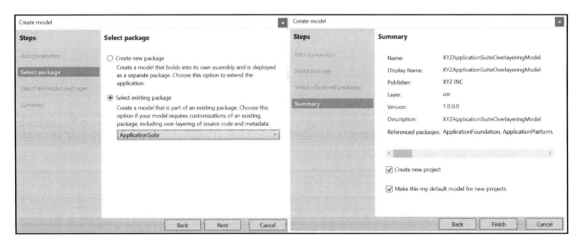

You can update the model description, display name and package references later using navigation option **Dynamics 365 | Model Management | Update Model Parameters**.

It it important to note that there has been two focus area for Microsoft since Microsoft Dynamics 365 for Finance and Operations, Enterprise edition is available in the market. First eliminating overlayering and second splitting the core into multiple models and packages. Eliminating overlayering and splitting the stack into multiple models provides many benefits, including faster compile time and a greater isolation of the code for servicing and deployment. In the Nov 2016 release Microsoft has hard sealed the platform and foundation models and application suite and other models will be hard sealed too as per the roadmap published by Microsoft product team.

Second focus area is package splitting where application suite is being broken into multiple independent packages and models, this enables Microsoft to split the Finance and Operations into multiple smaller applications similar to what is done in CRM application. For example, Microsoft already announced Dynamics 365 for Talent and Microsoft Dynamics 365 for Retail which are used to be HCM and Retail module in Dynamics 365 for Finance and Operations. In future we expect many more such smaller applications carving out of Microsoft Dynamics 365 for Finance and Operations, Enterprise edition product.

Extension capabilities

Extensions are way to customize Dynamics 365 for Finance and Operations, Enterprise edition in future, Microsoft is committed and working on scenarios where customer, partners and ISV solution will need extension capabilities. Every platform updates are delivering new extension capability as requested by customers.

Extensions provide the following capabilities:

- Creating new model elements.
- Extending existing model elements.
    - Adding a new enum value in existing enums
    - Modifying an existing extended data type
    - Modifying existing field or adding a new field in existing tables
    - Add index on existing tables

- Add relations on existing tables
- Modifying properties on existing tables
- Add method on existing tables
- Add a new datasource on the form
- Add form caption and change control properties
- Extending electronic report
- Extending reports by creating a copy of existing reports
- Customizing business logic. Ways to customize business logic include:
  - Creating event handlers to respond to framework events, such as data events
  - Creating event handlers to respond to event delegates that are defined by the application
  - Creating new plug-ins
  - Using method wrapping and chain of command

 For latest updates and extension capabilities check the extensiblity home page on documentation site. `https://docs.microsoft.com/en-us/ dynamics365/unified-operations/dev-itpro/extensibility/ extensibility-home-page.`

Project

When you create customization in Dynamics 365 for Finance and Operation, Enterprise edition, similar to other application development in Visual Studio, you start with project. Project helps you organize and manage the elements that you're working with. A Finance and Operations project in Visual Studio can contain elements of only one model. If you are working with multiple models, you must create multiple project.

Create a new project

There are several way, how you can create new project for Finance and Operations. The following are the two common methods :

1. Using Visual Studio menu **File** | **New** | **Project** and selecting **Dynamics 365** template **Installed** | **Template** | **Dynamics 365** | **Unified Operations**.
2. Select a element in **Application Explorer** and click **Add to new project** or **Create extension in new project**.

Similar to other application projects in Visual Studio, enter the name and location of the project and select whether you want to create a new solution or add the project to existing solution as shown in the following screenshot:

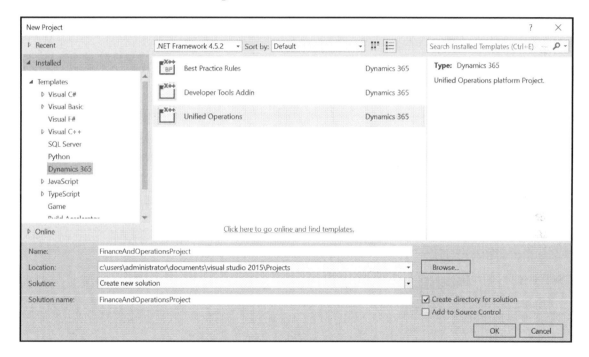

There are several important properties on the Finance and Operations project. To see and change these properties, select the project node and right click and then select **Properties** to open the project **Property Pages**. The following screenshot shows properties for the Finance and Operation project:

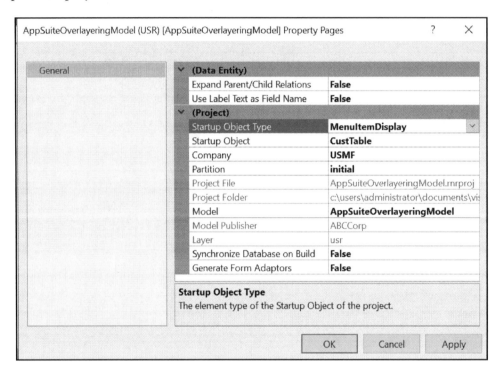

The following table describes some important properties:

Property	Description
Start Object Type	This define type of object that will be used as the startup object when the project is run. Form, Class and MenuItems are available options to select.
Startup Object	Based on object type, you can select object from the project that will be invoked when the project is run.
Company and Partition	This company and partition is used to display data, when project is run.
Project File and Project Folder	Location of the project file and folder on the disk.

Model	The model that the project is associated with. All elements in the project must be in the selected model. You can change the model if there are no elements in the project.
Synchronize database on Build	A value that indicates whether the synchronize operation for tables will be performed when the build action is performed for the project.

Adding new or existing element in the project

To add a new element to project, right click on the **Project** and click **Add** and then select **New item...**. This will open Dynamics 365 items from the template as shown in the following sceenshot:

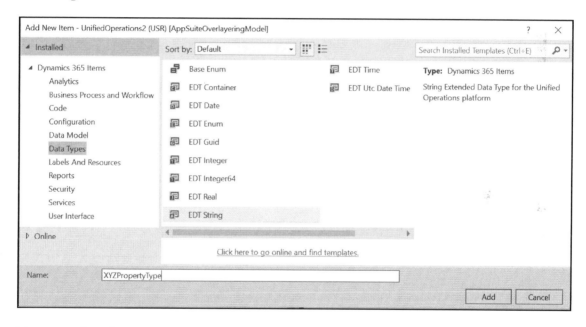

You can select the type of object you want to add, enter name of the object and then click **Add** button to add element to project.

To add an existing element, you can search the element in the application explorer and then click **Add to project** or drag and drop the element to project (element must belong to same model as project), or click customize (when you customization using overlarying and project model belong to same package as element) or click create extension (create extension element in the current project).

Import/export project

To transfer elements from one development environment to a different development environment, you can use a project package file. Project package files have the .axpp file name extension. A project package contains all the elements from the project. To export a project, select the project to export, right click and select **Export Project** option. This will open up dialog to enter file name and folder and save to export.

When you import the .axpp file in another development environment, the elements from the project package file will be imported into the same model that they were exported from. If that model doesn't exist in the installation, it will be created during the import process. To import .axpp file, select menu **Dynamics 365 | Import Project...**, this open the import dialog where you can locate file, select appropriate settings, select elements and click **OK** to complete the import. The following screenshot shows the project import dialog in Visual Studio:

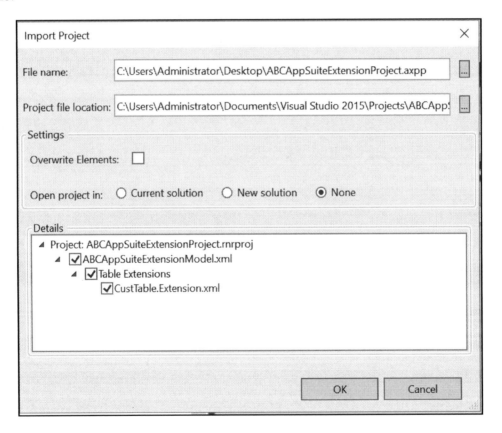

Development planning

The key objective of the development phase is to ensure a scalable, maintainable, and high-performing application. The next thing, after getting the development environment and the version control strategy finalized, is defining development plan and ground rules for the development team. The following are some basic guidelines and rules that need to be established by the solution architect and the project manager before the development.

Be agile

Irrespective of methodology selected for overall implementation, we recommend development phase to be executed in CRP or agile methodology. These methodology uses a series of Sprints to deliver implementation capabilities in incremental steps.

The following are some guidelines for using the CRP or agile methodology:

- For large implementation projects, create an implementation team for each functional area, for example, finance, supply chain, warehouse management, retail, and so on.
- Define Sprint cycle in full week increments. It is common to use 2 to 4 week sprints.
- Create solution backlog containing all customization and configuration activities and define priority based on business value.
- Do daily scrum meeting to discuss what each person in the team is working on and any roadblock if they have.
- Do sprint planning session and selects product backlog item from the backlog to work on the next sprint, plans the activities required to complete.
- Use automated unit testing, functional testing and automated build process
- At the end of each sprint present the solution to stakeholders to review the work and get early feedback.

Establishing the code review process

Effective code review during the development phase helps identify issues earlier, and avoids rework and bug fixes during the later phases of the project. It is important for the project team to define the code review process and the guidelines for the project at the beginning of the development phase. The code review should not be limited to checking the naming conventions, indentation, and other best practices errors or warnings, which can be easily caught by the best practices tools. The process should primarily be focused on achieving the following quality objectives:

- **Solution approach**: The code should be implemented in the correct way. If the existing business logic or processes are modified, they should be modified at the appropriate level. The code should be aligned as per the technical design documents.
- **Extensibility**: The solution should be extensible and appropriate.
- **Easy to read and follow**: The code should be easy to read and follow.
- **Error handling**: The code should be able to handle errors appropriately. It's easier to catch such issues during the code review process as compared to the testing phase.
- **Education for team**: The code review process helps in educating the development team members with review feedback from more senior resources. It needs to be used as a training exercise. Set up a culture where the code reviews and feedback sharing become a learning experience rather than a blame game.

One of the common issues that we have seen in the field is that the code reviews are ignored during the development phase, and are considered towards the end of the development cycle, or close to going live. Most of the time, the code review feedback at such later stages is just not feasible. It is difficult to make changes to the code that is already tested and stable. The best way is to embed the code reviews as part of the development cycle, and the learnings from the previous reviews can be used by the developers in further coding.

Development process

So far we understand the architecture and technical concepts related to development in Dynamics 365 for Finance and Operations, Enterprise edition. Now its time to explore the development process itself. The key objective of the development process is to ensure a scalable, maintainable, and high-performing application.

The following diagram shows the steps that a developer goes through while developing custom solutions:

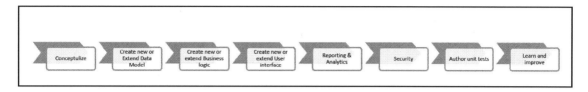

In this section, we will go through these steps and analyse how it relates to developing a custom solution in Finance and Operations, what capabilities system offers and best practices to follow during each steps.

Conceptualization

The first step of the development process is conceptualizing the solution. You must understand the problem that you are trying to solve. At this stage, you need to identify the where and the what—where in the standard flow you need to add your code, and what code can be reused from the standard one. Remember Finance and Operations provides numerous application frameworks and patterns that can be reused when developing any new functionality or extending any existing functionalities. If you do not understand the existing application pattern and frameworks, you may create a functionality that was not necessary, or one that already exists in the application.

While working with the customization requests, there are typically two kinds of scenarios presented to the developers. The first scenario is a standalone functionality, where new forms, tables, and business logic need to be developed and later integrated into the core modules. In the second scenario, the existing processes within the application need to be extended to support the requirement. In both cases, it's important for the developers to understand how the business logic for the core module and functionalities is implemented in the application. Understanding the implementation of the core functionalities and the framework is extremely important for the developers so that they can efficiently utilize, reuse, or extend these functionalities in their custom solution. In any case, customizations need to be added on a temporary basis. The customizations should be easy to isolate and remove when they are not needed anymore, or when the required functionality is added to the product in a later release.

Create or extends data model

Data model is the process of analyzing and defining the data structures as per your solution requirement. Similar to earlier version of AX, in Dynamics 365 for Finance and Operations, Enterprise edition you can create or extend existing data model using extended data types, base enums, tables, views, and data entities. Data entities are new artifacts introduced in operations. Data entities provides abstraction from the physical implementation of database tables and hide the relational model by flattening out the schema. Either you are ISV building vertical solution or customer or partner developing custom solution, create appropriate data entities to cover your custom data model. Simply creating data entities enables the following possibilities by default:

- Ability to use data entities for configuration and data migration
- Use data entities as OData services and recurring Integration
- Office integration
- Analytics and Power BI

If you need to extend the existing data models, many extensibility features are supported on data models elements for example, extending base enums, changing properties, adding relations, creating new field in tables, views, and so on.

Create or extends business logic

The business logic is a part of a program or code that encodes the real-world business scenarios. In Dynamics 365 for Finance and Operations, Enterprise edition, the business logic can be written at multiple levels, such as the form UI, table method, classes, SSRS reports, and so on. The following headings describe the best practices when you customize the business logic in operations:

- **Reusing the code**: As explained earlier, Dynamics 365 for Finance and Operations provides numerous application frameworks. When developing the custom features, you should be able to extend the existing frameworks or reuse the code for your customization. The suggestion is to try not to reinvent the wheel, but investigate and utilize what is already available in the system.

- **Use extensions**: Dynamics 365 for Finance and Operations, Enterprise edition, added several enhancements to improve extensibility of business logic and continue to add features in monthly platform update to improve further. You can extend or customize business logic by defining event handlers and plug-in classes. You can now author event handlers on several pre-defined events on tables, forms, form data sources, form controls, and others. Plug-ins are also a new extensibility concept that enables replacing or extending the business logic of the application.

- **Customizing the code**: When the base layer code needs to be replicated or used in other places, it is always better to extend the existing classes and modify the derived class for the change in behavior, rather than creating completely new classes and then copying the entire code from the base class. Extending the standard business logic by extending the class will make it easier to upgrade the code. If you have created an extension, only the modified code must be restructured. Create classes and methods so that the same piece of code can be reused in multiple places. Avoid creating long methods. They make the code difficult to read, hard to debug, and extremely difficult to upgrade and maintain. Do not keep the commented code if you want to avoid the upgrade and maintenance costs. Keep the older version of the code in version control.

- **Where to add the custom code**: Create the customizations at the appropriate location. Create the code for reuse as much as possible, but create it at the lowest appropriate location. For example, if something is required only in a form, do not put it at the table level.

- **Using .NET projects and assemblies**: Last but not least, several business logic can be implemented in .NET programming languages much easily than in X++. Now in you can easily build extended business logic in C# or any other programming language and use it with operations project as a reference.

Create or extend user interface

The user interface for Microsoft Dynamics 365 for Finance and Operations, Enterprise edition differs significantly from the interface for Microsoft Dynamics AX 2012.

The client in Dynamics 365 for Finance and Operations, Enterprise edition is an HTML web client that runs in major browsers such as Microsoft Edge, Safari and Chrome. The move to a web client has produced the following changes to client forms and controls:

- Form controls are split into logical and physical parts. The physical presentation of forms and controls is now HTML, JavaScript, and CSS that runs within the browser. The X++ logical API and related state run on the server.
- The logical and physical parts are kept in sync through service calls that communicate changes from each side.
- The server tier keeps the form state in memory while the form is open.

While there are lot changed how forms and controls runs, for developers, creating a new user interface or form is similar to Dynamics 365 for Finance and Operations, Enterprise edition. You continue to create forms, menu items, menues to build user interface. The form metadata continues to be used to define controls and application logic.

You create form, add data sources, design form layout by adding controls and add business logic by overriding the methods. Some control types, properties, and override methods have been removed, primarily due incompatibility with the new platform or for performance reasons. For example, ActiveX and ManagedHost controls can no longer be used to add custom controls, because they are incompatible with the HTML platform. Instead, a new extensible control framework has been added that lets you add additional controls.

 Operations documentation site, provides comprehensive technical details related to user interface and can be accessed by the following link: https://docs.microsoft.com/en-us/dynamics365/operations/dev-itpro/user-interface/user-interface-development-home-page

The following section provides some of these user interface development concepts for operations.

Navigation concepts

Several new navigation concepts are introduced in Dynamics 365 for Finance and Operations, Enterprise edition. The following are the key navigation concepts in Dynamics 365 for Finance and Operations, Enterprise edition:

- **Dashboard**: Dashboard is new a concept and is the first page that users see when they access the client. The dashboard contains tiles that show important details from the system.
- **Navigation pane:** The navigation pane provides access to workspaces, main menu elements, recently opened forms, and user-defined favorites.
- **Workspaces**: Workspaces are activity-oriented pages that are designed to increase a user's productivity by providing information that answers the targeted user's most pressing activity-related questions and allows the user to initiate their more frequent tasks.
- **Tiles**: A tile is a rectangular button that behaves like a menu item button. It is used to navigate to or open pages. In addition, tiles can display relevant data, such as counts or **key performance indicators** (**KPIs**).

The following screenshot shows the navigation page and dashboard:

The following screenshot shows workspaces and various tiles used within workspaces in Microsoft Dynamics 365 for Finance and Operations, Enterprise edition user interface:

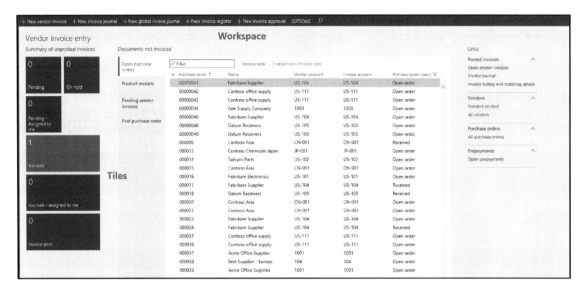

TIP

When you create custom solution, you should follow the conventions for these pages to present a consistent experience for the user.

Form patterns

Form patterns are new concept in Dynamics 365 for Finance and Operations, Enterprise edition. Form patterns provide form structure, based on a particular style (including required and optional controls), and also provide many default control properties. Form patterns are mandatory to specify, when designing a form element. The reason why it is mandatory because form patterns help guarantee that forms have a responsive layout. Finally, patterns also help guarantee better compatibility with upgrades. If your user interface design does not correspond to a given form pattern you can select custom form pattern, however this means that you should test the form for responsive layout on different devices, browsers and form factors.

There are several form patterns and sub patterns to choose from, visit the following web page to know details about form patterns and subpatterns:
`https://docs.microsoft.com/en-us/dynamics365/operations/dev-itpro/user-`
`interface/user-interface-development-home-page.`

User interface extensibility

Many times, you get requirements to add additional fields, validations, or change the layout of existing forms. Most of these requirements can be achieved by metadata extensions. Business logic on the forms can be extended by subscribing to standard events at form, datasource or control level.

For details around the extensibility follow extensibility page:
`https://docs.microsoft.com/en-us/dynamics365/operations/dev-`
`itpro/extensibility/extensibility-home-page`

Control extensibility

In Dynamics 365 for Finance and Operations, Enterprise edition, typically you use existing control to design the user interface but developers using modern tools such as HTML5, CSS3, and jQuery can also define entirely new control to provide specific visualizations of business data.

For more details visit Microsoft documentation on creating new control:
`https://docs.microsoft.com/en-us/dynamics365/operations/dev-itpr`
`o/user-interface/control-extensibility`

Sample code also available on the Github to create extensible controls:
`https://github.com/Microsoft/Dynamics-AX-Extensible-Control-`
`Samples`

Reporting and analytics

Reporting and analytics is major area of customization for organizations implementing ERP solutions. Dynamics 365 for Finance and Operations, Enterprise edition platform provides a collection of reporting solutions to address the various reporting needs of an ERP solution. From development and tooling perspective, the following tools are used for reporting and analytics.

SQL server reporting services

SSRS continues to be the platform for producing advanced operational and business document reports in Dynamics 365 for Finance and Operations, Enterprise edition. The process for developing a report in the current version of Dynamics 365 for Finance and Operations, Enterprise edition is easier than it is in AX 2012, because you can create and validate a reporting solution entirely in Visual Studio. In Finance and Operations, administration of SSRS is also simplified by hosting the services on Microsoft Azure compute service. SSRS framework also provides document printing and distribution services for producing precision documents which are intended for email, printing, archive, and bulk distribution. If you have requirement to change the existing reports, extension of SSRS report is not possible. Best practice is to leave the out-of-the-box reports as is, and create a copy of it to modify as per your requirement as a new custom report. Menu item extensions can be used to redirect the business logic to run custom report instead of standard report.

Power BI

Power BI is used create interactive visualizations and self-service report for Microsoft Dynamics 365 for Finance and Operations, Enterprise edition. Power BI can connect to multiple data sources, both on premises and in the cloud, to create combined reports and dashboards. Developer or power user can use Power BI desktop to author stunning Power BI visualizations and distribute it within the organization. Once these reports are published to `http://powerbi.com/`, they can be pinned to the Dynamics 365 for Finance and Operations, Enterprise edition client to provide interactive visuals that are related to business processes. You can also write X++ extensions for embedded reporting scenarios that require:

- Drill-down navigation into detailed pages in response to user interactions.
- Report filters based on user and session context information, such as company or date range.
- Ability to navigate directly into a specific tab within a Power BI report via menu items.

Several new concepts are introduced in Dynamics 365 for Finance and Operations, Enterprise edition to enable aggregate data for analytics and BI perspective. Developers needs to understand these concepts and constructs to extend or enable analytical data for their custom solutions. The following are some key concepts related to business analytics:

- **Aggregate measurement and dimension**: Aggregate measurement is a model that contains a collection of measures together with their corresponding dimensions. As a developer, you can model these measure and dimensions using Visual Studio.

- **Aggregate data entities**: Aggregate data entities are read-only data entities that are used for reporting purposes. You can create aggregate data entities by directly referencing aggregate measurements and aggregate dimensions. You can consume aggregate data when charts and other client controls simply adding them as a data source.

- **KPIs**: A developer can model a KPI definition in Microsoft Visual Studio. After a KPI is defined, users can customize it at run time.

- **Entity store**: Entity store is database dedicated for reporting and analytical purpose. In Finance and Operations, you can setup batch job to synchronize data entities and aggregate entities to entity store DB. Every Finance and Operations installations comes with a default entity store db. Entity store can be used for writing power BI and any other analytical and reporting needs.

> More details about other reporting and analytics capabilities are described in next chapter. You can also follow the developer documentation page to learn more about reporting options and tools:
> `https://docs.microsoft.com/en-us/dynamics365/operations/dev-itpro/dev-tools/developer-home-page#analytics`

Security

Similar to Dynamics AX 2012, in Microsoft Dynamics 365 for Finance and Operations, Enterprise edition security definition is a development task, and the ground work for the supporting security definition of the custom objects should be done as part of the development process.

In the Dynamics 365 for Finance and Operations, Enterprise edition, role-based security is based on the following key concepts:

- **Security roles**: The security roles that are assigned to a user determine the duties that the user can perform and the parts of the user interface that the user can view. All users must be assigned to at least one security role for accessing Microsoft Dynamics 365 for Finance and Operations, Enterprise edition.

- **Duties**: Duties correspond to the parts of a business process. The administrator assigns duties to security roles. A duty can be assigned to more than one role.

- **Privilege**: In the security model of Microsoft Dynamics 365 for Finance and Operations, Enterprise edition, a privilege specifies the level of access that is required to perform a job, solve a problem, or complete an assignment. Privileges can be assigned directly to roles. However, for easier maintenance, it is recommended that you assign the privileges to duties and duties to roles.

- **Permissions**: Each function in Microsoft Dynamics 365 for Finance and Operations, Enterprise edition, such as a form or a service, is accessed through an entry point. The menu items, web content items, and service operations are collectively referred to as entry points. In the security model for Microsoft Dynamics 365 for Finance and Operations, Enterprise edition, permissions group the securable objects and the access levels that are required to run a function. This includes any tables, fields, forms, or server-side methods that are accessed through the entry point.

- **Policies (Data Security Policy or XDS)**: These are used to restrict the data that a user can see in a form or a report. With this feature, you create a query with restrictions. Then, you create a security policy that can be applied to a security role. For example, if you wanted to limit your accounts-payable clerks from seeing the retail vendors, you could create a query on the vendor group table with a range that limits the retail vendors. You would then create a policy that includes this query and the security role.

Microsoft provide various add-ins in Visual Studio for developers where they can get details about specific objects used in any particular role ,duty, and so on which help them to research any security issues.

Security for custom objects

While the administrators can maintain the security role assignment for individual users, most of the work for creating the security objects needs to be done by the developer. The following security related tasks need to be created by the developers:

- The developers should create the appropriate privileges and add entry points to associate the functionality.
- Custom duties and roles should be created for custom functions, before they can be assigned to the users.
- The security policy nodes should be created by the developers to use the XDS security models in Microsoft Dynamics 365 for Finance and Operations, Enterprise edition.
- You can extend existing roles and duties using metadata extension model.

Roles, duties and privileges can also be created via the client UI and exported and imported to other environments. There are data entities for exporting/importing them.

Auther unit tests

Many improvement are done in Microsoft Dynamics 365 for Finance and Operations, Enterprise edition to help developer or test engineer author automated test cases. Developers can write unit test code using SysTest Framework and catch error early on the development process and improve quality. A custom unit test adapter is available in Visual Studio. This adapter lets test authors use the standard **Test Explorer** window in Visual Studio to schedule X++ tests and analyze test results. Developers can author tests by using **SysTestAdaptor**. You can also generate test code from task recorder recordings. These test cases can then be added to build systems for validations. For details steps on how to author unit test follow the Microsoft documentation link stated which is as follows:

```
https://docs.microsoft.com/en-us/dynamics365/unified-operations/dev-itpro/perf-
test/testing-validation
```

Learn and improve

ERP customization is big investment, bad customization can cause stability issue and business disruption. Solution architect and developer should apply the best practices and do code review to catch any such code and improve upon. In this section, we will learn some best practices to be followed during development cycle

- **Best practice check**: Run your code through the X++ best practices process, evaluate all the best practices errors and warnings, and take the appropriate action.
- **Naming variables and objects**: Use consistent metadata names, variable, method names throughout the application. Follow standard code patterns. Use meaningful and self-explanatory variable names. For example: `SalesTable salesTable` and not `SalesTable table1`.
- **Commenting the code**: Code comments enhance the readability of the code and are very useful for those involved in modifying or maintaining the code. Comments should be used to describe the intent, algorithmic overview, and the logical flow. Add XML documentation for class, class methods, and table methods.
- **Labels and text**: Use labels for all text such as labels, form caption, info-log, and so on and provide code comments.
- **Database**: The following list provides the best practices guidelines related to the database:
    - Avoid using direct SQL calls from the X++ code
    - Direct SQL statements do not respect application security
    - Consider specifying a field list in select statements to increase the performance
    - Use or create appropriate index bases on select statements and queries
    - Use `firstonly` where applicable to increase the performance
    - Use aggregates in the selection criteria instead of letting the code do the aggregation
    - Use table joins instead of `while` loops
    - Use `Update_Recordset`, `insert_recordset`, and `delete_recordset` wherever applicable

- **Exception handling**: Use appropriate exception handling when dealing with transaction processing.

Build and continuous updates

As the development phase of your project starts, you need ability to build your final solution including customization (Creating deployable package) and deploy to test environment for validation and testing. Building solution manually every time, developer change something in the source code is time consuming and is not worth specially when there is simple and easy way to automate. In large implementation projects, when you have multiple team working on multiple features, this build automation becomes more critical. In this section we will go through the automated build and testing process of Dynamics 365 for Finance and Operations, Enterprise edition.

Automated build

Unlike previous version, where source control and automated build process was left optional for vendors and customers, Dynamics 365 for Finance and Operations, Enterprise edition standardize the development application life cycle by providing the build automation out the the box using VSTS. No matter you using cloud VM's or downloaded VM's on premise for development, you can use build machine in the cloud build VM to automate the build and deployment process.

When a Build VM is deployed in Developer topology through LCS, it is pre-configured and ready to start a build. You can change the default configuration at any time from the Visual Studio IDE or the VSTS interface. The build machine is also auto-configured with default settings for build agent, build controller, build process template, and build definition. Tests that are integrated with build definition are executed after the build is successful. Technically, you can turn you downloaded on-premise VM as build machine but you have to do all these setup manually.

The following screenshot shows, build definition and configuration deployed on the VSTS account when you deploy the build machine:

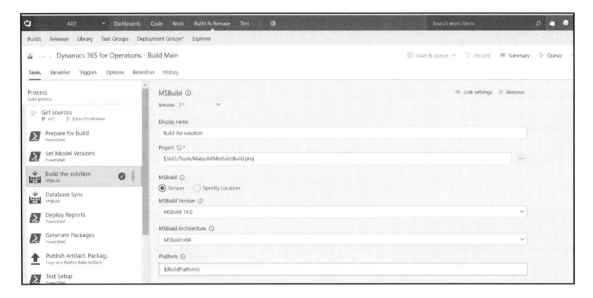

As shown in the screenshot, default build definition contains all the standard steps which you need to build solution including generating deployable packages. You can use this standard build definition to create build right away or customize it as per your specific needs. Automated build definition can also discover and execute all unit test and automated UI tested if you have.

If you are customer and using ISV solution for your implementation project, your ISV will provide their solution model. You can simply add their source code in VSTS source control and build process will pickup those models and build the final deployable package.

One build VM can support multiple build definitions for multiple branches, as long as the version of Dynamics 365 for Finance and Operations, Enterprise edition matches.

Continuous updates

One of the primary focus of Micrsoft with the release of Dynamics 365 for Finance and Operations, Enterprise edition is to enable customers to easily uptake the enhancements and fixes Microsoft has done in the product. Extensions, model-split and hard sealing concept make that vision a reality. Microsoft is releasing, platform binary updates in monthly cadence, this means you can uptake new features and bug fixes, without breaking your code. Once application suite is hard sealed, you will probably get monthly binary releases for application suite as well.

Now you do not have to go through expensive upgrade process to uptake these features. Specially if you in development phase, recommendation is to uptake these platform and application updates as soon as they are released so that you can utilize these new features when you Go Live.

Guidelines and best practices

The following are some common guidelines and recommendations for the development process:

- First and foremost, use extensions model of customization, even if it is possible to overlayer some of the models in the version you are doing your development on. If you have to overlayer because extensions is not possible, overlayer just to add hook and keep your business logic in extension classes.
- If you are part of the FastTrack, work with Microsoft fast track team member assigned to your project to raise any bugs or extension points as soon as possible.
- If customization you are working on is common enough and you think it should have been part of the standard solution. Submit it Microsoft using website `https://ideas.dynamics.com/ideas/dynamics-operations`.
- Build plan to uptake latest binary and X++ releases in your development cycle.
- Use version control and appropriate branching strategy for the development process.
- Implement a code review process to manage check-ins and control what needs to be released to the test environment.

- Implement comments during code checking, providing a brief description of the code, the linking feature, or defects to track the changes appropriately.
- Implement the formal release process (cadence of releases, manager approval, and so on) to avoid destabilizing the test environment due to frequent releases.
- Consider scheduled builds, continuous integration, gated check-in, and so on.
- Use automated unit testing and functional testing.

Summary

In this chapter, we began with understanding the architecture and new development concepts. Developer experience is completely changed, Visual studio is new development environment, X++ has become managed language and fully compile into CIL just like C#. Extensions is new customization, overlayering is still possible but going to be eliminated soon. Development is done now in pre-configured VMs, you can deploy a development environment in the cloud or download a VHD and do development on-premise. Visual studio team services is used for source control and automated build. We learned in detail, about the development process in operations, starting with conceptualizing the solution, understanding the importance of effective data design, implementing business logic, user interface development ,analytics and reporting. We learned the common best practices and recommendations for coding in X++. In the end, we learned how build automation can be used in the development life cycle along with along with the common guidelines and best practices.

In the next chapter, we will learn about testing and training phase of an implementation project. The next chapter covers, various tools, techniques and best practices which you need to know during testing and training phase of your project.

10
Analytics, Business Intelligence, and Reporting

In the previous chapter, you learned about development in Dynamics 365 for Finance and Operations, Enterprise edition using the latest, and recommended, extension approach and the non-recommended over-layering approach.

In this chapter, we will cover analytics in Microsoft Dynamics 365 for Finance and Operations, Enterprise edition and leverage the capabilities of Power BI in informative decision making using the following topics:

- Information insights in Dynamics 365 for Finance and Operations, Enterprise edition
- Platform empowerment for analytics
- Excel
- Power BI
- Cortana intelligence
- Data insights leveraging Azure
- Modern reports and SSRS
- Electronic reporting
- Financial reporting
- Best practices in analytics for Dynamics 365 for Finance and Operations, Enterprise edition

Information insights in Dynamics 365 for Finance and Operations, Enterprise edition

Data is everywhere and turning data into insights is a challenge for BI solutions. A good business intelligence solution should empower users to make informed decisions with the latest and accurate data from your Dynamics 365 solution.

Data needs vary--it may be needed in real time, near real time, or on scheduled intervals--and a BI solution for Dynamics 365 for Finance and Operations, Enterprise edition (AX) should be able to give the choice to the end users. Also, data may be needed to be extracted as it is at the transaction level or at an aggregated level.

Last but not least, the ability to view data in a platform of choice is needed, be it a mobile app, web app, desktop app, or any other device. In addition, the data retrieval should be fast, accurate, and reliable. Decisions in the modern world are taken in split seconds. So, quick data access and conversion to information is a key in the selection of a business analytics platform.

Microsoft cloud solution stands out in this regard, as it can give the best of both worlds. A dedicated BI solution on cloud, tightly coupled with Dynamics 365 and Azure will be able to offer multiple choices to the author, and deploy and consume information.

Let's now learn about the various enablers of analytics, from a platform perspective.

Platform enablement for analytics

Having plentiful choices can sometimes be overwhelming, hence it is the job of a specialist/advisor to use a select tools from a plethora of tools and tailor-fit them to the analytical needs of the customer.

Let's explore key data options available in Dynamics 365 for Finance and Operations, Enterprise edition (AX) for usage in analytics:

- **AX database (AXDB)**: This is the main OLTP transactional database of your Dynamics 365 for Finance and Operations, Enterprise edition in SQL.

- **AX data warehouse (AXDW)**: This is the Entity Store for data warehousing, available out of the box for Dynamics 365 for Finance and Operations, Enterprise edition in SQL. It supports in-memory processing for large-volume scenarios. It uses aggregated data entities and SQL **Non-Clustered Column Store Index (NCCI)**.

- **Read only secondary (ROS)**: This is a read-only database used by the **Application Object Server (AOS)** to redirect certain read-only queries off the transactional database.
- **Bring Your Own Data Warehouse (BYODW)**: This allows enterprises to combine information from Dynamics 365 for Finance and Operations, Enterprise edition (AX) by exporting data to an Azure SQL database and then pulling it to their own data warehouse for decision making.

The following table explores these data options as data sources and their usage scenarios:

Tool	Author	Datasource/Dataset
Excel/Office 365	End user or Power user	Frontend or web app for Dynamics 365 for Finance and Operations, Enterprise edition (AX), PowerPivot, Entity Store (AXDW), and OData
Power BI	Power user	OData, Entity Store (AXDW), and DirectQuery to Azure SQL (AXDB)
Management Reporter	Power user	Frontend or web app for Dynamics 365 for Finance and Operations, Enterprise edition (AX)
Embedded BI	Developer	Entity Store (AXDW)
SSRS reports	Developer	AX Azure SQL (ROS), Visual Studio - application explorer, Azure SQL (AXDB), and Entity Store (AXDW)
Cortana analytics	Developer	Entity Store (AXDW), OData, Azure SQL data warehouse, Azure data lake, and Azure data factory
Azure Machine Learning (AML)	Developer	Cortana analytics, Entity Store (AXDW), OData, Azure SQL data warehouse, Azure data lake, and Azure data factory

With the increasingly rich and populated Microsoft Cloud Technology landscape, new opportunities are presented in ways that organizations can make informed decisions at the speed of light.

Let's explore all the possibilities of using the Microsoft cloud to empower intelligent information insights and action:

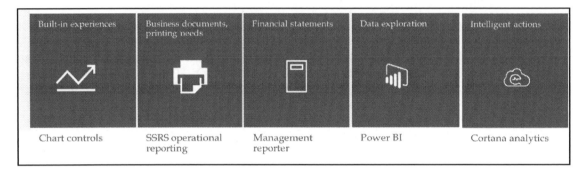

As shown in the previous image, the broad areas of analytics are:

- Built-in experiences using SSRS report, KPIs, charts, and more.
    - KPI's are Key performance indicators and have always been the backbone of all kinds of analytical reporting needs.
- Business documents including modern reports.
- Financial statements for ad hoc and systematic reporting of financials.
- Data exploration using a powerful visualization drive by Power BI.
- Intelligent actions as recommendations or tasks taken by Cortana cognition.

 There are lot of self-service capabilities in Dynamics 365 for Finance and Operations, Enterprise edition, which can be leveraged directly by the end users in their day-to-day operations and periodic reporting.

We foresee modern world business users' need of a BI tool, which can enable the following:

- A cloud analytics service (SaaS-based) that can seamlessly talk to the cloud service of Dynamics 365 for Finance and Operations, Enterprise edition.
- Transactional data in Dynamics 365 for Finance and Operations should be available as a native or first class data source in the BI tool.
- Be able to prepare, distribute, and consume industry templates across organizations and also within an organization

- Security is a long and iterative process, and any BI tool respecting security within Dynamics 365 for Finance and Operations, Enterprise edition is needed
- Information seekers would like to see the dashboards/visuals right within Dynamics 365 for Finance and Operations, Enterprise edition instead of opening several apps
- Mobile is unanimous in the modern world; hence there is a need for a BI solution that can offer interactive visuals over all platforms (Android, iOS, Windows)
- A BI service/solution that offers choice to author reports, be it online or on the desktop
- Ability to fully utilize in-memory processing for faster throughput, leveraging aggregated measures
- Ability to query using simple natural language to represent and filter the data with ease
- Ability to use *R programming*, a data science language for statistical computing, widely used by data scientists

The answer to all the capabilities is available out of the box in Microsoft's cloud BI offering (Power BI).

We all know how much user friendly and great Excel is, and if it could be leveraged seamlessly in your business applications, it will empower the users and increase productivity a lot. Let's explore the various options of using Excel with Dynamics 365 for Finance and Operations, Enterprise edition.

Excel

Excel has always been the ultimate choice to view data easily and quickly, convert it into information using charts and pivots, make informed decisions, and share the decisions with the other stakeholders.

The following screenshot depicts various Excel options available out of box:

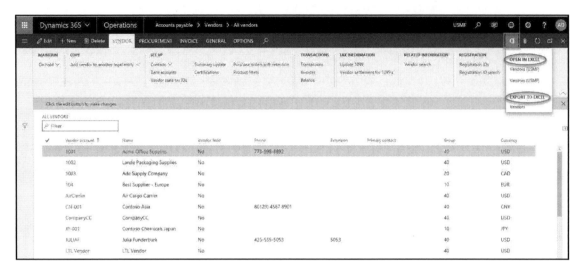

With Dynamics 365 for Finance and Operations, Enterprise edition, you get two choices while working with Excel:

- Export to Excel:
    - One-way export of data seen in the web form to Excel
    - Native functionality in all forms open via a web browser

- Open in Excel:
    - Bidirectional export of data to Excel using the Office Excel app for Dynamics.
    - The Microsoft Dynamics Excel Data Connector App (Excel App) is used to **Create, Read, Update, Delete** (**CRUD**) Dynamics 365 for Finance and Operations, Enterprise edition.
    - The connector uses OData services that are created for any entity left in the default state of `public` (`DataEntity.Public=Yes`)
    - Users can update, create, and publish new data.
    - Open in Excel experience is implemented using document templates and data entities.

In any of the preceding Excel approaches, the user security in Dynamics 365 for Finance and Operations, Enterprise edition is respected, which is a huge process and compliance enabler. However, for the Edit in Excel option, the user needs additional security as assigned to the data entity/entities in focus.

The following screenshot shows the Excel Data Connector app for Dynamics 365 for Finance and Operations, Enterprise edition:

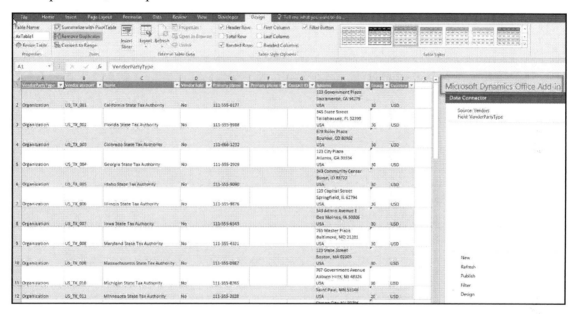

We'll quickly reiterate some of the salient features and benefits of OData and data entities, which you learned in `Chapter 6`, *Configuration and data management*:

- OData are REST-based services exposing all public data entities of Dynamics 365 for Finance and Operations, Enterprise edition (AX) and supporting the **Create**, **Read**, **Update**, **Delete** (**CRUD**) operations to the outside world.
- Data entities are conceptual abstractions and encapsulations (denormalized view) from the physical implementation of database tables representing key data concepts and functionalities

- OData are useful in setting up document templates, which are explained as follows:
  - The Excel Data Connector App is injected into a workbook when a generated Open in Excel experience is triggered or when a workbook is created using **Common | Common | Office integration | Excel workbook designer form**
  - When a template listed in **Common | Common | Office integration | Document templates form** (DocuTemplate) has **ShowInOpenInOfficeMenu** set to yes and has the same root **datasource** (table) as the current form, it will be added as an option in the **Open in Excel** section of the page

Let's now explore an analytical tool that makes life easier for informative decision making in the next section.

Power BI

Power BI is a suite of business analytics tools to analyze data and share insights. It has dashboards that provide a 360-degree view of the business with the most important metrics in one place, updated in real time and available on any device. The Power BI service publishes reports securely to your organization and sets up automatic data refresh so that everyone has the latest information. Interactive visualizations, dashboards, reports, and datasets are some of the tools in the Power BI collection:

Power BI dashboards are interactive dashboards and visualizations that can be created and updated from many different data sources in real time. One can create apps that integrate with a Power BI dashboard in real time, including Dynamics 365, using any programming language that supports REST calls.

One should always check the source type and its synchronization pattern of any data being used in analytical systems and always factor refresh interval of each of the input data.

Power BI has several components that make up a full **Business Intelligence (BI)** suite:

- Power BI (service):
    - Unify all of your organization's data, whether on the cloud or on the premises and publish reports securely to your organization with automatic data refresh for everyone to access the latest information
    - View and share dashboards across your organization, and connect to pre-built reports from experts
- Power BI Desktop:
    - A feature-rich data mashup and report authoring tool available as a Windows desktop app
    - Connect and transform data, create advanced calculations, and build stunning reports in minutes
- Power BI Embedded:
    - Create impactful and interactive data visualizations against your application data in Power BI Desktop, without writing any code
    - Easily explore application data through a free-form drag-and-drop canvas and produce rich data models using formulas and relationships
- Power BI Mobile:
    - A mobile app for all the major mobile platforms to view Power BI dashboards at your fingertips, no matter where you roam or with which device
    - Native apps provide live and interactive mobile access to your important business information
    - Integrate a Power BI tile or a report with an app with an IFrame HTML element
    - You can create a custom mobile app to display real-time Power BI tiles and reports on the user's mobile device

- Power BI gateways (on-premise):
    - Integrating helps you deliver your solutions faster while focusing on your core value
    - A gateway keeps the data fresh by connecting to on-premise data sources, without the need to move the data
    - Large datasets can be queried easily
    - Data transfer between Power BI and the gateway is secured through Azure Service Bus with encrypted credentials
    - Enterprise gateway is an option to serve large groups of users to refresh on-premise data sources
    - For data sources other than Azure connections that use DirectQuery, an Enterprise Gateway must be installed and the data sources must be registered to establish a data connection
- Power BI real-time streaming:
    - Stream data and update dashboards in real time with inbuilt connection with Azure services.
    - It is useful for devices and sources of streaming data, such as factory sensors, social media sources, service usage metrics, and anything else from which time-sensitive data can be collected or transmitted. For example, **Industrial Internet of Things (IIoT)**, wherein systems, solutions, and humans all interact with each other.
- Power BI REST API:
    - It gives the power to use Power BI in any mobile app, web app, or client application
    - Open standards-based REST API to integrate your application or service with Power BI
    - REST API calls are made on behalf of an authenticated user by passing a token in the *Authorization* header
- Power BI publisher for Excel:
    - Save snapshots of important PivotTables, Charts, cell ranges, and more across all of your Excel spreadsheets to a Power BI web dashboard with just a few clicks

Let's now explore some Power BI interactive dashboards and visualizations where users can create personalized dashboards to monitor the organization's most important data.

A dashboard combines on-premise and cloud-born data in a single pane of glass, providing a consolidated view across the organization, regardless of where the data lives. Each metric or insight is displayed on the dashboard as a tile.

We'll now share some readily available capabilities in Power BI:

- Out-of-the-box dashboard from Power BI along with Dynamics 365 for Finance and Operations, Enterprise edition for retail business area. The following visual showcases various metrics in different visualizations, highly interactive and connected with each other:

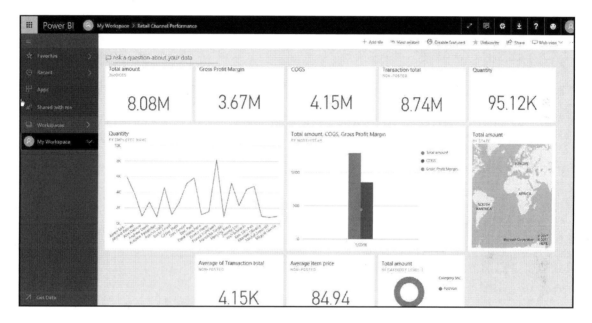

- Power users can also use a simple Q&A in Power BI to come up with interactive visualizations, by enabling the capability as shown below:

- You can ask a query, for example, `sum actual by company by period`, and it will give you the following visual for your business data in focus:

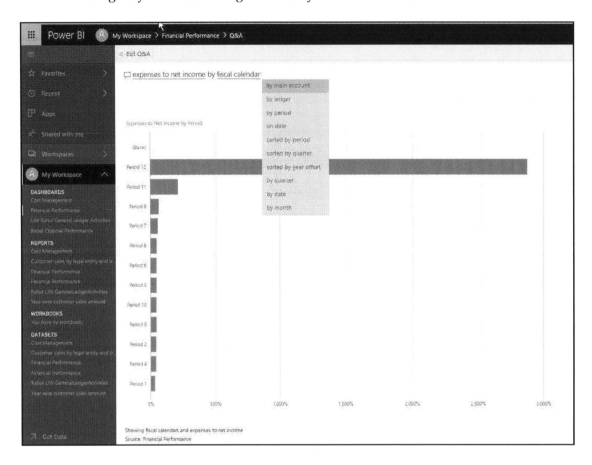

- Another out-of-the-box dashboard available as services from Microsoft Power BI is for the *financials* area, which is shown in the following screenshot with various KPIs and analytics:

- Another out-of-the-box dashboard available as services from Microsoft Power BI is for the *cost management* area, which is shown in the following screenshot with various KPIs and analytics:

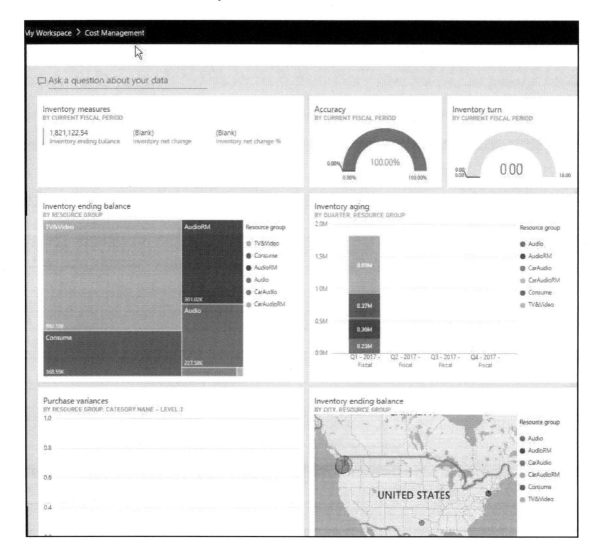

Apart from using the available services, you can quickly create a financial dashboard using OData, comprising a couple of data entities from Dynamics 365 for Finance and Operations, Enterprise edition and built in no time:

Let's now explore the variants and pricing of the aforementioned variants in Power BI.

Power BI choices

At the time of writing this book, Microsoft has three variants of Power BI, namely a free cloud service model, a monthly subscription model per user (PRO), and a model for enterprise scale usage (PREMIUM).

Power BI PREMIUM is capacity based pricing per node per month or it can be purchased based on the number of virtual cores. It is billed monthly on an annual commitment. Organizations can choose to apply their dedicated capacity broadly or allocate it to assigned workspaces based on the number of users, workload needs, and other factors, and scale up or down as the requirements change. This service is expected to be available in the late Q2 of 2017 for all geographies currently supported by the Power BI service.

We would like to share a comparative analysis of the two variants, FREE and PRO, as your quick reference guide in the next subsections.

Pricing

The following is a list of pricing elements in Power BI along with its side-by-side comparison between the free and paid versions:

	Power BI (Free)	Power BI PRO ($9.99/user/month)
Data capacity limit #	1 GB/user	10 GB/user
Create, view, and share your personal dashboards and reports with other Power BI users	Available	Available
Author content with the Power BI Desktop	Available	Available
Explore data with Natural Language 1	Available	Available
Access your dashboards on mobile devices using native apps for iOS, Windows, and Android	Available	Available
Consume curated content packs for services such as Dynamics, Salesforce, and Google Analytics	Available	Available
Import data and reports from Excel, CSV, and Power BI Desktop files	Available	Available
Publish to the web	Available	Available

 A dataset is automatically created in Power BI when you use Get Data to connect to and upload data from a content pack or file, or you can connect to a live data source.

Data refresh

The following is a list of data handling and refresh/update capabilities in Power BI along with its side-by- side comparison between the free and paid version:

	Power BI (Free)	Power BI PRO ($9.99/user/month)
Consume content that is scheduled to refresh	Daily	Hourly*
Consume streaming data in your dashboards and reports	10K rows/hour	1M rows/hour
Consume live data sources with full interactivity	Not Available	Available
Access on-premises data using the Data Connectivity Gateways (Personal and Data Management)	Not Available	Available

* Up to eight times (hours) per day.

When refresh data is triggered, its updating the data in the dataset that is stored in Power BI from the data source. This refresh is a full refresh and not incremental. Any visualizations in your reports or dashboards based on the data are updated automatically.

There are two choices of streaming in live data using:

- Real-time streaming datasets. This feature set allows users to easily stream data into Power BI via the REST APIs, Azure Stream Analytics, and PubNub, and to see that data is instantly light on their dashboards.
- Utilize Live/DirectQuery to get real time information in Power BI from source systems.

Collaboration

The following is a list of collaboration capabilities in Power BI along with side by side comparison between the free and paid versions, which is mostly available for the PRO/paid version:

	Power BI (Free)	Power BI PRO ($9.99/user/month)
Using Office 365 Groups in Power BI	Not Available	Available
Create, publish, and view organizational content packs	Not Available	Available
Manage access control and sharing through Active Directory groups	Not Available	Available
Shared data queries through the data catalog	Not Available	Available
Control data access with row-level security for users and groups	Not Available	Available

For more details, latest information, and recent changes, we recommend that you visit https://powerbi.microsoft.com/en-us/pricing.

Based on the previously mentioned capabilities, we foresee organizations using the Power BI free service to build their sample visualizations to use for learning and training purposes. However, for detailed testing and production purposes, Power BI PRO is the way forward. Its ability to handle large datasets, quick refreshes, direct queries, and collaboration capabilities makes it a standout for real-world usage. Also, you can test out Power BI by obtaining a 60-day trial.

We suggest that every implementation of Dynamics 365 for Finance and Operations, Enterprise edition (AX) always leverages as much as possible from Power BI, as it enables *everyone* to collect, analyze, visualize, and publish data. Also, we recommend that you leverage the Power BI DirectQuery capabilities and author reports that execute directly on the Entity Store database.

Cortana Intelligence Suite

Cortana Intelligence Suite (CIS) is a collection of tools and services offered by Microsoft, which transforms data into intelligent actions. Cortana also offers predictive capabilities with the help of state-of-the-art machine learning algorithms.

While Power BI is a great tool, the demand for intelligent insights never reduces to seek actions and predictions. With Azure, one can leverage several options in advanced analytics by coalescing Azure services as shown below:

- **Cortana Intelligence**: This is an actionable and intelligence-driven suite based on advanced analytics.
- **Azure HDInsight**: This is a cloud Spark and Hadoop service for big data processing.
- **Azure Machine Learning**: This is used for predictive analytics.
- **Azure Data Factory**: This composes and orchestrates data services at scale.

The following image shows the usage of advanced Azure analytics capabilities along with Power BI:

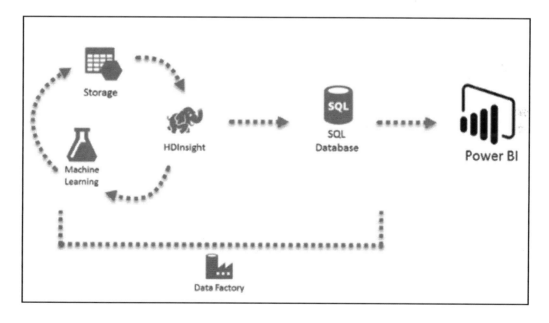

Cortana works on data in Azure stores, such as Azure DB, Azure DW, and Azure Data Lake, as well as on-premise data sources such as SQL Server.

With Entity store, customers can effectively leverage Cortana and complement with data from devices as well as other systems (for example, CRM), as needed.

The following are some of the key elements of CIS:

- Azure Machine Learning
- Azure HDInsight
- Azure Stream Analytics
- Azure Data Lake
- Azure SQL Data Warehouse
- Azure Data Catalog
- Azure Data Factory
- Azure Event Hub
- Power BI
- Cortana
- Cognitive Services
- Bot Framework

The following image shows the data source (left), the information source (middle), and the decision making result (right). Here, historical information about sales is pulled from Dynamics 365 for Finance and Operations, Enterprise edition using Entity Store into Cortana intelligence, where cognitive services work along with data factory, processing huge amounts of data under predetermined algorithms and suggesting recommendations to the POS user screen:

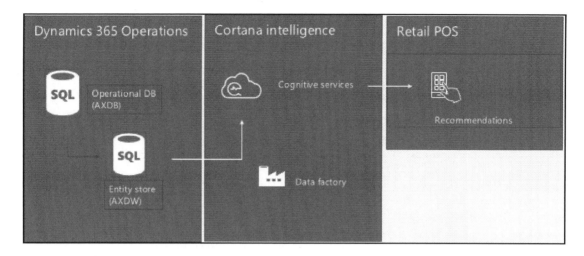

A use case scenario example for CIS is a POS (Point of Sale) user asking you to check out another item, which is mostly sold along with one of the items in your shopping cart.

The Cortana intelligence suite is a great value-add in Dynamics 365 and we strongly recommend that you include it in your analytics journey.

Data insights leveraging Azure

Machine learning is a technique of data science that helps apps, devices, and computers become smarter by learning from existing data in order to forecast future behaviors, outcomes, and trends.

Azure Machine Learning (**AML**) is a cloud predictive analytics service, which makes it easy to create and deploy predictive models as analytics solutions. AML uses algorithms to analyze historical/current data to identify patterns and to forecast future events.

Currently, there are predictive/cognitive capabilities available out of box in Dynamics 365 for Finance and Operations, Enterprise edition (AX), which use a combination of the Retail module, AML, and Cortana. In order to enable these capabilities, one can follow these steps:

1. One has to turn on **Enable Recommendations** in **Machine learning | Retail parameters**.
2. With this turned on, while making **Point of Sale** (**POS**) transactions, the user punching in sales will get recommendations of similar products bought together.

3. This recommendation setting on POS needs to be configured in a screen layout designer by using recommendation control in the **Transactions** screen.

AML benefits the forecasting process a lot with industry-proven algorithms that aid human decisions.

Microsoft has a lot of tools, cloud services, and APIs on Azure, which can be used along with Dynamics 365 for highly complex needs in analytics.

Some of the key tools are as follows:

- Azure Data Factory:

    - Cloud service for processing structured and unstructured data from almost any source
    - You can understand it in terms similar to SSIS for managing all your data on the premises and cloud

- Azure Data Lake:

    - Azure Storage with almost infinite space to handle streaming data (low latency, high volume, and short updates)

    - It is geo-distributed, is data-locality aware, and it allows individual files to be sized at petabyte scale

    - An enterprise-wide repository of every type of data collected in a single place

- Azure SQL data warehouse:
    - It is a cloud-based, scale-out database capable of processing massive volumes of data, both relational and non-relational

    - Leverages the **Massively Parallel Processing** (**MPP**) architecture for all kinds of enterprise workload

- HDInsight:

    - It's a fully managed Hadoop cluster service that supports a wide range of analytic engines, including Spark, Storm, and HBase

    - It uses the **Hortonworks Data Platform (HDP)** distribution to manage, analyze, and report big data, providing a highly available and reliable environment for running Hadoop components

- Cognitive services:

    - Microsoft Cognitive Services APIs are a suite of several general-purpose machine learning APIs that are made available in Microsoft Azure and can be used for any number of applications

    - These APIs simplify the whole process by abstracting away the complex machine learning models and the operationalization aspects so that the users can focus on real business problems

We all have a journey to make and so does the decision making process, which starts with data, then information, and then actions:

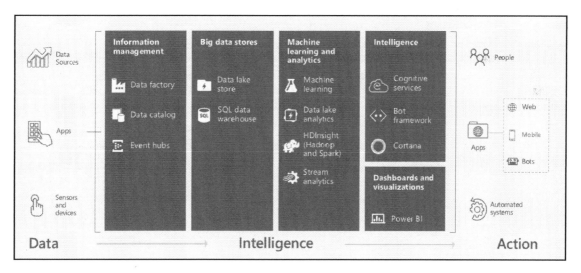

The preceding image shows how data is converted into intelligence and action which is at the core principle in Cortana Intelligence Suite and Azure tools using AML. At the heart of any decision making process is the ability to see data representation to intelligence and also be able to act on the recommendations.

Together these tools/services helps in delivering advanced analytics with actionable intelligence and predictive/cognitive capabilities.

Modern reports and SSRS

The need for reporting in predefined formats, taking document printouts and transactional details is never expected to go out of demand.

Dynamics 365 for Finance and Operations, Enterprise edition utilizes **SQL Server Reporting Services** (**SSRS**)-hosted Azure compute service. This service runs in the Azure compute emulator together with the application server. Therefore, there are no SSRS service administration prerequisites.

The process of running a report is as simple as clicking a link, providing parameters and filters, and running it. The reports could also be scheduled to run at periodic intervals. One can also decide the format of the report output.

One can also install/configure the modern design template, which can be downloaded from LCS and installed in the environment. This is a step forward in allowing configuration-driven branding of SSRS reports, useful when information needs to be shared with external parties.

The following screenshot shows a sample modern design report:

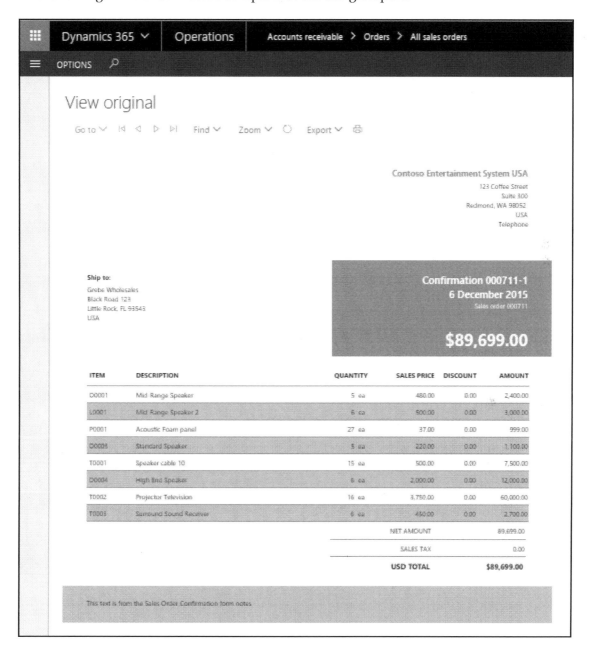

For more details on modern report design, visit `https://ax.help.dynamics.com/en/wiki/installing-the-modern-report-design-templates`

Reports are deployed in a package to cloud and their development process is quite easy. The entire process of developing a report in the current version of Dynamics 365 for Finance and Operations, Enterprise edition can be done in Visual Studio 2015.

When combined with ER, one can use an electronic medium to transmit these reports/documents. There is a dedicated workspace to configure several ER needs, supporting a wide variety of formats.

Electronic reporting

Electronic reporting (ER) is a tool to configure electronic document formats in accordance with the legal requirements of various countries/regions. This engine supports statutory/country-specific electronic documents, enabling you to manage these formats during their lifecycle.

ER has the following salient features:

- It is a good tool for producing TEXT, XML, and OPENXML worksheet formats
- It is designed for business users familiar with Excel-based formulas
- It easily adheres to changes in regulatory requirements
- Versioning is available to manage definition lifecycle

Other applications of electronic reporting include:

- Financial auditing
- Tax reporting/GST/VAT
- Electronic invoicing
- EDI (Electronic data interchange)

Let's now take a brief look at the steps of configuring ER:

1. Sign in to Dynamics 365 for Finance and Operations, Enterprise edition and go to the **Electronic reporting** workspace:

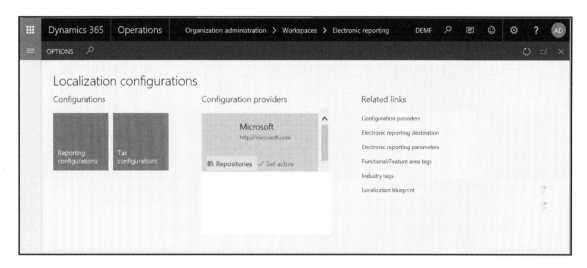

2. On the Microsoft tile, click **Repositories**:

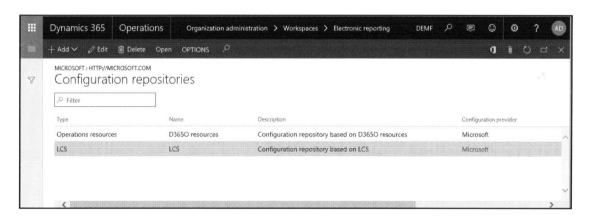

3. Go to **Configuration repository** to pick and choose statutory requirement-specific templates for importing to your environment:

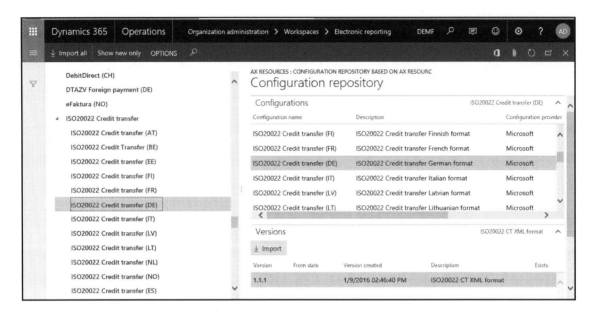

4. From the ER workspace, click on the **Configurations** tile:

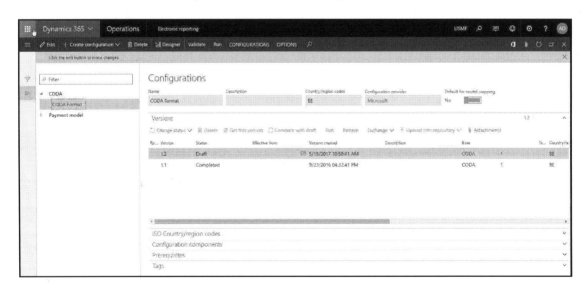

5. Click on **designer** from the ribbon:

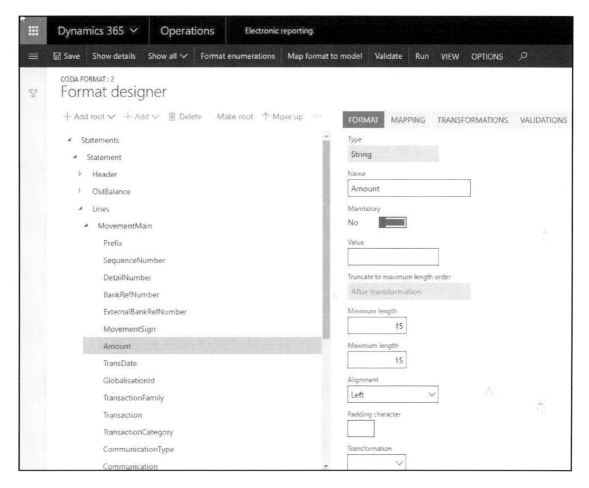

The following is a summarized list of available ER configurations that are available in Microsoft Dynamics 365 for Finance and Operations, Enterprise edition:

- Government Compliance: XBRL reporting and others
- Tax Authorities: Tax reporting, revenue/turnover, and more
- Banks: Payments, receipts, trade reporting, and more
- Customers: Electronic invoicing, EDI 810, EDI 857, and more

- Vendors: Electronic invoicing, payments, EDI 850, EDI 861, and more
- Localization through **Global Tax Engine** (**GTE**): Delivered via a taxable document model, which is a key input to the tax engine and leverages various taxable document types and tax document models

 For latest information on the various offerings of ER, we recommend you to visit https://docs.microsoft.com/en-us/dynamics365/operations/ dev-itpro/analytics/general-electronic-reporting. This capability is sometimes referred to as ER as well as **Global Electronic reporting** (**GER**), which are one and the same.

Mobile platform

Microsoft Dynamics 365 for Finance and Operations, Enterprise edition includes support for mobile apps, allowing reusability of business logic and modeling the app right from the core product. The mobile app is being made available for most popular mobile operating systems.

This mobile platform enables rich offline and mobile interactions, and an easy-to-use designer experience. The mobile platform also makes it easy to change forms and mobile app definitions to include customizations that are made to the larger product.

Developing these apps is not quite tough; developers can create simplified forms in Microsoft Visual Studio and then design mobile pages that expose this functionality. The mobile app platform doesn't assume connectivity to Dynamics 365 for Finance and Operations, Enterprise edition. Activities such as navigation, data view, and data entry don't require server connectivity after data has been cached.

The mobile platform communicates with **Application Object Server** (**AOS**) to get the metadata (pages and fields on the mobile page) and to get the data for the fields on these pages.

Navigation in the mobile app consists of four simple concepts, namely, dashboard, workspaces, pages, and actions, as shown in the following image:

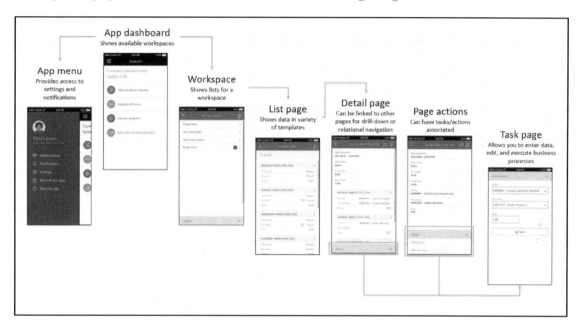

We foresee the mobile platform for Microsoft Dynamics 365 for Finance and Operations, Enterprise edition not only being used for actions and capturing data but also benefiting quick inquiries in the platform and device of your choice.

After you log in to the app, no workspaces are visible. To view workspaces on your mobile app, you must first publish the desired workspaces to the Dynamics 365 for Finance and Operations, Enterprise edition app. You need the system admin's permission to publish the workspace.

Here are the steps to publish out-of-the-box mobile workspaces to make them available in your smartphones:

1. Start Dynamics 365 for Finance and Operations, Enterprise edition.
2. Go to **System administration | Setup | System parameters**.
3. Select **Manage mobile workspaces**:

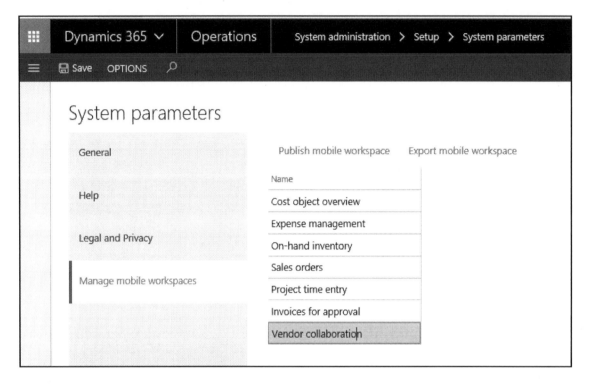

4. Select the workspaces to publish to the mobile platform.
5. Select Publish workspace.
6. In your smartphone, download the Microsoft Dynamics 365 for Finance and Operations, Enterprise edition app. The following screenshot shows the app on Google Play Store (`https://play.google.com/store/apps/details?id=com.microsoft.dynamics365.operations.mobilehl=en`):

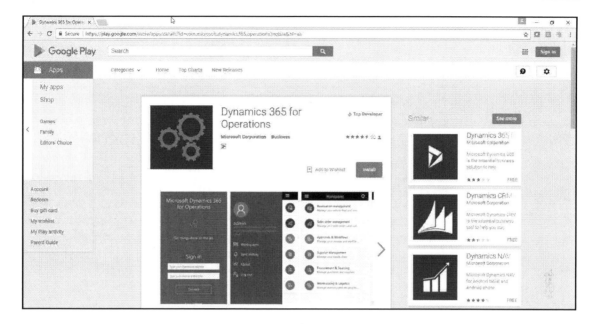

7. Sign in to the mobile app by specifying the URL for Dynamics 365 for Finance and Operations, Enterprise edition (AX) and a valid user having access to it.

The following screenshot shows the workspace area in a typical smartphone:

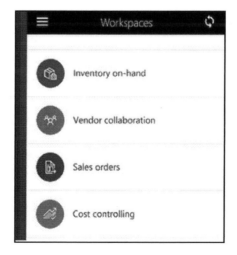

For more details, we recommend that you visit `https://docs.microsoft.com/en-us/dynamics365/unified-operations/dev-itpro/mobile-apps/platform/mobile-platform-home-page`.

Speaking of mobile, it cannot be connected to the cloud or internet all the time and hence the need for offline capabilities. Let's explore various offline capabilities and their synchronization with Dynamics 365 for Finance and Operations, Enterprise edition.

Offline and mobile apps

Dynamics 365 for Finance and Operations, Enterprise edition (AX) mobile app creates user sessions (and opens forms) only in short bursts while the app is being synced with the server (via data read for pages or via data write/update for actions). This is in contrast to the web client, which is highly connected to the Dynamics 365 for Finance and Operations, Enterprise edition server and maintains an open user session that has open forms on the server.

If there are no actions to sync with the server, and if the local data cache is up to date, the mobile app won't communicate with the Dynamics 365 for Finance and Operations, Enterprise edition server as the user navigates around the app (unless the user triggers an explicit pull-to-refresh).

When using the mobile app, the form logic runs only when the action is being synced with the Dynamics 365 for Finance and Operations, Enterprise edition server.

The following list describes the only times when you should expect form logic to run. Dynamics 365 for Finance and Operations, Enterprise edition form logic runs right before a page is opened on the mobile app for the first time:

- When a user first opens a page, the mobile app reaches out to Dynamics 365 for Finance and Operations, Enterprise edition and opens the associated forms. During this process, logic such as form init and data source init is all run in the usual manner.
- The mobile app framework reads the required data directly from the controls on the forms and sends the data back to the mobile app.

- The mobile app caches the data and shows it in a page on the mobile app.
- Future attempts to open the page will load the cached data. These attempts won't run the form logic again, unless the user explicitly refreshes the page or the cache expires. Currently, the default value for cache expiration is set at 30 minutes.
- Form logic is executed when any action is submitted to the server from the mobile app.
- When a user opens an action and fills in the data in that action, no form logic is run. A user can complete an action while he or she is either offline or online. The system behaves the same way in both the cases.
- After the user clicks **Done/Save** on the action, the mobile app queues a data synchronization operation. This operation will be synced with the server when the mobile app is connected to the internet.
- When an internet connection is detected (which can happen immediately after the action is completed) the mobile app sends the data synchronization operation to the Dynamics 365 for Finance and Operations, Enterprise edition server for processing.

To minimize synchronization times, it's best not to include any UI logic on the form.

Financial reporting / management reporter

Financial reports provide insights into an organization's financial state at any point of time or at the end of the defined financial periods.

This was earlier known as management reporter, which in turn originated from a tool called **FRx**. You will find a lot of useful information on the web upon searching either of the keywords.

Let's now look at the prerequisites to create and generate financial reports for a legal entity:

- Fiscal calendar
- Ledger
- Chart of accounts
- Currency

The financial reporting menu is available in a lot of places in Dynamics 365 for Finance and Operations, Enterprise edition, and users can gain access to it with appropriate privileges and duties assigned to their security roles.

In order to jumpstart financial reporting, Microsoft provides 22 default financial reports, which can be modified to suit the business needs of any customer. These modifications are made in a report designer client:

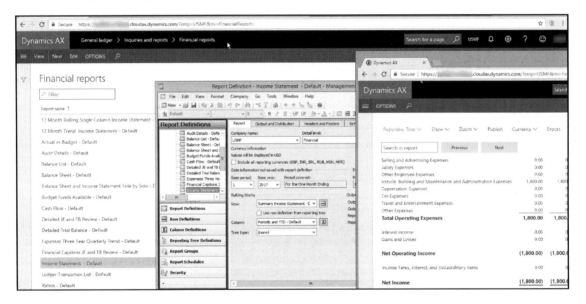

The preceding screenshot is an all-in-one visual showing the **Financial reports** listing on the left, **Report Definition** in the middle, and the actual report output on the right:

- Row definition:
  - A row definition defines the descriptive lines, such as salaries or sales, on a report. It also lists the segment values or dimensions that contain the values for each line item, and it includes row formatting and calculations:

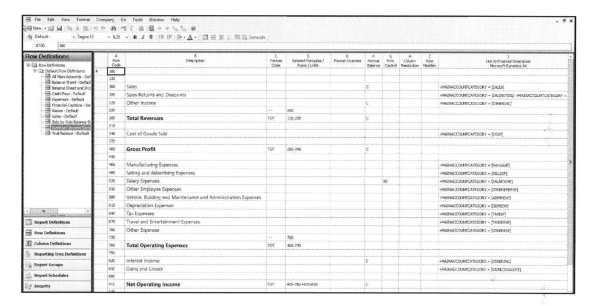

As shown in the preceding screenshot, in the the row definition, you can create row codes and description, and suggest the link to Dynamics 365 for Finance and Operations, Enterprise edition in the outer-most column, on the right. This is similar to creating rows in Excel.

- Column definition:
  - A column definition defines the period of extracting data from the financial dimensions. It also includes column formatting and calculations:

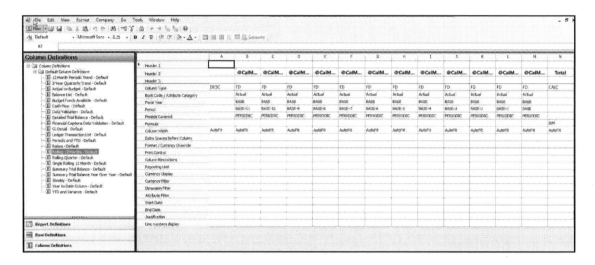

As shown in the preceding screenshot, in column definition, you can create a number of columns as in Excel and suggest the type and date criteria along with other attributes.

- Reporting tree definition:
  - A reporting tree definition resembles an organizational chart. It contains individual reporting units that represent each box in the chart. The units can be either individual departments from the financial data or higher-level units that summarize the data from other reporting units.

- There are two ways of creating the reporting tree:
    1. Directly create one in Report Designer.
    2. Leverage a read-only organization hierarchy from Dynamics 356 for Operations (AX):

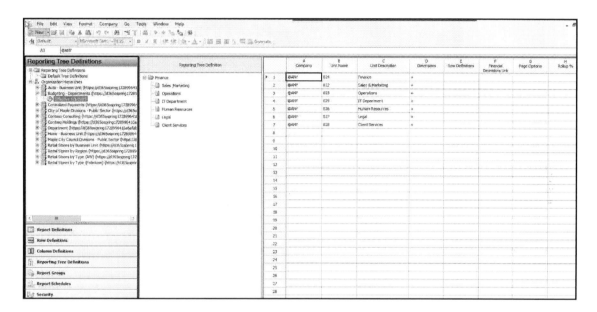

The preceding screenshot shows a reporting tree, wherein you can create a hierarchical listing of companies and units to use them for slicing and dicing your financial information.

- Report definition:
    - A report definition uses a row definition, a column definition, and an optional reporting tree definition to build a report. It also provides additional options and settings to customize a report:

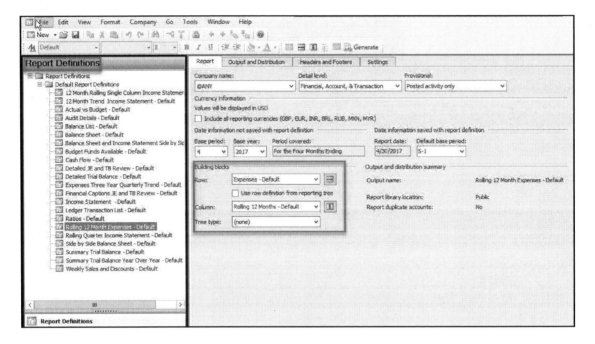

As shown in the preceding screenshot, the report definition is the binder of all the building blocks, bringing together the row definition, column definition, reporting tree, and various run attributes of your financial information.

We recommend that every initiative involving financial reporting in Microsoft Dynamics 365 for Finance and Operations, Enterprise edition should leverage the financial reports application available out of box.

These financial reports are closely and natively integrated with Microsoft Dynamics 365 for Finance and Operations - Enterprise edition. This tool is highly flexible, supporting interactive viewing and drill down capabilities and also extremely user friendly.

Best practices in analytics and information insights

Based on our experience, we would like to share the following best practices in this area:

- Analytics is a journey and not a destination. One has to keep on optimizing and evolving from the existing methods of seeking, consuming, and acting upon data.
- It's going to be rare to find just one solution to all the information needs; hence, one must choose from the best-of-breed choices.
- Leverage financial reporting or management reporting for all kinds of financial insights for an enterprise.
- Leverage Excel for all one-time and quick end user-based reporting.
- Leverage Power BI for all interactive visualizations and dash boarding.
- Leverage SSRS for the printing of all documents and for day-to-day operational needs.
- Leverage mobile apps for all actionable needs across devices and platforms in a mobile-natural way.
- Leverage Cortana analytics and Azure Machine Learning for all information actions and predictions using algorithms.

The world of analytics is fascinating, with a number of choices and reasons to get confused. Hence, due diligence in the right selection of the platform, tool, and fitment is crucial to getting the information needed for informed decision making.

Summary

In this chapter, we explored various information insights available out of the box in Dynamics 365 for Finance and Operations, Enterprise edition and the role played by the Microsoft analytics platform. With the empowerment of Excel, Power BI, Cortana intelligence, Azure, and other tools, it becomes super easy to make informed decisions.

With additional capabilities delivered from modern reports, ER, and financial reporting or management reporting, it becomes a full-suite analytics tool to make information available on time and in the medium of your choice.

Analytics, as a subject, evolves much faster than any other area; hence, we recommend that you always leverage tools and services offered by Microsoft rather than building them, as it increases the agility and accuracy.

In the next chapter, we will focus on end user-related activities, spanning testing and training.

11
Testing and Training

Quality, budget, and scope are the fundamental constraints on every ERP project. Most of the time, when the scope is increased and the budget stays the same, the quality gets compromised on. One of the biggest mistakes that people end up making is that they reduce the testing and training budget when there is budget pressure.

In many post-release, postmortem meetings, you would hear, *If I was to do this again, I would spend a hundred thousand dollars more on testing.* You have the opportunity to do it right and not regret it later.

In this chapter, we will cover the following for testing:

- Importance of testing
- Types of testing
- Automated testing strategies
- Test planning guidelines and recommendations

Similar to testing, training is another key aspect for the successful implementation of an ERP system. Ensuring that the users are comfortable with the new platform and understanding the new business processes and their role in the organization is essential for attaining a good working platform. Many a times in ERP implementation, users are not only dealing with system change, but also with process change. Training needs to be delivered to support this cultural shift.

The process of unlearning the old practices and learning new ways of doing things may take several iterations. Hence, training and an evaluation of adopting learnings of that training are very essential. We will discuss the following important aspects of training in this chapter:

- Importance of training
- Training and help system in Finance and Operations
- Planning and executing training

While discussing this topic of testing and training, our focus will *not* be on generic areas; we will talk about them at a higher level and focus on the Dynamics 365 for Finance and Operations, Enterprise edition-specific elements.

Importance of testing

Testing is the process of validating the system and processes to meet the business requirements. It includes testing the custom as well as the standard features, along with the migrated data, integrations, reports, and security aspects of the solution. It is an area that is most often underestimated and, as a result, hampers the success of your project.

A very common misconception is that testing starts after the development phase is over. The primary goal of testing is to provide feedback on the product as soon as possible. Identifying any issues in the requirements phase prevents them from becoming a part of the design. Similarly, identifying any issues in the design phase prevents them from being coded. The cost of fixing a defect depends on the phase where it has been detected; the cost of fixing a defect in the early phases of **SDLC (Software Development Life Cycle)** is much lower than in the later phases. The farther you go with the backlog of testing/validation; the more debt you carry on the project. Mostly, such a debt gets unmanageable, and it becomes difficult to predict/commit to the schedule.

Majority of the ERP implementation projects fail because of the improper test planning and testing. To understand the importance of ERP testing, it is important to understand the different types of testing typically performed in ERP implementation projects.

Types of testing

ERP implementation projects require different types of testing during the testing phase of the project. Each type represents a different objective, scope, and depth of testing.

The following diagram highlights the different types of testing in a typical implementation project:

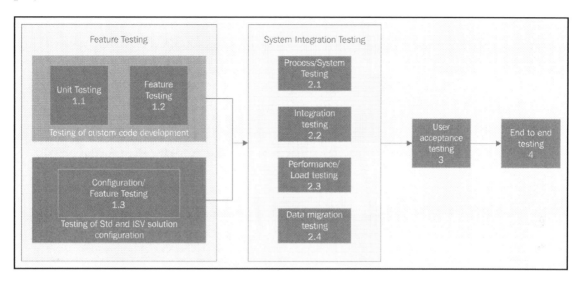

As shown in the diagram, we can categorize testing into four main categories: feature testing, system integration testing, user acceptance testing, and end-to-end or cut over testing. The following subheadings describe these testing types in detail.

Feature testing

Feature testing, also known as function testing, is standalone testing of individual features performed by the QA resources or business analysts. Primarily, there are two sets of features to test here: custom features being developed by the project development team to fill the gaps, and standard or ISV solution features being configured by the business analyst.

Testing of custom developed features

Testing of custom features by the project team involves unit testing, which is standalone testing of code artifacts, and is usually performed by the developers to ensure that individual code elements are working as expected. In software engineering terms, unit testing typically refers to automated testing. It provides many benefits that include finding bugs earlier, providing a safety net of tests for changes that are made later, and improving design. Over the long term, unit testing improves customer satisfaction and developer productivity.

Along with the unit testing, individual custom features need to be configured and tested to ensure that these custom features work according to requirements.

Testing of standard and ISV solution features

While the development team is doing custom feature development, business analysts are usually busy working on collecting configuration and master data and setting up the standard solution as per the requirements. The second part of feature testing is about testing the standard and ISV product features. This includes configuration such as parameters, reference data, workflows, security, and master data, and then testing transactions such as sales orders, purchase orders, production orders, and journal entries.

System integration testing

After feature testing, the next part is to test various subprocesses and processes together. By this time, the core configuration is already done, some level of data migration is also done, key custom features are developed, and various systems and solutions are integrated. There are various parts of system integration testing, and they usually get tested in parallel. The following are the testing categories that typically falls under system integration testing.

Process/system testing

Process or system testing involves testing subprocesses and processes. In this phase, typically all major processes are tested with system configuration and master data. Depending on the implementation scope and requirements, the testing team will test processes such as record to report, order to cash, procure to pay, and plan to produce. The objective of this testing cycle is to identify the correct configuration of parameters, missing master or reference data and any additional bugs or potential gaps.

For a simple business process example, consider the testing of the *Order-to-Cash* process beginning with a single order transacted through its entire cycle. The process starts with creating a sales order, picking and shipping the product, and then invoicing the order. Along the way, the system updates the inventory and accounting. Finally, payment is collected from the customer, the payments are applied, and customer balance is updated within the accounts receivable module.

As you can see, the complete cycle for a major business process may include many steps and touch various modules. During this testing, you will discover missing configurations and setups as well as code issues.

Data migration testing

Either you are replacing the old legacy system or upgrading from the previous version, the business will need legacy data migrated to the new system. Data migration testing is basically testing the data integrity and data quality. No matter how you decided to migrate the data, the testing team needs to analyze the migrated data and perform validation and transactions at the end of the data migration to ensure that the data migrated is complete and accurate to do future transactions. For example, if open sales orders are migrated from the legacy system, you need to ensure that you are able to ship and invoice these orders and ultimately, collect cash.

You also need to ensure that numbers, such as order count, account balance, and inventory levels, match between the legacy system and new system to make migration complete and accurate. A solid data migration strategy should also define the parameters for the success of data migration testing.

Integration testing

Testing the integrations with other systems that have been developed is just as important as the features and functional testing of the product itself. Integration testing is performed across applications to verify the seamless flow of information. All individual applications must be tested independently and made ready for integration testing. You will need an integrated environment across applications to perform this testing. For example, Finance and Operations requires integration with the CRM system; in this testing process, you will probably create customers in the CRM system and expect them to flow to Finance and Operations.

Next, you will probably test creating products and inventory in Finance and Operations and ensure that it flows back into the CRM system so that sales people can sell it to customers. Finally, you will create quotes in the CRM system and expect to get sales order created, shipped, invoiced, and payment collected in Dynamics 365 for Finance and Operations, Enterprise edition.

Performance/load testing

Performance testing or load testing is a process of identifying performance issues and solving them. It is important to conduct performance and load testing and tuning before going live to eliminate the issues that can impact the business negatively. It does not matter whether you have high volumes or not; you still need performance testing. At this stage of the project, the development of custom features is complete and functional testing is in progress. This is the time to validate the overall performance of your Finance and Operations system. The primary goal is to ensure that the solution will accept peak load without any major issues.

The key objective of this exercise is to establish a baseline for the key business scenarios, and to test and execute performance tuning and optimization to achieve the following:

- Creating a baseline of your core business scenarios
- Simulating users and transactions in terms of concurrency and volume, and determining the load that the system can handle
- Executing performance tuning and optimization

At the end, we have to validate all the preceding considerations and ensure that the system is ready for production. It is imperative to try to accurately identify the volume of transactions as they relate to the new system. Use the legacy system as a base starting point, and estimate the transactions in the new system by taking into consideration how transactions are generated on the new platform.

User acceptance testing

User acceptance testing (UAT) usually starts when the system integration testing is almost complete and minimal viable product is ready. The goal of UAT is to engage the users across business groups using the new system to run the business. This is an opportunity to provide them with hands-on experience for learning the new system as well. The more testing that the users perform, the more comfortable they will be with using the new system. Unlike other types of testing that are done by experienced application consultants and testing teams, UAT is done by actual business users and hence planning and execution of the UAT is very critical. The *Guidelines and recommendations* section of this chapter covers UAT planning and execution in detail.

End-to-end testing

In addition to UAT, you will need another round of testing to verify the end-to-end execution of a business process; this is called end-to-end testing. The key difference between UAT and End-to-end testing is that UAT is more focused on validating individual business processes, while end-to-end is focused on validating all of them together once each of them has been stabilized and tested.

Automated testing strategies

ERP systems are complex, and it is not always easy to test these systems. To conduct robust testing, you need the testing staff to not only know the system but also know the business process. Manual ERP testing consumes a lot of implementation time and budget. Test automation helps improve the quality of the product and reduces cost and time.

The following are the advantages of ERP test automation:

- The first and foremost advantage of automated testing tool is reduced testing time, and as you all know, *time is money*
- Automation removes the human error from the equation, which means more reliability and accuracy of test results
- Automated testing makes it easier to uptake future updates, bug fixes, and enhancements, as you can test and be confident that your core business processes will not break with the new enhancements in the product

Going through the advantages, you will say that automation is best; why do you even need manual testing? But it is not as rosy as it sounds. Testing automation, especially for an ERP system, is not an easy task. It is complex and requires experienced staff, time, and hence, money to write automation script. You will also need continuous maintenance of test scripts as and when changes are introduced to the features.

Automation testing has clear benefits, but it is important to find the right balance as to what processes or features you should automate, and what is not important. It is also important what framework your ERP system has for test automation and how easy it is to write these automation scripts.

Test automation features in Finance and Operations

Compared to the earlier version of Dynamics AX, Dynamics 365 for Finance and Operations, Enterprise edition has taken a major leap in providing several automated test capabilities as part of the product.

The following diagram shows two concepts related to automation test: various test cycles, targets, and the corresponding tools available in Finance and Operations for automation; and the reduction of automation test counts as you move up a pyramid:

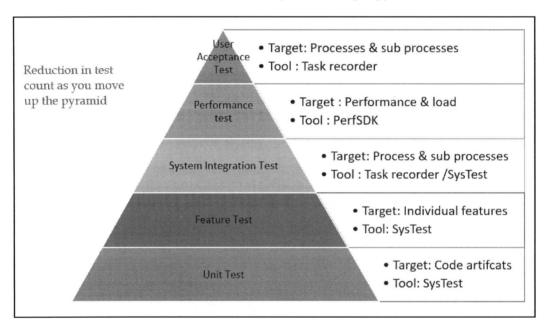

As illustrated, different testing phases (left-hand side) have different targets and tools for automation testing (right-hand side). Overall, the following are the key tools/concepts:

- SysTest framework
- Task recorder based testing
- PerfSDK

Let's understand these tools and concepts in detail as we go further.

SysTest framework

SysTest framework is Unit Test framework in Dynamics 365 for Finance and Operations, Enterprise edition. SysTest framework was available in the earlier version as well, and it provides developers the ability to write unit test code for the business logic. The following improvements have been made to SysTest framework in Finance and Operations:

- Integration with the Visual Studio test explorer to discover, schedule, execute test cases, and analyze test results
- Automatic data rollback for SysTest tests, and use of SQL savepoint transaction
- Capturing exceptions properly (for asserts), regardless of the transaction scope
- Ability to integrate automated test with version control and build process
- Simplified scope of testing when using extension programming model, as your business logic is separated
- Ability to discover the existing tests for an object in your project; discovery uses cross-reference data and displays result in test explorer

The automated testing integration with build is of utmost importance, especially in large enterprise engagements.

The next screenshot shows a sample test class with two test methods related to business logic in Finance and Operations:

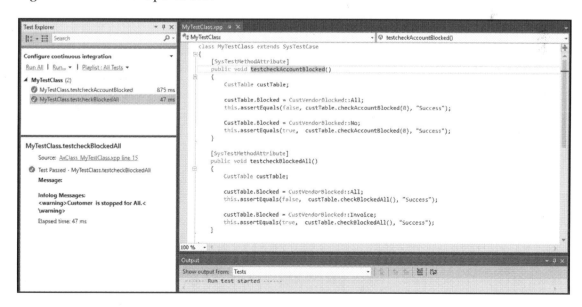

As shown, the right-hand side shows the test class and test scripts. To create a test class, you simply add a class object, extend the **SysTestCase** class, and add test cases by creating a method and decorating it with **[SysTestMethodAttribute].** To the left, you can see Visual Studio test explorer, which discovers the test cases automatically. You can select one test case to run or run them all.

Task recorder-based (coded UI) testing

Task recorder-based test automation is new in Dynamics 365 for Finance and Operations, Enterprise edition. This is basically coded UI testing. Using task recorder one can record a business process as you perform it, using the browser client. After the recording is complete, you can play back, create a Word document, or download and attach it to your BPM library as a task guide. You can also download a developer recording and import the recording file (.xml) into Visual Studio to create an X++ test. The task recorder import tool translates any recording gestures, validations, or tasks into the appropriate test code.

The following screenshot shows how developers can import task recording into Visual Studio and generate automated test code:

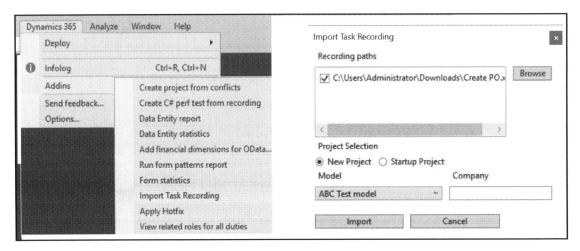

As shown, the **Import Task Recording** menu is available under **Dynamics 365 | Addins | Import Task Recording**. In the **Import Task Recording** dialog, browse the task recorder file, select your test model, and click on **Import** to create the automated test code.

The following screenshot shows test code created by the import utility after importing a task recording to create a purchase order in Finance and Operations:

As illustrated, the code generated by the import utility utilizes X++ form adaptors, type providers and SysTest unit test framework. The given bullets explain the concepts and the relevance of these concepts to support coded UI test automation:

- **X++ form adaptors**: Form adaptors are wrapper classes over forms, which provide a strongly typed API that can be used to test form functionality. Form adaptor classes provide a strongly typed API for forms using the logical control on the server. It enables form-based tests to be executed completely *headless*, which makes tests run much faster and more reliably.

  Microsoft ships form adaptor classes for all the faorms available in Finance and Operations in separate packages, for example, application foundation form adaptors, application platform form adaptors, application suite form adaptors, and so on. Test Essentials is another package which has helper methods to execute test code.

Microsoft removed adaptor models in its July 2017 update and replaced them with Type providers. Type providers are a new way to interface with forms in unit tests without a form adaptor model. Adaptor models are removed because they are expensive to run and maintain. In general, the type provider framework requires less processing time, and is more flexible to use than the form adaptor models. For details, follow the blog article at `https://community.dynamics.com/ax/b/newdynamicsax/archive/2017/07/12/updating-tests-from-form-adaptors-to-type-providers`.

- **SysTest framework**: Automated code generated by task guides basically uses the same unit test SysTest framework for setup data, validation, and assertion. In many cases, automated test script generated by task guide is sufficient; however, developers can add more complex logic, such as random data generation, to automate advanced test requirements.

 For more details and step-by-step guidance on how to import a task guide, follow the documentation on the Finance and Operations official documentation page at `https://docs.microsoft.com/en-us/dynamics365/operations/dev-itpro/perf-test/testing-validation`.

PerfSDK

PerfSDK is the performance or load testing tool for Dynamics 365 for Finance and Operations, Enterprise edition. It lets you test and validate all critical business processes for performance in a single user or multiuser test run. You can utilize PerfSDK in your project by adding a new, or modifying the existing, business scenario and simulating load testing. Now, let's get to the key highlights of PerfSDK:

- PerfSDK toolkit and sample codes are available on the developer VM under `C:\PerfSDK` or `J:\PerfSDK`
- It uses Visual Studio and Visual Studio Team Services to run load testing
- Sample code is available to test key scenarios such as distribution, financials, and inventory replenishment and warehousing
- You can create a task guide for additional scenarios and import task guides to create C# script for performance testing

For detailed steps on how to set up and run load testing using PerfSDK, follow the tutorial at `https://docs.microsoft.com/en-us/dynamics365/operations/dev-itpro/perf-test/perfsdk-tutorial`.

You will need a Visual Studio Enterprise edition license to run load testing in Visual Studio.

Integrating test with build process

After unit tests and coded UI are developed and checked into source control, you can integrate these tests with an automated build process so that every time build runs, these test cases are executed automatically.

The following screenshot shows test automation steps under default build definition for Dynamics 365 for Finance and Operations, Enterprise edition:

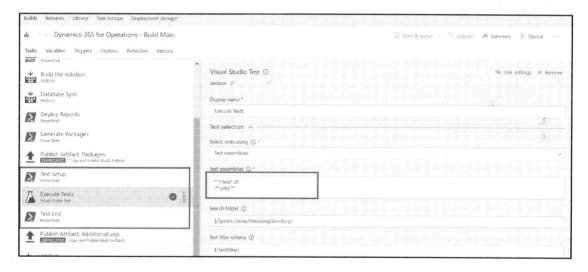

As shown, build process will find any assemblies that contain the test word and execute them.

Test planning guidelines and recommendations

Testing is a big topic, and each testing type requires special focus to achieve the right objective of the test cycle. To achieve success and get the desired result during the testing phase, it's very critical to plan. No matter how good the tools or testing method you use are, if there is no planning, you will not be able to achieve and measure objectives. In this section, we will cover various test planning guidelines and recommendations during the testing cycle.

Test planning and scenarios

To conduct proper testing, it is important to do proper planning before the test cycle starts. The following are some guidelines to keep in mind when planning for the testing phase:

- During the planning phase, create a test plan to define the scope, resources, and tools to be used for the testing, and to identify how bugs will be tracked. Establish the criteria for defining S1/S2, P1/P2 bugs, depending on the business criticality (severity and priorities).
- Dedicate QA resources for each area in a way similar to what we do for the functional analysts and developers. You need them to start on the project right from the beginning to understand the requirements and design that is being put in place. Plan the scope of automation testing, and dedicate resources and time for automated test script.
- Identify the external resources that need to be engaged during testing. For example, testing with banks for checks/electronic payments, positive pay files, EDI trading partners, customers/vendors, and any other parties to whom you send/receive data, such as D&B (credit) and third-party invoice printing. Start engaging them as early as possible, and align their schedules into the project plan.

Building test scenarios and test cases is important for executing a good test plan. The following tips will help you in developing effective testing scenarios:

- Prepare test scenarios and test cases parallel to the design and development phase of the project. Review test cases with the business analysts and the business SMEs, as applicable.

- The goal should be to identify and document each scenario in detail in the form of test cases, rather than stay at a very high level. If you don't document the test cases, there is a high chance of missing them during execution.
- Maintain a traceability matrix with the number of requirements, function specifications, technical specifications, test scenarios, and test-case IDs.
- Identify the test data to be used and the specific deviations in data to maximize the coverage of your testing. Say, for example, if a company has four product lines and all are sold differently, you will need to have scenarios that address each product line.

The UAT planning and execution

There is quite a bit of planning required to perform a successful UAT. Just throwing the business users into a room with computers and test scripts will not get you the results of an effective UAT. Let's look at what all goes in during UAT planning and execution under the following headings.

Planning

As we stated earlier, planning is critical to perform successful UAT. During the planning, you are not only required to identify what test cases to execute, but also to list out the right resources and the required training and logistics, such as the UAT environment, to perform testing. The following details should be considered when planning for UAT:

- Providing training to business users before the UAT. Untrained business users will take more time to test, which can result in low confidence in the new system.
- Ensure that the UAT/Sandbox environment is ready for the UAT. Data migration should be completed, and the required configuration done and tested. Ensure that business users have the appropriate security roles assigned.
- Plan multiple rounds of testing, scheduled a few weeks apart to fix issues. It is not uncommon to find a few pieces missing once the business starts looking at the solution. The goal should be to fix everything in between both the cycles so that the business does not experience the same issues, and the test cases are not blocked due to those issues.
- Ensure proper sequencing in the test cases. For example, you start with the data migration validation and then move on to customer/product creation, then to order processing, shipping, invoicing, processing returns, commission reports, financial postings and financial statements, tax reporting, inventory value reports, and so on.

- The people who run the business should be engaged to verify the system; the team should have cross-functional knowledge and knowledge of case scenarios. For example, your top performing, most brilliant sales talent pool needs to be involved in testing the order entry system. They will know all the different scenarios and *gotchas* from the current system, and they can help you break the system.

- Avoid relying on the temporary staff for testing; you need FTEs to review your new world. Engage the temporary staff in backfilling the FTE jobs to run the day-to-day business tasks, not in reviewing the future of the company.

- Encourage the business to bring in as many real examples as possible. For example, the AP can bring in a day's worth of a stack of invoices for processing, running a check on the migrated Open AP and newly created AP invoices to review the results, and on the real customer orders for order entry. This will help verify credit limits, customers/ products, on-hand inventory migration, and the related scenarios.

- Define the process for logging the bugs (record using task guide or screenshot, provide a reference to the test case, the step that failed, description of the issue being reported, any input file used for uploads, business impact, and so on, for every issue that is being submitted by the users). Users need to be educated on bug-tracking tools and the overall triage process. The more information you have, the less time will be required for the development team to analyze and fix the issues.

- Use a separate environment for UAT testing, rather than the regular testing environment. Limit the number of people having access to this environment; you don't want users creating random transactions and messing up UAT test scenarios.

UAT kickoff

It is important to set the expectations of testing before starting the UAT. The key messages that should be put across during the UAT kickoff are as follows:

- Finding bugs is the goal of performing UAT. If you find them in UAT, it's a great thing. Don't get frustrated because you've found issues and thus, get stuck in testing.

- Focus on first verifying all the critical business scenarios before getting into exceptional scenarios that won't happen frequently. Follow the 80/20 rule to define focus. This is also a good time to remind everybody about the goals for the project.

- Review the reports from the previous testing and communicate any open areas:
  - Communicate the schedule for testing and retesting.
  - Cover the tools/processes to be used for logging bugs, triage, and communication after fixing the bugs.
  - Set the sign off and exit criteria (communicate upfront that they need to sign off at the end of it). Set the client expectations with regard to the types of bugs expected to be fixed versus deferred. If this is not clear, you might struggle to obtain sign off with low severity bugs open. Usually, severity 1 and 2 bugs must be closed for sign off, while severity 3 and 4 bugs can be postponed or handled post sign-off.

Execution

To achieve results from a good plan, you need to execute the plan well. As explained earlier, you might have to do multiple rounds of UAT testing with the same group to ensure that business users are comfortable with the new system and any issue found during the testing is addressed. To do so, you have to ensure progress of the UAT execution and that the identified issues are tracked. During the execution of UAT, consider the following points:

- Track the testing progress along with the test cases that passed/failed. Publish reports on progress, bugs reported, and resolved bugs (for retesting).
- Actively manage blocking issues. You need to stay on top of the issues that are blocking the testing of certain areas; try to be creative in finding workarounds to continue testing.
- Issue a triage and managing issue list. Have multiple reviews with the team every day for issue statuses and resolutions. Set daily meetings with the business leaders to discuss issues and provide updates on the progress made. You need to hear their firsthand feedback on the issues being experienced.
- Ensure that the formal release process is defined and validations are performed to verify that the release has not broken the environment. This will ensure that precious testing time is not lost due to the broken UAT environment.
- Track dependencies between test cases. You may have a dependency between the test cases that will need coordination among the different business groups for testing. For example, when a sales order is created, you need to verify with the warehouse to ship it, and then the AR can see the invoice and collect against it.

- On larger projects with a multilocation roll out, it is a good idea to execute testing at a central location. However, you should also perform some testing locally, especially features that require local resources, such as local printing.
- Poor analysis and design for complex areas will get exposed in UAT and cause a lot of rework/continuous break-fix. Identify such critical areas and put in dedicated resources to get extra focus on such critical path items.
- In one of our implementation experience, a focus team was defined for testing and fixing the revenue recognition and deferral scenarios. It was one of the most complex parts of the project, and was dependent on many other processes, such as correct product and customer setup, order entry with different combinations of products and the way billing frequency was chosen by the customer, order entry and CRM integrations, and invoice distribution and rounding of totals. Every time a scenario was fixed, another was broken in deferrals; issues in the upstream processes, such as order entry, impacted the testing of deferrals functionality. The focus group helped track this subproject with additional visibility and helped fix issues faster.

Sign-off

A successful UAT is one where the business can show that they are comfortable with the application features, and thorough testing has been done with good involvement of the business users across areas. The key deliverable of UAT is the business sign off on the (**UAT**) and test results. There may be cases where items do fail, but the team agrees to a conditional sign off. Track any bugs that are critical for going live as a part of this conditional sign off. Most importantly, all areas should have been tested by now. There is a difference between knowing the open issues and being unable to test specific areas due to open issues.

End-to-end test planning and execution

You need to complete the testing of individual features and all the areas need to be stable to truly start end-to-end testing. In reality, you end up making some exceptions sometimes, but this is not ideal. Pick a selected core group for end-to-end testing. Everyone involved needs to know the end-to-end business flow. Usually, the finance team has a bigger role to play here, as they have a visibility into all the parts of the organization.

Plan for at least two rounds of end-to-end testing with some time in between to fix the bugs. Define the exit and success criteria prior to getting into end-to-end testing (such as 100 percent test execution, more than 95 percent pass rate, and no more than five critical bugs open).

Execution and real-life examples

The goal of end-to-end testing is to simulate real business, right from data migration to new product and customer creation, using this data for placing orders, fulfillment, invoicing, receiving cash, reverse logistics, transactions using migrated data, verify reporting, and so on.

Similar to UAT, you need to publish reports on the test results and follow a triage process. Areas that are blocked during testing need to be unblocked and tested again. Assess whether you have met the exit criteria and review it with the executives.

The project team should come up with all the key business scenarios that should be tested. The following are a few examples of areas that you should focus on during end-to-end testing:

- **Customer invoicing**: The timing and accuracy of invoicing customers is such a critical business function because it has a direct impact on the customer and on the cash flow of the company. On the other hand, invoicing is a downstream function--you have a dependency on products, customers, tax, fulfillment processes, and so on--which must work correctly before you can produce the invoices.
- **Commission reporting**: As commission reporting has an impact on the paychecks of the sales floor, you need to verify the accuracy of the commission reports with migrated orders and invoices. It should be a top priority, as you want the sales team to trust the system and focus on selling, rather than tracking their orders on spreadsheets for an expected commission or worrying whether they'll be paid. Commission reporting can be even trickier for orders shipped in the previous system, and you may have to pay a commission upon receiving customer payments.

- **Inventory costing and valuation**: Each customer has a different way of using weighted average, FIFO, and other inventory costing methods. It impacts the P&L, their bottom line, how executives are compensated, the inventory value on the balance sheet, and so on. Efforts need to be put in during UAT and end-to-end testing to validate that inventory costing is done according to the needs of the company and is understood by the financial controllers and the rest of the stakeholders.
- **General ledger postings**: You need to verify the posting for each type of transaction, and run month-end reconciliation reports (to verify that the general ledger and subledger are in balance).
- **Key reports**: Identify the key reports that are important to run the business, and validate the data based on the transactions that were processed in end-to-end testing.

Engage domain experts during end-to-end testing, such as tax auditors for tax integration testing. They will be able to put together a great test plan and execute it through unique scenarios to ensure that you have configured the system correctly.

Training

Training drives the successful adoption of the new system and processes. The learning capacity of the audience and the amount of changes being introduced to them dictate the amount of time you need to spend on training and retraining. The more people you have up to speed on the new processes and system, the smaller are the chances of them making mistakes, and the volume of support calls will be highly reduced. Ultimately, this results in a smoother adoption of the new system.

The ERP project is an opportunity for organizations to get people up to speed on end-to-end processes and train them on cross-functional areas. If you have a great system designed but people are not able to use it, can you call it a success?

The training and help system in Finance and Operations

The help system in Dynamics 365 for Finance and Operations, Enterprise edition has improved significantly. It is easier to train users how to use Dynamics 365 for Finance and Operations, Enterprise edition than ever before. Significant investment gone into designing an aesthetic user interface, navigation concepts, and tooling related to the help and training system. In this section we will discover how these concepts and tools help during training.

Modern clients and navigation concepts

Browser-based user interfaces are easier to use when compared to desktop applications. Dynamics 365 for Finance and Operations, Enterprise edition, provides a modern browser-based HTML5 client and mobile application to access application functionality and data.

Listed here are some advantages of browser-based applications, as compared to desktop applications:

- You do not need client application to be deployed to every user. Users can simply bookmark the application URL and access it anytime.
- Browser-based applications are platform independent, which means they can be accessed from any device and platform.
- Application usability is rated higher with the browser-based client as compared to desktop applications.

On the new browser-based client, Dynamics 365 for Finance and Operations, Enterprise edition introduced many new modern navigation concepts focused on productivity and usability of the system. The following bullets represent new navigation concepts in Dynamics 365 for Finance and Operations, Enterprise edition:

- **Dashboard**: The dashboard is new a concept and is the first page that users see when they access the client. The dashboard contains tiles that show workspaces that a user has access to. This removes the clutter, and users do not have to remember the navigation paths for regular activities and can simply click on the dashboard tiles, open the workspace, and start their work.

The following screenshot shows the dashboard for a user with an account role that shows the workspaces which they have access to:

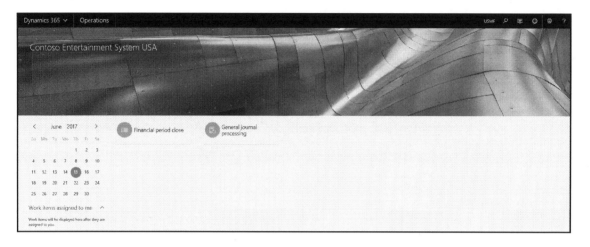

- **Workspaces**: Workspaces represent a business activity or logical group of tasks that a particular business user performs daily. Workspaces are designed for efficiency and productivity. With workspaces, business users do not have to remember different navigation paths to perform their tasks. For most users, they can simply be on one workspace and do all their daily work. Workspaces have the following primary goals:
  - Reduce the need for navigation
  - Enable the user to understand the current state of their activities on one screen
  - Perform light tasks in the workspaces to avoid round-trips to deeper pages
- **Form and action search**: Another great new feature added in Finance and Operations that business users are very happy about is the `search` field to find forms, and even the feature of searching for the action buttons on the form. Users simply type the keyword and all the forms containing that keyword will be displayed as a dropdown from which the user can select the right form they want to open.

As illustrated in the following screenshot, search field is available right after the company selection button. For example, users simply types `Ledger`, and the system displays all the menu options that have the word `Ledger` in it:

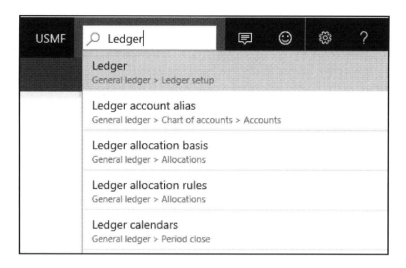

Not only can a user search the menus and open the form, they can also search for the action button on the form if there are too many buttons. Users do not have to remember which tab that button is on; if they simply remember the keyword, they can type it under the button search on the form, and the system will show all the buttons on the form with the keyword.

As shown in the following screenshot, if a user wants to find the **View activities** button on the vendor form, which is under **General** | **Activities** | **View activities**, they can simply type the keyword in the search box and get to the button without navigating to tabs and then clicking on the button:

In-product help

Another key feature that will help training go more smoothly is the in product help system, which is built for new users learning the system. The in-product help system pulls articles from the Dynamics 365 for Finance and Operations, Enterprise edition site on `https://docs.microsoft.com`, as well as from task guides stored in the Business process modeler in **Lifecycle Services (LCS)**.

The following screenshot shows the in-product help button available on the right-corner of the page. A user simply clicks on the help button to access task guides from LCS and articles from the public site in the context of user language and the form he/she is trying to get help on:

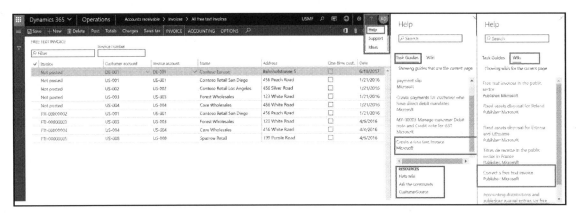

As shown in the screenshot, if the user is new and does not know how to create a free text invoice, they can simply open the free text invoices form and click on **Help**. This will bring up the **Help** pane and show **Task Guides** and **Wiki** articles, all related to free text invoices. Users can simply select the task guide to guide them through, or access the knowledge article from the wiki page.

The business process modeler

In LCS, you can use the business process modeler to create, view, and modify the business-process libraries and flowcharts for Dynamics 365 for Finance and Operations, Enterprise edition. The business process modeler helps you align your Finance and Operations processes with industry-standard processes, as described by **American Productivity and Quality Center** (**APQC**). There are more than a thousand business processes that are available, and you can tweak them as per your needs. As referenced in the earlier chapters, the business process modeler can be used right from the Gap/Fit analysis phase of the project to track all customizations, add visio process diagram, task recording, Word documents, or external links.

BPM library makes training easier in the following ways:

- Linking one or more BPM libraries in the LCS to your Finance and Operations environment
- Central repository for business and system process documentation
- Business process documentation and links can be attached to BPM libraries that are available in the **Help** page
- Associate task recording and guides with business processes that are available on the help page.
- Convert BPM process flows to Microsoft Word documents and for use as printed training material

The task recorder and task guides

The task recorder and task guides are an integral piece of the Finance and Operations help and training experience. Using task recorder, you can record actions that you take in the product's UI. When you use task recorder, all actions that you perform are captured. The specific UI fields and controls that are used are also captured. Task recordings can be played as **task guides**. A task guide is a controlled, guided, interactive experience through the steps of a business process. The user is instructed to complete each step by means of a pop-up prompt (*bubble*), which will move across the UI and point to the UI element that the user should interact with. The bubble also provides information about how to interact with the element, such as **Click here** or **In this field, enter a value**. A task guide runs against the user's current dataset and the data that is entered is saved in the user's environment.

This screenshot shows a user running the task guide to create a free text invoice and task guide helps user navigate and guide to create a new free text invoice:

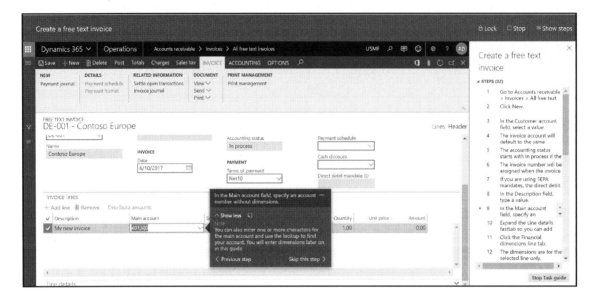

Documentation website

Another enhancement that Microsoft did, which will make training users much easier, is a brand new website for all its standard features. The following are some key highlights for the new documentation site:

- Microsoft documentation now focuses on business processes as well, rather than just explaining what the form does. Business users can really go through this and understand how they can use the particular business function.

- Microsoft documentation is integrated in the product and provides users with contextual help on what it means if a business user is learning how to create a free test invoice; he gets the help for free text invoices right there in the product.

- Help is personalized based on the user language in the system; for users who are set up with the Japanese language, when they access the help, Japanese documentation is presented.

- With the new model of help maintained in GitHub, a customer can copy Microsoft help content and create their own help repository and link it in the product; this way, you are accessing your custom help, which is relevant to your business processes, and not a generic one.

Planning and executing training

In the earlier section, we learned all of the great tools and enhancements that Finance and Operations brings for training users. Along with great tools, you need a good plan to conduct a successful and effective training. In this section, we will go through some of the essential training planning and execution guidelines to ensure that you get effective and proper training using those great tools.

Training plan

Training planning is an essential part of ERP implementation. It is more important because you are training business users who are used to a different process or system, and are completely new to this new system and processes.

Put together a training plan that covers the following points:

- **Understanding the audience**: How quickly are your users likely to catch up with the changes? The training plan needs to be defined accordingly to support their transition.
- **Train the trainers**: Consultants train the trainer who the business superusers or internal business analysts. The idea is to train superusers through multiple rounds of CRP sessions, training and testing to get them up to speed on the system in order to be trainers. The trainer approach will ensure that the business SMEs or internal business analysts have gotten up to speed well enough. It will reduce the dependency on the consulting team post go-live, and internal resources can be your tier one support.
- **Scope of training / areas to be trained**: You need to account for both system and process changes. There are three usual cycles of the training process: UAT training, end user training, and post go-live (training for areas that are struggling).
- **Logistics**: This includes factors such as meeting rooms/travel, centralized versus location-specific, and much more.
- **Training schedule and timing**: Timing is key. In some areas, you may need to train the users multiple times to ensure that they are comfortable. On the other hand, areas that have not changed much may need light training close to going live, to ensure that the users don't forget.
- **Training assessment**: This pertains to the ways and methods that you will use to get feedback on the training process.

- **Training material and user manuals**: Reviewed with the business SMEs, they may come in different forms, for example, checklists, visio for business processes, documents with screenshots, recorded videos, mapping between the old and new world, and/or a combination of multiple methods. The development of the training materials should be agreed to at the beginning of the project, in the planning phase, so that appropriate time and resources are built into the plan.
- **Signing off**: Define the sign off process and the criteria for training sign off. It is one of the major considerations for go-live.
- **Handling change:** The usual human psychology is to resist change. ERP implementations are not only system changes but, many a times, process changes as well. These changes may shift jobs or workload from one department to another. It is important to factor this resistance in the planning. Training is a good opportunity to help prepare people for the change. The more training you provide, the higher is the confidence that the users will have in embracing the change, and you will receive less pushback.

Training preparation

A lot of preparation goes into executing a smooth and effective training. This preparation includes validating system readiness, verifying the roles, putting together multiple forms of training materials, creating and maintaining a stable training environment with valid data, and so on.

Ensure that the system is ready and stable enough (testing complete) prior to training a larger audience. You also need to gauge the business's readiness for training and help them prepare; the following are some tips to do so:

- If a smaller group is being trained prior to UAT, the expectations may be different, as the system has not been tested as yet, and you may want to communicate the known open issues. However, when training larger groups, try to do it post UAT, when the system is stable enough and the processes have been finalized.
- Create a forum for the users to participate in and get more hands on experience from training through go-live. Arrange *Lunch n Learn* or other such team activities that will encourage more practice. From my experience, business leaders who encourage their teams for extra practice after training, and take the initiative to drive it, will have a lot less issues to deal with post release.
- Have a process to capture and respond to bugs/queries that are raised in the training. Most likely, you will find some critical items that were not known before.

- Let every user be configured with their to-be production security role. Avoid the use of the system admin role during training. Of course, roles should be tested prior to doing this.
- Use the business process flows at the beginning of every session. Give a ten thousand feet high walkthrough of the overall business process and of the piece that you plan to show before getting into application and details.

The training environment

Having a stable training environment is important for successful training. A lot of time will be wasted in training if the training environment is not in a good working order. Take a look at the following tips to be kept in mind when managing your training environment:

- You need to treat it like production; many people will be using it at the same time, and you want it to be stable while the training is going on or when the users are practicing after training.
- Keep it updated with the latest code and data. Have a communication plan for any downtimes for deployments to ensure that the users are aware.
- Have it available for the users to practice after training.
- It should share an integrated environment with the other applications. For example, if you plan to use Dynamics CRM in Production for order entry and integrate it with Finance and Operations for fulfillment, ensure that you have the training instance of the CRM connected to the Finance and Operations training environment. This will ensure an end-to-end training experience for the users.

Change management

In every phase of the project, you are dealing with actual users who will use the system and are the folks who'll be experiencing the most change. The usual human psychology is to resist change, be it a new process or new system. As part of an implementation project team, you can find many issues raised by users not completely aligned to the scope of the project, the signed requirement, or the solution design specs, and the success of your project is dependent on how these changes are managed.

For a CRP lead/project manager, it is very important to review and highlight any such change and take it through the change management process, as any change may impact the system design, timeline, budget, risk, goals, and many more factors. These changes must be addressed carefully, as the implementation of any change without proper analysis can potentially derail the project effort.

Training is a good opportunity to help prepare people for the change. The more training is provided, the higher is the confidence of the users in embracing the change and the system, resulting in less pushback. Let's explore the various options for managing change with users of the system, as follows:

- **Empathy**
    - Listen carefully to what the end users are asking and trying to achieve.
    - They may be going through nervousness, apprehensions, and fear, and hence the need to stay calm and show empathy; many of the concerns can be sought out with effective communication.

- **Signed scope**
    - Always be on top of signed scope, whether you are an advisor/partner/customer implementation team member, and any unresolved request is a new candidate for change, which must then go through the change management process.

- **Impact**
    - Once the change is identified, it must be adequately documented, added to **Requirements Traceability Matrix (RTM)**, and analyzed with the right stakeholders.

- **Workarounds**
    - Once the change is analyzed and identified to be included in scope, the project manager should rebaseline the project, while the implementation team should look out for various solution options.
    - Similar to the original requirements' analysis, the change must also be analyzed for suitability in the original solution; also, where it's a system gap, always look for suitable workarounds to try and have minimum impact, to agree to solution specs and yet be able to address the change.

- **Pushback**
    - If a change is identified as not critical, not system related, not urgent, or not factual, the change management team, CRP lead, advisor, and project manager must try to push the change back to the business and end user.

 Change management may shift jobs or workload from one department to another, and hence is an important topic in any transformation initiative.

A popular methodology is **Organization Change Management (OCM)**, which is used in training plans to ensure that the project stakeholders know what to do when a change is reported or adapted by the users of the system. In large projects, we have seen a dedicated team for OCM who report directly to the steering committee, possess solid business knowledge and system backgrounds, and are efficient in soft skills. When there is no dedicated OCM team, there should be a designated person who owns this OCM effort, known as the change management lead.

The CRP lead, change management lead, and project manager must utilize a lot of political power to fight battles where the change requested from end users is not something that is a *must have*, is out of original scope, and the impact to the business is not high and is not needed immediately. This is possible when changes are properly logged, analyzed, and approved before any effort is spent on implementing the change.

Summary

In this chapter, we reviewed the importance of the testing and training phase of the project and how to execute successful testing and training through effective planning and execution using the available tools. The ERP system goes through different testing phases, such as feature testing, system integration testing, UAT, and end-to-end testing, to ensure the overall quality of the configuration and custom features. Testing the ERP system can be costly, and automation testing can mitigate that. Many improvements and new features have been added to Dynamics 365 for Finance and Operations, Enterprise edition to enhance the automated testability of the product. Unit test framework is improved and integrated with Visual Studio to author unit tests for code artifacts and integrate with the build process. Task recorder-based test automation lets developers create a test script by simply importing the task recorder recording in Visual Studio. At the end, we learned the importance of test planning and guidelines for how to conduct successful testing. We discussed the ways to make UAT and end-to-end testing most effective by uncovering issues prior to going live.

In the training section, we discussed the importance of training and different enhancement and tools available in Finance and Operations for effective training. The new **In-Product** help pane integrates with LCS and Microsoft documentation to provide context-based help to users. At the end, we discussed the importance of training planning, execution, and best practices.

In the next chapter, we will learn about the final phase of the project--Go live. Go live is the final milestone of the project, and it's important to plan and execute to avoid any business disruption. In the next chapter, we will cover Go Live planning, execution, and tooling concepts in details.

12
Go Live

Go Live is one of the last events that needs to be executed as part of the ERP implementation project. This is the moment when you are going to turn on the switch and start using the new ERP system. It is exciting; however, it is also the most hectic and intense period in the entire ERP project and deserves a fair amount of planning and attention to go smoother. So far, the project team has been working extremely hard designing, developing, and testing, and a lot of time and money has been put into the project. A successful Go Live can make all that hard work and investment worth and smoothen the adoption of the new ERP system.

In this chapter, we will cover the following topics:

- The production environment and responsibilities
- The Go Live activities
- The organization's readiness to Go Live
- Go Live planning and execution

Production environment and responsibilities

Before diving deep into the Go Live planning and related activities, it is important to understand the production environment. Dynamics 365 for Finance and Operations, Enterprise edition offers three distinct deployment options: cloud, local business data (on-premises), and Cloud and Edge (hybrid). All the deployment options use the same application code base and tooling; However, the process, roles, and responsibilities of managing these production environments are different. In this section, we will walk through the difference in processes and understand the roles and responsibitlites to manage the production infrastructure and deployments.

Cloud deployment

In the cloud deployment model, Microsoft is responsible for actively monitoring the health of production environments. In case of any issue in the production environment, the Microsoft service engineering team is alerted. The team will investigate the issue and work with the customers and partners to find a resolution. Microsoft is also jointly responsible for sizing any application and for infrastructure updates. The customer and the partner will not have direct access to the production servers, but will be able to monitor the performance and activities through the LCS environment monitoring and telemetry tools. For application updates such as deploying a hotfix or updates to Dynamics 365 for Finance and Operations, Enterprise edition, the customer typically deploys and tests the changes in the sandbox environment and then creates a service request to schedule the production deployment. The Microsoft service engineering team works on applying the deployment in the scheduled deployment window. Finally, the customer validates and provides sign off to close the release.

The following diagram shows the production environment lifecycle and lists out the roles and responsibilities of Microsoft, customers, and partners in this process:

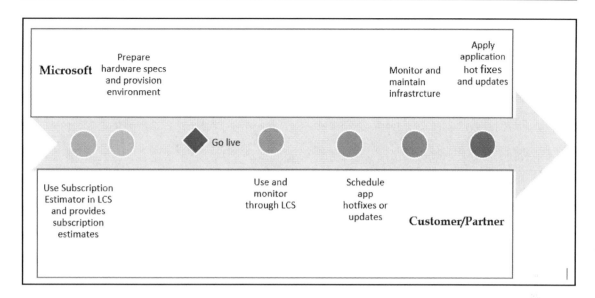

As shown in the diagram, the production environment provisioning starts with the customers and partners collecting the subscription estimation data and uploading the same into the LCS subscription estimator tool. In the subscription estimation, you typically describe your implementation project, for example, the number of legal entities, countries, languages, users, master data, and transactions, including the batch and integration volume. This data helps the Microsoft team to create the appropriate hardware specs for the production environment.

Once the production environment is provisioned and all the development, testing, and training activities are completed and signed off, the project team works with Microsoft to deploy the final code, configuration, and master data. The customers or partners then perform additional data migration, configuration, and integration setup as part of the Go Live activities. Once the customers start using the production environment, they can monitor the performance and activities through LCS, and schedule and hotfix or update the deployment though a regular servicing model. In case of any environment-specific update, such as applying a critical security patch and other maintenance, the Microsoft team notifies the customer and schedules the maintenance window accordingly.

Local business data

Unlike in the cloud deployment model where Microsoft manages the production environment and controls the deployment and servicing, in local business data, all the responsibilities lie on the customers and partners. Local business data deployment means deploying Dynamics 365 for Finance and Operations, Enterprise edition on the customer's own data centers or with any other cloud infrastructure provider.

The on-premise deployment option uses Microsoft Azure Server Service Fabric standalone clusters to deploy the operations on the local infrastructure. Service Fabric standalone clusters can be deployed on any computer that runs the Windows server.

 Service Fabric is a next-generation Microsoft middleware platform for building and managing enterprise-class, high-scale applications.

The following diagram shows the timeline for local business data deployment mode:

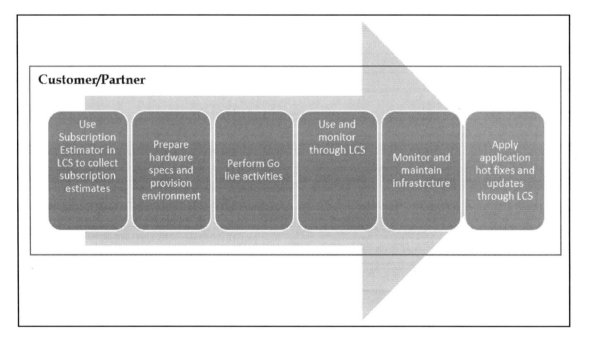

As shown in the diagram, the process of managing the production environment is similar to what we have in the cloud deployment model; however, just like any other on-premise application deployment, the customers or partners are responsible for the infrastructure and application updates. As a customer or partner, you are responsible for defining the environment specifications and the provisions of the environment. LCS tooling is provided by Microsoft to plan, provision, and deploy the changes on the production environment. As shown in the diagram, you still start with filling out the subscription estimator to help you figure out the hardware specs that you need for your implementation.

 Refer to the following link to get the minimum system requirements to provision a production environment for local business data:
`https://www.microsoft.com/en-us/download/details.aspx?id=55496`

Once the production environment is provisioned and all the other project activities are completed and signed off, you will perform the final Go Live activities to deploy the final code and data, and start using the system. The LCS monitoring and telemetry tools can still be used to monitor the production environment performance and activities. You can also use LCS to deploy any changes to the production environment. In addition, your IT team can monitor and manage the production infrastructure, such as applying critical patching, infrastructure upgrade, and so on.

Cloud and Edge deployment

The Cloud and Edge deployment model starts with the cloud components deployed on Azure to provide enterprise-level functionalities, such as complete enterprise view, business intelligence, and disaster recovery. In addition to cloud deployment, some operations such as retail and manufacturing can be deployed on the customer's infrastructure for business continuity or for integration with the local systems. From a production environment perspective, one can safely assume that it will be a hybrid scenario, where Microsoft is responsible for the production cloud components' infrastructure, while the customer manages the infrastructure for edge deployment at local data centers. LCS will still be a common tool, bringing both the worlds together to provide unified monitoring and application lifecycle management.

Go Live activities

Now we understand about the production environment, and the roles and responsibilities involved. Let's focus on the Go Live activities, that is, what all needs to be done as part of Go Live. Depending on the size of the project and the scope of Go Live, there can be hundreds of activities that need to be performed during Go Live. On a high level, the following list represents the various key activities performed during Go Live:

- **Final code deployment**: You need to deploy the final signed-off application, including all your customizations, ISV solutions, and so on. For cloud deployment, you have to submit a service request to deploy the final build on the production environment before Go Live.

- **Dependent application changes**: As part of your implementation project, you may have some new or existing application changes that integrate with or support Dynamics 365 for Finance and Operations, Enterprise edition, for example, changes to your front office applications, application code for integration, and so on.

- **Golden configuration and master data**: As part of the project, you must be maintaining a golden configuration and master data environment that is already tested. You need to bring this golden configuration to your production environment. This golden configuration can also include your initial data migration if you have built-in incremental data migration. For cloud deployment, you can bring the database backup of your golden configuration environment, apply it to the production environment before Go Live, and then update any additional final configurations and settings on top of it.

- **Additional setup and integrations**: After the golden configuration and master data is loaded, you may need to set up some additional configurations, such as integration settings, batch jobs, and so on. An ideal scenario would be to have most of the configurations as part of the golden configuration, but there could still be some configurations that may need to be updated or created for the production environment.

- **Final data migration and cut-over**: Once you have your golden configuration and the initial data migration in the production environment, you may have to run the final data migration to catch up on any new transactions generated in your legacy system for the final cut-over. You will probably be doing this activity with a system downtime so that no new transactions are generated in the legacy system.

- **Validation and sign-off**: Once the final data migration is done, it is time for business users to run validation and create some staged end-to-end transactions to make sure that the system is ready for production use.

Running multiple rounds of simulation or mock releases before the final Go Live will help you identify any gaps or issues in the release steps.

The organization's readiness to Go Live

There is always a tremendous amount of pressure to make the Go Live date; often, somebody's job is on the line. However, the readiness of the organization for a new system needs to be evaluated carefully prior to flipping the on switch. Readiness for Go Live is based on the fact that all the prior activities are completed as per the satisfaction of the key business users and stakeholders, and they are confident enough to pull the switch on and ready to use the new system.

Sign offs

One of the most important criteria to determine an organization's readiness to Go Live is to know whether your key end users and stakeholders are comfortable and are signed off on the new ERP system. The following list covers a few important considerations and criteria to evaluate whether you are ready to Go Live:

- **UAT sign off**: Make sure that the business users have tested the system using real business scenarios, including integrations, reporting, data migration, and so on. All the business leaders should have signed off on the testing for their areas. Any open issue needs to be documented. Review any critical issues that are open, and identify their impact on Go Live and whether there are any possible workarounds.
- **Training sign off**: The business teams should be comfortable with the training that they've received and should have access to the training documents. People play a key role in your ERP success, and the end users, across all areas, need to be comfortable with using a new system and the business process changes. All the business leaders should have signed off on the training for their teams.
- **Go Live plan**: This is a step-by-step, hour-by-hour plan that is reviewed with all the IT/business teams involved in the release, including the roll back plan and an overall timing to fit within the downtime window. The Go Live plan should include the validation scenarios and processes defined by the business. Use the Go Live plan in the previous iterations of the release simulations (including UAT and data validations). Make sure that the Go Live plan is signed off by the business and IT stakeholders.

- **Support plan**: The support plan includes the support resources per area, their location and schedule, the issue communication process (templates for providing issue description, screenshots, business impact, severity, and the information and tools for tracking or logging issues), triage, and loop back with the business teams. You need to ensure that there is an adequate budget approved for support (prior to going live). You don't want to be in a situation where you have to discuss dollars with the customer/business leaders while the business is impacted due to system issues.

  Also, you need to have a budget to not lose the resources that would be required for fixing the issues. Review the support plan with all the stakeholders and users to ensure that the process for the logging issues and communication is clear. Set up business and IT war rooms at different locations; the handover process between support teams can help with better communication.

- **Operations team's readiness**: The IT operations team needs to have enough knowledge to support the new system. The team should be comfortable with the monitoring of services/processes within the application and in LCS. It is important to get a sign off from the IT operations team

- **External sign offs and communication**: External sign offs as applicable for the business are a must, for example, sign off from the bank for check/electronic payments testing, EDI customers, vendors testing, and auditors. Get sign offs from the respective parties.

Any sign off exceptions need to be documented and presented to the business team and the management for making decisions. Discounting any of these areas could result in an unquiet environment post Go Live and negatively impact the business.

The decision to Go Live

The decision to Go Live or not to Go Live is one of the most important decisions in the project lifecycle, and it should not be taken lightly. Wrong decisions can jeopardize the success of the entire project. The decision to Go Live is highly dependent on the quality of end-to-end testing and user/organizational readiness, as mentioned earlier.

The implications and costs of a failed or unstable Go Live are often far worse than a minor delay in the schedule. Sometimes, the project manager or the delivery team can be under pressure to deliver on time. However, if things are not good, it is important to take a step back and delay Go Live rather than risking the project's success.

The following are some personal experiences that I would like to share in this area:

- Once, I was in a room full of executives, making a decision about pulling the trigger on a new system. Everyone was under pressure from the CEO to say, *We are ready*. However, most of them were not ready. They did not have enough time to go through the testing due to a lack of staff, but everyone said yes (there was a fear of getting fired; this was way back in 2009 when the economy wasn't doing well). I failed to push back as well. Any guesses as to what happened next? The customer went live, and it was very painful to stabilize them--but, lesson learnt!

- A similar situation occurred again, a couple of years later. Of course, I was smarter this time. The CIO called for a meeting to check the readiness on the project. Everyone said they were ready (the CIO was driving the dates very hard, and again there was fear of getting fired). It was my turn--I bravely stood up and said no, handing over a list of areas I wasn't comfortable with and which needed more testing. The CIO called for another meeting to better understand what was needed to finish those areas and decided not to Go Live. We ended up extending the schedule by six weeks based on what was on the list. The CIO thanked me (and still continues to) for standing up and challenging the decision to Go Live based on the bugs that were reported/fixed in those six weeks.

- On another project, I was involved in the capacity of an executive reviewer; I challenged their readiness, but the CEO did not want to listen. I told them that it was their call, and we would support the release if they signed a liability waiver, as my team was not comfortable with them going live (due to lack of testing from the business team). When we gave them a piece of paper to sign, the CEO chose to reconsider his decision. The customer ended up delaying the release by four weeks. The CEO who was not very happy when he received the push back, but now he feels thankful to my team for *watching his back*.

There are more instances like these that we can share. The point is that you need to think about the client and the impact on their business. As a consultant, you are their advocate, and you need to protect the customer from hurting themselves (even though it's not what they wanted to hear, you are doing it in their best interest). This is the time to utilize the relationships and respect you have earned from the customer to protect them. Don't be shy.

It is even trickier when you have to stand up for someone else's deliverables. For example, say the customer owns certain deliverables internally, which are not production-ready. You need to request the delay due to their internal deliverables, as you don't want the project to fail due to specific areas.

Saying that you need more testing is easy. The tough part is to decide how much more time you need. You won't get such an opportunity again. Thorough planning needs to be done to identify all the pieces that are incomplete and to put together a plan to come up with a realistic date. Many project managers fail in this exercise; just hitting the snooze button and delaying this by a few weeks may cost you a job eventually.

Picking realistic dates that will work for the business is important. You don't want to perform an ERP Go Live right before or during the peak periods of the business. Challenges from Go Live will have a severe impact on the business. There are many examples of companies going out of business due to an ERP Go Live during or just before the busy holiday season.

Business contingency planning

Part of your Go Live planning must address the business contingency planning. Conduct a pre-mortem session to brainstorm areas that may go wrong, and to find ways in which the team can reduce the likelihood or mitigate the business impact if the issue occurs. Review the critical business functions that are important for the organization and develop contingency plans to run the business if you did not have the computer systems in place momentarily. The goal of this exercise is to plan for the unknowns that may come your way. The following are a few examples to help with the brainstorming process:

- **Additional workforce considerations**: Look at adding temporary staff or approve overtime for areas that have changed the most or processes that would need more hand holding. I quote one of my customers, If I was to make a mistake on spending here, I would rather make it by spending more than less.
- **Additional technology resources to support Go Live**: You may have a lot of things uncovered during Go Live. It is like having an insurance policy: it's good to have it, but it's better if you do not have to use it.
- **Third-party considerations**: You have SLAs for the next day deliveries to the customers; work with your shipping carriers, and have them stand by to schedule a delayed pick up in case you need it.
- **Inventory levels**: You have a great dependency on planning and the stock levels; consider beefing up your inventory prior to Go Live.
- **Communication team**: Have them stand by in case you need to communicate with the outside parties (customers and vendors) or even internally. You may not want to let the customers know ahead of time about the ERP release, as they would consider it as an upcoming glitch and go somewhere else.

- **Cash flows**: It may take a little longer to get paid for a few weeks (or months) after Go Live due to system or training issues. You need to have an additional line of credit available in case you need it.

- **Key processes and proactive planning**: Identify the key processes and their first occurrence to provide some hand holding and validation. For example, after processing the checks for the first time, ensure that you can validate them against the checks that have passed the testing. The first time you are ready to start invoicing, try a few orders first and verify the results before you open the flood gates of batching hundreds of orders. In the case of files that are supposed to be sent out (such as EDI or positive pay files for the bank), verify those that were sent and were accepted faultlessly at the receiving end.

- **Going back to the previous system after a few days or few hours into using the new system**: Once you move to the new ERP system, it may not be possible to go back to the previous system. It is not easy to perform a reverse migration from a new platform to legacy. Make sure that everyone understands that once you are live, there is no going back. Everybody is in it together and issues need to be resolved on the new system. This helps in avoiding unproductive discussion of going back to the previous system after going live.

- **Running parallel**: It seems like an easy solution for business contingency planning. However, it may not be practical, unless you are staffed high and the transaction volume is not high. Running in parallel usually adds more burden and stress on your staff while they are trying to deal with the new system. In general, it will cause more issues/noise (as users may make more mistakes under stress) than helping. If you had to go for running both the systems in parallel, the amount of time to run in parallel should be kept to a minimum. Quite often, running in parallel is looked at as a replacement for inadequate testing; you think you are better off not doing testing in production (and hoping everything would be fine). There is sometimes a belief that running in parallel helps validate the new processes against the old system processes. This is a fallacy, as a part of the point of implementing a new system is to improve the processes that may fundamentally change the way you do business. So, it is like trying to compare apples with oranges.

- **Release validation**: As mentioned earlier, going back to the previous system or running in parallel is not easy. How can you verify that there are no critical issues as part of the release itself? It is ideal if you can hold certain transactions from the previous day. For example, let the AP team enter real vendor invoices, perform a check run based on what's due, enter orders that were received from the customers during system downtime, enter the incoming EDI transactions, and so on. The goal is to have good samples and real transactions to verify the system behavior.

These are some ideas based on my past experiences. You need to review these with the business leaders and determine what is applicable to your business in order to make appropriate arrangements.

Go Live planning and execution

Putting together a detailed plan that can be used for multiple simulations prior to Go Live is important. It gives you an opportunity to get the Go Live plan validated and address any bugs/issues due to missed steps in the release plan. It also allows you to make changes to the plan, allows more time to review with multiple groups and identify the missing elements, and helps educate the team about the dependencies and the big picture.

Planning

As part of the release, you may be performing hundreds of tasks, so it is important to track their progress, dependencies, and corrective actions. Go Live planning involves the following:

- Putting together all the steps in the plan
- Defining the sequence and dependencies between the steps
- Determining the time needed for each step
- Defining the owners and ensuring that all the concerned parties have a clear understanding of what is required

Multiple reviews with the IT and business teams can ensure that you have identified every task that needs to be performed as part of the cut-over and that everyone involved understands the big picture of all the tasks involved in the release. Using such a plan for UAT, end-to-end testing, and pilot releases can help you identify any gaps in the plan as you practice the overall release execution process. This includes the communication required across groups, such as turning off certain integrations of the legacy system, the setup of a new system, data migration, data validation, release testing, or a roll back process. All the steps need to be documented in the Go Live plan and should have relevant information, as described in the following table:

Column	Description
Task type	The type of tasks you are dealing with.
Description	This is the task description.

Owner(s)	This defines the owners of the tasks.
Start date/time	This is the planned start time for the task. It is important to keep track of the timing on tasks that are on a critical path. Any delays in critical path items will impact the overall schedule of the release.
Time needed	This is the time needed to execute the task.
Comments	These are the comments and/or additional information.
Detail steps	These are the detailed steps to execute the overall task if applicable. Attach or link to the detailed document if required.
Status tracking: Status, actual start time, finish time	Keep track of the actuals in the release simulation cycles to adjust your plan, and work with the technical teams to reduce the time taken by the critical path items. During the production release, keep track of the actual timings for each task.

The following are some typical task types you will be putting in your Go Live plan:

- **Pre-release**: Identify all the tasks that can be completed prior to getting into the system's downtime window for release. For example, communication for the upcoming changes, setup of the future production environments, moving the golden configuration and master data, and any dependent application code or configuration that has no hard dependency. Also, add the tasks for tracking all the necessary sign offs.

- **Release**: Identify the tasks to be completed during the system's downtime window for release, such as taking the systems down, ensuring that all the transactions are complete and that your source for data migration has the latest information, running the extraction and migration tasks, communicating at specific intervals during the release, taking backups during the release, and identifying good checkpoints when backups should be taken (in case you have to go back to the previous state), say for example, before starting the posting of transactions, as you can't unpost them easily if you found an issue.

- **Validation**: These are the tasks for validation, such as IT validation and business validation (verify the vendors and addresses, open balances, the validation of processes/functionalities that were identified in the release validation, and so on).

- **Decisions (Go/No-Go)**: Identify the multiple check points when you need to make Go/No-Go decisions with the executive/project team.
- **Post release**: These are the tasks to be performed after the final decision has been made to Go Live. These tasks may go on for multiple days into using the new system, for example, the communication for release, turning on automated processes, verifying acceptance of the outgoing EDI files by customers, verifying the acceptance of positive pay files by each of the banks, and so on.
- **Roll back:** You may have to roll back to a state prior to the release in unfortunate events like when something goes wrong during the release, when critical issues are identified, or when external, uncontrolled dependencies have caused issues. In any case, you need to have rollback steps defined and practiced in the release simulation phase in order to have an uninterrupted availability of the systems to the business. The time needed for the rollback procedure needs to be considered in the release process and the Go/No-Go decisions must be made in a timely manner to allow the completion of the rollback procedure.

The following are some guidelines for putting together your Go Live plan:

- A smaller number of manual steps and more automation is ideal to ensure that you don't have too many steps to perform and track.
- Minimize the dependencies; if activities can be completed in the production environment, mention them as a pre-release item. For example, if an integration solution requires creation of a new database, and if it can be done prior to the release, mention it as a pre-release item.
- You may be implementing ISV solutions or integrations with third-party systems, or integrating with an application managed by a different team in the same organization. Coordinate with the different teams to understand the dependencies and activities needed to deploy their solution. There should be one single deployment plan for all the components that need to be deployed as part of the release.
- Keep the overall deployment plan simple. Add additional attachments or links for the detailed steps that need to be performed.
- Create a repository to collect the artifacts and documentation required for completing individual tasks, including release notes, validation plan document, configuration checklist, code artifacts, and so on.

- Put together a visual summary of the detailed plan. It helps in communicating with the stakeholders.
- Every step, including logistics such as booking hotel rooms and ordering pizza, should be put on the plan with their owners.
- Ensure that you have not burnt your key resources with the release. Spread out the tasks in a way that allows for some downtime for the key resources. The real journey starts after putting the system into production, and you need everyone to stay energized for those first few weeks of transition.

Executing a release

More simulations, prior to going live, will make the final execution easy. It also helps prepare the recipe for the no panic pill. No matter how much preparation goes into planning a release, there may still be a few last-minute new discoveries. It is important how you react to them and maintain a *no-panic* environment. Consider following while executing a release:

- Track the tasks as per the Go Live plan and their dependencies.
- Send communications a multiple number of times (on track/ahead or behind, and the like) during the release window (communicate the frequency to all the stakeholders).
- Schedule conference calls with the leadership team to provide updates (you need to be giving them proactive updates rather than having them at your back, chasing for updates) as well as the Go/No-Go decisions at specific intervals.
- Engage the IT SMEs and business SMEs for data validation. You need to record these tests (reports from the previous system and the new system), and save the test results. You will need them for your audit.
- Run through the release validation tests to verify that a functionality is working as expected. If you can hold a good sample of transactions from the previous working day, try to process them in the system and take them end-to-end. You can hold half a day worth of orders from a day prior to Go Live, enter them manually in the new system, and try to take them all the way through invoicing. Verify the reverse logistics as well. Verify the access to reports and integrations across multiple systems.
- Stay alert for upcoming surprises, and handle them sooner.

The following figure shows an example of the Go Live plan execution and the communication plan:

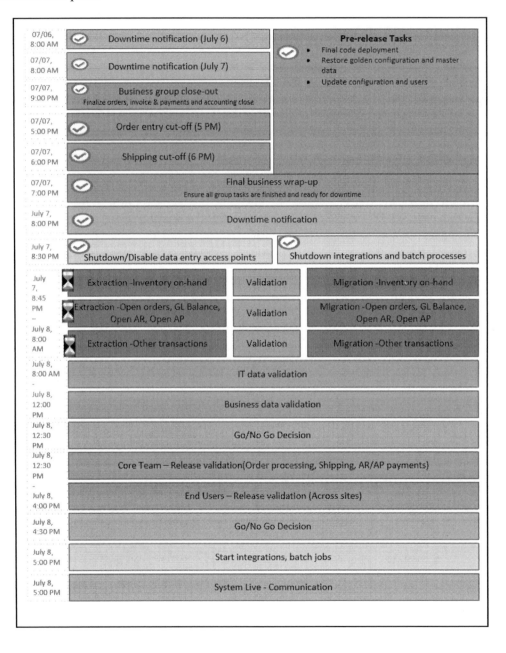

As shown in the figure, you can use this kind of format for tracking the execution of the Go Live plan as well as for communicating the progress of the execution with the stakeholders.

The importance of communication

Communication is a crucial part of the Go Live planning. Following is one of the references I would like to provide on why communication is so important when avoiding turning smaller issues into bigger challenges.

In one of the upgrade projects, we had a very small downtime window to perform the upgrade. It was shortened further, as updates in the data warehouse were going to take time, and we had to keep aside some time for rollback as well. However, with multiple iterations (thanks to the great technical team that was on the project), we were able to squeeze time to meet our requirements. Most of the core technical team was up the whole night to perform the upgrade and went to bed after the handover to the team in the morning. It was almost bug-free until users showed up at the warehouse and started shipping. The requested delivery date printed on the shipping labels was the same day; the warehouse couldn't start shipping.

Multiple emails and phone calls were received with messages such as *Warehouse can't ship, Warehouse is down, Need to call FedEx for delayed pickup, Should we stop picking,* and so on. This noise went on for two hours. It was hard to get a clear understanding of the real issue, until we reduced the audience and got on to call.

In AX 2009, Microsoft added multiple dates on the sales orders, such as estimated shipping date, requested shipping date, confirmed shipping date, and so on. One of these custom date fields to be printed on the shipping label was mapped incorrectly to the default value (that is, the system date). This date was the delivery date given to the post, which, obviously, couldn't be the same date. It was just one line of code change for the developer, once the real issue was explained.

 Based on our learning from past experiences, managing communications after Go Live is the most critical.

Summary

In this chapter, you learned about one of the final phases of the implementation project, Go Live. Go Live is exciting, but is also the most hectic and intense period of the project. Cloud has changed the way a production environment is managed and updated. Roles and responsibilities have changed. We started with understanding how a production environment's responsibilities vary based on the deployment model you selected for your project. In the cloud deployment model, Microsoft is responsible for managing the production infrastructure, and in on-premise deployment, the responsibility is on the customers and partners. We discussed Go Live activities to understand what all goes during the Go Live phase of the project. The decision of going live or not is not easy and needs many considerations. We went through the topic to describe all you need to understand to make that decision, the different sign offs you need, how it can be difficult for project managers and stakeholders to make a decision to not Go Live if things are not good, and the importance of planning business contingency. In the end, we discussed how you can put together a plan and mitigate the risks through multiple simulations and reviews. This was followed by tips for the execution of a Go Live plan and the importance of managing communication.

You are now live and the business has a stable system to use. Going live is an important milestone. Now, you have a solid ERP platform in place. It opens up the door for business transformation opportunities through the power of the new modern ERP.

In the next chapter, we will go through post Go Live and discover how to monitor the production environment and deal with post-production issues.

13
Post Go Live Support

In the previous chapter, you read about going live and cutover activities and how best to manage these activities.

In this chapter, we will cover post go live activities spanning support, issue identification, tracking, resolutions, and the whole 360-degree issue lifecycle.

We will cover the following topics:

- Resources for support
- Support tools and LCS
- Issue/support lifecycle
- Production environment support with Microsoft
- Support analytics using monitoring and diagnostics
- Best practices in post Go Live/support

You just went live and you should note ERP/business applications are not the destinations; they are a journey. Hence, you must constantly keep it updated, enhance it, derive maximum value, and proactively maintain it. This requires a strong support plan, support advisor or partner, and leveraging all avenues for getting the best support.

Resources for support

Support in the cloud world is expected to be quick, one-touch enabled, and with minimal impact to operations. However, one needs to know and leverage various tools available for seeking support.

I would like to mention a saying and use it as an analogy for support in Dynamics 365 for Finance and Operations, Enterprise Edition, *It takes a lot of effort to get the top position, it takes even more effort to maintain that position.* To provide context with Dynamics 365, you may have successfully gone live, but it takes a significant effort to ensure smooth operations post Go Live. Using the Star Wars analogy in ERP implementation, *Never underestimate the force,* never under-estimate any issue until its impact and root cause is fully known.

In this chapter, you'll explore various options for seeking support, tools used in support, an end to support lifecycle, and best practices in support.

With a lot of choices, comes a lot of decision-making time; hence, we would like to empower you with various helpful resources to enable you to maintain your Dynamics 365 solution.

One can seek knowledge using a number of options as follows:

- **Issue search (LCS)**:
    - Always search with keywords in LCS for the issue/situation to see whether it's a known issue and for possible solutions/workarounds from the principal
    - Here, you not only search for an issue but also its triage history, fixes, and solution information for resolution

- **Microsoft help documentation/wiki**:
  - This is a single place for all help content for Dynamics 365 for Finance and Operations, Enterprise edition
  - It has several user guides that can help you learn how to make Dynamics 365 for Finance and Operations, Enterprise edition work for your business
  - `https://docs.microsoft.com/en-us/dynamics365/operations`
  - Always make it a point to have explored help documentation from Microsoft

- **Forums**:
  - Always search whether the issue/situation you are facing was ever faced by someone and whether a potential analysis and solution is available in these forums. These forums include but are not limited to:
    - Microsoft Dynamics Community (`https://community.dynamics.com/`)
    - MSDynamicsWorld (`https://msdynamicsworld.com`)
    - **AX User Group (D365UG/AXUG)** (`https://www.axug.com/`)

- **Blogs**:
  - We recommend you to keep a list of blogs of all the MVPs of Dynamics 365 for Finance and Operations, Enterprise edition (AX) to get the latest and greatest information at your fingertips
  - For blogs from Microsoft about Dynamics 365, visit `https://explore.dynamics.com/`

- **Google/Bing search**:
  - If nothing can be found, just try searching the entire web using a good search engine to find a solution to your situation

- **Advisor/MVP/experts**:
  - When a solution is identified and you are unsure whether to go with it or not or a solution is not found, it is best to approach an expert from the area/capability

- **Dynamics Learning Portal (DLP)**:
  - DLP has evolved a lot and is a great knowledge repository for partners to leverage detailed documentation from Microsoft about its product and features
  - This portal is available to Microsoft Dynamics partners only

- **Roadmap**:

    - We are all curious about the future and what may come next, hence, visiting the roadmap site is going to help you plan your future solution growth
    - Visit `https://roadmap.dynamics.com` for more details

- **Feedback**:

    - If you want to help Microsoft in improving Dynamics 365 and its family of products and solutions, you could visit `https://ideas.dynamics.com/ideas/` and share ideas, suggestions, and feedback

- **Portals**:

    - For customers: `https://mbs.microsoft.com/customersource`
    - For partners: `https://mbs.microsoft.com/partnersource`

See whether your team/partner has evaluated all the preceding options before logging a support incident, as issues could be analogous to an iceberg; what you may see is not what the issue and its impact may be.

Let's now explore various support tools available in LCS that are recommended in your implementation journey.

Support tools and LCS

The support lifecycle uses a number of tools to empower users and implementation teams to collaborate on issues, resolutions, and quick turnarounds for closure. These tools/apps include Dynamics 365 for Finance and Operations, Enterprise edition, LCS, and VSTS/VSO to deliver a great support experience to all stakeholders involved.

Let's see how one can create an issue in LCS using the following options:

- **Directly from within Dynamics 365 for Finance and Operations, Enterprise edition (AX)**:

    - Cloud deployment of Finance and Operations provide ability for users and administrator to search about any ongoing issue using browser client. **Issue search** in the client provide the same search functionality as available **Issue search** tool in LCS.

- If any hotfix available based on the search context, user can submit a request for the hotfix. This step creates a hotfix request within LCS project **Support** page for further investigation and analysis.
- User can also create and submit issue from the client, Issue created from the client are available in the LCS under **Support** tile.
- Issues that are created through the Finance and Operations client contain metadata about the Dynamics AX environment. When these issues are selected in the issue grid, the **Troubleshoot** button becomes available.
- When you click on **Troubleshoot**, the event monitoring page opens. This page lets you access events and logs that are related to the issue. The page shows activities, error messages, and other information that has occurred within the last two hours since the issue was reported.

- **Directly from within LCS**:
    - When a support or work items tile is clicked on in LCS, you will be taken to the **Work items** screen.

- The **Work items** screen comprises of four areas, as shown in the following screenshot:

Now, let's explore each of the preceding **Work items** option and their use case scenarios in the following section:

- **Open work items**:
    - Based on the LCS project settings to map different work items in VSTS, this is the only place where information flows from VSTS to LCS for a visibility purpose
    - Work items of type bug or task created within VSTS are available in LCS.

- **Support issues**:
    - Issues created directly in LCS or via Dynamics 365 for Finance and Operations, Enterprise edition (AX) are seen on the list as seen in the preceding image under the **Support issues** tab
    - These issues could be product issues escalated to Microsoft via a support ticket or could be implementation/solution issues that your advisor/partner can help in resolving

- **Service requests**:
    - There are three kinds of service request available at present to leverage:
        - **Database point-in-time restore request**: This is for database backup restoration for your production
        - **Database refresh request**: This is to restore copy of production data in Sandbox environment
        - **Other request**: Generic request that does not belong to the preceding two requests

- **Hotfix requests**:
    - From the environment tile in an LCS project, two options are shown under the monitoring section: Application X++ updates and Binary updates. Refer `Chapter 14`, *Update, Upgrade, and Migration* for more details on hotfixes, updates and upgrade.
    - For an application X++ hotfix, apply the package in a development environment. After resolving any conflicts, generate a deployable package from Visual Studio and upload the package to the asset library software deployable package.
    - For a binary hotfix, upload the hotfix directly to the asset library under software deployable package. These could be Microsoft provided platform updates and so on.
    - There is one more type known as the metadata hotfix--the installation, and deployment of this and other hotfixes are explained in detail in the `Chapter 14`, *Update Upgrade Migration*.

The following is a screenshot showing an application X++ hotfix search screen, the ability to click and select one or many hotfixes, and then, download the package:

 In `Chapter 2`, *Implementation Methodology and Tools*, we have looked at LCS and the various tooling it offers. We recommended you to get conversant with all the key LCS tools for your implementation and post-implementation activities.

For detailed information about hotfixes and updates, refer to `Chapter 14`, *Update Upgrade Migration*.

Issue/support lifecycle

There are a series of steps and precautions to be taken while seeking support in Dynamics 365 for Finance and Operations, Enterprise edition (AX) to make the most of all available tools and options.

Let's see from a bird's eye view, an end-to-end picture of issue/support lifecycle using the following image:

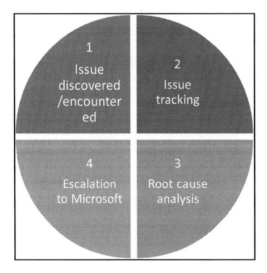

We'll now look at each of the preceding lifecycle considerations starting from issue discovery to its tracking, to root cause analysis then solution finding and issue closure.

Issue discovered/encountered

Whenever an issue or a problem is identified in Dynamics 365 for Finance and Operations, Enterprise edition (AX), we recommend you to use the LCS issue search tool to look for information and solution options.

The LCS issue search tool has a search field to search the issue encountered, as follows:

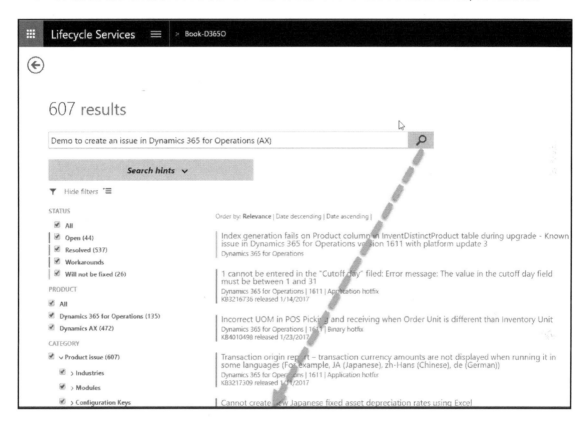

We recommend you to record task guides to add as additional details about the issue spanning:

- Save the steps, symptoms, setups, and output
- Save task guide with developer recording

Save the recorded task guide as both Word document and as an XML/developer document.

The following is a screenshot of the task guide tool in Dynamics 365 for Finance and Operations, Enterprise edition and its various capabilities to record, play, and save the recordings:

After having captured the details about the issue, it is time to raise a support issue right within Dynamics 365 for Finance and Operations, Enterprise edition (AX). We do it in the following steps:

1. We recommend that the end user or super user should be empowered to create a support request.
2. Refer to the following screenshot as the starting point to raise a support from within the solution. You can access the support fly-out by clicking on the **?** question symbol at the top-right corner and by selecting the **Support** option:

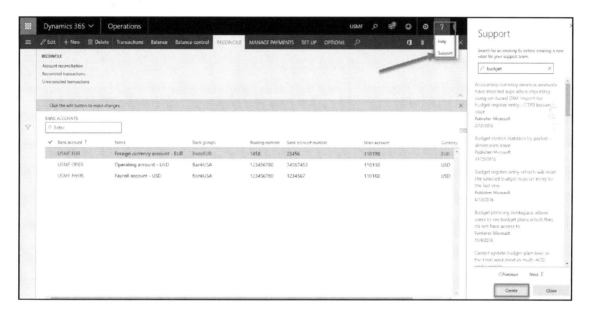

As seen in the preceding screenshot, you will notice context-specific help based on the screen opened and from where the issue is being created.

- Once no resolution is found, you may create a support issue by clicking on the **Create** button as highlighted in the previous screenshot. This will open up the **Contact support** screen and you need to provide a couple of details, as follows:

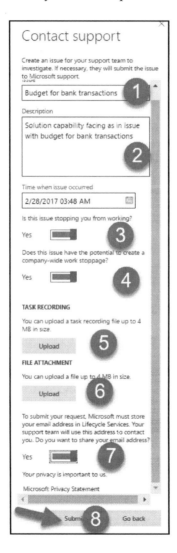

Once the issue details are captured and the issue is logged in the support system, it is important to track the issue.

Issue tracking

In Dynamics 365 for Finance and Operations, Enterprise edition, when a user clicks on **Submit** in the contact support screen, a support issue is automatically created as a work item as seen in the LCS support tile:

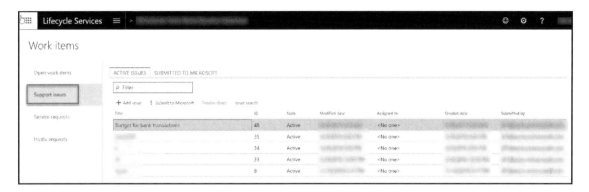

 With VSTS sync, the issue will also get created in VSTS as a work item type issue.

Let's see how the issue created in LCS looks in VSTS.

The following is the image of the issue automatically created in VSTS, and once it is in VSTS, you can leverage all your CMMI level practices to manage the issue lifecycle:

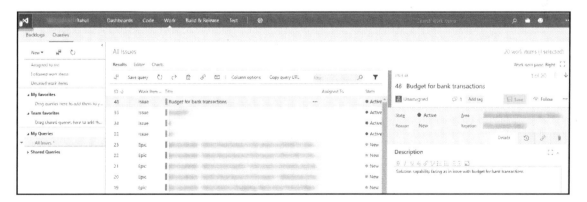

Capability Maturity Model Integration (**CMMI**) is a process level improvement training and appraisal program. It is administered by the CMMI Institute and was developed at **Carnegie Mellon University** (**CMU**).

We recommend you to always collect the following details along with the issue and post issue analysis for a quicker resolution and traceability:

- Task guide (user and development recordings)
- Issue triage
- Issue classification
- Problem isolation
- Root cause analysis
- Solution workaround or recommendations
- Training issues

After capturing the issue and logging it within LCS and VSTS, it is important to isolate the problem, find the root cause of the issue, and analyze impact and solution options.

Root cause analysis

VSTS should be used for all your project activities, goals, deliverables, code, documents, and collaboration as well as for your single source of support. We recommend the following steps in performing root cause analysis along with problem isolation, as follows:

Once the issue is available in VSTS, it should be classified and updated with more details. All ownership, assignments, and linking with existing BPM artifacts are recommended to be done in VSTS.

Advisor/partners/implementation team members must recreate the issue in a non-production environment, isolate the problem, and capture issue insights. The identified root cause should be updated in the VSTS work item for resolution.

Following a screenshot shows an issue work item being edited in VSTS with numbering to highlight key information fields.

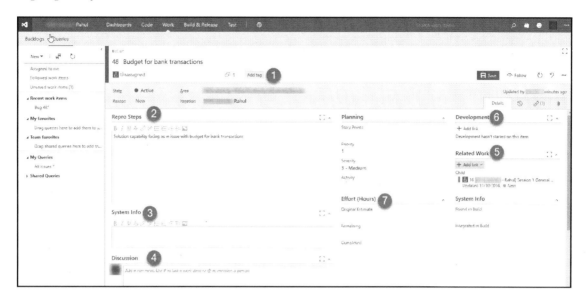

As shown above, VSTS allows lot of detailed information to be captured any kind of issue and some of the recommended ones are as below:

1. Add tags for ease in reporting and searching.
2. Steps for reproducing the issue/defect.
3. Information regarding state of system.
4. Any historical as well as future discussions can be captured and maintained.
5. Document links and attachments to this and other related issues.
6. Information from development perspective are also expected to be captured here.
7. Expected effort to triage, reproduce and solve the issue.

The above information helps in performing root cause analysis (RCA) quickly and accurately thus enabling faster turnaround time in issue resolution.

Based on the root cause analysis, if the issue seems to belong to the principal or Microsoft, then, it should be logged as a support ticket.

Escalation to Microsoft

If identified that the issue relates to an out-of-the-box product functionality, then in LCS support listing, the issue should be flagged for submission to Microsoft. A selection of your support plan/SLA and contract needs to be made (for example, premier versus non-premier) while submitting the issue.

For a showstopper issue submitted to Microsoft, always ensure you seek support from the solution architect from the Microsoft Dynamics R&D team assigned to your implementation and your partner and advisor.

The following is a screenshot where the **Submit to Microsoft** button is highlighted, which further opens a selection screen to select the contract type:

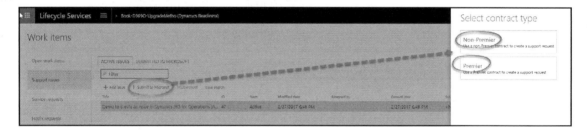

After the contract type is selected, you will be taken to the issue search screen, wherein the user can search for resolution one more time before deciding to write to Microsoft. The idea here is to get the resolution if it's already available, saving a lot of time and faster issue closure and also saving your incident count:

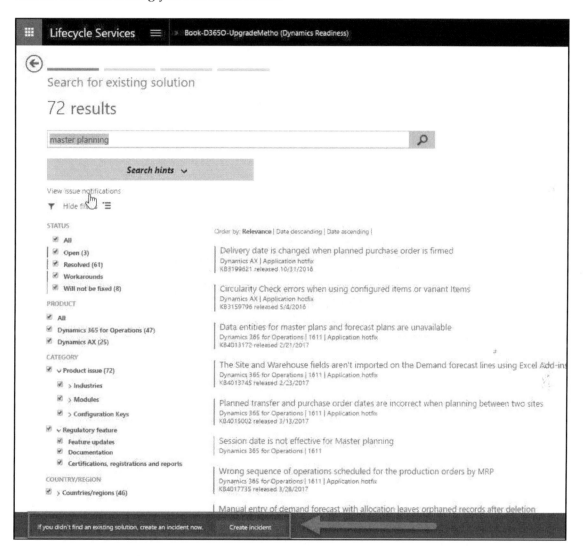

As seen in the preceding issue search screen, you get an additional option to create an incident, which otherwise is not available when just going through the issue search.

After the user clicks on **Create incident**, a screen will appear asking for more information such as severity, contact details, and other information that is typically needed when submitting an issue to Microsoft:

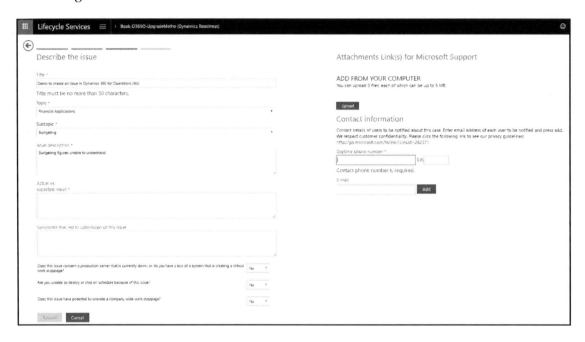

We'll now look at what has changed in the cloud world when your production environment is managed by Microsoft.

Production environment support with Microsoft

If you are using the cloud only version of Dynamics 365 for Finance and Operations, Enterprise edition, then in order to perform any activity on production environment, you need to work with Microsoft as they are the owner of the environment and you won't have any access to the production environment other than the URL for your solution.

Any interaction with the production environment can be done with a Microsoft service engineer. Hence, any communication with a **Dynamics Service Engineer** (**DSE**) needs to be tracked, organized, and be user-friendly. Thus, there is a need for a service request so that the customer, partners, advisors, and implementation teams can raise a request for any service needs in the production environment.

Following visual shows the three types of request which can be initiated in LCS as a service request:

The preceding screenshot shows the fly-out when a user clicks on the **Add** button in the **Work items** screen under the **Service requests** section.

> For any solution issues, one should use the **Support issues** capability, while for any production environment-related request, one needs to use **Service requests**.

With ongoing support and a lot of moving parts and issues, it is important to gain insightful information. Hence, support analytics play a significant role in decision making and also proactive support.

Support analytics using monitoring and diagnostics

In the cloud world, advisors, partners, and customer implementation teams need to leverage all possible available data in LCS to monitor and diagnose an environment. Telemetry data is the basis of monitoring and diagnostics in LCS.

Support analytics comprises three information tenants: monitoring, diagnostics, and analytics, which are explained in the subsequent section.

Monitoring

Microsoft supports two types of monitoring to view the health of an environment through LCS via availability and health monitoring. We'll now look at each of these.

- **Availability monitoring**: This type of monitoring performs a check against the environment to make sure that it's available at all times. If the check fails, the Microsoft service engineering team is immediately notified:

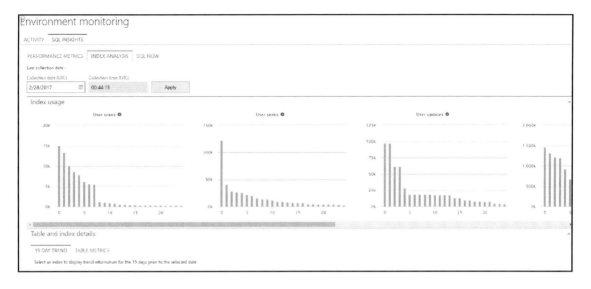

The various preceding charts are for index analysis on SQL Azure for a production environment. The **Index usage** view shows the most expensive indices on the environment based on seeks versus scans along tables with the highest row count. Also, one can gain information of the state and run on SQL Azure as well as performance metrics.

The feature **SQL NOW** gives the ability to troubleshoot SQL Azure issues in real time by looking into which queries are blocked and which queries are blocking them. It also provides a view in tables that have locks on them.

- **Health monitoring**: In addition to availability checks, some basic health checks must be performed. These basic health checks include CPU level, memory consumption of the virtual machines (VMs), and the total number of deadlocks in a five-minute period.

Microsoft Telemetry Infrastructure collects health metrics from the environments and if a metric crosses a threshold value, the Microsoft service engineering team is alerted so that the issue can be investigated.

Diagnostics

Telemetry data helps build a storyboard view that shows what that user and other users were doing when the issue was reported. In addition to user activity tracking, a rich set of SQL data is also available for performance troubleshooting using **SQL NOW**:

As shown in the preceding screenshot, **Environment monitoring** gives you information about the state spanning user load, activity load, SQL, server utilization, and so on spread across a configurable time scale.

Refer to `Chapter 2`, *Implementation Methodology and Tools*, for LCS - tooling called system diagnostics and its usage, which also plays a significant role in proactive monitoring.

Analytics

Analytics is another critical use case for the telemetry data that is collected. Currently, only Microsoft can perform analytics, so it can gauge and understand feature usage and performance through Microsoft Power BI.

For Dynamics 365 for Finance and Operations, Enterprise edition, Microsoft is responsible for actively monitoring the health of production environments at all times as it is a managed cloud service.

 The customer, however, is responsible for monitoring and troubleshooting the health of non-production environments.

Best practices in post Go Live/support

We recommend the following best practices while managing support/issues in Dynamics 365 for Finance and Operations, Enterprise edition:

- Always use VSTS sync with LCS BPM; this ensures end-to-end traceability
- Leverage Dynamics 365 for Finance and Operations, Enterprise edition or LCS to raise any support issues
- Issue should always be supported with information regarding its impact, symptoms, and task guides with steps and developer recording
- Issue management should be done in VSTS until its closure and an issue should only be closed by the originator
- Issue tracking should cover ownership assignments and artifacts linking with requirements, test cases, and other issues/bugs
- Ensure a rigorous release and test process to ensure minimum impact to working solutions
- Always use telemetric data in the form of monitoring and diagnosis to be proactive in managing your Dynamics 365 for Finance and Operations, Enterprise edition production instance

Summary

In this chapter, you learned about post go live activities, support planning, issue management and tools to use throughout the lifecycle of an issue. We covered capabilities in LCS, such as **Issue Search**, **Work items**, **Support**, and various other kinds of services request. We also touched upon hotfixes and the three types, namely binary, X++ application, and metadata, which will be covered in the next chapter in detail. The role of VSTS is crucial to be on top of your support/issue lifecycle. Issues generated either in Dynamics 365 for Finance and Operations, Enterprise edition or directly in LCS, must be synchronized in VSTS with proper documentation and steps using task guides and should be tracked and maintained in VSTS for its root cause analysis till closure. We also covered the steps of submitting product-related issues to Microsoft using support tooling in LCS as well as how to raise various kinds of service request related to your production environment on Azure managed by Microsoft.

Also, various options to manage your environment from monitoring, diagnostics, and analytics was covered highlighting SQL NOW, environment monitoring, and so on. The resources shared in the first section of this chapter are your knowledge repositories for any support situation and continuous learning.

In the next chapter, we will look at the upgrade and migration capabilities in Dynamics 365 for Finance and Operations, Enterprise edition.

14
Update, Upgrade, and Migration

In the previous chapter, you read about post go live activities, support, and best practices to keep the ERP value momentum going. The post go live phase is an interesting phase, as it is never static. Its dynamic nature calls for continuous improvement of your business platform, keeping up to date with the latest trends, and having a healthy system to fuel your organization growth.

In this chapter, we will cover activities involving evaluation of migration options from prior versions of Dynamics 365 for Finance and Operations, Enterprise edition. This spans updates to your solution and upgrades from a prior major version or migration from a version which existed before.

We will be sharing knowledge on upgrade and migration using the following topics:

- Understanding update, upgrade, and migration
- Updating to the latest Dynamics 365 for Finance and Operation version
- Upgrading/migrating from Dynamics AX 2012 or AX 2009
- Upgrading/migration planning
- Upgrading from Dynamics AX 2012
- Migrating from Dynamics AX 2009
- Best practices in upgrade and migration

Understanding update, upgrade, and migration

Before jumping to the details on different sections, let's understand the terminology used in this chapter; update, upgrade, and migration are technically enabled by what version of Dynamics 365 for Operation your organization currently has.

- **Update**: We will use the term update as a process of keeping your Dynamics 365 for Finance and Operations, Enterprise edition up to date with latest releases. With new concepts, such as models and new programming model extensions, it is easier than ever for organizations to adopt continuous innovation from Microsoft. In the following section, we will explore in detail the process of updating Dynamics 365 for Finance and Operations to the latest version.

- **Upgrade**: The term upgrade is used when upgrading to Dynamics 365 for Finance and Operations from an earlier version of Dynamics AX 2012. In this scenario, Microsoft supports the direct upgrade path by providing the tool set for code and data upgrade.

- **Migration or re-implementation**: The migration term is used when you are upgrading to Dynamics 365 for Finance and Operations, Enterprise edition from Dynamics AX 2009 or an earlier version. In this scenario, there is no code upgrade or data upgrade path. The customer has to re-implement the customization in finance and operations from scratch. Microsoft provides data migration tools to support data migration of configuration, master data, and open transactions from AX 2009 to Finance and Operations.

If you are planning to get the latest version of Dynamics 365 for Finance and Operations, it is important for you to know which option is applicable and which activities and efforts will be needed. Depending upon the type, the activities vary, skill sets vary, and tooling may also vary.

Let's explore the different upgrade types, which version they target, what is done in that upgrade types as well as its processing techniques in the following table:

Criteria/type	Update	Upgrade	Migrate
Version	Earlier versions of Dynamics 365 for Finance and Operations	Dynamics AX 2012	AX 2009, AX 4.0, AX 3.0
Type	Code, data	Code, data	Reimplement code, migrate data, adapt new process
Processing	Automatic	Partially automatic	Manual
Tools	LCS, Visual Studio, and data upgrade tool	LCS, Visual Studio, and data upgrade tool	LCS, Visual Studio, and data migration tool
Effort	Low	Medium to high	High

As shown previously, the efforts vary significantly due to processing options, efforts, and activities involved when migrating to the latest version of Dynamics 365 for Finance and Operations. If you are already on an earlier version of Dynamics 365 for Finance and Operations, it's easier than ever to get the latest version. New architecture and technology stacks help to make the upgrade easier. Upgrading from AX 2012 will require code upgrades, and data upgrade processes and tooling is provided to help the upgrade process.

Code upgrades from an earlier version, such as AX 2009 or AX 4.0 are not supported; you need to re-implement your customization in the new version and do data migration to the extent of configuration, master data, and open transactions only. Re-implementation is similar in nature to a fresh implementation, as it would entail a number of milestones overall, with a standard fresh ERP implementation.

Let's now explore each of the update types involved in an upgrade, in the subsequent sections.

Updating to the latest Dynamics 365 for Finance and Operation version

One of the key advantages of the Dynamics 365 for Finance and Operations new architecture is to make updates easier. Now, you can uptake new product innovations, features, and updates easier than ever before and keep your system current. Microsoft Dynamics 365 for Finance and Operations, Enterprise edition is serviced as a cloud offering. In this section, we will walk through the process of applying platform updates and application updates. To understand the process better, let's first understand the basics and different scenarios for updates. Updates in Dynamics 365 for Finance and Operations can be categorized into the following three scenarios:

- Updates to the latest platform
- Updates to the latest application
- Updates to a specific application hotfix

Let's explore these scenarios in the following sections.

Updates to the latest platform

The Dynamics 365 for Finance and Operations platform consists of a kernel level binary as well as X++ metadata related to core functionality, such as batch framework, workflow engine, and integration layer. Since February 2017, platform updates are released on a monthly basis. The platform release includes any bug fixes for the previous platform and new minor features. The following are the three most important characteristics of platform updates:

- **Minimal/no change**: After platform update 3 (Nov 2016), a application platform is hard sealed which means it cannot be overlayered. This makes it easier to update latest platform release as there will be no to minimal changes if you are on update 3. In the platform updates, Microsoft makes sure that any code change does not break changes and ensures that any extension you build on top of the platform will not break with the new platform. The expectation is that you don't even have to compile. You can simply apply the update using LCS in a non-production environment and test and sign off and then, get the updates applied to the production environment.
- **Cumulative**: Platform updates are cumulative, which means the latest version contains all the previous version code. You don't have to apply these updates one by one, just apply the latest one.

- **Backward compatible**: Platform updates are backward compatible which means that an older version of the application can run on newer versions of the platform.

Platform update 1 and platform update 2 allowed overlayering of platform X++ code. Later, platform updates had the platform level X++ locked for overlayering. If you are upgrading from platform update 1 or platform update 2, your developers will need to refactor the overlayering as extensions before you can upgrade. If you are upgrading from platform update 3 or higher to a later platform update, you can do so without refactoring your X++ code.

The following are the various choices to search and receive the latest platform updates:

- In **Lifecycle Services (LCS)**, open your project **Asset library**, click on **IMPORT** and select the platform update package from the shared asset library which is released by Microsoft.
- Searching for `platform update` in LCS **Issue Search** tool/tile.
- Using the **Binary updates** tile in your LCS environment page.

The following image shows the binary updates screen which gives a list of binary updates applicable to your environment; you can click on **Download binaries** to download the updates:

Platform updates (released monthly) and binary updates (if you chose to deploy a hotfix before it's available as part of monthly updates) are applied the same way. To apply the latest platform updates, you can either import the Microsoft released package from the shared asset library or download the latest binary hotfixes and import it into your project asset library. Then, you can use the manage environment option to apply the update package to a developer, build, or test environment.

Refer to the following image with steps to select and apply a binary deployable package:

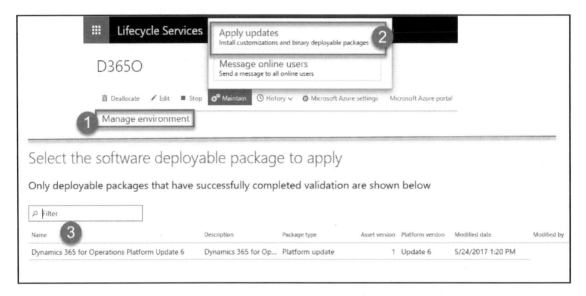

As shown previously, the first step is to click on the **Maintain** button on the LCS environment page. The second step is to select an option to apply updates, and the third step is to select the binary deployable package or your customizations deployable packages.

Upon confirmation, LCS will show a deployment screen showing the servicing environment with platform update and service status with various steps and options to download a log and runbook, as follows:

Once you have applied the latest platform update or binary update in your development and build environment, you can move it to deploy the latest deployable package to your sandbox environment and perform testing. After a successful test cycle, you can upload a request to Microsoft to deploy the changes in the production environment.

Updates to the latest application

This scenario applies to customers who are currently living on an earlier release and want to perform a full upgrade to the most recent platform and application versions.
The Dynamics 365 for Finance and Operations application consists of binaries of application components, such as SSRS, management reporter, and X++ metadata for application modules, such as AR and AP. Application updates are released two times in the year, namely Spring and Fall release, where Microsoft releases any major functionalities.

Updates to the latest application will require code and data upgrades. If you have overlayered the code, you may have code conflicts that needs to be resolved. Let's learn a bit more about the code and data upgrade process.

Upgrading your code

A code upgrade is needed when you are upgrading your application to a new major or cumulative release. As of July 2017, it is possible to overlayer the application suite model for customization. Overlayering enables the possibility of code conflict in your customization with the latest application code. The code upgrade process basically identifies such conflicts and then, manually resolves them by merging or refactoring your code.

The code upgrade process goes through following high-level steps:

1. Using the code upgrade service in LCS to upgrade your code.
2. Deploying a new development environment running the new version that you are upgrading to. You will use this environment to complete code merging and refactoring of your custom code.
3. Completing the code migration steps that require connecting your new development VM to VSTS, getting the upgraded code, resolving any code conflicts, preparing builds, performing tests, and creating a deployable package.

When you are upgrading from an earlier application version of Dynamics 365 for Finance and Operations to the latest version of the application and have significant customization, you may have to do a lot of code refactoring due to model split done in the application suite. For example, in RTW (Feb 2016) version, various modules such as human resources and retail were part of the application suite but in update 2 (Nov 2016), these modules are broken into their own model. In this case, the customer upgrading from RTW to update 2 had to do a lot of refactoring in their customization code.

Even if you do not have any overlayering in your application model, it is still recommended to run your application code to upgrade a service. The code upgrade service will also remove any previously applied metadata hotfixes, which is required when upgrading to the latest application version.

After the application suite is hard sealed (Fall 2018), a application update scenario especially the code upgrade will change. We would expect minor updates releasing monthly similar to the platform update as you won't have any code conflict to worry about. Probably, major updates will still be released two times in a year, however, applying the application update should become easier.

For details and the latest information on the code upgrade process, follow the Microsoft documentation page at `https://docs.microsoft.com/en-us/dynamics365/unified-operations/dev-itpro/lifecycle-services/configure-execute-code-upgrade`.

The next step, after the code upgrade, is to upgrade data which is described in the following section.

Upgrading your data

Application updates may introduce database schema changes and if so, existing data needs to be updated to comply with the new schema. The process of updating your application data according to the new data model is called the data upgrade. When you are upgrading the new application version, after completing your code upgrade you need to run data upgrade. It is strongly recommended to perform the data upgrade on a development environment. In case of any issue, it is much faster to make corrections and rerun the process in a development environment.

The following are high-level steps to perform data upgrade in a sandbox environment:

1. Export the database to a `BACPAC` file from the existing sandbox environment you wish to upgrade.
2. Redeploy the sandbox environment, delete the old environment, and deploy a new environment with a target platform and application version. Include your upgraded custom deployable packages from your asset library to be deployed to the environment.
3. Import the database from a `BACPAC` file into the newly redeployed sandbox environment.
4. Run the data upgrade package.
5. There may be additional components to use in your environment which requires further steps to upgrade.

 For detailed instructions, visit the Microsoft documentation page at `https://docs.microsoft.com/en-us/dynamics365/unified-operations/dev-itpro/migration-upgrade/upgrade-data-to-latest-update`.

Updates to a specific application hotfix

Apart from the monthly platform release and application major releases, you can receive and apply application hotfixes as they become available. These hotfixes usually address specific issues reported by customers or minor functionality release. When needed, these hotfixes can be found on the LCS issue or your environment details tiles.

Application hotfixes or the X++ hotfix can be downloaded individually as they are X++ updates. To download a specific application hotfix, you can click on the X++ updates button on the LCS environment page; it takes you to a screen similar to the issue search screen, wherein an issue/update can be searched and selected to be part of a package.

You can select more than one X++ update in a package.

In the following screenshot, here are the things that need to be changed:

- The first highlighted section is a keyword and is used to select an application or X++ related issue/hotfix/update.
- The second highlighted section is to validate the background of the hotfix and accordingly add to your package.
- The third highlighted section is to download the package to apply to your environment.

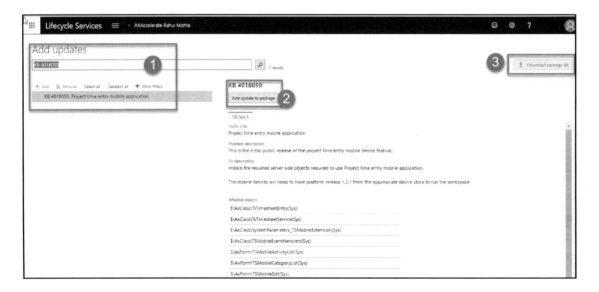

After downloading the X++ updates package, it needs to be applied to your development environment. This is applied as a metadata hotfix containing the `.axscdppkg` file:

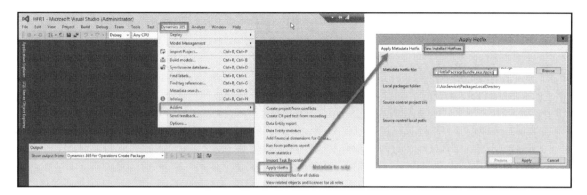

As shown in the preceding screenshot, to apply a metadata hotfix, open Visual Studio (in administrator mode), go to Dynamics 365 in the ribbon, select **Addins**, and then select **Apply Hotfix**. Here, you will be prompted with a dialog screen asking for the location of the **Metadata hotfix file** and your **Local packages folder** (in a cloud environment, path is typically `J:\AOSService\PackagesLocalDirectory`).

After the install command is invoked, the package installation process begins. As part of the installation process, some XML files in your metadata store folder will be updated to reflect the changes that were made in the fix itself.

If you're using VSTS or TFS, these files will be added to the list of included changes in the pending changes window in Team Explorer.

After verifying the hotfix listed on the **View Installed Hotfixes** tab, you are now ready to perform various tests to ensure the effectiveness and impact of the hotfix. After validating the metadata hotfix, you need to create a deployable package to deploy it to the sandbox and other environments. When using version control, you can check in your pending changes to VSTS using Team Explorer in Microsoft Visual Studio. Other developers can synchronize their code base with VSTS to get the latest changes in their development environment. Using the build environment, you can build a deployable package and deploy the final changes to other environments.

If using a build environment for build and test automation, the build automation process can build metadata hotfix files which are in your VSTS project; however, a hotfix can be built only if the descriptor file of the model that it belongs to is checked in to version control.

If the metadata hotfix package contains changes to objects that have been customized in higher-layer models, then the installation process automatically generates conflicts which must be resolved after the hotfix installation. Development tools allow you to create a project that groups all items that have conflicts by clicking on **Visual Studio | Dynamics 365 | Addins | Create project in conflicts**.

In the dialog box, select a model to check for conflicts and click on **Create project**. A project is generated that contains only those elements in the selected model that were found to have conflicts after the hotfix was applied. Open the designer for the conflicting element to view conflicts and resolve them using the tools that are provided.

> More information can be obtained at `https://docs.microsoft.com/en-us/dynamics365/operations/dev-itpro/migration-upgrade/install-metadata-hotfix-package`.

In the preceding section, we covered the update process and various techniques to seek and apply them. In the next section, we will cover the process of upgrading from version AX 2012 to Dynamics 365 for Finance and Operations, Enterprise edition.

Upgrading/migrating from Dynamics AX 2012 or AX 2009

In the previous sections, you learned how to update to the latest version of Dynamics 365 for Finance and Operations when you are already live or implementing a previous version of Finance and Operations. Now, let's explore what it takes to upgrade to Finance and Operations from the previous version of the product such as Dynamics AX 2012 or Dynamics AX 2009.

When to upgrade or migrate

Every technological system should be used in its best state. The decision and timing can be deferred but you should always try to be using the latest version. At the same time, the decision to upgrade is not easy; it's important to carefully examine and evaluate the pros and cons before embarking on an upgrade project. The following section mentions a few considerations to keep in mind before an upgrade:

- **Benefit to the business operation**: You should not just upgrade or implement a new technology platform. Instead, there should be a clear benefit to the business by upgrading to a new version. A thorough analysis of the new features that can be useful for the business needs to be done and a vision scope for the upgrade should be put together. Some of these features may be new to the business while some could replace your existing customization or third-party systems. The benefits could include moving operations from on-premises to the cloud, new features and functionalities, increased efficiency and productivity, and transparency through better reporting. The benefits should also justify the time and cost required to execute the upgrade project. A proper roadmap to realize the benefits and returns on the investment should be established.

- **Are operations ready for the change?**: Change is not easy. Upgrades often bring new user interfaces, functionalities, and processes with them, and it's not easy for a business to tackle these changes. The following are some key considerations:
    - Identify the competing business projects that would have to be reprioritized or delivered as part of the upgrade. Opportunity cost needs to be evaluated (as you would have to redeploy the IT/business resources and run into code freeze as part of the upgrade project).
    - An upgrade is not a technology project and needs good involvement from the business. The business should be ready to commit resources to the upgrade project.
    - Conduct an independent post-implementation review, and scope out what you would want to fix from the initial implementation as part of the upgrade, such as redoing specific customizations and doing the customization through extension.

- **Stabilization of the newer version**: In reality, it takes a few months for any new release to stabilize. You wouldn't want to get burned with early-on product issues as part of the project or let the business be affected due to the issues in production. If you choose to be early adaptors, ensure that you have enough support and blessings from your partner and the Microsoft team, in case you run into issues. For newly released modules, try to defer the implementation post upgrade until it is mature/stabilized enough.

- **Continued technical support**: For many organizations, this is one of the key reasons for the upgrade. It's important and critical for the customer to have continued vendor support and assistance if something goes wrong. For Dynamics AX, Microsoft provides mainstream support for five years or two years, whichever is longer, after the successor product is released. Microsoft also provides extended support following the mainstream support for five or two years, whichever is longer, after the second successor product (*N+2*) is released. You can go for extended support but you must know that upgrading to the latest version gets more and more complicated if you skip many major versions. For existing customers of Dynamics AX, it would be good to know the maximum support duration from Microsoft across their version. The following are the various AX versions and their primary support deadline dates:

Dynamics AX 2012 R3	Mainstream support ends on October 12, 2021	Extended support is available until January 10, 2023
Dynamics AX 2009, AX 2012 R1 and R2	Mainstream support ends in April 10, 2018	Extended support is available until October 12, 2021

From the preceding table, April 2018 is when the mainstream support of versions prior to AX 2012 R3 would end, which means that you should be starting your upgrade initiative at least six to twelve months before to safely transition to Dynamics 365 for Finance and Operations, Enterprise edition.

We recommend you visit Microsoft Support website to get the latest support dates at https://support.microsoft.com/en-us/lifecycle/search/?p1=17873.

Upgrading/migration planning

Upgrading or migrating from Dynamics AX 2012 or AX 2009 is not an easy task especially when you have large customization. Just like an implementation project, an upgrade project needs proper project strategy and planning. To execute a successful upgrade project, you need a proper project plan, change management, test, training, and deployment planning. Even before you start the upgrade project, you have to evaluate if you are ready for an upgrade and evaluate what activities you have to do.

The following image displays the key areas to be considered when planning to upgrade to Dynamics 365 for Finance and Operations:

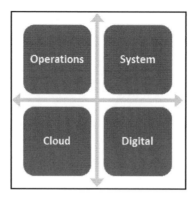

As shown in the preceding image, four quadrants spanning operations/business, system, cloud, and digital factors to assess and capture readiness metrics to ensure that the change initiative involving the upgrade runs smoothly. It is important to plan around each area; let's explore various considerations during upgrade planning in these areas.

Operations

Upgrading the ERP system is not an easy task; it requires buy in from the operations team. The operations team need to understand the benefit and also plan for potential operations impact, business process changes, and business team involvement for validation and training. The following section will explain some key considerations from the operations perspective.

Business benefit

Every organization seeking digital transformation needs to optimize their financials and operations to drive growth. Dynamics 365 for Finance and Operations is a modern ERP that can work as a driver in your digital transformation journey. It is important for the business team to understand the key benefits and objectives of the upgrade project. There can be several potential business benefits of upgrading to Dynamics 365 for Finance and Operations, as follows:

- Potential new out-of-the-box functionalities
- Opportunity for business process reengineering/optimization; use this initiative to redesign your business operations

- Opportunity to bring your ERP and CRM application together with homogenization of business applications and consolidation into one platform using Dynamics 365 for Finance and Operations
- Modern user experiences with modern browser-based application and mobile platform
- Ensure business continuity and system availability with the power of cloud, across geographies and time zone
- Adopt modern and new technologies and be able to innovate quickly with cloud

The IT team should work with the operations team to make sure that they understand and realize the benefit and objective of the upgrade project.

Business engagement

Many times, upgrade projects are branded as a technology upgrade. For the very same reason, it's hard to get the business engaged in upgrade projects. This might be true to some extent when you are doing a minor upgrade, such as upgrading platform upgrade of Dynamics 365 for Finance and Operations. For major version upgrades, such as AX 2012 to Dynamics 365 for Finance and Operations, business engagement is critical. You will need business agreement on various decisions, such as identifying unused features or customization, Fit/Gap analysis of custom features and new features, defining the scope, data archival and purging, training, and UAT.

System

Upgrade planning requires many considerations from a system perspective. This includes deciding between upgrade or reimplementation, managing existing customization, transaction data, system integration, and analytics and reporting. Let's explore these sections further.

Upgrade versus reimplementation

Sometimes, it might be better to plan a fresh implementation of the latest version than upgrading from the old version. The following are the scenarios where reimplementation can be a better approach rather than upgrade:

- If there is no direct upgrade path available. For example, for a customer using Dynamics AX 2009 or 4.0, there are no tools available to directly upgrade his code or data to Dynamics 365 for Finance and Operations; rather, he has to reimplement his customization in the new version.
- When you have heavy customization, several customizations can be eliminated and replaced by standard features.
- If the data quality of the current system is bad and it would require too much effort to clean the data to prepare for the upgrade.
- If there are changes in the fundamental master-data elements. For example, moving away from smart product numbers or implementing the product structure differently using product dimensions, changes in inventory costing, changes in the legal entity structures due to business reasons, such as splitting distribution, manufacturing, and sales of companies.

Managing the scope

What functionality is available in the version you are upgrading to versus what is in the scope of the upgrade project is the issue that needs to be decided.

In my experience, delivering the current functionality available to the business is the first step towards the new platform. No one would like to go backward on the features they already had. However, you should negotiate for not implementing brand new features as part of the upgrade project itself. These new features can come as a next step after the upgrade, even if these features are available out-of-the-box in the new version of Dynamics 365 for Finance and Operations. You need to consider the time needed for the implementation of such features and the impact to the overall timeline of the upgrade. I would rather run parallel projects to implement several new features once I have moved to the latest version, than delay the upgrade itself. This approach allows you to divide the scope into smaller projects for the new features and is easier to manage as well.

Managing customization (fit-gap)

Most upgrade projects that I have reviewed had a common theme. The new version was implemented in the old way, that is, all the customization from the previous version were ported on to the new version—as is. This is not the correct way.

As part of the upgrade analysis or planning, you need to spend a good amount of time finding a match for the existing custom features and deprecate the custom features. Most likely, Microsoft may have developed a feature that you had to customize years ago. This is your opportunity to unlock the power of a newer version and maximize your investment in the platform by tearing off customizations. While it may sound like a no brainer, many projects fail to do so, as it needs additional work to migrate the existing data from custom tables to standard ones. A few minor customizations that are in place may be needed on top of a standard feature if the standard one does not completely replace what you have. Hence, shortcuts are taken and all of the old custom code is ported into the newer version.

Also, there are customizations that may not be used anymore. Those need to be identified and removed or left behind as part of the upgrade project. Plan what customization can be replaced or re-implemented with the new version. You should do a detailed fit-gap analysis for new features and see how these features can benefit the business and if there are any gaps. Plan if they can be addressed during or after the upgrade. Fit-gap analysis is also relevant for custom features in the old system—compare these features with any equivalent features in the new version. Identify the gaps and plan to address them as part of the upgrade. Sometimes, such a list of features can be overwhelming and may add significant scope to the upgrade project.

You also need to make sure that new customizations are done using the new extensibility model. The application suite customization using overlayering will be discontinued after the Spring 2018 release. If you are upgrading to an earlier application version you will be able to do overlayering but this means you cannot uptake new application releases after the application is hard sealed. Refer to `Chapter 9`, *Building Customization* for more details about the extension concept and roadmap for sealing the models.

ISV Solutions

Evaluate your ISV solutions and check if it is still needed. There may be an out-of-the-box solution in the new version which you can easily adapt rather than carry over the ISV solution in the new version. If you still need it, check with them for their readiness on Dynamics 365 for Finance and Operations. You don't want to upgrade ISV code yourself. This is amongst the initial factors as part of your system readiness that should be checked as it can be a deal breaker if one or more of your ISV solutions are not yet ready for Dynamics 365 for Finance and Operations, Enterprise edition.

If you have customized the ISV solution heavily to fit your needs, you might have to plan this as well. A good approach will be to get the compatible ISV version and then add your customization on top of it.

Managing the data

Evaluate the data in terms of quality and volume. Clean the data in the source system if possible. Consider purging or archiving the source data from the production dynamics AX environment to minimize the data upgrade time of the production environment. This would help reduce the time needed for each data upgrade iteration and the downtime needed for performing a production upgrade apart from improving the data quality in the next version.

Impact on integrations

You may have a lot of other applications in your ecosystem that are integrated with Microsoft Dynamics AX. Integration technology is completely changed in Finance and Operations from its previous version. AIF document services which were the primary integration framework in AX 2012 and AX 2009 is deprecated and replaced with OData services and recurring integration using data entities. If your integration uses custom services in Dynamics AX 2012, these are still available and can be used as is or with little bit refactoring if needed. As part of the upgrade to Dynamics 365 for Finance and Operation, you probably need to rebuild all integration in the new version. Take a stock of all the integration you have and analyze and plan how they need to be replaced in the new version.

Impact on Power BI and reporting

Reporting and analytics are another area where you can expect major changes when upgrading from Dynamics AX 2012. Dynamics 365 for Finance and Operations introduced modern BI and reporting capabilities. It utilized the SQL Server reporting services for regular document reporting while analytics is powered by Power BI. If you have customized out-of-the-box SSRS reports in AX 2012 - code upgrade does not upgrade these reports; you have to manually do it.

If you have invested in data warehouse and analytics in AX 2012, you may have to do some work to upgrade this solution to work with Dynamics 365 for Finance and Operations. For example, you may want to utilize the new power BI capabilities provided out-of-the-box or extend this further for your analytical story or use **EntityStore** to your own data warehouse and build analytics from there.

Analyze reports that need to be migrated and evaluate the usage of Power BI and other Azure data tools to do away with some reports. You must revisit your data warehouse platform to leverage out-of-the-box provided **EntityStore** or using aggregated data entities to leverage your own data warehouse.

Cloud and digital

From digital and cloud considerations, we mean being ready for continuous innovation, agility, and resource commitment. In this section, we will explore these considerations further.

Deployment options

While the whole world is embracing cloud and digitization, it is important to have the power of choice for your business platform. This is due to one abstract thing change to which organizations constantly evolve and adapt to market situations.

In the prior version of Dynamics 365 for Finance and Operations, Enterprise edition, customers only had one choice--Cloud through Microsoft public Cloud (Azure). The earlier versions of Dynamics AX (viz. 2012, 2009, 4.0, 3.0) were all client-server architecture with some web footprint. Though there were limited choices on the ERP architecture, customers and partners leverage other technologies to enable more choices to suit the business needs.

This landscape has changed since July 2017 with the availability of two more choices with your popular ERP platform. These choices are on-premises (also known as local business data) and a hybrid model (also known as a Cloud + Edge model).

With this, customers now have three choices and also an opportunity to be on a single platform leveraging full Microsoft stack and seamlessly integrating with their other apps.

The following is an image of the three choices:

As part of the upgrade planning, you have to analyze and decide the best suitable option as per your organization requirements. For more details about architecture and a general idea about these deployment choices, refer to `Chapter 3`, *Architecture and Deployment*.

Upgrading from Dynamics AX 2012

Microsoft Dynamics 365 for Finance and Operations, Enterprise edition provides an upgrade path to customers who currently run Microsoft Dynamics AX 2012 to move their data and code. The upgrade process is built on the following elements:

- Tools to upgrade your custom application code from AX 2012
- A process to upgrade your existing 2012 database with full transaction history

The overall upgrade process can be better visualized as a three-fold approach comprising of analyze, execute, and validate.

- **Analyze**: Analysis part of the upgrade project is about going through upgrade planning considerations described in the last section and evaluating the estimates around code upgrade and data upgrade activity. To start with upgrade project analysis and estimation, you can create upgrade/migration project in LCS and select migration methodology. You can then upload your Dynamics AX 2012 model store (application code) to the Code upgrade tool and select option estimation only. This process will run through your 2012 code and generate reports which list out all the activities you have to perform to upgrade your code base to the latest version of Dynamics 365 for Finance and Operations.

  You can also use another tool called **Upgrade analyzer tool** to analyze your existing 2012 database to prepare you better for the upgrade. The upgrade analyzer tool runs against your AX 2012 environment and identifies tasks that you should do to prepare the AX 2012 environment, to help make the upgrade experience smoother and less expensive. At a high level, the tool provides help with the following features:

  - **Data cleanup**: Identify data in the system which can be removed to reduce the database size. This primarily includes logs and temporary processing data and can be safely deleted.
  - **SQL configurations**: Identify and suggest any SQL configuration changes to help reduce the time that is required for the upgrade Go Live process.
  - **Deprecated features**: It identifies features that you're currently using but that aren't available in finance and operations. Therefore, the process helps you discover gaps in functionality earlier. It also provides suggestions for alternatives.

These reports should give you a high-level overview and effort needed for the upgrade. These reports can also be used to estimate your overall effort, prepare project plan, and get customer buy-in.

- **Execute**: Once you get customer buy-in and are ready to start the upgrade project, you need to go through the following activities as part of the execution phase:
  - **Code upgrade**: Span the source objects to upgrade
  - **Reimplementation**: When there is no possibility of upgrading an element, it must be addressed with its new equivalent or alternate
  - **Data upgrade**: This includes data extraction, transformation, and data loading scripts/service
- **Validation**: Once you are done with code and data upgrade, it is time to test and validate new application code as well as data. If you have significant customization, integration, and ISVs to upgrade, your testing process should be similar to an implementation project, where you will go through system integration and user acceptance testing along with user training.

Let's go deeper and learn more about the process of code and data upgrade in the next section.

Code upgrade

Before you start the code upgrade process, remove unnecessary models from your model store in Dynamics AX 2012. These may be test models created by developers, conflict models that get generated when you import hotfixes, or any other model, which has features you don't use. The fewer models you have, the easier the upgrade process; chances are that a majority of the code will be auto-upgraded, leaving you with minimal manual effort. Make sure to upload a fully compiled model store that has no errors.

The code upgrade process starts with the LCS upgrade tool, a service that runs on the Cloud. The LCS code upgrade service takes a Dynamics AX 2012 model store as input, performs the following tasks, and prepares the solution for Dynamics 365 for Finance and Operations, Enterprise edition. Following image shows the code upgrade tool process in LCS:

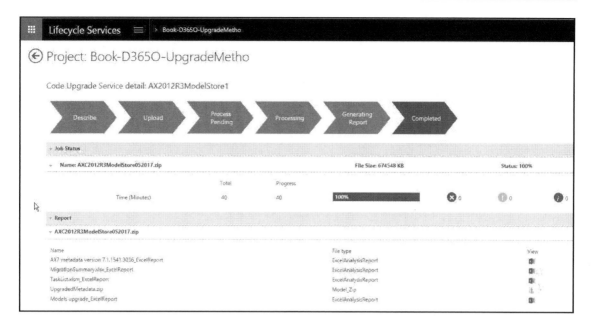

As shown in the preceding image, the code upgrade service in LCS comprises several steps starting from describing the title of an upgrade, uploading AX 2012 model store artifact, processing, and generating report suggesting migration summary, the upgraded model in ZIP format, and more.

This is what happens behind the scenes during the code upgrade process:

- **Convert to XML**: The first thing the LCS code upgrade tool does is to convert your AX 2012 metadata as XML files.
- **Re-baseline model store**: In this step, the model store is split into individual packages. This is nothing but a model split and is essentially the process of rearranging legacy metadata into individual packages.
- **Auto migration**: At the time of writing the book, the code upgrade service migration code used an overlayering principle. However, it's on the roadmap for Microsoft to enable the tool to do code upgrade using the extension approach.
- **Conflicts and TODO**: The tool identifies all elements that contain conflicts, error, or object which need refactoring and adds TODO's in the code for further manual resolution.
- **Conflict project and VSTS**: It creates conflict projects in Visual Studio and finally, check-in the upgraded code to VSTS as a new branch, produce VSTS task, and produce a report for further analysis and fixing.

You can also download your upgraded code as ZIP file from the code upgrade tool. Within your upgraded code folder, you will find three folders:

- **Export**: Project that contains the XML files after exporting from Microsoft Dynamics AX 2012. This contains the metadata in XML format before it is upgraded.
- **Metadata**: Upgraded code (the metadata XML file) on the latest version of Microsoft Dynamics 365 for Finance and Operations, Enterprise edition.
- **Projects**: Two solutions that you can use during the upgrade. One solution, **CodeMergeSolution**, is the solution that contains projects with the elements that have conflicts and need to be resolved. The other solution, **UpgradedSolution**, contains a collection of projects, one for each upgraded model.

In VSTS, the folder structure should look as follows:

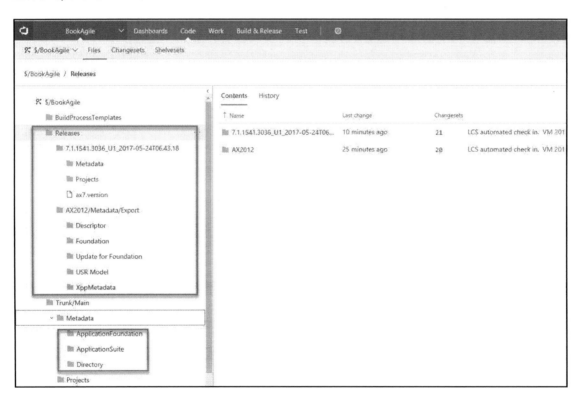

As of July 2017, the code upgrade service uses the overlayering approach to upgrade code from AX 2012, and one has to invest a lot of manual effort to refactor old code from the overlayered approach to the extension approach. In future, it is expected to upgrade code using the extension-based approach.

After the LCS code upgrade is completed, developers can configure their individual development VMs and connect to source control and get the latest upgraded code. Depending on the complexity of the solution, the following are typical development work items left to do manually to get a fully functional code in finance and operations.

- **Resolve conflict and compile error**: The key objective of the manual code migration process is being able to compile the upgraded solution. Compile errors are usually due to code conflict, use of deprecated API's in custom code, or missing references due to model split. The recommendation is to fix compilation errors in the lower packages first and then move higher. For example, start with application platform then application foundation then directory, then application suite and so on. For a large project, where multiple developers are working, work items created within VSTS can be used to split tasks within development teams. Work items are also sorted by priority, starting from the application platform conflicts first.

  To find and resolve code conflicts in the application code, there are number of tools available with Visual Studio. Code conflicts can be seen on the object in **Solution Explorer** as well as in the header bar of the designer view – with the symbol [!] at the end of the object name.

If there are conflicts, one can filter the object view to only the conflicts by typing `cf:` in the search field. To work and solve code conflicts, right-click on a method and select **Resolve code conflicts...**. This results in a window with three panes: left pane showing current baseline version, right pane showing current customizations, and the middle pane is a three-way merge with the original baseline before the code upgrade:

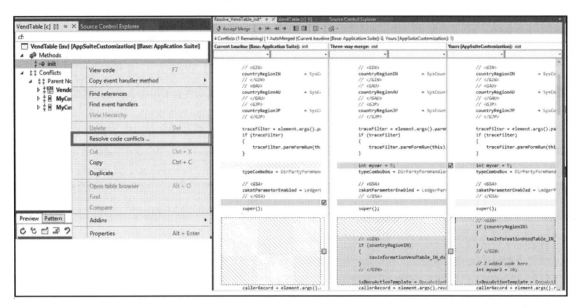

- **Update from patterns**: Second key effort after resolving the code conflict is to fix form pattern. Form patterns provide form structure, based on a particular style (including required and optional controls), and also provide many default control properties. Selecting appropriate form patterns and sub patterns is highly recommended on the custom migrated forms as this guarantees the responsiveness on various browser and form factors. This is one of the most important and time-consuming tasks along with report migration in the entire code upgrade process.

- **Refactor your customization as an extension**: Currently, code upgrade service upgrades the code using the overlayering programming model. However, after Nov 2016 release, platform and foundation layers are hard sealed which means you cannot overlayer any objects belonging to these models. As per Microsoft product team roadmap, Application models will be hard sealed by Spring release of 2018. This means that if want to continue up taking new releases, you must move all your customizations using the extension model. In some cases where it's not possible to use extensions, for example, a delegate is not available, you can probably do a small overlayering to add the hook yourself and move rest of the code to an extension. You can request these extension points to be added in the standard code from Microsoft through various feedback channels. Microsoft has been highly focused on making the extension story more and more strong so that all customization scenarios can be addressed.
- **Reimplement integration**: If you were using document services in AX 2012 for the system to system integration, the bad news is that feature is deprecated in Dynamics 365 for Finance and Operations. You have to rework and build the integration using new integration framework that uses the data entities and OData services. Also, probably, you are moving from AX 2012 on-premises to Dynamics 365 for Finance and Operations hosted in the Cloud; this also changes the integration story. Refer to `Chapter 8`, *Integration Planning and Design* for more detailed understanding of how integration works in Dynamics 365 for Finance and Operations.
- **Reimplement reporting and BI solution:** In Dynamics AX 2012, primary reporting mechanism is SSRS reports. If you have customized the standard reports in Dynamics AX 2012, they are not automatically migrated, you have to delete any customization and recreate it. In fact, the recommendation is to create a new report by copying the standard report and use extensibility models to point your business logic or UI to trigger a new report. Apart from the SSRS reports, if you have been using analytical cubes in Dynamics AX 2012, they are also deprecated and replaced with data entity and Power BI. For a detailed review of reporting and analytical capabilities and how you can leverage them in Dynamics 365 for Finance and Operation, refer to `Chapter 10`, *Analytics, Business Intelligence and Reporting*.

Like code upgrade, another important aspect of the upgrade is data upgrade which is explained in the next section.

Data upgrade

Once your code upgrade is completed, or at-least solution is completely compiled and all the tables conflicts are resolved, you can start with the data upgrade process. Data upgrade is the process to run the data upgrade scripts to transform an earlier version of the Microsoft Dynamics AX database to the current version. For easier understanding, Data upgrade process can be separated into following three activities.

Developing data upgrade script for custom schema changes

If you have done upgrade project in the earlier Dynamics AX version, for example, AX 4.0 to AX 2009 or AX 2009 to AX 2012, you might already be familiar with data upgrade scripts. Data upgrade scripts (Release update X++ classes) are similar in Dynamics 365 for Finance and Operations. These are business logic to transform and update earlier version data to match the new version application schema. The following are the scenarios when you need to write data upgrade script for your custom code:

- Change the name of a table or field
- Delete a table or field
- Add or change unique indexes or change a non-unique index into a unique index
- Restructure where data is stored; for example, move data from one field to another
- Correct old data inconsistencies
- Populate new tables with existing data
- Populate new fields with existing data or a default value that is different from the default value for the data type

 Microsoft provides all the data upgrade scripts for any such schema changes they have done from Dynamics AX 2012 to Dynamics 365 for Finance and Operations. As part of your code upgrade and refactoring, if you have made any such changes, you have to write a data upgrade script for that change.

 Data upgrade script are executed during the downtime window, so it highly important to use set-based operations in the data upgrade scripts. Follow the patterns and practices in out-of-the-box data upgrade script.

Running the data upgrade process

Running the data upgrade process can be further separated into two steps: the first step is running the pre-upgrade process that runs on Dynamics AX 2012, and the second step is referring as data upgrade process that runs on Dynamics 365 for Finance and Operations environment.

The pre-upgrade process within Dynamics AX 2012 is enabled through a hotfix installation. The purpose of this process is to copy some of the information needed from Dynamics AX 2012 model DB to transaction DB so that you have to copy only transaction db for an upgrade. Pre processing steps do the following:

- **Copy model elements from model db**: To maintain element IDs between the existing AX 2012 environment and the upgraded Finance and Operations environment
- **Copy security role from model db**: To preserve security role assignments for users
- **Create user to email mapping**: To provide a form, where you can map existing AX 2012 users to equivalent Azure AD users.

The next step is the data upgrade process, which finally upgrades your Dynamics AX 2012 transaction database to Dynamics 365 for Finance and Operations db. The following image shows the data upgrade process:

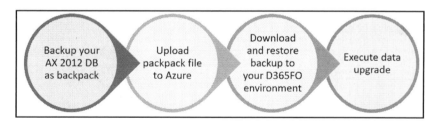

As shown in the image, the first step is to back up your AX 2012 data as `BACPAC` file and then, upload it to the Azure environment and restore the backup. Once the data is available in the SQL Azure database, you can execute the upgrade process in Dynamics 365 for Finance and Operations to get the data upgraded code.

If you are using the on-premise version of Dynamics 365 for Finance and Operations, then instead of moving the AX 2012 database to SQL Azure, you would be restoring the db to local SQL database for further processing.

Running the data upgrade process in a sandbox environment is slightly different than running in a development environment, especially the steps to copy the AX 2012 database and restore part. The key difference is that development environment runs on the SQL server and the sandbox environment runs on the Azure SQL database. Refer to documentation steps at `https://docs.microsoft.com/en-us/dynamics365/unified-operations/dev-itpro/migration-upgrade/upgrade-data-sandbox?`.

Execution of the data upgrade process is similar to what gets executed when you upgrade from an earlier application version to the latest version of Finance and Operations. The difference is when upgrading from Dynamics AX 2012, major version upgrade scripts are executed as compared to minor version upgrade scripts when upgrading from and to Finance and Operations.

The process of executing the upgrade process is through a special deployment package. You can get the latest update script from your target environment that is running the latest Finance and Operations update; download the latest binary updates from LCS and find the `MajorVersionDataUpgrade.zip` folder in the package. After this, you can run deployment of this special deployable package which executes the data upgrade process.

The following page provides details step by step documentation to install a deployable package:

`https://docs.microsoft.com/en-us/dynamics365/unified-operations/dev-itpro/deployment/install-deployable-package`

Data upgrade steps provided here in the book are just a high-level overview; there may be additional steps required for data migration depending on the version of source and target. Always refer to the latest documentation from Microsoft on this topic at `https://docs.microsoft.com/en-us/dynamics365/unified-operations/dev-itpro/migration-upgrade/data-upgrade-2012`.

```
At the time of writing this book, data upgrade was only
available from Dynamics AX 2012 R3; earlier versions, such as AX
2012 R2 or RTM are on the roadmap and will be available in the
near future.
```

The entire process of data upgrade is done, including backup and copying of your database to Azure will require downtime, hence it is important to execute your data migration multiple times and improve scripts to make sure downtime window is within the accepted downtime window.

Data upgrade is the most important process of an upgrade project. Testing the data upgrade is, basically, running the data upgrade processes on the copy of production data in a development or test environment. The key to have an optimal data upgrade experience is to plan well in advance, run multiple test cycles building on the lessons learned, and then, plan the live data upgrade in complete detail, building in time for unexpected, last minute issues. Testing the data upgrade process in development environment must have following key goals:

- Testing of the data upgrade scripts
- Identifying potential issues/bottlenecks in the data upgrade scripts
- Ensuring data integrity and completeness of the upgraded data
- Identifying the time required for each activity and calculating the final downtime
- Preparing the data for system and regression testing
- Planning for the final data upgrade in the production environment

To achieve these objectives, plan multiple rounds of the data upgrade cycle to test all the data upgrade steps consistently and to identify and tune the approximate downtime needed for the upgrade process in a live environment. Plan for an evaluation and optimization window with each test data upgrade. The objective is to reach an acceptable downtime window, agreed upon with the business team. More effort will be required to reduce the downtime window. Use a copy of production data for testing the data upgrade process. Try to use the latest copy of production with each round of the data upgrade testing.

Data upgrade in a production environment is done by Microsoft; ensure appropriate advance window to execute the final data upgrade in a production environment.

It is in the Microsoft roadmap to provide self-service tools for customer and partners to do the entire data upgrade in a production environment with little involvement from the Microsoft team. Check the latest capabilities in the Microsoft documentation or roadmap website.

Validation and final cutover

After you are done with the code upgrade and multiple rounds of test data upgrade, it is time for validation and final cutover. Validation of the data upgrade project goes through the regular process of system testing, integration testing, performance testing, and user acceptance testing, including training just like an implementation project. Chapter 11, *Testing and Training* in this book covers these topics in great detail. In addition to this, data upgrade needs to be tested thoroughly to ensure that new data matches with old data and business transactions can be performed in the new system using migrated data.

Now, let's come to the final cutover process, the final process of getting a new system live. This cutover process consists of the tasks that occur after Microsoft Dynamics AX 2012 is turned off but before Microsoft Dynamics 365 for Finance and Operations, Enterprise edition, is turned on. The following illustration shows the overall process for cutover to go-live as it will occur in the production environment:

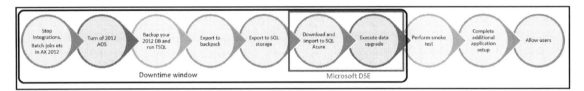

The final cutover process involves both customer/partner technical, functional and the Microsoft DSE team working together. The process starts with customer/partner team stopping all integration and batch jobs and then turning off AOS to shut the operations down in Dynamics AX 2012. After this, they take backup of 2012 DB, run TSQL script, prepare the BACPAC file, and upload the BACPAC file to the SQL storage. After this, Microsoft DSE will download and import to SQL Azure the data upgrade process and execute it. Once the data upgrade process is finished, customer/partner can do the smoke test to validate if the system is up and running.

After this, there are many additional functional configurations that can be done by customer and partners. These additional configuration includes configuring batch processes, integration, and turning on functionalities. Finally, it also includes declaring go live in the new system and allowing users to start doing transactions.

 It is important to document all the steps necessary to be performed during the final cutover in advance and run through this exercise couple of times to make sure that the final cutover goes smooth. Automate and practice deployment steps as much as possible before final cutover to save time and manual error.

Go live on the new system is not just planning the activities what needs to be done in the system, but it requires detail planning and communication with the operations and stakeholders. Chapter 12, *Go Live*, covers these activities in great detail. These guidelines and recommendations are applicable and relevant to implementation as well as any major upgrade or migration project.

Migrating from Dynamics AX 2009

If you are still on Microsoft Dynamics AX 2009, mainstream support for this version is going to end on 4th Oct 2018. This means that if you have not already planned, you need to start planning to migrate to the latest version. Unfortunately, there is no code upgrade path from Dynamics AX 2009 to Dynamics 365 for Finance and Operations, which means that you have to reimplement the customizations in the new version. The silver lining is that there is a data migration tool to assist you with data migration from AX 2009 to Dynamics 365 for Finance and Operations.

Another approach could be to transition first to Dynamics AX 2012 and then upgrade to the latest version of Dynamics 365 for Finance and Operations. If you have high customizations, this approach can be costly both in terms of money and time and for the same reason not recommended.

Planning and code migration

When planning to migrate from Dynamics AX 2009, all the upgrade/migration planning activities described in the earlier section are relevant and needs to be evaluated. Many new functionalities have been added to the product since AX 2009, so special focus needs to be given to customization analysis and fit gap to evaluate what customizations can be deprecated and replaced with existing out-of-the-box features. It is also important to identify a new feature that can be utilized after moving to the new platform. As stated earlier, to better manage the scope of migration, it is recommended to separate implementation of these additional features after the migration, if possible.

Since you will be re-implementing the customization in the new environment, you should follow the new development best practices and extensibility framework to redevelop your solution. Note that if it is not possible or extremely difficult to use an extension for your customization, you can upgrade to a Dynamics 365 for Finance and Operations version which supports overlayering, but note that major application releases in Dynamics 365 for Finance and Operations are supported for 3 years since the date of release. For example, if you upgrade to application release July 2017, this version will be supported till July 2021. This gives you enough time to refactor your code to replace it with the extensions.

Now, let's explore the data migration tool which is provided by Microsoft to help you migrate data from AX 2009 to Dynamics 365 for Finance and Operations.

Data migration

You learned that there is no code upgrade path from AX 2009 or older AX versions but the good news is that there is a tool available that can help you migrate your data to the latest version of Dynamics 365 for Operations.

The migration tool includes following types:

- **Configuration and setup**: Ledger, customer groups, vendor groups, and so on
- **Master data**: Customer, vendor, project, accounts, and so on
- **Opening balances**: Ledger balances, inventory on hand, prices, and so on
- **Open documents**: Open sales order, Open purchase order, AR, AP invoices, and so on
- **System configuration**: number sequences, users, user groups, security, and so on
- Anything that is entity (historical transactions data is not recommended)

It is not recommended to migrate historical transactions using this tool as it will be very difficult to manage the data and referential integrity. If you need your historical transaction for historical or audit purpose, you can either leave one instance of AX 2009 running for inquiry and reporting, or you can use data warehouse to combine the Dynamics AX 2009 and Dynamics 365 for Finance and Operations data, and then use Power BI reports to display historical data inside Dynamics 365 for Finance and Operations. There may be still some instances, where you need historical data for transaction processing; these scenarios need to be evaluated case by case; one solution could be to migrate relevant information to custom tables and then, change the business logic to use those custom where needed.

The following image shows the high-level architecture of the data migration tool:

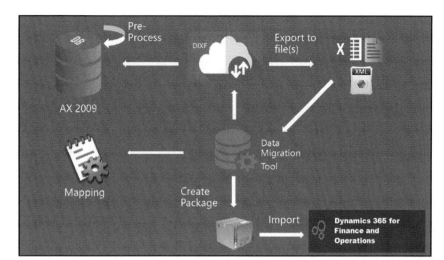

As shown in the image, the data migration tool is essentially a solution which you need to install in your AX 2009 environment. There are primarily two components of this tool, first data export and import service and second, a new module within AX 2009 environment which includes data migration checklist and several forms to manage the data migration preprocessing. The DIXF service is the same tool which is available in AX 2012 and Finance and Operations; it is ported back to AX 2009 for data migration solution. You first use the AX 2009 data migration module to define what needs to be migrated, then export using the DIXF service as a data package, which finally gets imported in the Dynamics 365 for Finance and Operations using data entities.

The following image shows the high-level process which you go through in the data migration process:

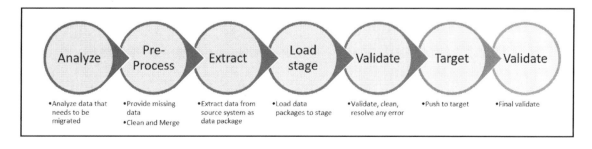

After installing the data migration tool in your Dynamics AX 2009 environment, the first thing you do is to analyze what data needs to be migrated. Next, you use different forms in the data migration module to prepare your database for migration. This includes selecting the legal entity to migrate, defining the mapping for new constructs, such as ledger setup, inventory dimensions, advanced warehouse management, and connection to your Dynamics 365 for Finance and Operation system.

After you are done with the initial setup, you can map Ax 2009 data with finance and operations entity. The tool comes with out-of-the-box map template to map out-of-the-box tables. If you have customized the standard tables or added a new table in AX 2009, you need to make sure that these additional fields and tables are available and represented by data entity in the target Dynamics 365 for Finance and Operations environment. The tool is capable of discovering these metadata changes in the target application, and map automatically. It also has advanced capabilities to define data conversion rule and mapping. Once you are done with the mapping, you can define the migration group which is nothing but a group of entities, and then extract the data as a data package.

Data packages are loaded to staging tables in Dynamics 365 for Finance and Operations, where you can validate and resolve any issue and clean data before loading to target tables. In the end, validate the data in the target system to make sure that everything is migrated as expected.

Some important capabilities of the tool are worth mentioning:

- Migration Tool does not expect you to migrate the full data in one go; different teams can work on different modules or areas and define migration groups and migrate data when ready.
- The tool can connect to your target environment and discover custom entities and fields and map it automatically. You can also change these mappings and use SQL queries to write an advance filter or mapping rules.
- The tool support versioning and incremental push, which means that you can migrate the initial set of data when you are live on AX 2009 and then, finally run the incremental migration to migrate the final data. This way you can better control your overall data migration time for the final run.

At the time of writing this book, this tool was in preview mode and not released to the public. Some features described here may be different than what is described in the book. Find the latest information about this tool on Microsoft official documentation site at `https://docs.microsoft.com/en-us/dynamics365/unified-operations/`.

Best practices in upgrade and migration

Upgrade and migration are quite a significant project. The following are our suggested best practices for them:

- Upgrade decision must be evaluated with pros and cons based on the business case and toolset availability.
- The major version from which you are migrating to Dynamics 365 for Finance and Operations, Enterprise edition is also a key input to deciding between a technical assisted upgrade or a re-implementation.
- Leveraging perfectly skilled resources in Dynamics 365 for Finance and Operations as well AX 2012 is crucial for a successful and timely upgrade.
- Whether it is an upgrade or a migration, always revisit new capabilities and frameworks to leverage while decommissioning old ones.
- Optimize your business fitment with available capabilities in Dynamics 365 for Finance and Operations and try and keep your solution mix as simple as possible.
- Never underestimate the need for substantial testing irrespective of the approach taken. Any major changes to your core business solution platform must be thoroughly tested and accepted by the business while undergoing any necessary change management.
- Always document all artifacts, key decisions, original data, and code backups and retain them for at least one good financial year end close.
- Our recommendation for data upgrade is to always maintain a repository to validate input loads, processed loads, exceptions, and test results.
- Never dilute your upgrade objectives and stay on course while engaging a good partner or advisor in your adoption journey to a new platform.

Summary

In this chapter, you learned various considerations when taking an upgrade project. These considerations include preparing a strong business case and combining with the deployment choices and accordingly making an informed upgrade decision.

It's crucial to understand what exact process is intended to be followed based upon on the decision which is often between update, upgrade, or migrate.

We also shared insights on various kinds of updates available and how to apply them through the upgrade processes involving code upgrade and data upgrade. We also covered various phases of an upgrade project. In the planning phase, we covered the importance of managing customization, managing scope, business engagement, and impact analysis.

As highlighted in best practices and recommendations shared throughout the chapter, we would like to you to consider while moving to the latest version. According to us, the upgrade is a must and the deciding factor is the timing of such an initiative. It's best to keep upgrade plan as isolated as possible with other ongoing initiatives so that dedicated and committed resources are leveraged to achieve the goal.

One should always factor that Dynamics 365 upgrades are not like any Windows or legacy application upgrade, where you will start the upgrade and your system will back up on the new platform in a few hours. Here, extensive planning, preparation, and resources are required and often the need to engage experts/advisers from the field.

Index